Motor
Learning
and
Control

Motor Learning and Control

Charles H. Shea
Texas A & M University

Wayne L. Shebilske
Texas A & M University

Stephen Worchel
Texas A & M University

PRENTICE HALL
Englewood Cliffs, New Jersey 07632

Library of Congress Cataloging-in-Publication Data

Shea, Charles H. (date)
   Motor learning and control / Charles H. Shea, Wayne L.
Shebilske, Stephen Worchel.
     p. cm.
   Includes bibliographical references and index.
   ISBN 0-13-605684-9
   1. Motor learning.   2. Motor ability.   I. Shebilske, Wayne.
II. Worchel, Stephen.   III. Title
BF295.S44 1993   92-2485
152.3—dc20   CIP

Acquisition editor: **Ted Bolen**
Editorial/production supervision: **Hilda Tauber**
Prepress buyer: **Herb Klein**
Manufacturing buyer: **Robert Anderson**
Design supervisor: **Christine Gehring Wolf**
Photo research: **Rhoda Sidney**
Photo editor: **Lori Morris-Nantz**
Interior design: **Richard Stalzer Associates, Ltd.**
Chapter opening art and cover design: **The Design Lab,**
   Warren, New Jersey

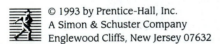

© 1993 by Prentice-Hall, Inc.
A Simon & Schuster Company
Englewood Cliffs, New Jersey 07632

Printed in the United States of America
10 9 8 7 6 5 4 3 2 1

ISBN 0-13-605684-9

Prentice-Hall International (UK) Limited, *London*
Prentice-Hall of Australia Pty. Limited, *Sydney*
Prentice-Hall Canada Inc., *Toronto*
Prentice-Hall Hispanoamericana, S. A., *Mexico*
Prentice-Hall of India Private Limited, *New Delhi*
Prentice-Hall of Japan, Inc., *Tokyo*
Simon & Schuster Asia Pte. Ltd., *Singapore*
Editora Prentice-Hall do Brasil, Ltda., *Rio de Janeiro*

Brief Contents

Preface xi

1 Motor Learning and Control in Perspective 2

2 Biological Foundations 22

3 Human Memory 50

4 Information Processing: An Overview 76

5 Sensation and Perception 96

6 Response Selection 124

7 Response Execution 146

8 Theoretical Perspectives on Motor Control 166

9 Speed-Accuracy Principles 182

10 Information Feedback 204

11 Practice Scheduling and Composition 232

12 Human Performance in a Social Context 260

13 Theory into Practice 278

Appendix A: Measuring Motor Behavior 294

Appendix B: Descriptive and Inferential Statistics 304

Glossary 312

References 323

Author Index 341

Subject Index 345

Contents

1 Motor Learning and Control in Perspective 2

Sherlock Holmes: DETECTIVE-SCIENTIST   3
Motor Learning and Control: The Field   5
Motor Learning and Control: The Family   5
Physiology   6
Psychology   7
Engineering   8
Education   8
Today   9
Motor Learning and Control: The Science   9
Scientific Thinking   10
Scientific Experiments   12
Sampling   13
Experimental Paradigms   13
Experimental Validity   16
Motor Learning and Control: A Behavioral Emphasis   18
Allowing for Individual Differences   18
Behavioral Level of Analysis   19
Information Processing Approach   20
HIGHLIGHT: Ethical Treatment of Human Subjects   16
FINAL COMMENT   21
KEY TERMS   21

2 Biological Foundations 22

Agnes de Mille: RECOVERY FROM A STROKE   23

Neurons   24
Neural Impulses   25
Synaptic Transmission   25
Functional Types of Neurons   27
Neural Control of Muscle Force   27
Motor-Unit Recruitment   28
Rate Coding   29
Major Subdivisions of the Nervous System   30
Central and Peripheral   31
Sensory and Motor   43
Autonomic   45
HIGHLIGHT: Computer-Based Methods of Brain Examination Without Surgery   32
HIGHLIGHT: Recovery From Brain Damage   46
FINAL COMMENT   49
KEY TERMS   49

3 Human Memory 50

Armstrong and Aldrin: THE LUNAR LANDING 51
How Memory Is Studied   52
Types of Memory   54
Sensory Memory   54
Short-term Memory   55
Long-term Memory   57
Depth of Processing   57
Encoding   58
Encoding in Short-term Memory   58
Encoding in Long-term Memory   61

vii

Recoding and Retaining   62
   Chunking in Short-term Memory   62
   Organization and Reconstruction in Long-term Memory   63

Retrieval   66
   Retrieval from Short-term Memory   66
   Retrieval from Long-term Memory   67

Forgetting   68
   Trace Decay   68
   Interference   69

Neurobiology of Memory   70
   Short-term Memory, Long-term Memory, and Neurons   70
   Working Memory and the Hippocampus   71
   Memory Loss and Disease   72
   Electrical and Chemical Regulators of Memory   74
HIGHLIGHT: Flashbulb Memories   72
FINAL COMMENT   74
KEY TERMS   75

4   Information Processing: An Overview   76

Jan Berry: "DEAD MAN'S CURVE"   77

Behaviorism   79

An Information-Processing Model   80
   Peripheral Processes   82
   Central Processes   82

Information Flow   84
   Serial Processing   84
   Parallel Processing   85
   Parallel-Distributed Processing   85

Reaction Time as a Measure of Processing Demands   87
   Sensation-Perception   88
   Response Selection   88
   Response Execution   89

Factors Influencing Processing   90
   Stages of Learning   90
   Movement Time   91
   Preparation Time and Anticipation   91
   Environment   92
   Task   95
HIGHLIGHT: Context Dependent Behavior   94
FINAL COMMENT   95
KEY TERMS   95

5   Sensation and Perception   96

Angeline AND WOLF HOUSE BAY   97

Measuring Sensations   99
   Sensorimotor Coordination   98
   The Method of Adjustment   99
   The Method of Limits   100
   The Method of Constant Stimuli   100
   The Method of Signal Detection   100

Methods for Measuring Psychophysical Functions   103
   Weber's Law   104

Exteroception   104
   Vision   104
   Hearing   109
   Cutaneous Senses   115

Proprioception and Kinesthesis   120
   Proprioception and Sensorimotor Control   122
HIGHLIGHT: Dart Throwing and Visual-Motor Coordination   110
FINAL COMMENT   123
KEY TERMS   123

6   Response Selection   124

Luke Skywalker: "STAR WARS"   125

Decisions and Translations   127

Uncertainty   127
   Event Uncertainty and Hick's Law   128
   Temporal Uncertainty   131
   Perceptual Uncertainty   133

Advance Information and Expectancies   134
   Precuing   134
   Known Probabilities   137
   Sequential Dependencies   138

Stimulus-Response Compatibility   139

Psychological Refractory Period   142
   Refractory Theory   143
   Expectancy Theory   144
   Single Channel Theory   144
HIGHLIGHT: Brain Work   135
FINAL COMMENT   144
KEY TERMS   145

7 Response Execution 146

Mary Lou Retton: A VAULT WITHOUT A
FAULT 147

Introduction 149

Role of Feedback in Motor Control 149
  Closed-loop Control 149
  Open-loop Control 152
  A Closed/Open Loop Continuum 154
  Hierarchical Control 155

Factors Contributing to Motor Control 156
  Mechanical Factors 156
  Neurological-Reflexive Factors 159
  Synergies 160

Factors Influencing Movement Production 162
  After-Contraction Phenomenon 162
  Tonic Neck Response 164
  HIGHLIGHT: Walking Machines 157
  FINAL COMMENT 165
  KEY TERMS 165

8 Theoretical Perspectives on Motor Control 166

Nan Davis' Story: OVERCOMING PARALYSIS
167

Closed-Loop Theory: Adams, 1971 168
  Memory States 169
  Criticisms of Adams' Theory 169

Schema Theory: Schmidt, 1975 170
  Sources of Schema Information 170
  Invariant and Variant Features 171
  Temporal and Spatial Demands of Movements 174

Mass-Spring Hypothesis 175

Coordinative Structures and Multilimb Control 177
  HIGHLIGHT: Training the Deaf to Speak 178
  FINAL COMMENT 181
  KEY TERMS 181

9 Speed-Accuracy Principles 182

Nolan Ryan: ARM WITHOUT END 183

Speed-Accuracy Trade-off 185

Fitts' Law 185
  Index of Difficulty 186
  Accounts for Fitts' Law 191

Impulse Variability Theory 192
  Effective Target Width and Movement Demands 192
  Force-Force Variability Relationship 194
  Accounts for the Force-Force Variability Relationship 194

An Apparent Speed-Accuracy Paradox 196
  Anticipation and Timing 196
  Factors Influencing Anticipation and Timing 196
  A Batting Example 200
  HIGHLIGHT: Speed and Accuracy in Controlling Machines 191
  FINAL COMMENT 203
  KEY TERMS 203

10 Information Feedback 204

Super Cockpit: THE VIRTUAL DISPLAY 205

Classifications of Information Feedback 207

Distinction Between Learning and Performance 208

Theoretical Issues 209
  Reward, Motivation, and Information 209
  Guidance Hypothesis and the Processing of Feedback 211

Knowledge of Results 211
  Absolute and Relative Frequency of KR 211
  Bandwidth KR 216
  KR Delay and Post KR Delay 218
  Summary KR 220
  Precision of KR 223

Considerations Related to the Error Measure Used 225

Knowledge of Performance 228
  HIGHLIGHT: A New Generation of Feedback 226
  FINAL COMMENT 230
  KEY TERMS 231

11 Practice Scheduling and Composition 232

Alex Rogan: THE LAST STARFIGHTER 233

Designing Effective Practice   234

Retention and Transfer   235

Scheduling of Practice   236

   Practice Distribution   236
   Contextual Interference   239

Composition of Practice   246

   Specificity Versus Variability of Practice   246
   Part-Whole Practice   252
   Mental and Observational Practice   254

HIGHLIGHT: The Men and Women Behind the Patriot Missiles   256

FINAL COMMENT   259

KEY TERMS   259

12 Human Performance in a Social Context   260

Muhammed Ali: "I AM THE GREATEST"   261

Why Study Social Influences?   263

The Social Nature of Some Basic Concepts   264

   Arousal   264
   Social Comparison   264

Goal Setting: The Influence of Social Context   265

   Group Polarization   266

Social Learning Theory   267

Performing Alone or With Others   268

   Social Facilitation Versus Social Inhibition   268
   Social Loafing: Robbing Individual Motivation   270
   Home-Court Advantage: Where We Perform   271

The Power of the Group   272

   Focus of Attention   272
   Concern with Evaluation   273
   Social Identity   273

HIGHLIGHT: Men and Women in Groups   274

FINAL COMMENT   277

KEY TERMS   277

13 Theory into Practice   278

Paradigms: OUTSMARTING THE FUTURE   279

Understanding the Problem or Question   281

Appropriate Application of Principles   282

Motor Learning Checklist   283

Is Theory Necessary?   283

   Theory: The Positive Viewpoint   283
   Theory: The Negative Viewpoint   284

Basic Research and Theory into Practice   285

   The Proposed Research and Communication Model   285
   Research Classifications   286
   Communication   287
   Contextual Interference Example   289
   General Concerns   289

HIGHLIGHT: Chaos in the Brickyard   290

FINAL COMMENT   293

KEY TERMS   293

Appendix A Measuring Motor Behavior   294

Types of Motor Behavior Measurement   294

   Physiological Correlates of Movement   294
   Reaction and Movement Times   294
   Response Errors   298
   Kinematic Measurements   302

KEY TERMS   303

Appendix B Descriptive and Inferential Statistics   304

Descriptive Statistics   304

   Central Tendency   305
   The Normal Curve   307

Inferential Statistics   308

   T-Tests and Analysis of Variance   308
   Correlation and Regression   309

KEY TERMS   311

Glossary   312
References   323
Author Index   341
Subject Index   345

Preface

A paradox exists between the complexities of human movement and the ease with which people move. Each time we speak, smile, dance, type, and so on, we are executing very complex, precise actions. Tasks like walking, talking, dancing, throwing a football, playing the guitar, riding a bicycle, shifting gears in a car, and many, many other tasks involve the performance of highly complicated skills. Although these skills are difficult to learn, with sufficient practice an individual can become extremely proficient. Indeed, in many cases these skills are seemingly performed with little cognitive effort.

The acquisition and performance of motor skills is the focus of this book. Understanding the processes involved in learning and performing motor skills will enable the reader to design and conduct more effective practice and rehabilitation experiences and to improve the equipment and technologies used in a wide variety of motor skills.

This textbook is intended primarily for college and university students in the fields of physical education, kinesiology, exercise science, psychology, physical therapy, and human factors engineering. The concepts presented and discussed should be particularly useful to students and practitioners who will design training programs in sports, dance, rehabilitation, industrial, or military settings. Furthermore, those concerned with the design, evaluation, and use of technologies related to skill development and human/machine interaction will also find the information invaluable.

The text is esentially, although not formally, divided into four sections. The first section consists of three chapters that provide the foundation necessary to understanding motor learning and control as a science, the biological foundations of human performance and learning, and the fundamentals of human memory. Section 2 is composed of four chapters that present an information processing framework in which the human is viewed as an active rather than passive processor of information. Section 3 comprises two chapters focusing on the theoretical proposals that have been presented to account for the control of movement and the principles of control related to speed and accuracy. Section 4 consists of four chapters that focus on the principles relating to the enhancement of the learning of motor skills and the applications of these principles to instruction.

Features of the Text

The text offers a fresh, new perspective on motor learning and control. We integrate information from psychology, physiology, and engineering to paint a refreshing new picture of motor skill performance and learning. Each chapter begins with an introductory story that provides an interesting, practical frame of reference for the concepts that follow. In addition, highlight boxes in each chapter feature a new or related application.

We have taken great care to write with the student in mind—to make the text contemporary, inviting, and relevant to students without sacrificing the content. We use color, figures, and pictures to heighten visual appeal and to enhance understanding.

Teaching and Learning Aids

Each chapter begins with a chapter outline and chapter objectives. Important terms are highlighted in the text, listed at the end of each chapter, and defined in a full glossary at the back of the book. In addition, two appendices have been included. Appendix A is devoted to methods of measuring motor behavior; Appendix B focuses on descriptive and inferential statistics. Two supplements are also available with the text: an instructor's manual and a laboratory activities manual.

Instructor's Manual. The instructor's manual includes teaching suggestions, class discussion figures that can be used as overheads or slides, test items, and additional supplemental readings. The teaching suggestions include interesting analogies and practical examples that are useful in supplementing the text material; also included are suggestions on using the laboratory activities and hints on using the class discussion figures to stimulate class discussion. The test items include multiple choice, fill-in-blank, and short-answer questions for each chapter.

Laboratory Activities Manual. A laboratory activities manual including a computer disk is available for instructors and students. The computer activities and associated text are designed to complement the textbook by providing opportunities for the student to experience first hand various types of tasks used in motor learning research. Activities include simple experiments and exercises relating to reaction time, information processing, Weber's law, Hicks' law, Fitts' law, and contextual interference as well as many other important concepts. Each activity has specific exercises for students to complete. Instructors may choose to have students complete these activities outside of class or they may be incorporated into classroom activities.

■ ■ ■

Acknowledgments

We wish to thank a number of people who contributed in many ways to the writing and preparation of the text. Leann Willoughby and David Wright from the Human Performance Laboratories at Texas A&M University assisted in almost every facet of the development and delivery of the manuscript. Without their help and encouragement the text would not have been completed. Leann typed, edited, and managed the many tasks that were required to complete the work on schedule. David reviewed, critiqued, and helped revise the text. We are also indebted to Chad Whitacre who assisted in the development of the computer software that accompanies the laboratory activities manual. We are also grateful to the many students at Texas A&M University who have used draft versions of our motor learning and control text. They were an invaluable source of information in the revision process.

We owe a debt of gratitude to the publishing team at Prentice Hall for their collaborative efforts in the careful review, editing, and production of this text. Ted Bolen, college editor, and his assistants Nicole Gray and Diane Schaible provided generous help and encouragement; Hilda Tauber, production editor, supervised with unfailing commitment the multiple details involved in getting from manuscript to bound book; Helene Capparelli handled the supplements. We acknowledge with thanks the photo research efforts of Rhoda Sidney.

We are also most grateful for the thoughtul criticism and helpful suggestions of the following reviewers for *Motor Learning and Control*: Tami Abourezk, California State University, Northridge; James Cauraugh, University of Florida; Gail Clark, Louisiana Tech University; Mark Guadagnoli, University of Nevada, Las Vegas; Leon E. Johnson, University of Missouri, Columbia; Robert M. Kohl, Wayne State University; Dan Southard, Texas Christian University; Richard K. Stratton, Virginia Polytechnic Institute; Tonya Toole, Florida State University; Michael G. Wade, University of Minnesota, Twin Cities; Stephen A. Wallace, University of Colorado, Boulder; David Wright, Texas A&M University; and Howard N. Zelaznik, Purdue University.

1

Motor Learning and Control in Perspective

Sherlock Holmes: DETECTIVE-SCIENTIST

Motor Learning and Control: The Field

Motor Learning and Control: The Family
- *Physiology*
- *Psychology*
- *Engineering*
- *Education*
- *Today*

Motor Learning and Control: The Science
- *Scientific Thinking*
- *Scientific Experiments*
- *Sampling*
- *Experimental Paradigms*
- *Experimental Validity*

Motor Learning and Control: A Behavioral Emphasis
- *Allowing for Individual Differences*
- *Behavioral Level of Analysis*
- *Information Processing Approach*

HIGHLIGHT: Ethical Treatment of Human Subjects
FINAL COMMENT
KEY TERMS

Sherlock Holmes: DETECTIVE-SCIENTIST

The day's routine had been disrupted as the winds howled and the rains pelted the great city of London. In late September fierce gales were not unusual. As evening approached, the storm shrieked and cried like an "untamed beast in a cage." Sherlock Holmes sat moodily at one side of the fireplace indexing his records while Watson sat reading one of "Clark Russell's fine sea stories until the howl of the gale from without seemed to blend with the text, and the splash of the rain, to lengthen out into the long swash of the sea waves."

Suddenly the doorbell rang. Who could have braved so violent a storm? It must be terribly important. "Come in!" called Sherlock Holmes turning the lamp so that it shone on the vacant chair upon which the visitor must sit.

The young man who entered was "well groomed and trimly clad, with some refinement and delicacy in his bearing." "I trust that I am not intruding. . . . My name is John Openshaw . . . I come for advice . . . and help."

"You have come from the south-west," said Holmes, "that clay and chalk mixture which I see upon your toe caps is quite distinctive. . . . draw your chair up to the fire and favour me with some of the details of your case." The young visitor positioned his chair to take advantage of the fire and began, "My case is no ordinary one."

"None of those which come to me are. I am the last court of appeal," said Sherlock

Because of his painstaking observation and research, and his analytical evaluation of data, Sherlock Holmes can be considered not only a great detective but a model scientist.

- ■ To understand the relationship between the subfields of motor learning and motor control.
- ■ To appreciate the relationship between motor learning and control and other scientific disciplines.
- ■ To examine the scientific process.
- ■ To understand the principles of scientific experiments.

Holmes. . . . "Pray give us the essential facts from the commencement, and I can afterwards question you as to those details which seem to me to be most important." After hearing the mysterious chain of events that began many years before and culminated in this visit, Sherlock Holmes dismissed the stranger into the night with the warning "take care of yourself in the meanwhile, for I do not think that there can be a doubt that you are threatened by a very real and imminent danger."

Sherlock Holmes lit his pipe as he sat contemplating the facts of the case, all the while staring into the red glow of the fire. "I think, Watson," he remarked at last, "that of all our cases we have had none more fantastic than this." Appearing to be absorbed in the scant few facts provided by their visitor, Holmes continued:

> The ideal reasoner would, . . . when he had once been shown a single fact in all its bearings, deduce from it not only all the chain of events which led up to it but also the results which would follow from it. As Cuvier could correctly describe a whole animal by the contemplation of a single bone, so the observer who has thoroughly understood one link in a series of incidents should be able to accurately state all the other ones, both before and after. We have not yet grasped the results which reason alone can attain to.

Early next morning Holmes set out in search of the missing pieces of the puzzle. It was clear that he had already visualized the pattern that had been so intricately woven into the bizarre chain of events, and anticipated the events still to occur. The famous sleuth described his method in these words:

> "It is of the highest importance in the art of detection to be able to recognize, out of a number of acts, which are incidental and which vital. Otherwise your energy and attention must be dissipated instead of being concentrated."

Upon his return, Holmes reviewed the facts he had uncovered and explained to Dr. Watson how each interlocked with the others. The mystery was solved! The facts fit together perfectly. Or did they?

■ ■ ■

You can read the entire adventure in the story entitled *The Five Orange Pips* written by Sir Arthur Conan Doyle in 1891. We have taken care not to reveal specifics in order to encourage you to read the story. This mystery is unique in that the great detective is unable to prove that his reconstructions of the crimes are truly accurate because all the characters involved had perished. Yet he presents such a logically convincing chronicle that few who read the account require further proof. For his painstaking observation and research, and his analytical evaluation of data, Sherlock Holmes is not only a great detective but also a model scientist.

Motor Learning and Control: The Field

Sherlock Holmes developed his reasoning skills to a very high degree, but he would not have been able to solve even the simplest of cases purely in his head. He needed to ask questions, look for clues, and, in many instances, make things happen by donning a disguise or baiting a trap. He communicated with and intervened in the world around him through actions. Motor actions and their production are the basis for this book. A smile, a spoken word, a gesture, a glance, a gymnastics routine—all are the result of a complex interaction of many processes.

Motor learning and control can be defined as the scientific discipline concerned with understanding the development and execution of the processes that lead to human movement. It is easy to see from the term itself and the definition that the discipline is really a combination of two closely related subfields: motor learning and motor control. **Motor learning** focuses on understanding the way in which the processes that subserve movement are developed and the factors that facilitate or inhibit this development. **Motor control** is concerned with understanding the execution of those processes that lead to skilled human movement as well as the factors that lead to

the breakdown of such skills. As shown in Figure 1.1, the two subfields are so closely intertwined that it is often unproductive to separate them. Factors that influence the control of a motor skill often influence the learning of that skill, and vice versa. The processes responsible for movement are constantly changing in very subtle ways, with each new experience holding the potential to change the way we respond.

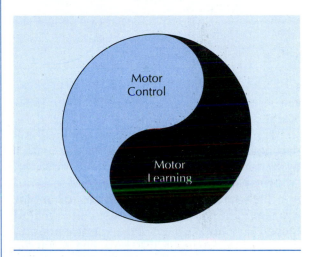

Figure 1.1 *The intertwined relationship of motor learning and motor control.*

Motor Learning and Control: The Family

Sherlock Holmes used his knowledge of literature, chemistry, psychology, biology, and geology in seeking a solution to a case. His knowledge in these areas was often the key to solving a mystery. Similarly, it is important for the scientist in motor learning and control to have a background in a number of related scientific disciplines. Scientists experimenting in the discipline of motor learning and control may be compared with detectives. They solve

mysteries of the mind and body. They rely on the knowledge that has been generated in many disciplines, particularly psychology, physiology, engineering, and education.

Figure 1.2 illustrates how motor learning and control interrelate with other scientific disciplines. We have placed it in the center of the scientific family, although we recognize that other disciplines could claim central position for themselves.

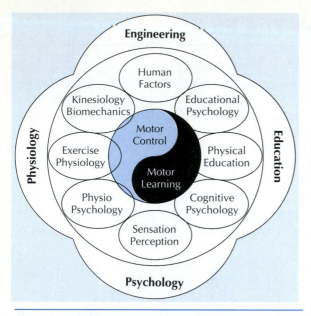

Figure 1.2 *Fields and subfields that are closely related with motor learning and control.*

The disciplines of education, engineering, psychology, and physiology all have a history much longer than that of motor learning and control. You might say that these disciplines are the parents or grandparents of motor learning and control. Scientists in each of these disciplines conceived experiments and theories that formed the foundation of the field of motor learning and control as it is today. In the following sections, we briefly spotlight the work of two scientists in each discipline. Of course many other individuals and groups have made important contributions to our understanding of motor learning and control. Our attempt is only to characterize the types of contributions made and to emphasize the importance of our closest scientific relations.

Physiology

A branch of the discipline of physiology, neurophysiology, has the closest ties to motor control. Work by Sir Charles Sherrington (an English physiologist, 1857–1952) and his colleagues on the role of reflexes in the control of

voluntary movements is still important in our thinking today. Sherrington is credited with the creation of a number of classical concepts of motor control including **reciprocal innervation** and **final common pathway**. Reciprocal innervation refers to the idea that when one muscle group is activated (turned on), the opposing muscle group is deactivated (turned off). The notion of a final common pathway suggests that the neural commands from the brain, sensory receptors, and reflexes converge at the spinal level to produce the set of commands sent to the muscle. Sherrington also coined the term **proprioception** as a result of his work on the sensory receptors that detect body position and orientation.

Sherrington concentrated on understanding the nerve-muscle interaction. He was not concerned with movement per se, but rather with the neurophysiological processes that result in the movement. A Russian physiologist, N. A. Bernstein (1897–1966), blended behavioral and neurological theory and techniques

Sir Charles Sherrington is credited with the creation of a number of classical concepts of motor control, including reciprocal inhibition and final common pathway.

in his study of complex movements such as locomotion. This work described coordinated movement in terms of both neurophysiological processes and biomechanical characteristics. Bernstein is especially noted for the formulation of general laws relating to the organization of human movement, self-regulation, and the role of feedback in motor control. Unfortunately, for a number of years many scientists were largely ignorant of Bernstein's forty years of research because his works were not translated into English until after his death.

Psychology

The branches of psychology that deal with physiological psychology, sensation-perception, and cognitive psychology are close kin to motor learning. Psychology can be defined as the scientific study of human behavior. Wilhelm Wundt (1832–1920) is credited with both establishing the first research laboratory in psychology in 1879 and writing the first book on psychology in 1862. Thus, he is considered by many scholars to be the father of modern scientific psychology. His work in sensation, perception, and attention and his use of reaction time to assess the speed of mental processes have direct application to the study of motor learning and control.

Toward the end of Wundt's academic career, a number of psychologists adopted an approach termed **behaviorism**. A behaviorist believes that a scientist must be concerned with observable events. Processes occurring in the mind, such as thinking or feeling, cannot be observed directly, but rather must be inferred from observable events. One of the well-known advocates of this approach was B. F. Skinner (1904–1990). His best-known work concerns **operant conditioning**, a type of learning in which an animal or person learns to make responses to get a reward or avoid punishment. Skinner was concerned with the strength of the relationship between stimuli and motor responses.

Wilhelm Wundt is considered by many to be the father of modern scientific psychology. He is credited with establishing the first psychology laboratory and writing the first psychology textbook.

An advocate of the behaviorist approach, B.F. Skinner is best known for his work concerning operant conditioning.

Engineering

In the late 1940s it became obvious that engineers, who were designing increasingly complex machinery, needed to consult with psychologists and other training/learning experts. Technology was being developed without considering the capabilities of the human operator. This need resulted in the emergence of industrial engineering and its subfield of human factors engineering. A. T. Welford (1914–   ), an Englishman trained in psychology, viewed individuals as active processors of information. He proposed the notions of **central intermittency** and the **single channel hypothesis**. The notion of central intermittency proposes that humans process information in discrete bursts rather than continuously. The single channel hypothesis maintains that while one set of information is being processed (e.g. a decision is being made), the processing of a new set of information is delayed. These concepts have played an important role in the design of complex machines, particularly aircraft. Clearly, the operator's processing abilities could be overloaded, and the engineers needed to consider this in their designs.

About the same time, P. M. Fitts (1912–1965) applied mathematical and information-processing principles to hand-arm movements. In what has come to be known as Fitts' Law (Fitts, 1964), he derived an index of difficulty for aiming tasks that considered both movement extent and target size. Decreases in target size and increases in movement distance increased the index of difficulty and movement time. This work paved the way for many more researchers' attempts to apply mathematical, engineering, and psychological principles to the understanding of human movement.

Education

Education has a very long history, but as a distinct scientific discipline its roots are much shorter. For many years educators were concerned primarily with the practice of teaching, leaving the study of principles of learning to the psychologists. In 1900 John Dewey delivered the presidential address to the American

John Dewey emphasized the need for formal programs of research on the education of children. He is considered by many as the father of educational psychology.

Psychological Association. His speech emphasized the need for formal programs of research on the education of children. Dewey was a proponent of an approach to psychology termed **functionalism**, which emphasized the function of thought. The functionalist asked: How do mental processes (thought) function to fill our needs? How do our mental

Paul Fitts utilized mathematical and information processing principles to develop what has come to be known as Fitts' Law.

abilities enable us to adapt to our environment? As a result of his work in this area, John Dewey is considered the founder of educational psychology.

Franklin Henry is considered by many as the father of motor learning and control.

Franklin Henry (1904–   ), who was trained in psychology but worked in physical education, is considered by many to be the father of motor learning and control. Henry influenced many faculty members and doctoral students who subscribed to his general method and point of view. Many of those directly or indirectly influenced by Franklin Henry (e.g., Richard Schmidt, Robert Christina, George Stelmach) assumed positions in physical education departments during the college growth boom of the 1960s. These leaders created Ph.D. programs and trained more students in Henry's tradition. His influence was pervasive by the 1970s. Henry is probably best known for his work with reaction time, which resulted in the memory drum theory of neuromotor reaction in 1960.

Motor Learning and Control Today

We have not forgotten our relationship to other academic disciplines. They continue to serve us and we continue to serve them. But often as an area of study emerges from other, more established disciplines, there is an attempt to seek a distinct identity. This happened for motor learning and control in the late 1960s. Professional organizations such as the North American Society for the Psychology of Sport and Physical Activity (1973) and the Canadian Society for Psycho-Motor Learning and Sport Psychology (1969) were formed. About the same time, the first motor learning textbook was written by B. J. Cratty (1965), and the Journal of Motor Behavior was started by R. A. Schmidt (1969).

Today, however, a renewed sense of academic unity seems to be emerging. Scientists in a number of different settings are discovering the value of collaborative research, resulting in many of the researchers in motor learning and control holding joint appointments in two academic disciplines. Top researchers in motor learning and control often publish in journals and regularly attend conferences more traditionally aligned with other fields. Different perspectives on a topic are viewed as refreshing. The arbitrary distinctions between disciplines seem to be on a decline.

Motor Learning and Control: The Science

While reading a Sherlock Holmes story, you get the sense that Holmes is intrigued by the cases that are brought before him. He seems to look upon each case as a challenge. His curiosity is aroused by the mystery. We are all aroused by mystery. We are curious creatures. When we observe ourselves, others, and the world around us, we continuously question: What? When? Where? Why? Do these sound like questions that only Sherlock Holmes would ask? No! These are the questions we all ask. We are curious to know the answers, to solve the mystery. In motor learning and control, we also ask questions about the processes that lead to movement.

What? What limits my memory? my speed of movement? my ability to process information?

When? When is a muscle strongest? is reaction time fastest? are movements most accurate?

Where? Where does the system break down when I get fatigued? forget?

Why? Why is one person more coordinated than another? more forgetful?

The need to answer these and many, many more questions leads us to observe, to speculate, to observe again, to speculate further. On some occasions, we even experiment, that is, we purposely try something new or manipulate some condition because our observations and speculations have resulted in a tentative understanding of the question. So we test our idea, our understanding.

We all conduct experiments. When we take a new route home from school and measure how much time we save or lose compared to our normal route, we are conducting an experiment. When we apply fertilizer to only one part of our garden and observe the change in the growth of the plants, we are conducting an experiment. Even a trip to the grocery store results in an experiment as we taste test two ice creams and judge one to be richer than the other.

Scientific Thinking

One way our everyday thinking and experiments differ from those of a scientist, is the manner in which the scientist is trained to think when posing scientific questions. Figures 1.3 and 1.4 depict the basic structure of scientific thinking and experimentation that plays a role in determining what questions the scientist will ask.

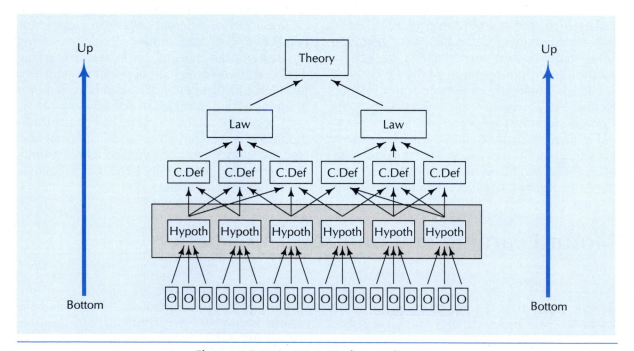

Figure 1.3 *Bottom-up (empirical) research process.*

The process begins with observations (see bottom of Figure 1.3)—information that arises from direct observations or from the literature. When speculation about these observations leads to questions, formal and informal hypotheses are developed. A **hypothesis** is a tentative prediction of behavior under a set of conditions. To test hypotheses, experiments are devised. The shaded area in Figure 1.3 is the point in the scientific process where experiments are conducted to test hypotheses derived from observation or literature. An **experiment** is an investigation in which a researcher manipulates one variable while measuring its effect on some other variable. Experiments are the most common method used to test hypotheses. Experiments provide evidence on which a hypothesis is rejected or held tenable. But science does not accept a hypothesis as true, even after repeated demonstrations. This is the point that Polya (1954) made when he wrote:

> Nature may answer yes or no, but it whispers one answer and thunders the other; its yes is provisional, its no is definitive. (p. 10)

If there is one demonstration that a hypothesis is not true, the hypothesis must be reworked or rejected. Many demonstrations that are consistent with a hypothesis only serve to keep the hypothesis viable. This is an important point that will be emphasized throughout the chapter.

At this stage, experiments are termed empirical experiments. **Empirical** means based on observation and/or literature rather than theory. Facts are generated for facts' sake. This is the most inefficient level of scientific inquiry, but much information is generated this way. These facts may appear to be isolated and of little use at the time, yet they are the very foundation of science (see Figure 1.3).

Science advances more quickly when the findings of individual experiments are linked together. **Coordinating definitions** are used to tie together isolated facts. Logical reasoning from isolated facts to a more general description is termed **induction**.

A hypothesis or group of related hypotheses that continues to be held tenable after being subjected to repeated experimentation

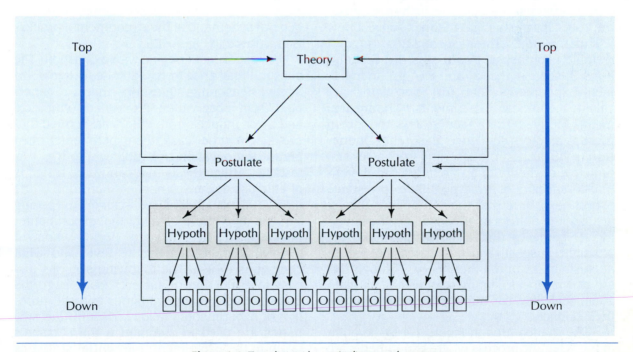

Figure 1.4 Top-down (theoretical) research process.

becomes a law. More specifically, a **law** is a statement describing a sequence of events in nature or human activities that has been observed to occur with unvarying uniformity under the same conditions. Similarly, associated laws are linked together by tentative explanations for the laws and, thus, the observation on which the laws were based. This explanation or **theory** is a statement of the processes that account for the lawful phenomenon. The term "theory" implies that there is considerable evidence in support of the explanation. In contrast, a hypothesis is a much more tentative prediction of behavior and does not necessarily consider explanations for that behavior.

The process to this point can be termed "bottom up" because the observations (facts) at the bottom, in conjunction with inductive reasoning, have driven the development of theory. The theory falls (is rejected) as its bases of support (hypotheses, coordinating definitions, and laws) are rejected. For young fields, the scientific process is largely bottom up.

For more mature fields the scientific process progresses in a *top down* fashion (see Figure 1.4). This means that theories suggest new postulates and these postulates suggest testable hypotheses. **Postulates** are assumptions based on theory and not grounded in fact. Experiments that test postulates are called theoretical experiments. **Theoretical** means derived from theory. The top down process involves deductive reasoning. **Deduction** is the process of reasoning from a general principle or theory to an unknown, from general to specific, or from postulate to testable hypotheses. Note that the top down process, just like the bottom up process, is self-correcting. Hypotheses that are rejected make the postulate suspect, and postulates that fail to be sustained can fell the theory. Through this top down process, many scientists (e.g., Platt, 1964) feel they can most efficiently advance their science.

The shaded area in Figure 1.4 is the point in the scientific process where experiments are conducted to test hypotheses derived from theory. Scientists like to ask critical questions and then very carefully plan and carry out critical experiments. *Critical*, in this context, refers to those questions and experiments that have the potential to reject one hypothesis, law, postulate, or theory in favor of another. This makes efficient use of the scientists' resources, since the experimental process is often very costly in terms of time and other resources. The identification of a critical question is difficult and requires a great deal of insight into and/or knowledge of the phenomenon at hand. Empty experiments are to science what empty calories (calories from candy, potato chips, etc.) are to our health and that of our children. They are often costly and may provide some immediate satisfaction, but they do little for our growth and development. The intent of the scientific community is to advance the understanding of the phenomenon to be studied in an orderly and most direct way.

Scientific Experiments

The shaded areas of Figures 1.3 and 1.4 are the points in the scientific process at which experiments play their most important role. A general schematic of the experimental process is illustrated in Figure 1.5.

An experiment begins with a question. The question may arise from either deductive or inductive reasoning. Questions that are generated from observation are termed empirical and those induced from theory are termed theoretical. In either case, the experimenter must phrase the question or hypothesis so that it is testable. A hypothesis that cannot be tested is of little use to the scientist. Perhaps one of the most difficult jobs of the scientist is posing testable hypotheses. Next, the experimenter must use the hypothesis to decide whom to test, what measurements to take, and what conditions to use. The following sections discuss the selection of subjects (sampling), the experimental plan (paradigm), and the problem of experimental validity. **Descriptive statistics** are used to summarize the measures taken in the experiment. **Inferential statistics** are used as the basis to reject or fail to reject

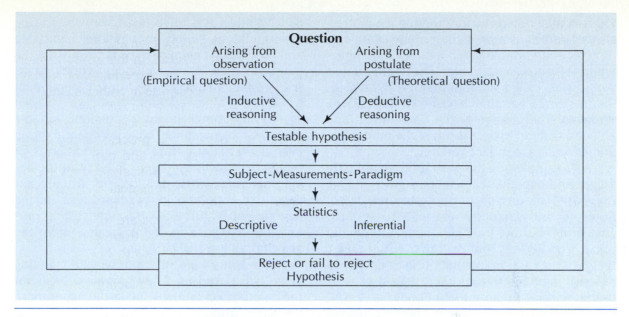

Figure 1.5 Schematic of the research process.

the hypothesis under consideration in the experiment. Information concerning common measurements in motor learning and control is presented in Appendix A. Descriptive and inferential statistics are discussed in Appendix B.

Sampling

An important question in every experiment centers on the selection and number of subjects to be tested. In an attempt to increase the generalizability of the results, the experimenter carefully selects a sample of subjects from a population of subjects. A subject **population** is comprised of all persons who meet a particular set of conditions (male, female, right-handed, blue-eyed, college student, etc.). A **sample** is a subset of a population. The experimenter desires to use a sample that is representative of the population since it is rarely feasible to test an entire population.

Often, a process called **randomization** is used to help ensure that each person in the population under study has an equal opportunity to participate in the study. This procedure makes it more probable that subject differences in the population will be distributed throughout the sample and thus will enhance generalizability. When possible, scientists randomly select subjects and then randomly assign them to groups. Also to be taken into consideration is the size of the sample needed for a particular experiment. Too few subjects might limit the chances of the sample's being truly representative of the population and also might limit the statistical tools that can be used to analyze the data. Increasing the sample size, however, may be costly in terms of time and in many cases money. What the scientist would like to do is select a sample size that is large enough to permit a representative sample to be chosen and appropriate statistical analysis to be conducted, but small enough to be reasonably tested. Methods are available to estimate the sample size necessary to utilize certain statistical techniques, but the questions related to the representativeness of the sample are much more difficult to answer.

Experimental Paradigms

Of the many scientific methods available to those studying motor learning and control, the experiment is by far the most commonly used.

The scientist begins by formulating a hypothesis that serves as a prediction of the change in a measured variable given a specific manipulation of another variable. The manipulated variable is called an **independent variable**; the measured variable is termed a **dependent variable**. The change in the dependent variable is assumed to be a result of the manipulation of the independent variable.

An example of a simple experimental paradigm and hypothetical results is given in Figure 1.6. Two groups of subjects are tested. Subjects are randomly assigned to groups. One group is randomly assigned to be tested under Condition A and the other group under the experimental manipulation in which Condition B is added to (Sternberg, 1969) or subtracted from (Donders, 1969) Condition A. The group of subjects tested only under Condition A is called a **control group** because their performance is used as a baseline to determine the influence of the experimental variable B. The subjects who receive Condition A + B or A − B make up the **experimental group**. The control and the experimental groups must be treated in exactly the same way except for the one variable under study, in this case Condition B. The hypothesis is that the introduction of Condition B influences (positively or negatively) the performance.

In the experiment just described, the scientist will have a difficult time convincing the scientific community that the manipulation of the independent variable (Condition B) caused, directly or indirectly, the change in the dependent variable. It is often not a very convincing experiment to simply manipulate a variable and observe the change. Who is to say that the manipulation of the independent variable was responsible for the change in the dependent variable?

The difference in the dependent variable may have occurred for the experimental group even if we had not introduced Condition B, or the groups may have been different in the beginning. These criticisms may be partially satisfied by including a baseline test in the experiment (Figure 1.7). Baseline testing permits the comparison of the groups under the same conditions.

The control group and baseline testing serve two purposes: They provide a basis for the comparison of results with the experimental group and offer a means for eliminating some of the alternative explanations of the results. With the inclusion of the control group and the baseline test, the scientist is more assured that the changes in the dependent variable can be attributed to the independent variable. Since both groups were tested under the same conditions except for the condition of interest and since both groups were similar at baseline testing, any difference between the groups at the end of the experiment can be argued to be a result of the experimental condition that was not shared (Condition B). Remember, conditions shared by both groups are controlled.

A transfer paradigm is used when the experimenter is interested in the impact of an in-

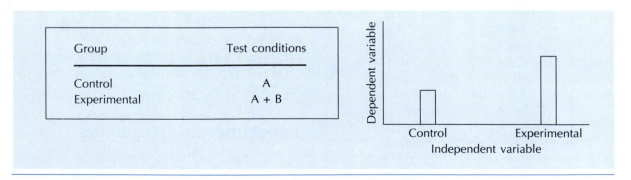

Figure 1.6 *Simple two-group paradigm (left) and hypothetical data (right).*

14

dependent variable on learning (Salmoni, Schmidt, & Walters, 1984). In the example in Figure 1.8, one group of subjects is given practice on a task under Condition A and another group under Condition A + B. From the hypothetical results, it is clear that the addition of Condition B retards performance. However, these results may not accurately reveal how well the experimental group could perform when Condition B is removed. The hypothetical results illustrate a rather dramatic reversal from acquisition to transfer. The experimental group, whose performance had been inferior to that of the control group throughout acquisition, now "out performs" the control when Condition B is no longer present.

To illustrate this concept (discussed in greater detail in Chapters 9 and 10), we will use a simple example from exercise physiology. Two groups of students with similar psychological and physical makeups are put on a running program for 16 weeks that will end in a 10-kilometer race. The students run the same workout each day, but the members of

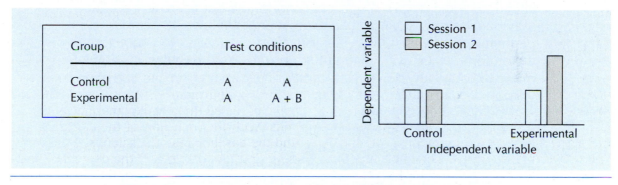

Figure 1.7 Two-group/pre-post test paradigm (left) and hypothetical data (right).

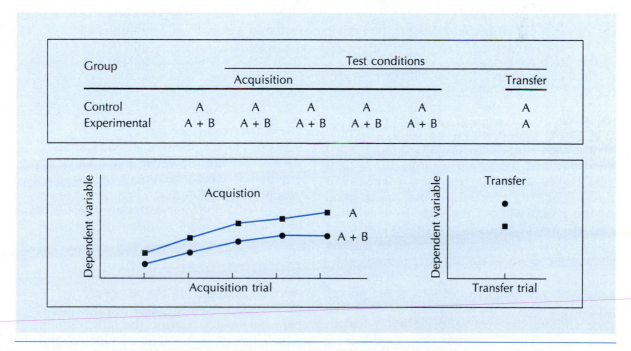

Figure 1.8 A transfer paradigm (top) and hypothetical data (bottom).

H I G H L I G H T

Ethical Treatment of Human Subjects

As a college student, you may be asked to be a subject in an experiment. This can be a very interesting and valuable experience, as well as your chance to play a role in the progress of science, but the experience may produce some anxiety. Anytime we enter into an unknown situation, some degree of anxiety is normal. What is anxiety producing about being a subject in an experiment? We have all heard of experiments in which the subject was exposed to something uncomfortable or even dangerous, tricked in some way, or simply made to look silly. Could you unknowingly appear on the scientific version of "Candid Camera"? What could happen to you?

Today many safeguards are in place to assure that you, as a subject, are protected from unnecessary risks. Professional organizations as well as agencies of the federal government have adopted and published guidelines for the handling of both human and animal subjects. Primary among the considerations for the ethical treatment of human subjects are the issues related to informed consent, risk, privacy, deception, and debriefing.

Informed Consent. It is the experimenter's duty to inform subjects in writing of the relevant aspects of the study they are requested to participate in and to obtain their written consent. This consent must

one group are required to wear weighted vests. Times for the workouts are recorded each day and the group wearing the weight vest makes progress over the 16 weeks but never is able to record times that are as good as the group without the vest. How will the two groups do on race day if they are tested under equal conditions (either with or without the vests)? We must run the race to find out!

It is easy to predict why the students running with the weighted vest recorded poorer workout times. How well will they do in the race without the vest? Did the extra weight they had to carry influence their fitness level or just their performance? Each of us can

guess the results of the experiment just described, but we must collect and analyze the data to be sure. However, it should be apparent that it would be unfair to test the two groups under different conditions (one with weight vest and one without). The test must be completed under common conditions.

Experimental Validity

Another factor that sets our everyday experiments apart from those of the scientist is the care taken to control the environment in which the experiment is conducted and the concern the scientist has for the generalizabil-

clearly indicate the nature of the study and that the subjects are free to withdraw their consent without penalty at any time.

Risk and Benefits. Experimenters are charged with the safety and well-being of the subjects involved in their study. Likewise, subjects should be informed of potential physical and psychological risks and/or benefits that may arise from the conduct of the study. The experimenter, subject, and perhaps even an outside review board must weigh the potential benefits versus the potential risk.

Privacy. Unless the subject specifically releases his or her data or other material related to the experiment (e.g., videotape), the experimenter is charged with confidentiality. The individual or group data may be presented provided that individual identity is withheld.

Deception and Debriefing. An experimenter should avoid deceiving subjects whenever possible. However, it is sometimes not possible to tell the subject the whole truth in advance. Prior knowledge may influence or bias the manner in which the subject responds. If it is necessary to deceive or simply withhold information from the subject, it is required that the experimenter conduct a debriefing session as soon as possible after the experiment. The subjects should be told what information was withheld and the reasons for doing so.

ity of the results. Control is necessary to ensure the internal validity of the experimental results.

Internal validity refers to the degree to which the manipulation of an independent variable in an experiment truly accounts for the changes observed by the experimenter. Internal validity increases as the experiment provides a more convincing demonstration that the observed change was a result of the experimental manipulation. Was the change in driving time a predictable result of the new route or did a car wreck or other irregular event influence driving time? Did the fertilizer cause the increase in plant size or was it that the plot had better drainage and more sun? Could it be that the second brand of ice cream we sampled tasted richer because it was the subjects' favorite flavor and not because it was truly richer? By more carefully controlling our experiment, we would increase internal validity and be better able to attribute the change to the variable under consideration. This is not to say that a carefully controlled experiment proves that a manipulation causes a specific change. Causality is very difficult to establish. By conducting experiments, scientists can find evidence that is consistent with a cause-and-effect relationship. It is possible to find evidence that disproves causality, but it is not possible to directly prove a manipulation of one variable causes the change in another.

External validity refers to the extent to which the results of the experiment are generalizable. Would the shortcut save time for other drivers, at different times of day, or in different weather conditions? Would the fertilizer produce similar results for different types of plants, soil conditions, or at a different time of year? Can we expect other customers who sample the ice creams to choose as we did if they prefer a different flavor, if the time of day were different, if the outside temperature were very cold, or if they had just come from the dentist? Generalizations are important to scientific study. A goal of research is to make statements that extend beyond the specific experiment and can be applied to a range of situations involving similar variables.

Ecological validity refers to the degree to which the conditions of the experiment are representative of conditions encountered in the real world. This term was popularized by Niesser (1967) because of a concern that laboratory research was becoming more and more distant from real life. Ecological validity increases when the experiment involves performances in real, everyday, and culturally significant situations. The ecological concern is that as the experimenter more carefully controls the experimental conditions and tasks, the results tell us less about how a person performs in everyday situations. This does not mean that all laboratory experiments are ecologically invalid but rather that laboratory experiments should be concerned with capturing the fundamental principles existing in more natural environments.

The reader should be aware that the controls used by scientists to increase internal validity often decrease external and ecological validity. This causes scientists a great deal of concern because they would like to generalize from their research to other situations, especially real-life situations, and to a wide range of subjects. However, questions of internal validity require careful control of the subjects and the environment in which the tests are conducted. The scientist wishes to conduct an experiment in which the results are clearly attributable to the experimental manipulation. Thus, the scientist is left with the dilemma of trading off internal validity for external and ecological validity or vice versa. This trade-off often causes scientists to include more groups or more testing conditions in order to demonstrate more clearly the influence of an independent variable and still be able to generalize the results to more than the specific testing conditions and subjects. But proof in a mathematical or logical sense is not necessary for scientific inquiry to advance. The scientist cannot prove that the sun will come up tomorrow, but we all have confidence that it will. Scientists have not been able to prove a link between smoking and lung cancer, but their experiments have left little doubt in our minds.

Motor Learning and Control: A Behavioral Emphasis

Allowing for Individual Differences

There is a tendency to approach behavioral science theory and research the way we read a cookbook: The notion is that each time we combine the specified ingredients and bake at a certain temperature, our cake will turn out exactly the same. For example, we might turn to Chapter 12 to find out exactly how social factors will influence our motor learning and performance. To our surprise, we discover that the research, like much scientific investigation, is aimed at predicting how *most people* will behave under specified circumstances *most of the time*. The results are not absolute.

But we know that although we share many similarities with other people, we also have many differences that make us unique. These *individual differences* may include physical factors such as our specific muscle development, genetic factors, personality, and experiences. Each of these factors can have a profound effect on our learning, control, and performance. A coach may identify a person who seems to have all the attributes to be a star gymnast, only to find that even with the most intense training, that particular person does not develop as expected.

The area of individual differences poses an exciting, and sometimes frustrating, task for us. After developing theories about how people "in general" act, we then use more refined probes to explore the role of individual differences. In doing this we may examine gender, age, race, experience, size, personality, and hundreds of other personal characteristics. Through this process we constantly improve and refine our theories and models. We can make more precise predictions, and develop more unique training programs. The focus on individual differences is an important and central one in the field of motor learning and control, and you will see these issues in each area we discuss.

However, keep in mind that science is a constantly developing process; it often finds more questions than answers. And because of this state, we are still uncovering information about the impact of individual differences on behavior. We talk about probabilities and tendencies rather than certainties. Thus, you may be frustrated not to find a formula that states that "Cindy Smith will develop in this way at this time, and if she follows this program, she will become this type of athlete." We can, however, talk about the probabilities of someone with Ms. Smith's attributes developing and behaving in a specific way. Thus, as you read this text, keep the concept of individual differences in mind and identify some of the questions that might be examined in future research on motor learning and control.

This text is concerned with human motor control—the learning and control of purposeful movements in intact humans: the fluid and powerful movements of a dancer, a basketball player, or a diver; the sequenced and patterned finger-arm movements of an artist, typist, or pianist; the everyday movements of everyday people and the wondrous actions of the most highly skilled. Movements are our link with the environment around us. We can explore, communicate with, and change our environment through movement. The ability to move allows us to eat, work, and play.

Although the focus of this text is meant to be on a broad range of motor performances, not just on those related to sport or work, we do concentrate on skilled movements. Adams (1987), in a historical review of skilled behaviors, suggests that a definition of skill in this context has three defining characteristics. First, it must have wide boundaries but not so wide as to include "a physician making a clinical decision or the skill of a mathematician." Second, a skill is learned. Thus, we will deemphasize movements that are primarily reflexive and those that can be considered primarily genetically defined (e.g., walking). However, our concern will be with all stages of learning. We do not concentrate on the highly skilled but rather on the processes that allow that skill to be accomplished. Last, skill relates to tasks that require movement for goal attainment. Thus, our concern is more with the processes of a pianist, athlete, or machinist than with those of a mathematician, philosopher, or writer. In addition, we are more concerned with the learning of a task than with training. The changes in performance capabilities of a distance runner or powerlifter after intense training are of less interest than a child's learning to ride a bike or a teenager's learning to drive a standard shift car.

Behavioral Level of Analysis

There are many levels at which the study of motor learning and control could begin (Pew, 1974). The focus of this text is primarily on the behavioral level of analysis. That is, we use the observables (stimuli and motor actions) in the movement environment in an attempt to understand the processes that contribute to motor learning and control. This requires that from our observations we must infer processes rather than measure the processes directly. The observables are the tools we use in an attempt to unravel the mysteries of motor behavior. We are first and foremost concerned with underlying processes that contribute to skilled motor performance. The behavioral level of analysis is sharply contrasted with the neurophysiological level of analysis in which the study of learning and control is carried out by directly measuring the functions of the senses, brain, spinal cord, and motor units. An advantage of the behavioral level of analysis is that intact humans and animals can be studied in more or less normal conditions. In many cases, the neurophysiological level of analysis requires special *in vivo* and *in vitro* preparations.

A true understanding of motor skills, however, requires experimental analysis on various levels. Pew (1974) suggests that "skilled behavior is the rich intermingling of these various levels of control as a function of the task demands, the state of learning of the subject, and the constraints imposed on the task and the subject by the environment." Thus, in this text we try to weave important findings from neurophysiology and biomechanics into our study.

Information Processing Approach

There are many approaches that could be taken to study motor learning and control. We primarily utilize an information processing approach. Throughout the text, we view humans as active processors of information rather than as passive recipients. We do not always respond to the same stimuli in the same way. We consider the current circumstances and past experiences stored in memory before formulating a course of action. We seek out information and interpret stimuli based on the context in which it is presented. The basic assumption of the information processing approach is that when an individual performs a movement, there are a number of cognitive processes that are required for the movement to be executed correctly.

Consider a tennis player about to receive a serve. The player must utilize sight and sound to determine how fast the ball is moving, where it is going, and what type of spin has been put on the ball. This information along with information stored in memory from similar past situations is used to plan and execute an appropriate return. These processes represent our ability to process information. Reflect on movements you make every day. What are the processes involved in those movements? Finding the answer is our task.

FINAL COMMENT

The field of motor learning and motor control is concerned with the processes involved in the learning and control of motor skills. The field grew out of and still is closely aligned with the disciplines of psychology, physiology, engineering, and education. Motor learning and control is considered a science because researchers in this field formulate questions, test hypotheses, conduct experiments, develop theories, and devise models. Experiments planned as a result of induction (bottom up) reasoning are termed empirical and experiments formulated as a result of deductive (top down) thinking are termed theoretical.

KEY TERMS

motor learning
motor control
reciprocal
   innervation
final common
   pathway
proprioception
behaviorism
operant conditioning

central intermittency
single channel
   hypothesis
functionalism
hypothesis
experiment
empirical
coordinating
   definition

induction
law
theory
postulates
theoretical
deduction
descriptive statistics
inferential statistics
population

sample
randomization
independent variable
dependent variable
control group
experimental group
internal validity
external validity
ecological validity

2
Biological Foundations

Agnes de Mille: RECOVERY FROM A STROKE

Neurons
- *Neural Impulses*
- *Synaptic Transmission*
- *Functional Types of Neurons*

Neural Control of Muscle Force
- *Motor-Unit Recruitment*
- *Rate Coding*

Major Subdivisions of the Nervous System
- *Central and Peripheral*
- *Sensory and Motor*
- *Autonomic*

HIGHLIGHT: Computer-Based Methods of Brain Examination Without Surgery
HIGHLIGHT: Recovery From Brain Damage
FINAL COMMENT
KEY TERMS

Agnes de Mille: RECOVERY FROM A STROKE

On May 15, 1975, at 5:50 P.M., a blood vessel burst in the brain of Agnes de Mille, a prominent ballet dancer and choreographer. For over sixty years, she had struggled to perfect her skills and to win support for her work. Now she was fighting for her life as blood gushed into her brain's soft tissues, tearing and compressing major centers. There was no pain, no awareness that something was wrong. The first clue came when de Mille tried to sign a contract with a new cast member. "I can't write," she said quietly. "My hand won't work." After sitting down, her symptoms became more alarming. "I have no feeling in my right leg. I can't feel on the right side. Am I talking funny? I seem to be talking funny."

Fortunately, Dr. George Gorham arrived within minutes and put de Mille in a New York hospital. Later he was joined by Dr. Fred Plum, chief neurologist, who took charge of the case, and Dr. Caroline McCagg, a specialist in rehabilitation medicine. The doctors watched CAT scan images of the blood spreading in de Mille's brain. "This is speech . . . possibly sight." As the blot grew larger, they said, "That is all speech and mobility." After observing the images, they prepared her husband for the worst: "There is blood in the spinal fluid, and that is usually fatal."

De Mille never became discouraged following her stroke. Her vital spark never dimmed even though her right side was paralyzed and she could neither see nor speak clearly. She simply blocked out doubt as she had learned to do in her work. The doctors at-

Agnes de Mille, a prominent ballet dancer and choreographer, learned physical discipline in her sixty years of dancing. The greatest test of her discipline, however, came during physical therapy after her stroke.

- To examine the anatomy and physiology of neurons.
- To appreciate the methods by which neurons are activated to control force.
- To examine the interaction of the central and peripheral nervous systems.
- To appreciate the interaction of the sympathetic and parasympathetic divisions of the autonomic nervous system.

tributed the modern medical miracle that followed to her vital energy. Her sight and speech returned quickly, but the paralysis persisted.

De Mille had learned physical discipline long ago as a young dancer. Now she concentrated every measure of that control on her physical therapy. Her determination peaked when a therapist said that she would never again rise on her toes to do relevés onto full point (a ballet step). Two months later she was doing four relevés and within six months she was doing eight.

Speaking of her remarkable recovery, Dr. Plum remarked: "Those who can learn from and follow her example will enrich their lives as Agnes de Mille has enriched hers and, by her radiance of spirit, mine."

■ ■ ■

De Mille's struggle for life raises important questions: How did the doctors know that her stroke threatened her speech, sight, and mobility? Why did damage on the left side of her brain paralyze the right side of her body? We will answer these and other questions when we explore the nervous system, a coordinating mechanism that controls body functions and behaviors.

The nervous system has many parts that maintain control by sending messages to one another. Even the simple action of picking up this book and opening it to this chapter required more messages in the nervous system than those sent over the Bell Telephone system on holidays. This chapter will discuss the mechanisms that keep our neural messages flowing. You know this flow is no small accomplishment if you have ever had to wait hours to get a phone call through jammed telephone lines. Our attempt to understand this accomplishment begins with an analysis of microscopic parts. We then move on to larger components of the system.

Neurons

Neurons are cells that receive and send messages throughout the nervous system. Your brain contains 100 to 200 billion neurons, and each one connects with many others. As a result, your nervous system has more connections between neurons than there are stars in our galaxy (Hoyenga & Hoyenga, 1988). Figure 2.1 shows a neuron's main parts. Some features occur in all cells: a cell nucleus, cell membrane, and cell body. Other components are unique to a neuron's function of receiving and sending messages. **Dendrites** are tiny branchlike fibers extending from the cell body that receive messages. An **axon** is a single extension that carries messages to thousands of terminal branches that reach out to dendrites of other neurons. The illustrated axon has a fatty covering called a myelin sheath, which

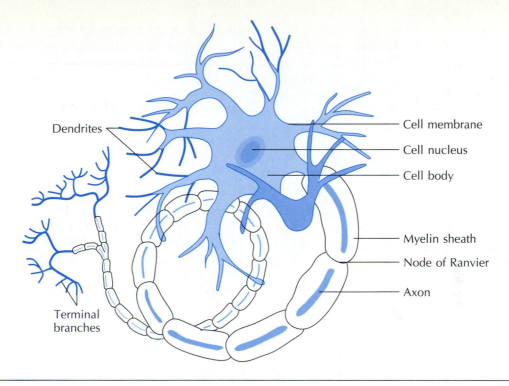

Dendrites

Cell membrane

Cell nucleus

Cell body

Myelin sheath

Node of Ranvier

Axon

Terminal branches

Figure 2.1   *A typical myelinated neuron.*

has gaps called nodes of Ranvier. Such myeli-nated axons carry neural messages faster be-cause the impulses skip from one node to the next. In fact, neural messages can travel as fast as 400 feet per second on myelinated axons and as slow as 3 feet per second on un-myelinated ones.

Neural Impulses

Neural messages enabled Agnes de Mille to rise to her toes to do relevés onto full point. They are enabling you to read and understand at this moment. In fact, they are the basis for all our perceptions and actions. It is rather as-tonishing, therefore, that the language of neural messages is a simple *off–on* code.

The *off* and *on* states are defined by the distribution of ions, or charged particles (e.g., sodium and potassium). Ions, with positive and negative charges, are inside and outside every neuron. An imbalance of these charges creates a **membrane potential**, which is an electric tension across the cell membrane.

During the *off* state, which is also called the *resting state* or the *state of polarization*, nega-tively charged ions are concentrated on the inside and positively charged ions are concen-trated on the outside. During the *on* state, which is also called the *action potential* or *state of depolarization*, positive ions rush inside one spot in the neuron. They are then quickly pumped out to bring the neuron back to its resting state. This process is immediately re-peated at a neighboring area until the action potential travels the entire length of the cell membrane (Figures 2.2 and 2.3).

Synaptic Transmission

When an action potential travels to the end of an axon, it reaches a synapse, which is a junc-tion between two neurons. Movement of a neural impulse across this junction is called synaptic transmission. The process has four steps. First, the action potential reaches an axon terminal, a tiny knob at the end of an axon's terminal branch. Second, a synaptic

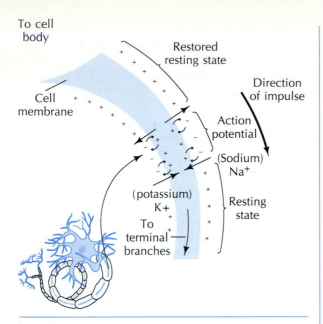

To cell body

Restored resting state

Direction of impulse

Cell membrane

Action potential

(Sodium) Na+

(potassium) K+

To terminal branches

Resting state

Figure 2.2 *When a point on the neural membrane is adequately stimulated by an incoming message, the membrane opens at that point and positively charged sodium ions flow in, depolarizing the neuron. This process is repeated along the length of the membrane, creating the neural impulse that travels down the axon, causing the neuron to fire.*

vesicle then releases a chemical transmitter substance. Third, the chemical crosses a synaptic space, a very small gap between neurons. And fourth, the chemical enters receptor sites on the dendrite (Figure 2.4).

A strong synaptic transmission will cause an action potential in the receiving cell. The strength must be above a minimum or threshold level. This threshold is sometimes compared to the minimum trigger pull required to fire a gun. A bullet will not fire if the trigger is not pulled hard enough. Similarly, an action potential will not fire unless synaptic transmission is strong enough.

The initiation of an action potential is an all-or-none event, which again is similar to firing a gun. A trigger pulled hard enough to fire a gun is hard enough to fire it at full force. Pulling the trigger harder will not make the bullet go faster or farther. Similarly, a neuron either fires an action potential at full force or it does not fire it at all. Stronger stimuli do not trigger stronger action potentials. They do,

however, trigger them at a faster rate. Thus, the strength of a stimulus is indicated by the rate at which neurons fire.

Firing rate is limited by an absolute refractory period, which is about 1 millisecond (1/1000 second) after one action potential during which another one is impossible. After this brief period, neurons enter a relative refractory period—that is, several milliseconds during which a neuron can be fired only by a very strong synaptic transmission. In other words, the threshold level goes beyond reach for one millisecond (the absolute refractory period), then remains very high for several more milliseconds (the relative refractory period).

The strength of a synaptic transmission varies with the chemical transmitter used at a synapse. Some transmitters shout loudly and get fast action. Others speak softly and nudge

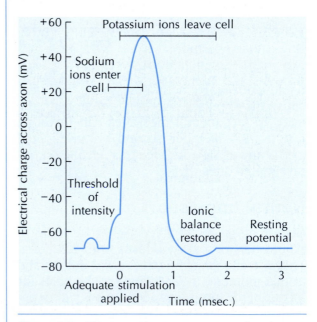

Figure 2.3 *The incoming message must be above a certain threshold to cause a neuron to fire. After it fires, the cell body begins to pump potassium ions out of the neuron until a state of ionic equilibrium is restored. This process happens very quickly and within a few thousandths of a second the neuron is ready to fire again. The small "bump" to the lower left represents an incoming message that was too weak to cause the neuron to fire. Adapted from Carlson, 1981.*

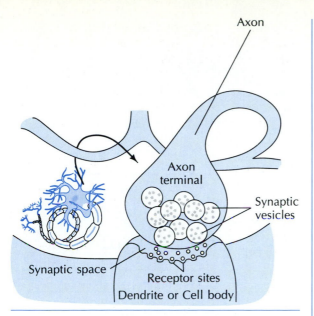

Figure 2.4 *Synaptic transmission occurs when a neurotransmitter carries a neural impulse from the axon of one neuron to the dendrites of another.*

neurons toward action slowly but surely. Some excite neurons as we have been discussing. Others inhibit neurons making them harder to fire. Remember, the neuron does not fire unless the threshold has been reached.

The most common transmitter is acetylcholine (Ach). It delivers a strong, excitatory message, usually to muscles. Then it is broken down into chemical parts, transported back to the axon, reassembled, and stored in the synaptic vesicles. Deadly poisons affect Ach. For example, botulism, a severe food poisoning, blocks the release of Ach and causes paralysis. Death can result from respiratory paralysis. In contrast, the venom of the black widow spider interferes with the breakdown of Ach. Too much builds up in synapses, and the muscles contract and become paralyzed. Again, death results in severe cases.

Other important transmitters are known as catecholamines. Some are excitatory; others are inhibitory. All are cleared out of the synapse by a powerful transport system. Cocaine works by blocking this transport system.

Other neural transmitters are dramatically affected by exercise. For example, long distance running elevates the level of **endorphins**, a word meaning "endogenous [internal] morphine." Morphine, of course, is a powerful pain killer (Colt, Wardlaw, & Frantz, 1981). Thus, as the name suggests, endorphins reduce sensitivity to pain (Besson & Chaouch, 1987). Running and vigorous walking also increase levels of norepinephrine. Low levels of this neural transmitter are related to feelings of depression. Some clinicians suggest, therefore, that you can raise norepinephrine levels and reduce depression by taking brisk walks.

Functional Types of Neurons

Three categories of neurons carry neural messages between the brain, spinal cord, and muscles. Sensory neurons, which are also called **afferent** neurons (the prefix *a*- means *to*) carry signals to the brain or spinal cord. Motor neurons, which are also called **efferent** neurons (the prefix *e*- means *from*), carry signals from the brain or spinal cord. **Interneurons** originate and terminate in the brain or spinal cord. We will encounter many examples of these categories when we consider the larger structures of the nervous system.

Neural Control of Muscle Force

We stated that neural messages control our actions. They controlled Agnes de Mille's dance steps, and they control your ability to pick up and read this book. To follow through on this point, let's discuss the role neurons play in controlling muscle force.

Muscles are composed of many intertwined fibers. A typical muscle fiber is innervated by one neuron, called a **motor neuron**. The stimulus is an action potential sent from the motoneuron to the fiber. A motor neuron and the muscle fibers it innervates form a

motor unit. The number of muscle fibers in a motor unit varies. More than one thousand fibers may comprise a motor unit in the lower leg while a motor unit from the hand or eye may contain one hundred or less fibers. Generally, the fewer fibers in the motor unit, the more precise the movements. Each motor unit, however, can exert force.

The nervous system controls a muscle's force by controlling motor units. It has two options. The first is motor-unit **recruitment**, the process of varying the number of activated motor units. The second is **rate coding**, the process of varying the rate at which each active motor unit generates action potentials.

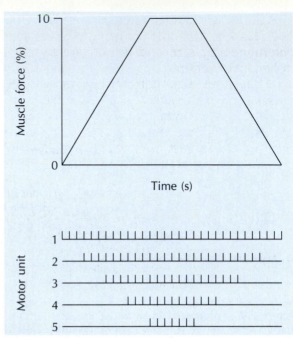

Figure 2.5 *Simplified motor neuron pool with five motor units.*

As a young dancer Agnes de Mille performed complicated steps with apparent ease. But even a simple dance step may require more messages to be sent in the nervous system than sent over the Bell telephone system on holidays.

Motor-Unit Recruitment

To recruit motor units means to activate them. They are usually activated and deactivated in a set sequence. The **size principle** is the most popular theory of how this orderly recruitment is controlled. Accordingly, the sequence depends on the size of the motoneurons. Motor units with the smallest motoneurons are recruited first and deactivated last. Motor units with the largest motoneurons are recruited last and deactivated first. Figure 2.5 shows a simplified motoneuron pool with five motor units. The smallest motor unit is 1; the largest is 5; and the intermediate ones are 2, 3, and 4 in order. The figure represents a special case in which motor-unit recruitment is the only factor affecting muscle force. Motor units are recruited in the order 1, 2, 3, 4, 5. Then, motor unit 5 is the first to be deactivated; motor unit 4 is deactivated next, and so on. Notice motor unit 1, the smallest, is active from the beginning to the end of the contraction, and motor unit 5, the largest, is only active during the brief period of maximal force. According to the size principle, the order of recruitment is predetermined by size and is not directly controlled by the brain.

Motor-unit size corresponds to specific muscle characteristics. For example, the smallest motor units, Type S, are slow-contracting, low-force, and fatigue-resistant. In contrast, the largest motor units, Type FF, are fast-contracting, high-force, and fatigable.

Rate Coding

Muscle force depends not only on the number of active motor units, but also on the rate at which motor units discharge action potentials. There are two kinds of rate codings. One is to vary the overall frequency of action potentials. Another method is to vary the temporal pattern of action potentials between different motor units. Let's consider each of these in turn.

Rate coding through the control of overall action potential is the most complex. Generally, muscle force increases as discharge rate increases. But the relationship between muscle force and discharge rate is different for two types of motor units: tonic and phasic. *Tonic* motor units increase discharge rate as muscle force increases at low levels. Then their discharge rate remains constant as muscle force continues to increase at high levels. In contrast, *phasic* motor units increase discharge rate as muscle force increases over the entire muscle force range. It is not known how these types relate to the classification of motor-unit size (e.g., Types S and FF). However, some other characteristics are known. Tonic motor units discharge smaller action potentials than phasic motor units. Tonic units are also recruited earlier and are less fatigable than phasic units.

Another form of rate coding is the discharge of two or more motor units at the same time. These synchronous discharges have been observed in muscles that were developed through strength training. It has been

Muscle force is determined both by the number of motor units used (recruitment) and by the frequency with which the motor units are innervated.

suggested, therefore, that muscle force increases when motor units are synchronized.

Although we have described recruitment and rate coding separately, these two options are executed at the same time. That is, muscle forces are often determined by a combination of both kinds of control processes. Surely, both options were used at the same time during Agnes de Mille's dance steps. And surely you will use both kinds at the same time as you go about your activities today.

You will also use billions of neurons throughout your nervous system. The next sections explain how you coordinate this complex neural activity.

Major Subdivisions of the Nervous System

Our billions of neurons interact efficiently because highly organized subdivisions of the nervous system regulate the interactions. De Mille's doctors could anticipate the consequences of her stroke because the function of critical structures is the same from person to person. This consistency also enables us to draw some generalizations about structure-function relationships. Figure 2.6 summarizes the major subdivisions. You might want to refer to this chart as we take up each component.

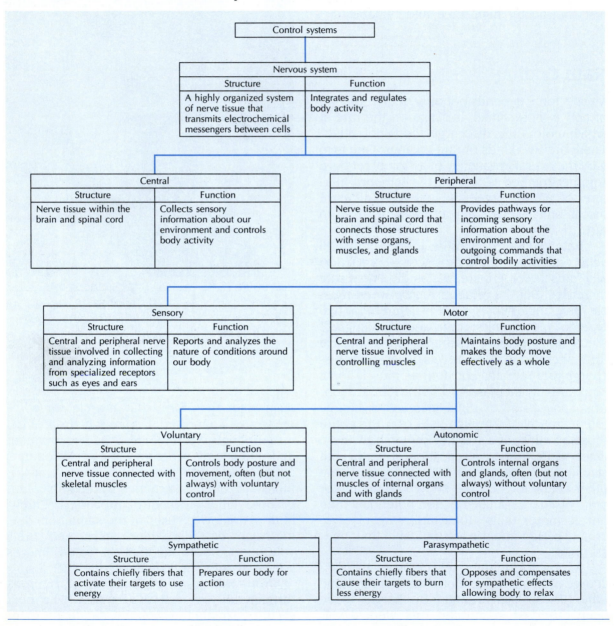

Figure 2.6 *Overview of the nervous system.*

Central and Peripheral Nervous Systems

Neurons of the brain and spinal cord make up the **central nervous system** (CNS). All other neurons are part of the **peripheral nervous system**. Let's concentrate on the brain first.

The Brain.   Figure 2.7 shows a photograph of a human brain, which is about three pounds of soft, spongy, pinkish-gray nerve tissue. You will find it more helpful to refer to the drawing in Figure 2.8 as we discuss the basic parts of the brain.

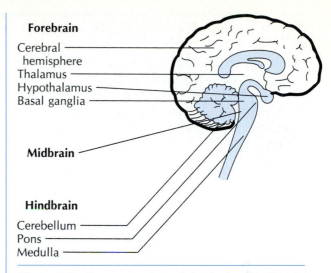

Figure 2.8   A cross section of the brain showing the hindbrain, midbrain, and forebrain.

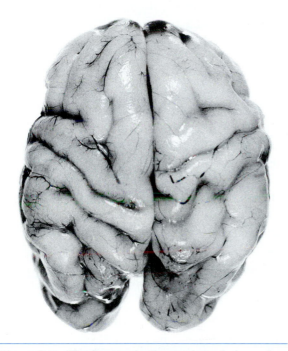

Figure 2.7   The human brain consists of about three pounds of soft, spongy, pinkish-gray nerve tissue. This incredible structure is the control center of our physical and emotional being.

Brainstem.   Figure 2.8 shows the brainstem, a pedestal-like structure connecting the rest of the brain to the spinal cord. The brainstem consists of four important parts:

1. *Medulla.* Directly above the spinal cord is the medulla, a slender tube no larger than your index finger. Even slight damage to the medulla can be fatal because its neurons control breathing and heartbeat, as well as posture.

2. *Pons.* The wider part of the brainstem above the medulla is called the pons. It consists of a cable of neurons that are critical in the control of movements. Injury to the pons can result in movement disorders such as "restless-leg" syndrome, which is characterized by extreme thrashing about during sleep.

3. *Cerebellum.* Two wrinkled hemispheres strapped onto the back of the pons are known as the cerebellum. This part of the brain regulates the force, range, and rate of our movements. Injury to the cerebellum leaves a person without muscular tone, strength, and coordination.

4. *Midbrain.* Above the pons the brainstem widens again in an area called the midbrain. We would face unconsciousness or death if our midbrain were damaged because so many vital nerve fibers run through it. The midbrain also contains the reticular formation, a mass of neurons involved in alertness, arousal, and consciousness.

Computer-Based Methods of Brain Examination Without Surgery

The computerized axial tomography (CAT) scanner, which was so new when Agnes de Mille had her stroke in 1975, is now readily available in most communities across the nation. In addition, many hospitals are acquiring other powerful computer-based instruments for studying the brain without surgical intervention. Health sections of newspapers and magazines are filled with articles describing these instruments in more detail than we can do here. But we can briefly describe some of the instruments and discuss how they enhance clinical diagnosis and experimental research.

Most of what is known about the brain was learned by observing the effects of brain damage. The fact that brain damage causes behavioral deficits has been known for at least five thousand years. The last two hundred years have provided the kind of area-by-area analysis that enabled doctors to predict de Mille's paralysis and loss of speech. CAT scanners and other computer-based instruments are not only fine tuning the examination of injured or diseased brains, but also are providing "windows" for observing normal brain operation.

Picture 2A shows a powerful technique for observing brain processes that was developed by adding computer-based filters to recordings of the brain's electrical activity. In the 1920s, the German psychiatrist Hans Berger produced an electroencephalogram (EEG),

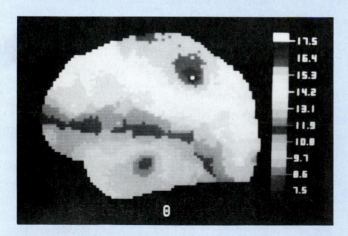

2A The electroencephalogram (EEG), an early brain monitoring technique, is based on the electrical activity of brain.

2B (opposite page). Physicians use computerized axial tomography (CAT) to safely view brain structure.

which is an amplified recording of waves of electrical activity that are picked up by electrodes taped to the head. An EEG reveals changes in these brain waves as a function of different activities. For example, Berger observed faster waves during problem solving than during relaxation. With the assistance of a computer, it is also possible to record evoked potentials, which are changes in EEGs that are caused by the occurrence of certain responses or by the presentation of certain stimuli. Computers determine the nature of evoked potentials by averaging over many trials EEG changes that occur when people make simple responses such as pushing buttons or when people are exposed to visual, auditory, olfactory, taste, or touch stimuli. Research laboratories and medical clinics measure EEGs and evoked potentials because these recordings can reveal both normal and abnormal brain functions.

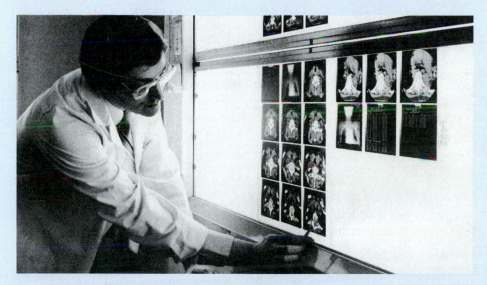

A CAT scan (Picture 2B) is a computer-generated representation of brain structures. An X-ray beam scans the brain while a computer records how much of the beam is absorbed. The amount of absorption depends upon the density of the scanned tissues, fluids, and bone. The computer is programmed to interpret the pattern of absorption and display its interpretation of brain structures in a color-coded image on a monitor. An advantage of CAT scans is that they can be done without injecting dyes and without presenting special risks or discomfort to the patient.

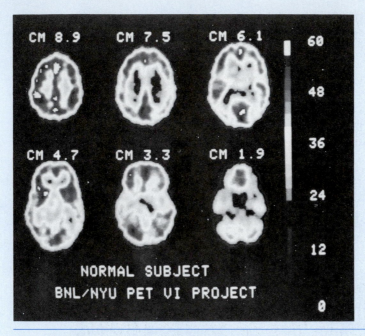

2C *Positron emission tomography (PET) detects the metabolic activity in the brain rather than brain structure.*

Picture 2C shows a PET (positron emission tomography) scan, which is a computer-generated representation of brain activity. First, a temporarily radioactive sugar is administered and then the brain is scanned to determine where the sugar is absorbed. Since sugar is a fuel for activity, the amount of absorption depends upon activity level—more active areas absorb more sugar. The computer interprets the pattern of absorption and displays its interpretation of brain activity in a color-coded image on a display monitor. Phelps and Mazziotta (1985) used PET scans to determine which brain areas are most active while people listen to music, do mathematical calculations, and daydream. Chugani and Phelps (1986), using PET scans on infants at different ages, found different rates of maturation for different brain structures. Maturation occurred by 5 weeks for the brainstem, by 3 months for most of the cerebral cortex, and by 7.5 months for the frontal lobes of the cortex.

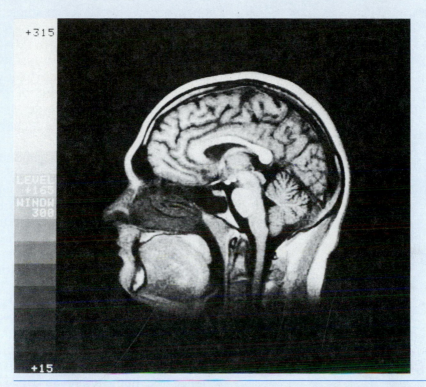

2D *Magnetic resonance imagery (MRI) provides the most detailed view of brain structure commonly available today.*

Picture 2D shows a computer display generated by magnetic resonance imaging (MRI). The head is put in a magnetic field that aligns the axis of rotation of all atoms that have an odd atomic weight. A radio frequency then makes all the aligned atoms spin. After the radio frequency is turned off, a computer monitors electromagnetic energy that is released when these atoms stop spinning. The computer interprets the underlying structures from the pattern of energy released and displays its interpretation in a color-coded image. Today, MRIs are providing the most detailed views of the living nervous system that are possible so far.

Downs syndrome is a genetic disorder that affects the development of the central nervous system. The genetic defect that results in Downs syndrome has also been implicated in Alzheimer's disease.

Forebrain. The rest of the brain is called the forebrain. We can identify important parts by continuing to follow Figure 2.8 upward. The hypothalamus, located directly above the brainstem, contains nerve centers that control body temperature and rate of burning fat and carbohydrates. Other maintenance functions are indicated by the consequences of injury. We might notice, for example, impairments of bowel movements, urinary output, sweating, and reaction to pleasure and pain. Two egg-shaped structures called the thalamus are located above the hypothalamus. The thalamus integrates incoming sensory information from all parts of our body. A damaged thalamus would distort our sensations of the world. The **basal ganglia** are four masses of gray matter located deep in the forebrain. They modify commands from other structures in the brain

in ways that are not completely understood. One result of these modifications is to regulate "background" muscle tone (Brown & Frank, 1987). When we write, for example, the basal ganglia prepare for hand movements by tensing the upper part of our arm. Mushrooming above the thalamus are two furrowed structures called the **cerebral cortex**, which accounts for about 80 percent of the brain's weight. This is where Agnes de Mille's stroke occurred. Its many functions include abstract reasoning and speech.

The cerebral cortex has right and left cerebral hemispheres. These two halves are defined by a gap that runs from front to back. The **corpus callosum** is a nerve cable that crosses this gap to connect the hemispheres. Figure 2.9 shows a side view of the right hemisphere. The gap between hemispheres is referred to in the figure as the longitudinal fissure. Another deep groove, the lateral fissure, runs obliquely behind the ear. And a third deep groove, the central fissure, runs vertically from the middle of the lateral fissure to the longitudinal fissure. You might have an easier time remembering these fissures if you visualize the hemisphere as a boxing glove. The lateral fissure forms the thumb of the glove. The central fissure runs across the glove's knuckle section.

Figure 2.9 also labels four areas:

1. The frontal lobe forms the fingers of the boxing glove; it is the area in front of the central fissure and above the lateral fis-

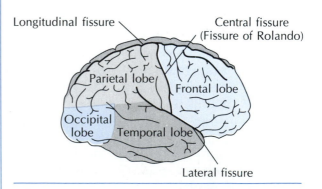

Figure 2.9 *Side view of a cerebral hemisphere, showing the various lobes and fissures.*

sure. It receives sensory messages after they have been processed by other parts of the cortex. It also sends messages to muscles.

2. The occipital lobe is the hindmost section of the brain and receives visual input. Using the boxing glove analogy, the occipital lobe is where the hand inserts into the glove.

3. The parietal lobe represents the back of the hand. It extends back from the central fissure to the occipital lobe. It responds to touch, pain, and temperature.

4. The temporal lobe is below the lateral fissure and in front of the occipital lobe. It looks like the thumb in our imaginary box-

ing glove. It has diverse functions including the control of speech and the processing of sounds and smells. De Mille's stroke originated in her left temporal lobe.

Figure 2.10 illustrates two bands on the top of the cerebral cortex. One, the motor cortex, controls our movements. The other, the somatosensory cortex, processes sensory information from the body. Penfield and Rasmussen (1950) determined the link between these cortexes and specific parts of the body as shown in Figure 2.10. Their technique allowed patients to remain awake during brain surgery for treatment of epilepsy. They determined that stimulation of the motor cortex moved specific muscles, and stimulation of

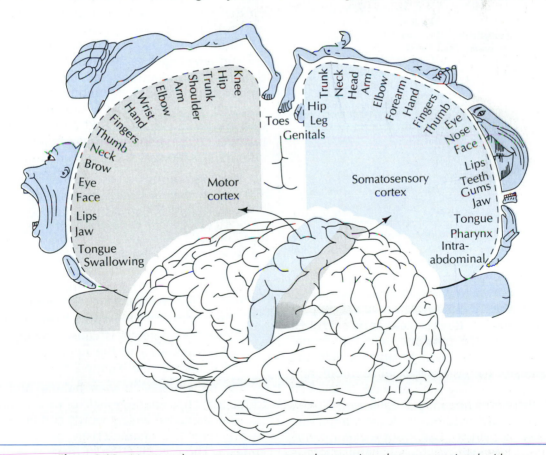

Figure 2.10 *Motor and somatosensory cortexes have regions that are associated with specific body parts. The relationships are shown by drawing body parts over the corresponding brain areas. The body parts are drawn smaller or larger to reflect the amount of brain surface devoted to each.*

the somatosensory cortex triggered sensations from specific body parts. For example, the surgeon would apply a small probe to the surface of the exposed cortex and the patient would report a numbness of the tongue, another position and the patient would report a tingling of the fingers. Notice that some body parts, such as the thumb, cover large sections of these cortexes. Other parts, such as the forearm, cover small sections.

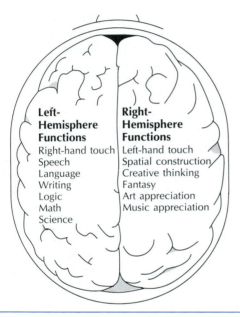

Figure 2.11 *The left and right brain hemispheres specialize in different functions. Split-brain research suggests that functions are divided as indicated.*

Roger Sperry (1970) also revealed important properties of the cerebral cortex through surgery to reduce epileptic seizures. Figure 2.11 illustrates his findings that the left and right sides of the cortex specialize in different functions. By cutting the connection between the hemispheres (the corpus callosum), Sperry reduced seizures without noticeably impairing everyday activities. Laboratory experiments indicated, however, that each hemisphere is strong in some areas and weak in others. These experiments took advantage of an amazing fact. Sensory and motor information from the right side of the body, the right visual field, or the right ear is processed by the left hemisphere and vice versa. That's why a stroke on the left side of de Mille's cortex affected the right side of her body. Sperry found that the two sides of the cortex are specialized in other ways as well. Consider, for example, some evidence that mathematical abilities reside in the left hemisphere. Sperry's patients could solve complex math problems when they were presented in the right visual field, but they could do no math more complex than adding two-digit numbers when the problems were presented in the left visual field. In 1981, Sperry won a Nobel Prize in medicine for his research, which not only revealed hemispheric specialization, but also paved the way for the development of life-saving techniques of brain surgery.

Studying the relationship between the cortex and language has also depended upon research with human patients, especially those with language disorders. Two pioneers in this research were Paul Broca (1824–1880) and Carl Wernicke (1848–1905). De Mille's case illustrates two well-known disorders named after these scientists:

1. **Broca's aphasia** is characterized by speech that is slow, labored, and slightly distorted. It is caused by injury to Broca's area in the left anterior lobe (Figure 2.12).

2. **Wernicke's aphasia** refers to speech that sounds normal until attention is paid to meaning. The speech includes wrong words and nonsense words, and the message seems to shift from topic to topic. Wernicke's aphasia is caused by injury to Wernicke's area in the upper part of the left temporal lobe (Figure 2.12).

De Mille's speech was halting and distorted, which is characteristic of Broca's aphasia. She also used wrong words and nonsense words, which is characteristic of Wernicke's aphasia. The combination of these two disorders reminds us that normal speech requires the coordination of cognitive and motor control processes.

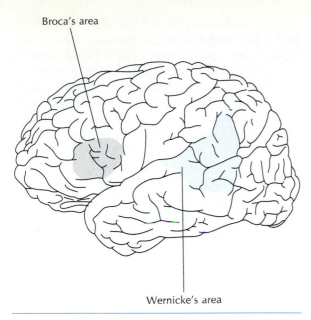

Broca's area

Wernicke's area

Figure 2.12 *Broca's area and Wernicke's area of the brain.*

The Spinal Cord. The **spinal cord** is made up of nerve tissue that runs from the brainstem through the backbone to the lower back. Figure 2.13A shows a cross section of the spinal cord. It seems to contain a bent "H" of gray matter surrounded by white matter. The gray area is composed of unmyelinated nerve fibers. The white area contains myelinated fibers. The white matter carries information to and from the brain. Ascending nerves carry sensory information up to the brain. Descending nerves carry commands down from the brain to the muscles. Paralysis is the unfortunate consequence of injury to the descending nerves. For example, the viral disease polio attacks descending nerves causing paralysis. Spinal injuries also cause paralysis. Injuries to the lower part of the spinal cord can paralyze the legs. Injuries higher up can paralyze the arms, legs, and breathing.

Spinal Reflexes. Our brain and spinal cord work together when we pick up this book. Our spinal cord responds without waiting for the brain when we jerk our foot away from a thorn. Automatic action with no conscious effort is called a *spinal reflex.*

Spinal reflexes take into account the fact that muscles work in pairs. One muscle group, the **flexors**, contract to decrease the angle of a joint. An opposing muscle group, the **extensors**, contract to increase the angle of a joint. These muscle groups come into play during the seemingly simple action of pulling our foot away from a thorn. Figure 2.13B illustrates how this response is controlled by a withdrawal reflex, a spinal reflex that moves affected body parts away from painful stimulation. A sensory neuron stimulates interneurons in the spinal cord's gray matter. The interneurons stimulate the motor neurons of the flexor muscles in the leg. They also innervate other interneurons that inhibit the leg's extensor muscles. This pattern of muscle innervations would withdraw our foot from the thorn. We also use an analogous withdrawal reflex to draw back our hand from a hot stove. The thorn example is more interesting, because we pull our foot up without falling down. We manage to stand because the withdrawal reflex in our legs always occurs with a crossed extensor reflex. This spinal reflex responds to painful foot stimulation by straightening the leg on the unprovoked side, enabling it to bear weight. Figure 2.13B shows that the interneurons that stimulate flexors and inhibit extensors on the injured side simultaneously inhibit flexors and stimulate extensors on the other side.

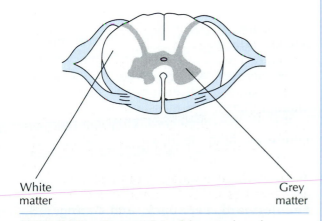

White matter

Grey matter

Figure 2.13A *Cross section of the spinal cord.*

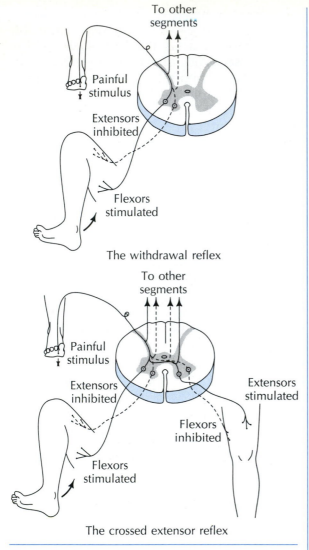

To other segments

Painful stimulus

Extensors inhibited

Flexors stimulated

The withdrawal reflex

To other segments

Painful stimulus

Extensors inhibited

Extensors stimulated

Flexors inhibited

Flexors stimulated

The crossed extensor reflex

Figure 2.13B *The withdrawal and crossed extensor reflexes.*

Figure 2.13B also shows innervations going from interneurons to other parts, or segments, of the spinal cord. These control the other movements that are needed to make a coordinated withdrawal from the thorn. For example, they might control arm and head movements to help us keep our balance. When we yank our hand away from a hot stove, messages to other segments would control actions of the shoulders, trunk, and legs to make a coordinated movement away from the painful stimulus.

If you have ever had a doctor hit your knee with a rubber hammer, he or she probably explained that it was to test a reflex. Figure 2.14A illustrates the patellar tendon reflex, a spinal reflex that contracts a stretched muscle. The hammer tap stretches the tendon, which in turn stretches the muscle and a sensory receptor located in line with the muscle. The receptor, called a muscle spindle, discharges when the muscle length is unexpectedly changed. The afferent discharge synapses in the spinal cord to innervate the stretched muscles. This results in the knee jerk response.

The stretch reflex (Fig. 2.14B) is a monosynaptic (single-synapse) reflex that differs from the others we have considered. They were all polysynaptic (many-synapses) because they had at least one interneuron between the afferent fiber and the motor neuron. Even though the stretch reflex is monosynaptic in contracting the stretched muscle, it employs interneurons to inhibit the antagonists of the stretched muscle. It can also affect muscles on the opposite side. Specifically it can have the opposite effect of inhibiting agonists and stimulating antagonists.

You have stretch reflexes throughout your body. For example, suppose you hold your arm out with your hand facing up. A weight dropped into your hand will pull your arm down, but a stretch reflex will quickly return it to its original position. Stretch reflexes also help you maintain an erect posture. If you lean forward, you stretch muscles and stretch reflexes pull you back. If you lean back, you stretch the opposite set of muscles, and stretch reflexes pull you forward. Similar stretch reflexes control left and right swaying.

Sometimes we are aware of the movements caused by stretch reflexes. In fact, the afferent fibers send messages to the brain as well as to the spinal cord. They can therefore inform the brain about the stretched muscle. However, many stretch reflexes, such as those in postural sway, are very small and occur without our awareness.

Feedforward, Feedback, and Gating. Simultaneous messages to the brain and spinal

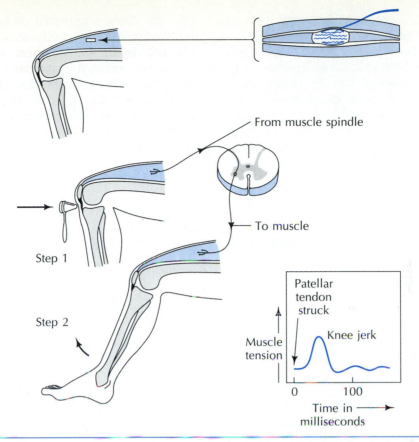

From muscle spindle

To muscle

Step 1

Step 2

Patellar tendon struck

Knee jerk

Muscle tension

0   100

Time in milliseconds

Figure 2.14A *The patellar tendon reflex. This reflex is produced by the activation of muscle spindles subjected to sudden stretching. In Step 1, a reflex hammer strikes the patellar tendon, stretching the muscle spindle fibers. This results in a sudden burst of activity in the afferent fibers that synapse on motor neurons inside the spinal cord. In Step 2, the activation of the motor units in the stretched muscle produces an immediate reflexive kick.*

The changes in muscle tension can be graphically recorded: Note the small secondary kick that may occur if the leg rebounds past its resting position.

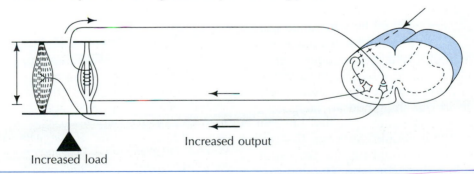

Increased output

Increased load

Figure 2.14B *The stretch reflex. If a load is placed on a muscle, the muscle is stretched. Stretching activates the receptors in the muscle (muscle spindles) sending a barrage of excitation via the spinal cord to the muscle. The muscle in turn contracts, resisting the stretch.*

cord can illustrate another important concept, feedforward. **Feedforward** is a process in which factors that cause a result prepare systems to modify the result. As an example, suppose someone startles you by unexpectedly putting a hand on your shoulder. You find yourself prepared to act before you know whether or not you want to. The startle response sends a message to the brain, and it also sends a feedforward message to the spinal cord. Spinal reflexes produce postural adjustments that prepare you for action. Should the brain act on the message it receives, it will find the body in a state of readiness.

The spinal cord also contains feedback circuits. These are processes in which factors that cause a result are themselves modified by that result. For example, Figure 2.15A shows a motor neuron that uses its response to decrease its own ability to be reactivated. The motor neuron sends out an axon with two branches. One goes to the muscle. The other goes to a Renshaw cell, which is an interneuron that inhibits the motor neuron that stimulates it. That is, when the motor neuron gets excited, it stimulates a Renshaw cell which in turn makes it harder for the motor neuron to get excited again.

The cell membrane mechanisms that cause an action potential produce this reaction. The feedback loop modifies these mechanisms, making the cell less likely to fire again. This feedback circuit protects motor neurons from becoming overexcited. The protective function is clearly illustrated when Renshaw cells are blocked by strychnine poison. The block eliminates the feedback circuits, and the motor neurons become overactive and produce violent muscle contractions.

Before considering the next circuit, let's set the stage in our imagination. Suppose a few drops of boiling water splashed on your left forearm. What would be your first response? Many of us would rub the sore spot, and this would reduce the pain. Did you ever wonder why? Or did you ever wonder why scratching relieves the pain of an irritated area? Melzack and Wall (1965) proposed an answer. They suggested that rubbing and scratching influence gate circuits in the spinal cord that open and close to regulate the flow of certain sensory information. Figure 2.15B shows a gate for pain. The gate contains a pathway for pain (C), one for fine touch and pressure (A), an interneuron (I), and a secondary pain cell (SP). Pathway A stimulates I and SP. Pathway C inhibits I and stimulates SP.

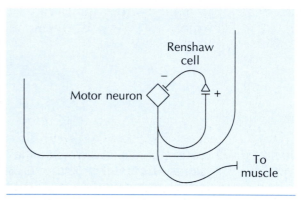

Figure 2.15A *Motor neuron with feedback circuits. Note that the motor neuron can decrease its own ability to be reactivated.*

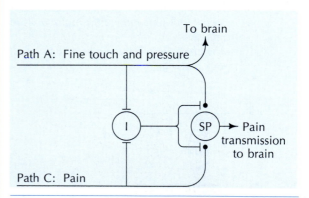

Figure 2.15B *A model of the gate proposed by Melzack and Wall (1965). Activation of the fine touch and pressure pathway excites the interneuron (I), but activation of the pain pathway inhibits it. The interneuron delivers presynaptic inhibition on transmission afferents to the secondary pain cell (SP). Thus, fine touch and pressure activity decrease pain transmission.*

Activity in I inhibits the transmission from both pathways to SP. When a touch signal on A increases relative to a pain signal on A, I is stimulated, the excitability of SP is inhibited, and pain signals from SP are reduced. Melzack and Wall provided evidence that such gates exist in the spinal cord. So the next time you relieve pain by rubbing or scratching, you can thank your spinal cord and its gate circuits.

The next section takes a more comprehensive view of the nervous system and considers both the brain and the spinal cord. It answers many more questions about why we perceive and act the way we do.

Sensory and Motor Nervous Systems

Most of our actions involve both the sensory and motor nervous systems, but we can analyze these systems separately. Figure 2.16 shows an important part of our sensory system. The highlighted structures are known as the **reticular activating system (RAS)**. This subdivision has the functions of directing attention and activating sensory parts of the brain by connecting the reticular formation with other parts of the midbrain, hindbrain, and forebrain.

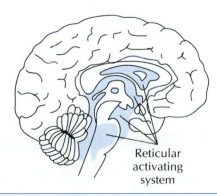

Reticular
activating
system

Figure 2.16 *The reticular activating system (RAS) activates all regions of the brain for incoming sensory impulses and plays an important part in alertness and selective attention.*

You use your RAS for directing attention when you prepare yourself to respond to one stimuli and ignore others. Imagine waiting anxiously at a traffic light on a street surrounded by billboards. Your RAS would prepare your brain to respond to the green light and would tone down its response to irrelevant billboard lights.

We often become most aware of a functional subsystem when we lose it. You have lost the alertness function of your RAS if you have ever had surgery under general anesthesia. Surgeons use drugs that block the RAS so they can operate without their patients' being awake and feeling the pain of the surgical procedures.

Voluntary Motor Control System. The voluntary motor control system is the central and peripheral nerve tissue that controls body posture and movements, often without our deliberate volition. De Mille and others who struggle to control their muscles remind us how dependent we are on this system. It enables us to dress, eat, and do other everyday activities. It also coordinates the high performance skills of athletes, pilots, dancers, and surgeons.

Figure 2.17 shows the organization of the voluntary motor control system. The typical flow of information is from the top down, that is, from the brain to the muscles. But the system is easiest to describe if we start at the bottom. We begin, therefore, with the final common path, the projections from the spinal cord to the muscles. It is a common path because all signals from the brain to the muscles go through the spinal cord. In addition to signals from the brain, the spinal cord also receives signals from sensory receptors and other areas of the spinal cord.

Now let's go to the top of the system. We see that signals originate in the cerebral cortex. These messages, which are represented by downward arrows, can be grouped into two tracts: one to the basal ganglia and the other to the cerebellum.

The basal ganglia are responsible for retrieving or initiating movement plans, scaling

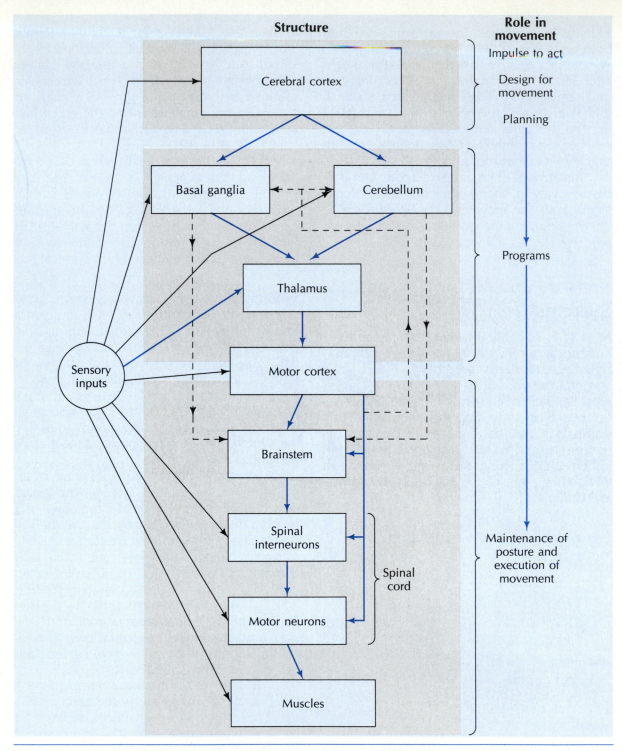

Figure 2.17 *Diagrammatic representation of the organization of the motor system, showing its major structures and connections.*

movement force and extent, and perceptual motor integration. Disorders related to damage of the basal ganglia include Huntington's disease and Parkinson's disease. These diseases are characterized by uncontrollable movements, shaking, and/or slowness in the initiation and completion of movements.

The cerebellum regulates muscle tone, coordination, timing, and motor learning. Cerebellar damage can result in coordination deficits, slurred speech, problems with muscle relaxation, and difficulties in learning motor skills.

The higher centers of the nervous system activate the motor cortex in much the same way a pianist depresses piano keys to produce a melody. The result is musical melody in the case of the pianist and a coordinated movement in the case of the nervous system.

The thalamus sends and receives sensory signals related to vision, hearing, and pain. It serves as a kind of relay or integration center for sensory and motor information. If the thalamus is affected by surgery, patients often experience difficulty naming familiar objects in a picture or thinking of common words.

The motor cortex is nervous tissue responsible for very localized function. As we saw in Figures 2.10 and 2.11, activation of a specific area causes a finger to move or a leg muscle to twitch. The higher centers of the nervous system activate the motor cortex in much the same way a pianist depresses piano keys to produce a melody. The result is a musical melody or a coordinated movement.

The brainstem is similar in structure to the brain of many lower animals. It controls many basic functions such as the involuntary activity of the tongue, larynx, eyes, and facial muscles. The brainstem also controls sleep and arousal and coordinates spinal activity responsible for walking, breathing, and the beating of our hearts.

In summary, the cerebral cortex is responsible for creating impulses to act and designing a general movement strategy. The basal ganglia and the cerebellum plan and integrate the movement while the thalamus, motor cortex, and brainstem are responsible for the specific characteristics of the movement. The neurons and muscles are the hardware that carry out the movement.

Autonomic Nervous System

The **autonomic nervous system** consists of nerves that stimulate and inhibit body parts to regulate functions such as heart rate, blood vessel dilation, sweating, digestion, and gland secretions, which are usually involuntary. It has two subdivisions that we consider one at a time.

Sympathetic Division. The **sympathetic division** is the part of the autonomic nervous system that favors physical activities in its pattern of stimulation and inhibition. It activates

Recovery From Brain Damage

A team of rehabilitation therapists and physicians worked together to help Agnes de Mille recover from the brain damage caused by her stroke. Similar teams across the world help millions of people recover from strokes and other causes of brain damage, including head injuries, tumors, viruses, bacteria, radiation, and poisons. Rehabilitation efforts are guided by an understanding of the mechanisms that contribute to recovery from brain damage. Your first guess about these mechanisms might be misled by what you see when you injure your skin. When you scrape your knee, for example, a scab forms and eventually new cells replace the injured ones. Unlike the skin, however, the brain cannot replace injured neurons. The brain must therefore restore as much function as possible by working with the cells that survive. How is this restoration accomplished?

Recovery from brain damage depends upon behavioral adjustments as opposed to structural adjustments in the brain. For example, people who lose peripheral vision can learn to make better use of their remaining central vision (Marshall, 1985). Patients often have trouble using their remaining skills and benefit from the guidance of a physical, occupational, or speech therapist. These rehabilitation therapists start working with the skills that remain immediately after the injury. They also assess and train additional skills that return gradually as the brain makes structural adjustments.

One mechanism for structural recovery is the restoration of function to uninjured neurons. Within hours after a brain injury, toxins from dead cells surround the surviving neurons. Behavior declines as the toxins spread, and behavior improves when the toxins are washed away over several days or weeks. Similarly, uninjured cells temporarily fail to function normally because their blood supply is decreased. In one case, language abilities were impaired because blood flow to speech areas was barely enough to keep cells alive. These abilities returned within six months as the blood flow gradually improved (Olsen, Bruhn, & Oberg, 1986).

Another mechanism for recovery is repair of injured neurons. Healthy neurons often have synapses that are not used. These silent synapses can be activated when other synapses are destroyed (Merzenich et al., 1984). In addition, neighboring neurons can sprout new branches to innervate synapses that are broken (Sabel, Slavin, & Stein, 1984). An injured neuron can also compensate for lost synapses by increasing the sensitivity of its remaining synapses (Zigmond & Stricker, 1973; Kozlowski & Marshall, 1981). Although the human brain does not regrow severed axons, such regrowth does occur in the peripheral nervous system and in the central nervous system of some fish (Scherer, 1986). Investigators are therefore trying to make such regeneration possible in human brains (Schwab & Thoenen, 1985). Let's turn to the therapeutic implications of these and other efforts to promote structural recovery in the brain.

Kalat (1988) reviewed research on promoting recovery from brain damage through direct intervention in the brain. One approach is to identify chemicals that will enable axons to regrow in the human brain. An important clue in this search was the observation that a damaged peripheral nerve increases protein synthesis while a damaged central nerve does not (Shyne-Athwal, Riccio, Chakraborty, & Ingoflia, 1986). Present research is being guided by the hypothesis that protein is necessary for axon growth. This hypothesis is supported by the observation that a certain protein is present in developing infant rats and in regenerating peripheral nerves but not in damaged central nerves. The hope is that the addition of this protein to injured areas in human brains will enable the regrowth of axons.

A second similar approach is a search for chemicals that will promote sprouting and increased sensitivity. This search has also been spurred on by promising findings. For example, chemicals have been discovered that seem to increase sprouting and decrease behavioral deficits (Sabel, Slavin, & Stein, 1984).

A third exciting approach is grafting of brain tissue. For instance, structural and behavioral recovery is enhanced when developing brain tissues from a fetus of a rat are transplanted in a damaged area of a rat brain (Gash, Collier, & Sladek, 1985; Deckel, Moran, Coyle, Sanberg, & Robinson, 1986). Similar results have also been obtained with monkeys (Gash et al., 1985). We might hope that transplants from monkeys to humans would work as well. Finally, some success has been achieved by transplanting tissues from one part of the nervous system to another in humans. For example, when Backlund et al. (1985) transplanted tissue from certain parts of the sympathetic nervous system to damaged parts of the brain in patients with Parkinson's disease, the patients experienced an immediate decrease in the muscle rigidity that is caused by the disease. Even though the benefits lasted only a couple of weeks, these results have raised hopes for the development of improved methods for promoting recovery from brain damage through direct intervention.

the heart and lungs, for example, because they are needed for physical activities. It suppresses digestion in order to save energy for the parts that are activated. Other patterns of stimulation and inhibition are shown on the right side of Figure 2.18. The sympathetic division works continually to stabilize body functions, but it is especially active in stressful situations (Wallin & Fagius, 1986). It triggers a flight-or-fight response that is designed to prepare the body for vigorous action. You feel the effects of this response when you get pumped up for athletic competitions or academic exams. The extra energy you feel is useful up to a point, but it is all-important to maintain stability.

Parasympathetic Division. The **parasympathetic division** is the part of the autonomic nervous system that stimulates and inhibits in a way that generally balances the pattern of the sympathetic division. The left

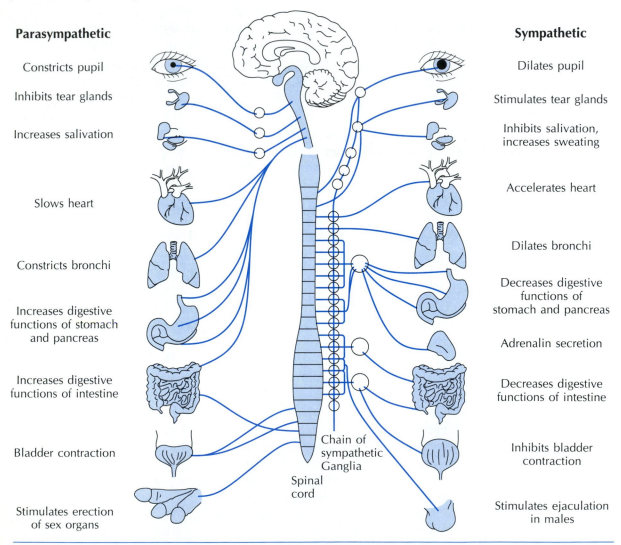

Parasympathetic

Constricts pupil

Inhibits tear glands

Increases salivation

Slows heart

Constricts bronchi

Increases digestive functions of stomach and pancreas

Increases digestive functions of intestine

Bladder contraction

Stimulates erection of sex organs

Sympathetic

Dilates pupil

Stimulates tear glands

Inhibits salivation, increases sweating

Accelerates heart

Dilates bronchi

Decreases digestive functions of stomach and pancreas

Adrenalin secretion

Decreases digestive functions of intestine

Inhibits bladder contraction

Stimulates ejaculation in males

Chain of sympathetic Ganglia

Spinal cord

Figure 2.18 *The sympathetic and parasympathetic subdivisions of the nervous system serve many of the same organs, but they affect them differently.*

side of Figure 2.18 shows the parasympathetic division's pattern of activation and suppression. Notice that the two divisions generally offset one another. As a result, the two divisions continually harmonize body functions. You feel the effects of the parasympathetic division, for example, when you finally relax after a big game or exam.

FINAL COMMENT

The central nervous system is responsible for the very complicated and integrated set of communications that allow us to feel, think, respond, and react. If disease or injury impairs the function of even the smallest subdivision of the biological systems, the consequences can be disastrous. Agnes de Mille's doctors were able to diagnose her stroke and trace her impaired functions because of their understanding of biological systems. Similarly, by studying these systems, we should be able to understand better the wonder of movement that allows us to experience and respond to the world around us.

KEY TERMS

neuron
dendrite
axon
membrane potential
synapse
afferent
efferent
interneuron
motor neuron

motor unit
motoneuronal pool
recruitment
rate coding
size principle
central nervous
    system
peripheral nervous
    system

basal ganglia
cerebral cortex
corpus callosum
Broca's aphasia
Wernicke's aphasia
spinal cord
flexor
extensor
feedforward

reticular activating
    system
autonomic nervous
    system
sympathetic division
parasympathetic
    division

3
Human Memory

Armstrong and Aldrin: THE LUNAR LANDING

How Memory Is Studied

Types of Memory
- *Sensory Memory*
- *Short-term Memory*
- *Long-term Memory*

Depth of Processing

Encoding
- *Encoding in Short-term Memory*
- *Encoding in Long-term Memory*

Recoding and Retaining
- *Chunking in Short-term Memory*
- *Organization and Reconstruction in Long-term Memory*

Retrieval
- *Retrieval from Short-term Memory*
- *Retrieval from Long-term Memory*

Forgetting
- *Trace Decay*
- *Interference*

Neurobiology of Memory
- *Short-term Memory, Long-term Memory, and Neurons*
- *Working Memory and the Hippocampus*
- *Memory Loss and Disease*
- *Electrical and Chemical Regulators of Memory*

HIGHLIGHT: Flashbulb Memories

FINAL COMMENT

KEY TERMS

Armstrong and Aldrin: THE LUNAR LANDING

A computer-controlled system on Apollo 11 took Neil Armstrong and Edwin Aldrin within 50 feet of the moon's surface, but it was their perceptual-motor learning and memory that got them the rest of the way. A computer failure forced Armstrong to take manual control of the *Eagle* lunar module with less than 60 seconds of descent fuel remaining. Armstrong, a 39-year-old civilian with 23 years of experience as a test pilot, had trained extensively for this possibility on a Lunar Landing Training Vehicle. Using pistol grip controls, he executed a U-turn, hovered 22 seconds, identified a suitable landing site, and touched down with 18 seconds of descent fuel to spare. He then reported: "Houston, Tranquility Base here. The *Eagle* has landed."

Armstrong and Aldrin spent the next 3 hours and 12 minutes readying the *Eagle* for a quick takeoff if an emergency required them to return to their fellow astronaut Michael Collins in the orbiting command module, *Columbia.* They then requested permission to skip their scheduled four-hour rest period. The astronauts had slept very little the night before, but they showed no signs of fatigue, and permission was granted. Armstrong and Aldrin donned their portable life support systems, depressurized their cabin, and opened the hatch.

Armstrong was the first to descend the *Eagle*'s ladder. On his way, he activated a TV

Those of us old enough to recall the night in 1969 can remember the words spoken by Neil Armstrong as he first stepped onto the moon's surface: "That's one small step for man, one giant leap for mankind."

CHAPTER OBJECTIVES

■ To identify the classifications of human memory.

■ To examine factors that determine the depth to which memories are processed.

■ To appreciate the methods of storing, organizing, and processing memories.

■ To examine the processes whereby information is retrieved or lost from memory.

■ To understand the factors that influence forgetting.

camera that recorded his historic progress. Millions of TV viewers on earth watched him reach the bottom rung and lower himself onto a bowl-shaped footpad. He then extended his left foot back and planted it firmly on the fine-grained surface of the moon. He then spoke the first words from lunar soil: *"That's one small step for man, one giant leap for mankind."* The time was 10:56 P.M. (EDT), July 20, 1969.

Aldrin joined Armstrong moments later and the two astronauts mesmerized TV viewers for the next 2 hours and 14 minutes as they bounded around in the weak lunar gravity. They set up experiments, snapped pictures, scooped up moon rocks, and gathered soil with a core sampler. Few Americans shut off their TV sets until the astronauts returned to the *Eagle* and closed the hatch behind them.

Many parts of the astronauts' mission had been, and would be, dangerous, but their decisive actions in crises had proven the value of astronaut-controlled space flight.

■ ■ ■

Armstrong's giant step illustrates amazing characteristics of perceptual-motor learning and memory. He did not have time to relearn the many geography and flying lessons that he had practiced on earth. He needed, and had, the information "at his finger tips" when he took manual control of the *Eagle*. Similarly, we are often required to remember skills and to produce them "on demand." This chapter examines **memory**, the system that enables us to retain information over time.

In ancient times, the Greeks and Romans established the art of memorizing long speeches. Their emphasis on verbal memory carried over to the first scientific investigations by Hermann Ebbinghaus in 1885. The study of memory for movement came much later (e.g., Adams, 1967). This chapter focuses on memory for movement, but also reviews underlying concepts that emerged from the work on verbal memory.

How Memory Is Studied

Scientists and teachers use similar methods for testing memory. **Recall tests** measure a person's ability to reproduce material. Teachers use this method with essay exams or fill-in-the-blank questions such as "Recall tests measure a person's ability to _____ material." **Recognition tests** measure a person's ability to pick the correct answer when several answers are given. Teachers use this method with multiple-choice questions such as "Recognition tests measure a person's ability to: (a) reproduce material, (b) imagine material, (c) pick the correct answer when several answers are given." **Savings tests** measure a person's ability to relearn material faster than it was learned the first time. Teachers rarely, if ever, measure savings. But they do count on it when they give comprehensive final exams. Students forget much of material learned early in a course, but they quickly relearn it for a comprehensive final exam. The fact that re-learning is faster than original learning indicates that something is remembered. Savings is often the most sensitive memory test. Students who can neither recall nor recognize material often show savings by relearning the material faster than they did originally.

Let's translate these familiar school examples into tests of memory for movement. Have someone help you learn to raise your hand 5, 6, or 7 inches above a table top with your eyes closed. Your assistant should place your hand at each height one time and tell you which height it is. He or she should then give you a recall test by saying each number and having you try to reproduce the movement. The assistant should mark your hand position on each test and show you your results after you have tried all three. At this point, your assistant should give you a recognition test by raising your hand each distance and asking you to say which distance each one is. Then continue a series of recall tests followed by knowledge of results until you perform all three movements

Fill-in-the-blank questions are examples of recall tests; multiple choice questions are examples of recognition tests. What would be examples of recall and recognition tests in the motor domain?

within an eighth of an inch twice in a row. Count the number of tests and learning trials it takes you to reach this performance criterion. Now wait a day or two and repeat the whole procedure. Your first recall test will probably be worse than your last one from the previous session. You might even make a mistake on the recognition test. But you will probably show savings by reaching the performance criterion in fewer trials during the relearning session in comparison with the number of trials required during the original session. Figure 3.1 illustrates hypothetical learning and relearning data from one subject. The subject required 9 blocks of 3 trials in the learning phase to achieve the criterion of less than 5 millimeters error. In the relearning phase only 3 blocks were required.

Notice that all three tests: recall, recognition, and savings, infer memory from performance. This inference is the best we can do because we cannot see memory directly. But the inference is not perfect because performance can be changed by things other than

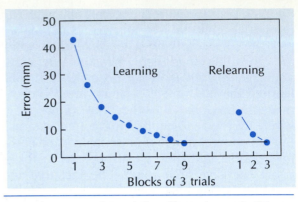

Figure 3.1 *Hypothetical data illustrating typical learning and relearning curves. The task is considered learned or relearned when error is smaller than the 5mm criterion.*

memory. For example, suppose you had the flu on the day you tried to relearn the movements of 5, 6, and 7 inches. You might remember the movements but be unable to make them because your hand is too shaky. Can you think of other reasons why performance does not perfectly reflect memory? Keep your eyes open for reasons as you read this chapter.

Types of Memory

Armstrong used different kinds of memory when he took manual control of the *Eagle*. For instance, he used memories of information he had learned much earlier during training on earth. These memories told him where the controls were and how they worked. He also used memories for information that he was gathering as he made his descent. These memories told him where there was a safe place to land. Figure 3.2 illustrates a **multiple memory theory**, which accounts for these different kinds of memory (Atkinson & Shiffrin, 1971, 1977). It states that there are three types of memory: **sensory memory**, which holds sensory impressions for only 1 or 2 seconds; **short-term memory**, which holds information for less than 30 seconds; and **long-term memory**, which holds information for long periods of time (perhaps permanently). Accordingly, Armstrong drew from his long-term memory to find how the *Eagle* controls worked. He used short-term memory to recall a safe landing place that he had seen within the last 30 seconds. He also used sensory memory to hold visual information through disruptions such as blinks.

Sensory Memory

You can demonstrate your sensory memory by waving your hand in front of your eyes. Your hand's sensory representation remains after your hand moves, so you see your hand in more than one place at a time. According to the multiple memory theory, sensory memory holds sensory information under special conditions for as long as for 1 or 2 seconds in order to allow time to transfer sensory input into short-term memory. The processes that transfer sensory input into short-term memory are called **recognition processes**. George Sperling (1960) showed that recognition processes can use information in sensory memory even after the original sensory input is turned off. Figure 3.3 illustrates Sperling's methods and results. He presented 12 letters in 3 equal rows for 50 milliseconds. He then asked subjects for either a whole report or a partial report test. In the whole report test, subjects named as many letters as they could, which was usually 4 or 5. Sperling believed that subjects saw more letters than that but forgot them before they could say them. He therefore also used a partial report test. In that test, a high-pitched tone indicated that subjects only had to name the top row; a medium tone indicated the middle row; and a low tone indicated the bottom row. When the tone came immediately after the letters went off, on three trials the subjects could report 75 percent of the letters, which meant that they recalled 9 of the 12 letters available. Sperling used the same logic as a teacher who takes the percent correct on an exam to represent the percent known on all the material. When the tone was delayed 150 milliseconds, the

number of letters available fell to about 8. That number continued to fall when the tone was delayed 300 and 1000 milliseconds until it reached 4 or 5, the number of letters available without a tone.

Sperling used similar procedures to determine the following properties of sensory memory: (1) Sensory memory lasts longer for brighter stimuli, usually 1 or 2 seconds. (2) A second stimulus wipes out the sensory memory for a preceding stimulus. This **backward masking** occurs when the second stimulus, the mask, is presented within 1 or 2 seconds after the first stimulus is terminated. Presentation of a mask is an excellent way for an experimenter to control the processing time available for a stimulus. (3) Sensory memory contains visual features that have not yet been named or recognized, such as curves and angles.

Sounds also produce sensory memories with properties similar to those of visual sensory memory (Massaro, 1970).

Short-term Memory

When visual or auditory features are recognized as letters or words, they are stored in short-term memory according to multiple

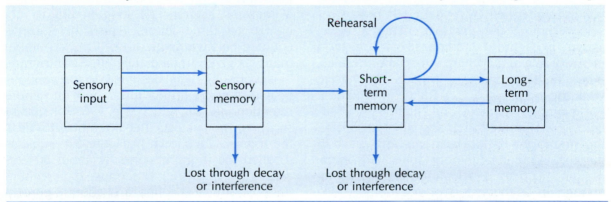

Figure 3.2 *Atkinson and Shiffrin's (1971, 1977) multiprocess view of human memory is shown in this model. Sensory information is briefly retained in some type of sensory memory system; some of it is then recoded into short-term memory, where it may be retained through rehearsal. The longer it remains in short-term memory, the more likely it is to be transferred into long-term memory. Although information can be lost from sensory and short-term memory through decay or interference, retention in long-term memory is assumed to be virtually permanent.*

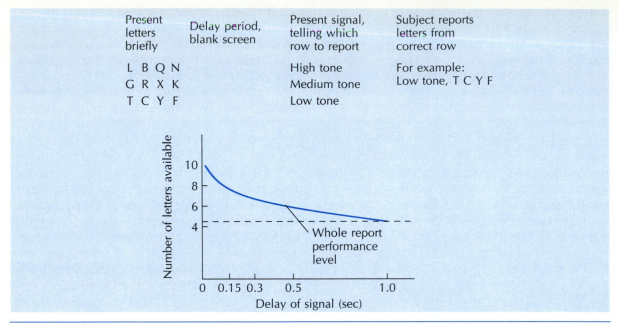

Figure 3.3 *Sperling's partial report technique is shown in the upper part of the figure. Below is a graph of the results: The number of letters recalled decreases as the signal to report is delayed. The dashed line represents the results of the subjects' ability to recall all 12 letters in the report (Sperling, 1960).*

memory theory. For example, when you look up a telephone number, its features enter sensory memory until they are recognized as numbers. Then they enter short-term memory where they last less than 30 seconds unless you **rehearse** them by repeating them to yourself. Although the multiple memory model shown in Figure 3.2 emphasizes short-term memory as a place where information resides, other multiple memory models emphasize what the individual does with the information. For example, Baddeley and Hitch (1974; Baddeley, 1981) named their second stage **working memory**—a short-term working space in memory. Working memory holds new information, such as a telephone number, long enough for us to use it. Working memory also provides a working space in which we can combine old and new memories in order to revise our long-term memories. We will use the term *short-term memory* when we discuss structural characteristics, such as the amount of information held, and *working memory*

when we discuss functional characteristics such as forming new long-term memories.

Peterson and Peterson (1959) developed a way to measure how long short-term memory lasts without rehearsal. Their subjects looked at trigrams, such as JTX, long enough to recognize all three letters. Then the subjects counted backwards by threes from a number that was given immediately after the trigram. This counting was designed to prevent rehearsal and continued throughout the entire retention interval, which was 3, 6, 9, 12, or 18 seconds. The subjects then attempted to recall the trigram. As shown in Figure 3.4, subjects recalled the trigrams correctly about 50 percent of the time after 3 seconds, 25 percent of the time after 9 seconds, and about 8 percent of the time after 18 seconds. Many experimenters have used the Peterson and Peterson procedure to show that we forget isolated facts such as trigrams in less than 30 seconds if we do not rehearse.

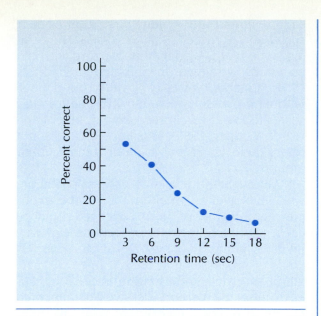

Figure 3.4 *Research has shown that people rapidly forget isolated facts if they do not rehearse them. In the graph here we see a rapid decline in the percent of correct recall of trigrams (Peterson & Peterson, 1959).*

Experimenters have used similar procedures for testing short-term memory for the location and distance of simple movements. For example, Toole and Lucariello (1984) found that subjects did not forget locations in a 15-second blank interval after making a simple linear movement, but they did forget the exact distance of the movement during the same interval. Although short-term memory for movement location is excellent during blank intervals, it is easily distorted when subjects are required to make a second movement (or imagine making a second movement) before recalling the first (Johnson, 1982). Short-term memory for movements is also lost rapidly for patients with mild to moderate Alzheimer's dementia, a degenerative nerve condition most common in people over age 60.

Long-term Memory

Rehearsal transfers information from short-term to long-term memory. If you repeat a phone number a few times, you will remember it long enough to dial it once. But if you repeat the number often, it will go into long-term memory and will be available for a long time. You can probably recall your own phone number from long-term memory as well as numbers of friends you call often. A search of your own long-term memory will also reveal that it contains many different kinds of information. For example, you probably remember what your friends sound like on the phone. You might remember the smell of a friend's perfume or cologne. (People forget very few smells even after a one-year period [Engen, 1980].) If your car has a bright-light switch on the floor, you could probably hit the switch on your first try without looking, even if you have not used it for a long time. Keele and Ells (1972) showed that people remember both the position of the target (the switch) and the distance that must be moved to reach it in such simple movement tasks.

Depth of Processing

According to the **levels of processing theory**, Armstrong remembered his training for a long time because he processed his lessons deeply (Craik & Lockart, 1972). He did not remember all the details that he saw during his descent because he did not have time to process them as deeply. The levels of processing theory does not distinguish between short-term and long-term memory. Both kinds of information are thought to be stored in the same kind of memory.

One memory lasts longer than another because it was processed more deeply. A surface level of processing would be illustrated if you would do nothing more than identify all the letter "e's" in this text. A deeper level of processing would be shown if you identified each word one by one. A still deeper level of processing would be obtained if you understood the meaning of the passage that you read. In general, deeper levels of processing are associated with making more connections with background knowledge. The concept of levels of processing could help explain why skilled athletes, who have richer background knowledge, process information more efficiently in perceptual-motor learning situations than do nonathletes (e.g., Singer, 1984).

Levels of processing theory can explain memory during typing. It is not uncommon for a skilled typist to transcribe a whole page without remembering more than a couple of words. Levels of processing theory would predict that these typists limited themselves to low levels of processing. Evidence supports this limitation. Skilled typists do not seem to process meaning. They can carry on a conversation without any serious disruption of their speed and accuracy (Shaffer, 1975). They can also type words arranged haphazardly as fast as words arranged meaningfully (Fendrick, 1937). Clearly, typists can transcribe a page without processing meaning. They limit themselves to lower level processing of letters and words (Cooper, 1983). This limitation does not retard their typing, but it greatly reduces their memory.

Although the levels of processing theory was developed as an alternative to the multiple memory theory, both concepts could be correct. In fact, in the next sections we draw on both points of view. We discuss various kinds of processes that are assumed to operate in short-term and long-term memory. For each process, we consider well-documented effects in motor memory that relate to these processes. Finally, we consider how theories of multiple memory and levels of processing might explain these effects.

Encoding

Encoding is the process of selecting stimulus information and representing it in a form that can be stored in memory. A television camera and recorder passively took in every part of Armstrong's famous first steps on the moon. The recording included a complete visual representation that could be played back at any time. Would your own memory be as complete? Would you remember everything, or would you remember only parts? Would your memory be a visual representation, or would it have some other form? Let's consider these questions separately for short-term and long-term memory.

Encoding in Short-term Memory

Test your short-term memory by trying to recall every word in the last sentence. Did you remember all the words, or just the important ones? Did you remember the words' appearance, sound, meaning, or all three? It is hard to answer these questions directly, but researchers have used some clever experiments to get answers.

Attention. Figure 3.5 illustrates a procedure that researchers use to study **attention**, the process by which we notice important information and ignore unimportant stimuli. The procedure is called **dichotic listening**. Earphones play separate messages in each ear. Subjects are told to ignore one message and shadow the other, which means to repeat each word immediately after hearing it. Moray (1959) used this procedure and then gave a surprise test of the irrelevant message. He found that the content of the irrelevant message was forgotten within 30 seconds. Subjects did not even have any recollection of the

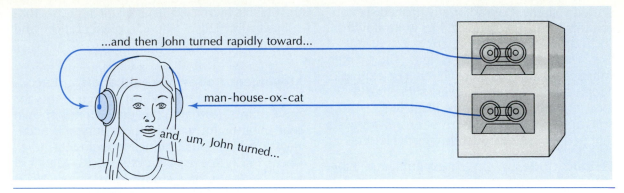

Figure 3.5 *Apparatus used in a typical dichotic listening experiment. Separate messages are played through earphones to each ear of a subject who tries to ignore one message and to repeat the other.*

content change in the irrelevant message from English to a foreign language. They did notice and remember, however, when the irrelevant message changed physically. For instance, they remembered changes from a male to a female voice. They remembered when the voice stopped completely or was replaced by a tone. These results suggest that people remember the physical characteristics, but not the meaning, of irrelevant stimuli.

Although people do not remember the meaning of irrelevant information 30 seconds after hearing it, they do process some of the meaning. Treisman (1960) found, for example, that the meaning of the irrelevant message can disrupt the processing of the relevant message. One relevant message began with the words "Poor aunt." This beginning created the expectation of a woman's name. At that moment, the irrelevant message said "Jane" and the relevant message said some unrelated word. This arrangement caused subjects to shift their attention briefly to the irrelevant message and to say "Jane." They usually recognized their mistake immediately and apologized. Have you ever made similar shifts in attention when you heard your name mentioned in a nearby conversation? We seem inclined to hear our own name, and it is hard to ignore stimuli that we are inclined to hear.

Generally, however, we are very successful at attending to relevant stimuli and ignoring irrelevant ones. The next question is: How do we represent relevant stimuli? Again, this question is difficult to answer directly, but experiments have provided answers.

Verbal Codes. In one experiment, Conrad (1964) analyzed recall errors and concluded that people use verbal codes to represent digits, letters, and words even when they are pre-

Treisman (1960) demonstrated that if a person attends to a message presented in one ear, a message presented in the other ear is not processed. However, a meaningful message (e.g., your name, a fire) could cause you to shift your attention.

sented visually. Conrad briefly flashed six consonants and asked subjects to write down all six in order. He found that errors rarely looked like the correct answer, but they often sounded like the correct letter. For example, people would rarely, if ever, substitute a "K" for a "B," but they would be likely to substitute a "T" for a "B." This pattern of errors suggests that people use verbal codes for the letters.

Visual Codes. Other experiments have shown that we sometimes use visual codes. For example, Kosslyn, Ball, and Reiser (1978) asked subjects to remember a map such as the one shown in Figure 3.6. The subjects then imagined a dot moving from one point to another on their remembered map. Figure 3.6 shows that the time it took to imagine the dot movement increased as the distance between

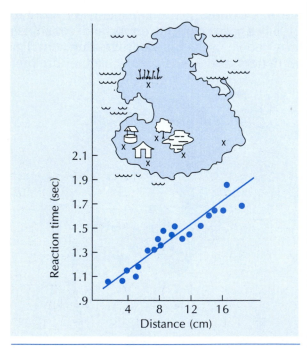

Figure 3.6 *People can use visual images to memorize maps. They can also imagine a dot moving from one location to another on the map's image. As the lower portion of the figure indicates, the reaction time from the beginning to the end of the imagined movement increases as objects on the map are shown farther apart (Kosslyn et al., 1978).*

the objects increased. This result suggests that subjects formed a visual representation and imagined the dot moving on it.

Movement Codes: Verbal Labels. Encoding is also important in short-term memory for movements. Research has consistently shown that meaningful verbal labels enhance accuracy of limb positioning movements (e.g., Shea, 1977; Reeve & Proctor, 1983; Magill & Lee, 1987). In one study, John Shea (1977) asked 45 right-handed female volunteers to do a manual lever positioning task with a relevant label, an irrelevant label, or no label. The relevant labels referred to positions on a clock. The irrelevant labels were unrelated nouns. The task started with a lever in the three o'clock position. It was held in the right hand. A blindfolded subject moved the lever until it hit a stop at one of five predefined positions, which were at two, one, twelve, eleven, and ten o'clock. She then returned the lever to the starting position, waited either 5 or 60 seconds, and then tried to reposition the lever. She had to remember where the lever had been because the stop was removed. In the label conditions, the labels were given while the subject held the lever against the stop and 5 seconds before the recall attempt. The constant errors showed that subjects tended to overshoot the target positions slightly on average. After 5 seconds, the conditions did not differ significantly. After 60 seconds, however, constant errors were lowest with relevant labels, significantly higher with irrelevant labels, and significantly higher yet with no labels.

How can we explain the beneficial effect of meaningful verbal labels? In principle, either multiple memory or levels of processing theories could explain the effect. According to multiple memory theory, one might suggest that meaningful labels increase the probability that the to-be-remembered information is stored and retained in short-term memory. From the levels of processing viewpoint, one might suggest that superior memory is the result of deeper processing for the meaningful labels.

Movement Codes: Location Versus Distance. Another well-documented effect involving codes is that locations are recalled better than distances. The women in Shea's study started each movement in the same place. They therefore could have remembered locations, distances between the starting position and the to-be-remembered location, or both. Many other studies, however, have separated these possibilities (e.g., Laabs, 1973; Smyth, 1984). The general strategy was to use different starting positions during the presentations and recalls. When subjects start in a different position, the experimenters can ask them to recall either the distance or the location. For example, suppose the women in Shea's study were presented a movement from three to twelve o'clock. Suppose further that the recall movement started at two o'clock. The women could then be asked to recall the location, and the correct answer would be twelve o'clock. Alternatively, the women could be asked to recall distance. What would have been the correct answer? It would have been eleven o'clock because the distance between three and twelve is the same as the distance between two and eleven. When such studies are done, subjects usually recall locations better than distances.

How do we explain the advantage of location over distance? Researchers have argued that location is remembered more easily because of the way the movements are represented in memory. They maintain that movements are represented in separate codes for location and distance that enable both location and distance to be recalled (e.g., Smyth & Pendleton, 1989). The advantage of location recall suggests that the location code is better. Again, either multiple memory or levels of processing theory could explain the advantage. According to multiple memory theory, one might suggest that location codes have a higher probability of being stored and retained in short-term memory. From the levels of processing viewpoint, one might suggest that location codes are more meaningful and that superior memory is the result of deeper processing for the meaningful codes.

Movement Codes: Active Versus Passive. Another coding effect involves active versus passive movements. The women in Shea's study made **active movements**, which means that they controlled their own movements. In contrast, **passive movements** are controlled externally. They are tested in experiments similar to Shea's by having the experimenter move the subject's arm. An everyday example is a swimming or golf coach who moves a student's arms through a stroke. Research on passive and active movements suggests that recall is best when the presentation and recall are the same. That is, active presentation and active recall or passive presentation and passive recall are better than active-passive or passive-active (e.g., Lee & Hirota, 1980). This result suggests that active and passive movements are coded differently. Recall is best when an active movement is based on an active memory code or when a passive movement is based on a passive memory code. A practical implication is that coaches should limit their use of passive demonstrations of active movements.

Encoding in Long-term Memory

Both verbal and visual codes are concrete in comparison with more abstract representations that are used in long-term memory. Sachs (1967) found, for example, that subjects remember the meaning but not the exact words of a text two minutes after hearing it. One sentence used in the study was "The author sent a long letter to the committee." Two minutes later subjects were able to distinguish sentences that had different meanings, but they could not distinguish the original sentence from a different one that had the same meaning: "A letter that was long was sent to the committee by the author." Similarly, you are probably remembering the meaning but not the exact words of this text. The next section discusses how likely you are to recode and retain the information.

Recoding and Retaining

Recoding is the process of changing a representation from one form to another. Thanks to recoding, we can see Armstrong's walk on the moon more clearly than the original television viewers saw it. Computers can record the original representation in a form that eliminates many of the distortions in the original. Similarly, we often recode information after we store it in memory. Our recoding is different in short-term and long-term memory. Let's look at these separately.

Chunking in Short-term Memory

Chunking is the process of grouping stimuli into meaningful units. Chunks can be digits, letters, syllables, words, or even sentences. For example, each letter is a chunk in the following string: REGGENEZRAWHCS. However, in the reverse order, the whole string is one chunk: SCHWARZENEGGER, the name of a famous body builder and actor.

Chase and Simon (1973) observed that expert chess players are no better than novices at remembering the positions of chess pieces that are arranged in random positions, but are far superior when the to-be-remembered pieces are arranged according to the rules of the game.

Our short-term **memory span** is the number of chunks that we can read through once and recall in sequence with no mistakes. George Miller (1956) wrote a paper "The Magical Number Seven, Plus or Minus Two" to explain that virtually all adults have a memory span between five and nine chunks. Chase and Simon (1973) tested an important implication of this principle of short-term memory. The implication is that individuals who chunk better also remember better. Chase and Simon observed that expert chess players are no better than novices at remembering the positions of chess pieces that are arranged in random positions, but they are far superior when the to-be-remembered chess pieces are arranged according to the rules of the game. Egan and Schwartz (1979) found similar results when they compared novice and expert abilities to reproduce randomly arranged or real circuit drawings. The experts were superior because they had learned to organize information into large, meaningful chunks; and better chunkers remember more.

Similar effects also occur in sports. A skilled basketball player, for instance, recognizes specific plays and notices meaningful patterns in the relative positions of players. If you show experts and novices a snapshot of players in random positions, they will remember the same amount. However, if you show both groups a snapshot of players in meaningful positions during a game, the experts will remember more positions (Allard, Graham, & Paarsalu, 1980). According to multiple memory theory, one could say that the experts organized their information into fewer and larger chunks. The more economically packaged chunks were remembered better because they took up less room in short-term memory. According to levels of processing theory, on the other hand, one could say that experts remembered more because the more meaningful information was processed more deeply.

Does Miller's magical number seven plus or minus two apply to memory for movements? Wilberg and Salmela (1973) argued that it does. They had subjects recall a sequence of 2, 4, 6, or 8 movements of a joy stick. Their results suggested that the memory span for motor memory is about 8 movements. That is, subjects can repeat a sequence of 8 movements without mistakes. We will need much more data before we will be sure that the memory span range of 5 to 9 is as universal for motor memory as it is for verbal memory. The best guess for now is that it is.

Organization and Reconstruction in Long-term Memory

People also recode information in long-term memory using processes of grouping and regrouping the information. These long-term memory processes are called organization and reconstruction. Those of us who saw Armstrong's first steps on the moon organized our memory for the event according to all the information we had learned about the moon's weak gravity, the bright sun, and so on. Later, we reorganized the information when we heard narrators explain specific experiments that were being conducted. Let's consider the process of organization first.

We organize our background knowledge about the world and use that knowledge to organize our long-term memory for specific events. Tulving (1972) distinguished two kinds of long-term memory:

1. **Semantic memory** is a person's general background memory about words, symbols, concepts, and rules.
2. **Episodic memory** is a person's memories about events, including the time and place that they occurred.

Many experiments indicate that semantic memory imposes itself on simple responses, including the formation of episodic memories. Let's consider three examples.

1. James Deese (1965) measured the organization of semantic memory using a **free association test**, a procedure requiring people to listen to one word and then say other words that come to mind. The test revealed the way general knowledge about words is grouped in semantic memory. Deese then gave another group of subjects a **free recall test**, a procedure requiring people to recall a list of words in any order they chose. The test revealed the organization of episodic memory because it showed how people grouped material learned at a specific time and place. Deese found that people imposed the organization of their semantic memory on their episodic memory. That is, people did not remember the words in the order that they were originally presented; they grouped their recall according to the organization of semantic memory.

2. Collins and Quillian (1969) showed that the organization of semantic memory also influences answers to simple true-false questions. They also showed that our semantic memory is organized in a hierarchy, a grouping of information into levels of categories and subcategories. Figure 3.7 shows an example of a hierarchy of information about canaries. Collins and Quillian predicted that we would use this structure in answering questions about canaries. They predicted also that it would take longer to answer questions at different levels. These predictions were con-

firmed: it takes longer to decide "A canary can fly" (level 2) than it does to decide "A canary can sing" (level 0). It takes even longer to decide "A canary has skin" (level 1). Other studies have shown that we also use hierarchies to organize episodic memory (e.g., Bower, Clark, Winzenz, & Lesgold, 1969).

3. We continue to reorganize our memory as time passes, and we are often unaware of these recodings. Elizabeth Loftus (1975, 1981) showed that such unconscious reconstructions often distort memories. In one study, Loftus induced memory reconstructions by the way she worded questions. Subjects saw a film of an accident and then they answered the following question: "About how fast were the cars going when they _____ into each other?" The blank contained one of five verbs: *smashed, collided, bumped, contacted,* or *hit.* The word *smashed* caused higher speed estimates than the other words. It also increased the probability that subjects reported seeing broken glass even though there was no broken glass in the film. In other words, the memory was reconstructed to include details consistent with an accident at a higher speed. The implications of the word *smashed* were drawn from semantic memory and these implications were imposed on episodic memory.

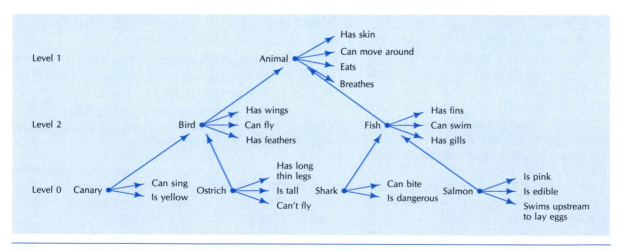

Figure 3.7 *A model of semantic memory. This type of organization is called a hierarchy (Collins & Quillian, 1969).*

Elizabeth Loftus has demonstrated that the way in which questions about an accident are phrased influence the way in which eye witnesses report seeing the events leading up to the accident.

Does the distinction between episodic and semantic memory apply to memory for movements? Yes, it is very similar to one made by Richard Schmidt (1975) in his schema theory (for further information on this topic see Chapter 8). Schmidt distinguished between memory for specific movement episodes (which might be called episodic memory for movements) and memory for an abstract generalization of a movement, which he called a **schema**. Schmidt's schema notion of an abstract representation of a movement is similar to Tulving's semantic memory notion of a general background memory of concepts and rules. Both of these are highly structured representations of general knowledge, and both representations are imposed on simple responses including the formation of episodic memories. We take up these similarities again later in the book when we discuss Schmidt's theory in more detail.

The similarities between motor and verbal memory have given researchers many important leads in studying motor memory. But the two kinds of memory processes also have important differences as we see in the next section.

Retrieval

Retrieval is the process of getting information out of memory. We can retrieve recordings of Armstrong's walk on the moon by pushing a button and a recording will play back all the information. Human retrieval processes are not as reliable. For example, you might have had the unpleasant experience of not recalling an answer during a test, but remembering it immediately after the test. Your ability to remember it afterwards suggests that the information was in your memory during the test but you were not able to retrieve it. We are often unaware of our retrieval processes, so researchers have designed special techniques to make inferences about the processes. Let's discuss those procedures separately for short-term and long-term memory.

Retrieval from Short-term Memory

Saul Sternberg (1966) found evidence that we search our short-term memory one item at a time. He asked people to memorize a short set of numbers. He then presented a test number and asked if it was a member of the memory set. Figure 3.8 shows how long it took people to answer this question when the number of items in the memory set was 1, 2, 3, 4, 5, or 6. It took about 440 milliseconds with one item and another 40 milliseconds for each additional item. Apparently, we search our short-term memory one item at a time with each item taking about 40 milliseconds. This kind of one-item-at-a-time "look up" is called a **serial search**.

Do we also make a serial search of our short-term memory for movement? Or do we make a **parallel search**, which is a simultaneous looking up of all items in a memory set? Lucariello, Toole, and Cauraugh (1983) suggested that memory for movement is searched in parallel. They used memory for a linear positioning task in which subjects were given a

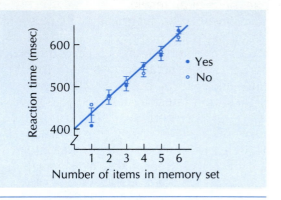

Figure 3.8 *Mean reaction time for positive responses (filled circles) and negative responses (open circles) (Sternberg, 1966).*

memory set of 1, 2, or 3 movements. Subjects used both hands during the experiment. They made the linear movements with their right hand, and then they lifted a finger on their left hand to indicate whether the movement was the same or different from the ones in their memory set. The critical measurement was the reaction time for identifying the movement as same or different. The serial search and parallel search hypotheses make different predictions about these reaction times. The serial search hypothesis predicts that reaction time should be longer for longer memory sets. The parallel search hypothesis predicts that reaction time should be the same for all memory set sizes. The results supported the parallel search hypothesis. That is, there was no difference in reaction time as a function of memory set size.

The sharp contrast between these results and those of Sternberg (1966) suggests that there might be a fundamental difference in the way we search our verbal and motor memories. The experiments suggest that we make a serial search of our memory for verbal material and a parallel search of our memory for movements. Sternberg's evidence for serial search of verbal material has been replicated many times, so we can be confident about those results. We can be less confident about there being parallel searches of motor memory until we see replications of the important Lucariello et al. results.

Other results suggest that there are some similarities between retrieval from verbal and motor short-term memory. For example, verbal and motor recall show similar **serial position effects**. For both, recall is best for the earliest and latest in a series, and it is worst for the middle part. The superior recall of the early material is called the **primacy effect**. The high recall of the latest material is called the **recency effect**. This pattern (see Figure 3.9) has been observed many times for verbal material (e.g., Craik, 1970). This pattern has also been observed for motor recall. In a study by Magill and Dowell (1977), blindfolded subjects moved a handle along a straight rod to nine stopping positions. Then they tried to recall the movements in the same order. The earliest movements were recalled the best (a primacy effect). The latest movement was recalled the next best (a recency effect). The five middle movements were recalled the worst.

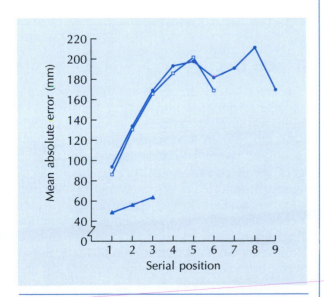

Figure 3.9 *Serial position curve for the recall of 3, 6, or 9 movement locations (Magill & Dowell, 1977).*

Retrieval from Long-term Memory

The procedures for studying retrieval from long-term memory have been every bit as elegant as Sternberg's procedure for short-term memory. One method was developed by Brown and McNeill (1966). They used the tip-of-the-tongue (TOT) phenomenon, which is the uncomfortable state of being on the verge of recalling something. They produced over 200 TOT states by giving definitions. For example, what word means "lying on one's back, with the face upward"? You are in the TOT state if you think you know the word but cannot recall it. (The word is *supine*.) After producing a TOT state, Brown and McNeill asked subjects questions about the word that was on the tip of their tongues. Their answers suggest that we search our long-term memory by the sound of a word as well as its meaning. For example, subjects gave words that sounded like the correct word such as *secant* for *sextant*. Subjects also gave the correct first letter over 50 percent of the time and the correct number of syllables over 60 percent of the time. Thus, we reveal aspects of our retrieval processes when we come close to retrieving information from long-term memory without actually finding it.

We also reveal our retrieval processes when we are given **retrieval cues**, which are aids to locating information in memory. Tulving and Pearlstone (1966) showed, for example, that we can use retrieval cues to organize our search through memory. They presented long lists of words from common categories such as animals, gems, and flowers. They presented the words in random order and told subjects that they could recall them in any order. They gave two tests. On the first one, half the subjects were given the category names at the time of recall; the other half were not. On the second test both groups were given the category names. The subjects given the category names on the first test did much better than the other subjects. Both groups did equally well on the second test. The important result was that subjects who could not recall words without help could recall them with the help of retrieval cues. Apparently, the information was in memory during the first test, but subjects could not find it until they were given retrieval cues to help them organize their retrieval.

We also organize our retrieval of movements. When dancers learn the Texas Two Step, for instance, they commonly learn the foot sequence first. For instance, men lead with the left, follow with a half step to the right, and so on. As they become familiar with the foot sequence they learn to perform these same sequences while turning or moving backwards. Finally, men learn to give lead signals to their dance partners by pressing gently on their backs or pushing their hands to indicate turns and changes in direction. Each of these parts are learned separately, but the dancers reorganize them as they practice. Timing, rhythm, and coordination improve as they group the lead signals and the foot movements together into fluid sequences. Novice Two-Steppers retrieve the foot part and the hand part separately but later retrieve the two as a whole.

Magill and Lee (1987) measured similar organizational effects in a simple laboratory task. Subjects were presented with 12 linear hand movements in random order. They then were asked to recall as many as they could in any order. A different random order of the same movements was then presented and subjects again tried to recall as many as they could in any order. This presentation and recall sequence continued for 12 trials. Subjects tended to ignore the presentation order, and they developed consistent recall sequences. The subjects with the most consistent recall orders were the ones with the most accurate recall of the criterion movements. In other words, better organization of memory and retrieval leads to better performance, not only for verbal memory, but also for motor memory.

Forgetting

Forgetting is the inability to remember or retrieve information from memory. Most of the memory experiments that we have already considered involve forgetting because subjects did not make perfect recalls. The only exception was Sternberg's experiment, which measured reaction time for small memory sets that were recalled perfectly. Subjects forgot answers in the other experiments. This section reviews two theories of forgetting: (1) **trace decay theory** holds that we forget because memory fades away in time if its strength is not maintained through use; and (2) **interference theory** holds that we forget because other memories get in the way, making the desired memory harder to locate. Let's review each of these theories in turn.

Trace Decay

The trace decay theory is essentially a "use it or lose it" idea. Early memory theorists saw memory strength as being similar to muscle strength. When you use a muscle, it gets stronger. When you stop using a muscle, it gets weak again. According to trace decay theory, memories also get stronger when they are used and weaker when they are not. Trace decay seems to be a reasonable explanation for forgetting in some, but not all, of the experiments we have considered so far. It works well, for example, to explain the Peterson and Peterson experiment in which subjects forgot within seconds if they were not allowed to think about the syllables that they were asked to remember. It does not work well, however, for the Tulving and Pearlstone experiment in which subject forgot items on one test but remembered them on a second test when they were given retrieval cues. These results seem more consistent with the interference theory.

Interference

Can you remember the name of the scientist who developed a schema theory of motor learning? You learned the name earlier in this chapter. You probably have not used the name again since then, so your memory strength for the name might have decayed. But decay of memory strength alone does not completely determine forgetting. You have learned a lot of other names in this chapter, and they might get in the way of retrieving the correct name, Richard Schmidt. According to interference theory, there are two kinds of interference: proactive inhibition and retroactive inhibition.

Proactive inhibition is the interference of a previous memory with memory for new learning. The names you learned *before* Richard Schmidt are potential sources of proactive interference. Another example of proactive interference may be found in our dance example. When a novice dancer tries to learn the Two Step after learning the waltz, information from the waltz commonly interferes. Figure 3.10 illustrates the experimental procedure for studying proactive inhibition with three procedural steps and two groups of subjects. In the first step, an experimental group learns Task B, such as a linear arm movement and a control group does some unrelated activity such as mental arithmetic problems. During the second step, both groups learn Task A, such as a different linear arm movement. For the third step, both groups recall Task A. Proactive inhibition is shown when performance on Task A is worse for the experimental group, which had learned Task B, than for the control group, which had not learned Task B.

	Experimental group	Control group
Step 1	Learn task B	Rest or engage in unrelated activity
Step 2	Learn task A	Learn task A
Step 3	Recall task A	Recall task A

Figure 3.10 *Proactive inhibition occurs when a previous memory interferes with the recall of a new memory.*

Proactive inhibition only affects similar information. Wickens (1970) showed, for example, that subjects are released from proactive inhibition when verbal material changes categories (e.g., from letters to numbers). Leavitt, Lee, and Romanow (1980) showed that release from proactive inhibition also occurs for motor memory. They showed that proactive inhibition affects memory for location and memory for distance. No proactive inhibition occurs, however, when subjects switch from one to the other. For example, memory for a location is worse when the recall attempt is preceded by recall attempts for other locations. It is not worse, however, when the recall attempt is preceded by recall attempts for distance. When subjects switch from one kind of recall to another, they are released from proactive inhibition.

Retroactive inhibition is the interference of new learning with old memories. The names you learned *after* Richard Schmidt are potential sources of retroactive interference. Once again, dance may provide an example of retroactive interference. When a novice dancer learns the polka after the Two Step, the polka may be source of retroactive inhibition when the dancer once again tries to Two Step.

The procedure for studying retroactive inhibition also uses three steps and two groups as shown in Figure 3.11. Both groups learn Task A in the first step. The experimental group learns Task B in the second step, while the control group does an unrelated activity. Both groups recall Task A during the third step. Retroactive inhibition is shown when

	Experimental group	Control group
Step 1	Learn task A	Learn task A
Step 2	Learn task B	Rest or engage in unrelated activity
Step 3	Recall task A	Recall task A

Figure 3.11 *Retroactive inhibition occurs when a new memory interferes with the recall of a previous memory.*

performance on Task A is worse for the experimental group, which learned Task B, than for the control group, which did not learn Task B.

Retroactive inhibition from Task B can produce systematic biases in the recall of Task A. For example, Stelmach and Kelso (1975) required subjects to move to one location while learning Task A and to move to another location for Task B. When the Task B location was shorter than the Task A location, subjects attempting to recall Task A tended to produce a movement short of the Task A location. When the Task B location was farther than the Task A location, subjects attempting to recall Task A tended to produce a movement farther than the Task A location.

You will be a victim of proactive inhibition if you forget the present discussion of interference because we just discussed retroactive interference. However, we learned earlier that old memories can help new memories. We learned earlier that old memories of category groupings can help as retrieval cues in the recall of new words. You will be a victim of retroactive inhibition if you let the present discussion of interference make you forget our earlier examples of old memories helping new memories. When test time rolls around, remember both. Sometimes old memories help as retrieval cues and sometimes they hurt as sources of proactive inhibition. In general, old and new memories help one another as retrieval cues when you use one to help you organize your memory for the other. In this case, your memory is like a filing system that you continually improve through cross-referencing. Old and new memories hurt each other through interference when you throw your memory together like a junk drawer. More and more junk in the drawer makes it less and less likely that you will find anything.

Let's try to take advantage of what we already learned about memory to learn more about the neurobiological basis of memory.

Neurobiology of Memory

Scientists are beginning to understand how learning and memory change our nervous system. So far we have been talking about memory as if it were an abstract information processing system. We have discussed encoding, recoding, and retrieval from short-term and long-term storage systems. This section adds some flesh and blood to our discussion. In Chapter 2, we learned that the nervous system controls and coordinates much of our behavior, and that the neuron is the basic building block of that system. We begin, therefore, by asking how memories change neurons.

Short-term Memory, Long-term Memory, and Neurons

Do neural changes reflect the distinction we have made between short-term and long-term memory? Greenough (1984) argued that they do. He hypothesized that (1) change in the excitability of cell membranes is the basis for short-term memory and (2) the establishment of new connections between neurons is the basis for long-term memory. The cell membrane is a gate that controls the transmission of messages across existing pathways in the nervous system. The gate can close so that a message will not go between neurons that are connected. The gate can also open more or less to regulate the flow of signals on existing paths. Researchers are trying to test the hypothesis that our short-term memories are determined by these membrane gate-keeping changes. They are also testing the hypothesis that our long-term memories are established when neurons grow new branches to reach other neurons. Scientists already know that learning does the things that are consistent with these hypotheses. Learning changes the excitability of cell membranes (Alkon, 1983). It changes the firing pattern of single neurons (Olds, 1973). And it changes the number of connections between neurons (Greenough, 1984). These results have encouraged scientists to push on in their efforts to understand the relationship between memory and neurons (Hoyenga & Hoyenga, 1988). Scientists are also studying the relationship between memory and specific brain structures. The next section reviews one branch of that research.

Working Memory and the Hippocampus

The **hippocampus** is a brain structure (see Chapter 2). A damaged hippocampus affects memory in ways that are often explained in terms of the distinction we have made between working memory and long-term memory. Memory loss from brain damage is called **amnesia**. There are two kinds: (1) **retrograde amnesia**, which is loss of memory for events that occurred before the injury and (2) **antrograde amnesia**, which is difficulty in remembering events that take place after an injury. A damaged hippocampus produces antrograde amnesia, suggesting that the injury impairs working memory and makes it difficult to form new memories.

Consider the case of H. M., a 28-year-old man who had his hippocampus removed in an effort to control his violent seizures. The procedure has never been repeated because H. M.

suffered a severe memory disorder after the surgery. H. M. had good recall of his earlier life up to about one to three years before the surgery. However, he had great difficulty forming new memories as indicated in the following clinical report:

Ten months after the operation, the family moved to a new house which was situated only a few blocks from their old one, on the same street. When examined . . . nearly a year later, H. M. had not yet learned the new address, nor could he be trusted to find his way home alone, because he would go to the old house. Six years ago, the family moved again, and H. M. is still unsure of his present address, although he does seem to know that he has moved. [He] will do the same jigsaw puzzles day after day without showing any practice effect, and read the same magazine over and over without finding the contents familiar.

On one occasion, he was asked to remember the number 584 and was then allowed to sit quietly with no interruptions for 15 minutes, at which point he was able to recall the number correctly without hesitation. When asked how he was able to do this, he replied, "It's easy. You just remember 8. You see 5, 8, and 4 add to 17. You remember 8, subtract it from 17 and it leaves 9. Divide 9 in half and you get 4 and 5, and there you are: 584. Easy."

In spite of H. M.'s elaborate . . . scheme, he was unable, a minute or so later, to remember either the number 584 or any of the associated complex train of thought; in fact, he did not know that he had been given a number to remember (Milner, 1970).

These effects suggest that loss of the hippocampus severely damaged H. M.'s working memory. He still had the long-term memories that he formed one to three years before the operation. Because of a badly impaired working memory, however, he virtually lost his ability to form new long-term memories.

This conclusion is also supported by a similar case of a man who lived five years after losing his hippocampus in a stroke. He had a good memory for events that occurred before the surgery, but he seemed to lack the working memory needed to store new memories (Zola-Morgan, Squire, & Amarai, 1986).

Flashbulb Memories

Many people have **flashbulb memories**, which are vivid memories of unexpected and emotionally important events. Let's try to tap some of our flashbulb memories with the following questions: (1) What were you doing when you learned that war had broken out with Iraq? (2) Do you remember where you were and what you were doing when you learned that the space shuttle *Challenger* had exploded? Many of us can answer these questions in vivid detail. For example, I heard a TV bulletin announcing that bombing had started in Baghdad. At that moment, I was taking an apple from my refrigerator. I dropped the apple and ran to the TV in my living room. My wife was standing in front of the TV turning up the volume. She was pale and shaking when she turned to me and said, "This is it."

Brown and Kulik (1977) found that most Americans over 40 can recall exactly what they were doing when they heard the news about President Kennedy's assassination. I am no exception. I remember clearly the moment the announcement came over my school's PA system. According to Brown and Kulik, this moment was set in my memory like a photograph taken with a mental flash camera.

Do you have vivid memories of sudden, emotionally charged events? If you do, you may be surprised to learn what recent research has shown about them: First, "vivid" does not necessarily mean accurate. Flashbulb memories are both vivid and accurate a week or two after events such as the *Challenger* explosion. They remain vivid, but they lose accuracy as time passes (Neisser, 1982, 1986; Thompson & Cowan, 1986; McCloskey, Wible, & Cohen, 1988). Second, much of what is remembered is rehearsed in conversation. If it is not rehearsed, it will not be remembered accurately eight months after the

Memory Loss and Disease

One disease that causes antrograde amnesia is Korsakoff's syndrome, which is brain damage caused by severe thiamine (vitamin B-1) deficiency that is characterized by apathy, confusion, and memory impairment. This disease is rarely observed except in alcoholics who go days or weeks without eating. Barbizet (1970) described a 59-year-old Korsakoff's patient with memory impairments similar to H. M.'s. For example, he easily recalled his youth, but he had trouble forming new memories. He forgot that he had long conversations

Vivid memories of events occurring many years ago may become accessible at class re-uinons. However, research has shown that these memories may not be accurate.

event (Bohannon, 1988). Special memory mechanisms are therefore not necessary to explain flashbulb memories. The memories are important, however. They are, according to Neisser (1982), the site where we identify our lives with the events of history.

shortly after he had them. He reread newspaper articles without knowing that he had read them before. When he sat in front of an empty plate, he did not know whether he had just finished eating or whether he was waiting to be served.

Schachter (1983) observed similar memory losses in an elderly patient with Alzheimer's disease, which we defined earlier. The patient remembered the jargon of golf, but he could not keep track of his game. He teed off five times on the same hole without knowing that he had teed off before. When he did remember having taken a shot, he often could not remember where his ball went or what kind of ball he was using.

These patterns of memory loss suggest that working memory was impaired in both of these patients, making it very difficult for them to form new memories.

Electrical and Chemical Regulators of Memory

The importance of working memory is also suggested by the effects of electrical and chemical regulators of memory. Memory can be either increased or decreased by electrical stimulation of the brain (Gold & McGaugh, 1975) or by chemical stimulation of the brain (Gold & McGaugh, 1977). These effects are greatest if the stimulation occurs when it would be most likely to affect working memory, shortly before or shortly after training.

FINAL COMMENT

Clearly, scientists are making progress in understanding both the cognitive processes of memory and the neurobiological basis for those processes. At the same time, much of what has been learned about memory processes is being applied to improving the learning and memory of the kinds of complex skills required by astronauts, for example. As modern technological systems have become more complex, computers have been introduced to monitor and control many functions that were previously controlled by people. Ironically, the net effect of this automation has been to increase the demand for training of human operators. As Armstrong's famous landing on the moon dramatically illustrates, (1) people remain very much involved in managing the complexities that computers do not handle, (2) their jobs are often difficult to learn, and (3) their role is continually changing (see Rasmussen & Rouse, 1981). Consequently, those who are committed to the computer revolution are faced with the problem of creating a training revolution as well. The severity of this problem is clear when we consider that most of the required training involves high-performance skills that are defined by three characteristics: (1) more than 100 hours are required to reach proficiency, (2) more than 20 percent of highly motivated trainees fail to reach proficiency, and (3) substantial qualitative differences in performance exist between a novice and an expert (Schneider, 1985). The technology for solving this problem is already available. The real problem, therefore, is ineffectively utilizing it. And the solution demands an increased understanding of the learning processes involved in acquiring a high-performance skill. The research reviewed in this chapter provides a foundation for understanding these processes and applying that understanding to the development of the kind of training demanded in modern society.

KEY TERMS

memory
recall test
recognition test
savings test
multiple memory
   theory
sensory memory
short-term memory
long-term memory
recognition
   processes
backward masking

rehearsal
working memory
levels of processing
   theory
encoding
attention
dichotic listening
recoding
chunking
memory span
semantic memory
episodic memory

free association test
free recall test
schema
retrieval
serial search
parallel search
serial position effect
primacy effect
recency effect
retrieval cues
forgetting
trace decay theory

interference theory
amnesia
active movement
passive movement
antrograde amnesia
retrograde amnesia
proactive inhibition
retroactive inhibition
hippocampus
flashbulb memories

4

Information Processing: An Overview

Jan Berry: "DEAD MAN'S CURVE"

Behaviorism
An Information-Processing Model
- *Peripheral Processes*
- *Central Processes*

Information Flow
- *Serial Processing*
- *Parallel Processing*
- *Parallel-Distributed Processing*

Reaction Time as a Measure of Processing Demands
- *Sensation-Perception*
- *Response Selection*
- *Response Execution*

Factors Influencing Processing
- *Stages of Learning*
- *Movement Time*
- *Preparation Time and Anticipation*
- *Environment*
- *Task*

HIGHLIGHT: Context Dependent Behavior
FINAL COMMENT
KEY TERMS

Jan Berry: "DEAD MAN'S CURVE"

Jan Berry was stretched out in a lounge chair enjoying the sun of Palm Springs. It was Easter weekend of 1969 and his twenty-eighth birthday. Palm Springs had been invaded by thousands of high school and college kids on their spring break. The transistor radios at poolside were blaring out a golden oldie, a million seller from nearly ten years before. Jan smiled on the inside but wasn't sure the smile made it all the way to his face. He had written and sung that song while he was still in high school. Back then he was riding high, making records, wheeling and dealing, riding the crest of the perfect wave. That was before—before the accident, all the heartache, the doctors, the therapy, and the hospitals.

In 1958 Berry and a friend, Dean Torrence, were the kings of the California good-time sound—surf music. Recording sessions with the Beach Boys were more like beer parties than work. Herb Alpert was one of their managers. Leon Russell played the keyboard, Glen Campbell the guitar, and Joe Osborne was on bass. Their interests (and also the subjects of their songs) included "riding the wild surf," "sidewalk surfin," "the new girl in school," "fast cars," and "drag racing." Jan and Dean sold approximately 10 million singles and 7 million albums between 1958 and 1966. They hosted a show that featured James Brown, Smokey Robinson, Marvin Gaye, the Supremes, the Beach Boys, and the Rolling Stones. Times were good and the pace was furious.

Jan Berry and Dean Torrence sold millions of records while they were still in high school. They were the kings of the California good-time sound, surf music, until the accident.

- To appreciate the varied ways in which humans process information.
- To examine the types of processing that lead to goal-directed human movement.
- To understand how reaction time can be used to estimate information processing demands.
- To appreciate the factors that influence the speed and efficiency with which information is processed.

Jan was obsessed with fast living and even faster driving. Dean was petrified by Jan's driving. On more than one occasion, Jan changed clothes while driving at nearly 100 mph. Three times Dean was in the car when Jan was involved in serious accidents.

In 1963, Jan and Dean released a song that turned out to be both a great hit and an omen. "Dead Man's Curve" reached number five on the national hit parade. In April 1966, after a meeting with his draft board, Jan roared through a curve on Whittier Boulevard just below the Sunset Strip in Hollywood. There was a terrible screech and deafening noise as Jan's 1966 Corvette Stingray rammed into a parked car. Minutes later, two ambulance attendants pulled Jan from the car. His head was cracked wide open.

When he finally awoke in the hospital, he was looking at his mother and father. He recognized them immediately and he knew who he was. But when he tried to speak the words did not come out right. He tried to get out of bed but was no longer sure how to move his arms and legs. He was frustrated—he thought that if he went to sleep and woke up a little later, he would find that it was all a bad dream. But that did not happen! He could think clearly; he knew what he wanted to say or do, but he did not know how to do it.

Things that he had never thought about before were now his center of attention. Before the accident, when he wanted to speak, the words just came out. When he wanted to move, his arms and legs responded. Now something was terribly wrong. The doctor explained that he had suffered some brain damage. The therapist called it aphasia. Apparently, a link in the information processing chain was damaged. It was as if his body could not understand the language of his brain. He thought he needed a translator. The therapist said he needed to relearn the language himself.

By 1969, after nearly three years of therapy and frustration, Jan could walk again but the movement of his right hand and right leg was still impaired. He could speak very slowly and often had difficulty finding the right word. But he could sing a little and was planning a comeback!

Not all stories have a completely happy ending. Jan attempted to re-record "Tinsel Town" in 1973, but the song was never released. He made his first live appearance at the Hollywood Palladium in the summer of 1973 with his old friend Dean. The audience could not understand why Jan moved so strangely and sang so slowly. They got the impression he was on drugs. Jan and Dean were booed off the stage. The following year he was recognized in Las Vegas and was asked to perform a number. Jan slowly made his way to the stage and said "Many years ago, I wrote and recorded a song that was to become the story of my life." Then he sang "Dead Man's Curve" to the best of his ability.

It is easy for us to take our processing abilities for granted. We pay little attention to the processes involved in responding to our environment until something happens to take those abilities away. Jan Berry experienced the painful realities of the disruption of a single processing link. In this chapter we will attempt to characterize the general stages in information processing. Remember these stages are discussed as though they involve discrete, independent processes, but this is not the case. Processing at one stage invariably influences processing at other stages.

Behaviorism

In 1938, a psychologist named B. F. Skinner published a book entitled *The Behavior of Organisms*. The book chronicled experiments that were thought to provide insight into the manner in which the environment acts on an organism to influence learning and shape behavior. The book had its roots in work conducted nearly 100 years earlier by a German scholar, Hermann Ebbinghaus (1850–1909). The approach taken by Skinner, termed **behaviorism** or sometimes *stimulus-response,* maintains that the environment controls our behavior more than any other force. The basic tenets of behaviorism are that (1) the mechanisms and principles of learning are similar for all species; (2) all learning, no matter how complex, can be understood in terms of two kinds of simple associations referred to as **classical conditioning** and **operant conditioning**, and (3) the only effective way to study behavior and learning is to determine the relationship between environmental stimuli and the resulting response.

To the behaviorist, concepts such as the *mind, thinking,* or *processing* are best ignored because they cannot be studied directly and therefore are outside the realm of real science. The vast majority of scientists who study motor learning and control, along with cognitive psychologists, reject this line of reasoning. They recognize that the environment may dictate the behavior of some organisms and animals. However, they maintain that many animals, particularly humans, actively utilize environmental information and memory to determine their behavior. The problem is that it is difficult to delve into the "black box" of the mind. This black box holds the secrets that determine the events and processing that occur between the presentation of a stimuli and the execution of a motor response.

Today's technology offers some possibilities of directly studying the internal processes of the mind (see Chapter 2), but these processes are still not well understood. Adequate knowledge and techniques for the direct study of complex human processes such as perception, response selection, and response execution are not currently available. However, by utilizing an information processing approach, these processes can be effectively modeled and studied.

The information processing approach is not new and was not developed specifically for studying motor learning and control. Theorists in many areas of cognitive science utilize information processing techniques because they believe that this approach facilitates the conceptual understanding of the processes underlying human performance. Recall that the information processing perspective views the individual as an active processor of stimulus information rather than as a passive recipient. The basic assumption of the information processing approach is that when an individual performs a movement, a number of cognitive processes are required for the movement to be executed correctly. Neisser (1976) describes the task of understanding human behavior as analogous to that of a person trying to discover the sequential operations a computer executes in arriving at a solution while at the same time being unconcerned with the computer "hardware."

An Information-Processing Model

Both before and after the accident, Jan Berry could process information. However, after the accident one or more links in the information processing chain of events were not functioning correctly. The model presented in Figure 4.1 represents a simplified attempt to depict the major events in human information processing. The model assumes that the individual accepts sensory input (information) via the various sensory receptors. The information is transmitted to the central nervous system (CNS) where it is acted upon or processed. These processes result in commands transmitted to the musculature that are tailored to the specific environmental demands and the intentions of the performer—hence, the label **information processing**.

In describing the model it is convenient to choose an arbitrary starting point for the flow of information. For example, while waiting at a traffic signal, the light turns green and impacts the sensory receptors in the eyes. This information is transmitted to the CNS and processed, and then impulses are transmitted to the muscles in your legs and feet that cause your foot to be taken off the brake so that you may begin to depress the accelerator. However, the model does not necessarily suggest a point at which a sequence of events begins that ultimately results in movement, but rather depicts a continuous flow of information. Sensory receptors are continually bombarding the CNS with volleys of input. The CNS is in a constant state of flux with information being processed, memory states being activated, and other memory states being stored. One result of the processing in the CNS is a nearly constant output to the muscles. As a result of a change in the state of any one of these processes, a sequence of events can begin that will result in movement. The movement, in turn, creates a whole new sensory perspective.

This simplified model of information processing is in the behaviorist tradition. The CNS is depicted as a black box. The model does little to distinguish between the operation of simple mechanical devices and the complex processes involved in the control of human movement. To illustrate this point, let's consider the heating and cooling system in a typical house (Figure 4.2). The system is composed of three primary components: temperature sensing devices, thermostat (selection/decision device), and heating/cooling machinery. The temperature-sensing devices are continually relaying information to the thermostat. The thermostat applies a set of rules (turn on heat at 65 degrees, air conditioning at 78 degrees, or do nothing between 65 and 78 degrees) to the input and at appropriate times turns either the heater or air conditioner on or off. What is different about the functioning of a thermostat and that of the CNS? The thermostat does not think, learn, or selectively process information. The thermostat passively applies a few simple rules; the same set of

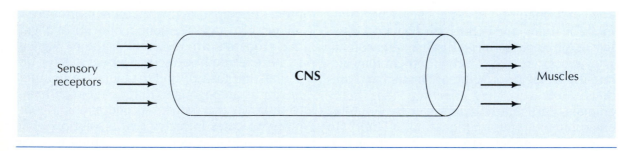

Figure 4.1 *A simplified information processing system.*

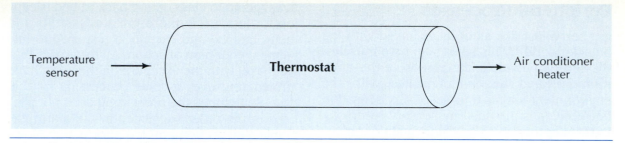

Figure 4.2 *A simplified temperature control system.*

conditions always results in the same response. Humans actively seek out information and selectively respond to stimuli. Indeed, this simplified model provides us with little insight into what might have gone wrong as a result of Jan Berry's tragic accident.

To understand better the source of Jan Berry's difficulties in processing information, it is necessary to describe more completely the general categories of processing that are engaged in producing movement. Two expanded information processing models are presented in this chapter (Figures 4.3 and 4.7). Both models depict essentially the same processes occurring to produce movement. However, the first model is a serial processing model (Figure 4.3) and the second suggests the varied processing flow indicative of parallel-distributed processing (Figure 4.7).

Traditional information processing models have generally depicted a serial flow of information (Welford, 1968; Marteniuk, 1976). The model illustrated in Figure 4.3 is a serial processing model. The model separates the processes into central and peripheral components. **Central processes** are categorized as sensation/perception, response selection, and response execution processes. **Peripheral processes** involve the activation of sensory receptors and muscles as well as the transmission to (afferent) and from (efferent) the central nervous system. The concentration in this chapter and in Chapters 5, 6, and 7 as well will be on the central processes, although a brief discussion of the important features of the peripheral components comes first. Could Jan Berry's difficulties be traced to peripheral or central sources?

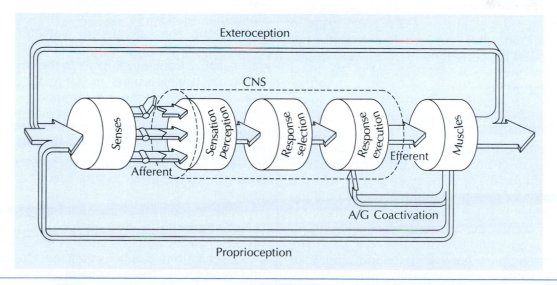

Figure 4.3 *An expanded information processing model. Note that this model implies a serial processing flow.*

Peripheral Processes

Jan Berry, just like all of us, is linked with the outside world by his senses and his muscles. His senses provide a description of the environment, and he communicates with the environment via his muscles. Every sensation he receives is provided by sensory receptors. **Exteroceptors** such as vision, audition (hearing), taste, and smell provide a description of the world around him, and **proprioceptors** such as the muscle spindles, Golgi tendon organs, and various pressure and temperature receptors provide him with the current state of his body.

On the other hand, muscles are his only means of communicating with the environment. He communicates through speech and song, facial expression, posture, and action. Jan uses movement not only to communicate with the environment but to change the environment and to seek out information. Every movement changes the environment in some way and provides sensory receptors with potentially new stimulation and perspectives. Jan's physicians determined that his sensory capabilities remained intact after the accident, but they were not so sure about his neuromotor system. Was the nerves-muscles system injured in the accident or was there some other factor that caused Jan's speech and movements to be impaired? Doctors were able to determine that Jan's problem was not peripheral. The peripheral nerves were intact and the muscles would respond to electrical stimulation.

Central Processes

With a little reflection, it is easy to see that a great deal of processing must occur between the stimulation of sensory receptors and the initiation of meaningful movement. Could the difficulties that Jan Berry experienced be a result of central processing problems? Consider the movements you make every day. The alarm (stimulus) goes off in the morning. Your brain senses and hopefully perceives the meaning of the stimuli. You consider alternatives (going to class, going back to bed, sleeping for just a few more minutes [sure!]) and then organize and execute a response to implement your plan of action. All responses that we make, with the exception of those we have termed reflexive, involve processing of this type. Sometimes the processing does not proceed in the order suggested in the alarm example (see section entitled Information Flow) and sometimes the demand on a particular type of processing are increased or decreased (see section entitled Factors Influencing Processing), but in general three stages or types of processing can be described. We believe that an in-depth understanding of these classifications of processes is so important that we have devoted an entire chapter to each.

In the following brief description of the classifications of processing, consider the problems that Jan Berry experienced as a result of his accident. He could see, hear, and sense the world around him; he could quickly decide what to do, but he ran into trouble when he attempted to move.

Sensation and Perception. The first major class of processing is termed **sensation-perception** and will be dealt with in depth in Chapter 5. Neural transmission from tens of thousands of sensory receptors must first be sensed and then perceived. **Sensation** involves the detecting and/or selecting of specific sensory transmissions from the continual barrage of transmissions impacting the central nervous system. So much information is available that the resources for information processing cannot possibly act on all of them. What happens when a friend whispers to you in class? Do you hear what the professor is saying or do you listen to your friend? Can you do both?

After stimuli are sensed can they be perceived? **Perception** involves long-term memory because sensations are given meaning. Thus, sensations can be organized, classified, and interpreted. The movement of a few dots on a computer monitor is perceived and rec-

High sensation and perception demands are placed on this industrial worker. Sensation involves the detecting and selection of specific sensory information from the environment; perception involves organizing, classifying, and interpreting those sensations.

experiences to formulate a course of action or inaction. Consider a batter in baseball. The batter must utilize information from sensation-perception processing of the pitcher's motion, movement of the ball, instruction from the coach, situation in the game, position of the fielders, the count, and so on to plan an appropriate action. Swing or don't swing? Take it to right field or left? Bunt or hit away? As the number of alternatives and complexity of the situation increase, so does the difficulty of response selection processing.

Response selection can involve a conscious decision or a nonconscious translation. **Decisions** are required when two or more alternatives are considered. **Translation** involves relating a particular stimulus to a particular response. Sometimes stimuli and responses are highly compatible. That is, a particular stimulus nearly automatically elicits a particular response. In Figure 4.5 (left), the compatibility between the lights and the response keys is relatively high. However, responses to the lights–keys arrangement in Figure 4.5 (right) will require a good deal of translation. Certainly, subjects will perform more slowly when the compatibility is low than when the compatibility is high.

ognized as a moving ball or an outline of a person or a hand (Figure 4.4). A sound is no longer a simple auditory sensation but a signal that class is over. The visual information representing the contours of a face now represents a specific friend. A light touch on your arm might invoke fear when you are working around a wasp nest or warmth when in the company of a loved one. Perceptual processing considers the current circumstances and past experiences in interpreting sensations.

Response Selection.   The second class of processing is termed **response selection** and is discussed in detail in Chapter 6. Response selection utilizes current information and past

Response Execution.   The third class of processing is termed **response execution** and is the focus of Chapter 7. The product of the response selection stage can be likened to the floor plan an architect devises for a house. It

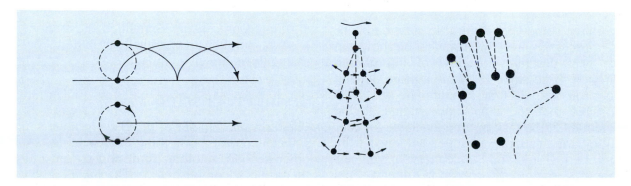

Figure 4.4   Three illustrations of how we actively impose organization on moving objects.

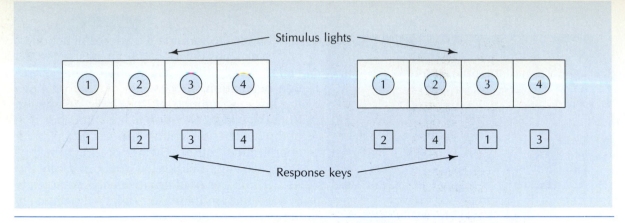

Figure 4.5 *Two stimulus response configurations differing in compatibility. The configuration on the left offers higher compatibility between the stimulus and response than the configuration on the right. Higher compatibility would result in faster reaction times.*

provides the general features of what the final product should look like but does not include the detail necessary to actually construct the house. The **action plan** is the detail—the step-by-step sequence of events that makes up the planned movement. The sequence of efferent commands must be coordinated both hierarchically and sequentially. In this context, *hierarchical* means that changes in posture must precede changes in limb position, or commands to stabilize the shoulder must precede commands to the arm and hand. Similarly, sequential organization involves the timing and ordering of the various efferent commands. People involved with computer programming or music should be familiar with the concepts of hierarchy and sequence.

It is this stage of processing that Jan's physicians determined was impaired. Jan has what they called an *output aphasia*. The part of the brain that translated the action plan into motor commands had been damaged. We take for granted the ease with which we speak, walk, or sing. So did Jan Berry before the accident.

Information Flow

We have somewhat arbitrarily classified central processing into three stages. But how can we best describe the flow of information through these stages? This is a more difficult question than it first appears. In fact, it is possible that the flow may change as the demands of the task or time available for executing the response change. Evidence from Sternberg (1969) and Sanders (1980) suggests that processing may proceed in either a serial or parallel fashion. More recent theoretical work by Karl Pribram (1988) suggests an even more flexible processing flow called *parallel-distributed processing*. Simplified illustrations of serial, parallel, and parallel-distributed processing flows are given in Figure 4.6.

Serial Processing

The term *serial* in **serial processing** means in a specified order: one thing happens first, another second, another third, and so on until the task is accomplished. Traditional assembly lines and conventional computers work in a serial fashion. It is easy to conceptualize human information processing as occurring in a

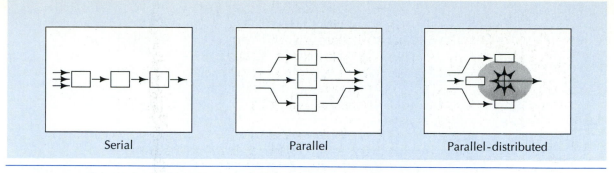

| Serial | Parallel | Parallel-distributed |

Figure 4.6 *Simplified serial, parallel, and parallel-distributed processing models.*

serial order. A stimulus impinges on sensory receptors; the receptors generate transmissions to the brain; sensation is converted to perception; perceptions are translated and/or utilized to decide on a plan of action; the plan of action is formalized and transmitted to the muscles; and the muscles carry out the prescribed action. For example, suppose that a fire alarm goes off while you are in class. What is the sequence of events that result in action? The expanded information processing model depicted in Figure 4.3 is a serial model.

Parallel Processing

Parallel processing occurs when two or more processes occur at the same time. Can response selection processing occur while sensation-perception processing is occurring or is one type of processing dependent on the information from the other? Manufacturing engineers and computer scientists have found that parallel processing can be much more efficient than serial processing. For example, in the automotive industry it is common for the frame, engine, and the body of a car to be assembled simultaneously. Likewise, computer scientists have discovered that the speed of processing can be increased by increasing the number of processors (CPUs—central processing units) that are simultaneously acting on information. There are many indications that, at times, humans perform like parallel processors of information. This is particularly evi-

dent, as we will see in later chapters, when there is little time to respond or when we are placed in a position in which we must anticipate upcoming events.

Parallel-Distributed Processing

The key principle of **parallel-distributed processing** is flexibility. At times the conditions are such that serial processing is most appropriate; at other times parallel processing is needed, while other demands could best be met with some combination of serial and parallel processing. This notion suggests that the demands of the task, the state of the environment, the past experiences of the performer, and the current intentions are all considered in determining the optimal flow of information. Sensory information from one set of receptors may flow directly to the response selection or response execution processing centers while other information may need to be perceptually processed first. The system is considered plastic because it can change as demands change. Parallel-distributed processing can be quite efficient.

The information processing model depicted in Figure 4.7 could be used to describe parallel-distributed processing because the flow of information is not restricted by the model. It is difficult to model paralled-distributed processing because allowances have to be made to permit the processing flow to progress in a variety of ways.

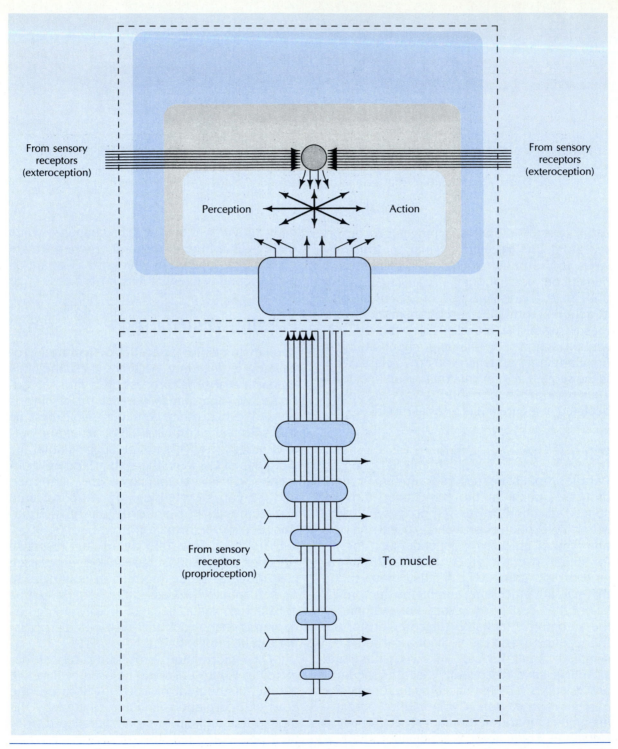

Figure 4.7 *An expanded information processing model. Note that this model implies variable processing flows indicative of a parallel-distributed processing model.*

It is also important to note that this model depicts a great deal of cross-talk throughout the information processing model. The term **cross-talk** describes the variety of neural communications that takes place in the spinal cord and brain. Cross-talk occurs at almost all levels of information transmission and processing. Simple reflexes are based on the concept of cross-talk. **Reflexes** are responses to stimuli that do not require information to be processed in the brain. Rather, reflexes occur nearly automatically. For example, the patellar tendon reflex (knee jerk) occurs when our patellar tendon (just below the knee cap) is tapped with a rubber hammer. The stimulus (tap) results in a very rapid afferent discharge from muscle spindles which in turn activates the motor neurons/muscles of the leg such that the leg jerks forward. This is contrasted to almost all other movements in which the sensory information is processed in the brain before commands are sent to the muscles.

Reaction Time as a Measure of Processing Demands

What events take place between the presentation of a stimulus to move and the beginning of a response? A basic assumption of the information processing approach is that all processing activities take time. The more "difficult" the processing, the more time is required. Thus, reaction time has the potential to be used as an indicator of the difficulty of various processing activities.

Consider the following example. As you are walking across campus, you see an object coming directly at you. What are the processes you engage in before responding? First, your senses (probably your eyes) must be stimulated by a change in the environment (the movement of the object). The information from the senses must be transmitted to the brain and then must be sensed and acted on perceptually (it must be determined what the object is and whether it represents a danger, etc.). The perceptual information must be used to decide on a plan of action (duck or attempt to catch the object?). The plan of action must be organized and executed so that the appropriate muscles are innervated at the appropriate time. The innervation signals must be transmitted to the muscles and the muscles must act.

For purposes of illustration, consider that it takes about 200 milliseconds for these operations to take place (Figure 4.8). Of that time only a very few milliseconds are taken up by the senses, muscles, and transmission to and from

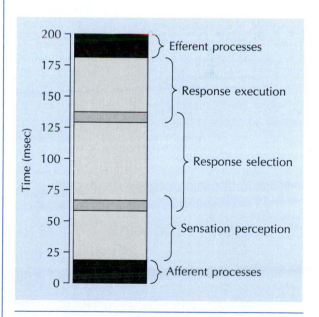

Figure 4.8 *Illustration of the time course of simple reaction time. Note that the central processes (sensation-perception, response selection, and response execution) compose the major portion of the total reaction time.*

the brain. Most of this time, perhaps as much as 95 percent, is utilized in sensation-perception, response selection, and response execution processing. This is a substantial amount of time. However it is difficult to determine which type of processing is most responsible for the delay. Was the sensation-perception processing most responsible, with the response selection and response execution processing occurring relatively faster? Or was the sensation-perception processing relatively simple and the response selection and response execution processing responsible for the majority of the delay? This is difficult to assess in natural settings but is possible under more controlled situations in the laboratory.

Consider three simple laboratory reaction time experiments, one focusing on each of the general classifications of processing: sensation-perception, response selection, and response execution. Note that **reaction time** (RT) is the time from the presentation of a stimulus until the initiation of a response. This is different from **movement time** (MT) which is the time from movement initiation to the completion of the response. An attempt will be made to manipulate one type of processing while holding the others constant. In this way we can better understand the cost (increase in RT) or gain (decrease in RT) to the overall information processing attempt. Remember, increases in RT are operationally defined as resulting from increases in processing demands and decreases in RT from decreases in processing difficulty. This method has been utilized to determine the impact of variables on information processing since 1869—the time of F. C. Donders.

Sensation-Perception

Subjects lightly rest the index finger of their preferred hand on a response key. They are instructed to depress the key as rapidly as possible when the stimulus is presented. The stimulus is either a light or a buzzer. One-half of the subjects receive 10 trials with the light stimulus and then 10 trials with the buzzer. The other half receive the buzzer first and

then the light. In each case the subject is informed before the trial begins which stimulus is to be used.

Notice that processing related to response selection and response execution is kept constant across the two stimulus conditions. For each condition, the subjects are informed ahead of time about which stimulus to respond to and the same finger is used in the same manner. Also, learning and/or practice is equally distributed across stimulus conditions. If average reaction time to the two stimuli is different, it is probably due to differences in the sensation-perception processing.

What are your predictions? (See Figure 4.9A.) Why? Should we respond to the light more quickly than the sound because light travels faster than sound? No! Remember that only a very small portion of the time required for information processing is taken up in the periphery. What else could account for the difference? What other stimulus conditions could be used? Would different colored lights or different intensities of the stimulus influence reaction time? This method allows the scientist to determine the qualities and/or characteristics that pose demands on our sensation-perception processing.

Response Selection

To test response selection, two response keys are used. The first finger of the right hand is rested on the right key and the first finger of the left hand on the left key. Subjects are instructed to depress the right key as rapidly as possible when the right light is illuminated and the left key when the left light is illuminated. One-half of the subjects receive a block of 10 trials under an unknown stimulus condition first and a block of 10 trials under a known stimulus condition second. The other half of the subjects receive trials in the known stimulus condition first and the unknown stimulus condition second. In the known stimulus condition, the subjects are informed as to which light will be illuminated on each trial. In the unknown stimulus condition, the subjects do not know which light will be illuminated.

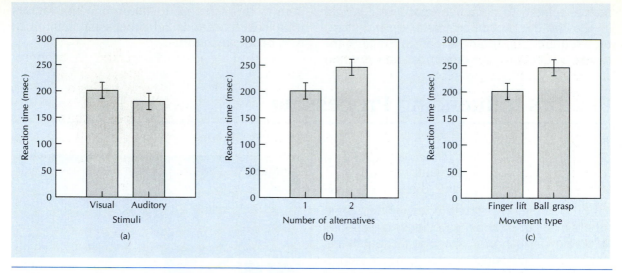

Figure 4.9 *Graphs illustrating the influence on reaction time of three classifications of processing: (a) sensation-perception (data from Woodworth & Schlossberg, 1954); (b) response selection (data from Leonard, 1959); and (c) response execution (data from Henry & Rogers, 1960).*

The intent in this experimental setup is to keep the sensation-perception and response execution demands constant while varying the demands related to response selection. The stimuli (lights) and the fingers used are the same under both the known and unknown stimulus conditions. Response selection demands are minimized in the known condition and increased in the unknown condition. If the average reaction time to the two conditions is different, it is probably due to differences in processing related to response selection.

What are your predictions? (See Figure 4.9B.) Why? What would happen if the number of keys and lights were increased to three or four? This method allows the scientist to determine the qualities and/or factors that pose demands on processing related to response selection.

Response Execution

In this experiment, one response key and one stimulus light are used. The first finger of the dominant hand is used to depress the response key. Subjects are instructed to release the response key as rapidly as possible when the light is illuminated. In the simple movement condition, the subject is required only to release the response key when the light is illuminated. In the complex movement condition, the subject is asked to release the key and move his or her finger as quickly as possible to pick up a tennis ball placed 20 centimeters from the response key. One-half of the subjects perform the simple task first and then the complex task. The other half perform the complex task first and then the simple task. Reaction times are recorded. Remember reaction time is only the time from the illumination of the light until the release of the response key and does not include the time required to make the movement.

Notice that the sensation-perception and response-selection demands remain similar across tasks. The same stimulus light and the response key finger are used under both conditions. If average reaction time for the two tasks is different, it is probably due to processing demands related to the planning and execution of the response.

What are your predictions? (See Figure 4.9C.) Why? What other movement factors would increase or decrease the processing demands related to response execution? Would increasing the movement distance, the accuracy required, or adding a load to the limb increase or decrease the demands? This method allows the scientist to determine the factors that pose demands on processing related to response execution.

Factors Influencing Processing

Many factors influence the manner in which the processing for a particular response is accomplished. Some conditions stress our sensation-perception processing capacities while others place greater demands on the response selection or response execution capabilities. This section introduces some general factors that have the potential to impact information processing.

Stages of Learning

Think about a specific motor skill you have practiced many times—such as typing, playing the piano, serving a tennis ball, or hitting a baseball. Many changes occur as a task becomes better learned. Compare your performance now and when you first attempted the task. Think about how you processed information when you were first introduced to the task and the manner in which you process the information now.

In 1964, Fitts proposed three stages of learning: the cognitive stage, the associative stage, and the autonomous stage. At each stage, the manner in which we process information may change just as our performance changes.

Cognitive Stage. The **cognitive stage** begins when the learner is first introduced to the motor task. The learner must determine the objective of the skill as well as the relational and environmental cues that control and regulate the movements. Think about attempting a new video game. What do the sounds and the changes in color or movement mean? What stimuli are important to attend to? What stimuli are simply distractions? What alternatives

The form of information that a coach provides to a player depends not only on the player's performance but also on the player's stage of learning.

are available? What are the best choices to make? When? Which controls do what? Is speed, steadiness, or accuracy important? The requirements of this stage of learning may place high demands on sensation and perception processing. So many stimuli are available, but so much is unimportant and distracting. Stimuli must be carefully selected and then organized and interpreted. At the same time, demands on response execution are low. It is too soon to concentrate on refining the movement.

Associative Stage.   The **associative stage** is concerned with performing and refining the skill. The important stimuli have been identified and their meaning is known. Conscious decisions about what to do become more automatic translations. Now the performer concentrates more on the task and response execution. How can the movements be timed better, made more efficient, or accomplished more quickly? In the associative stage, the emphasis shifts toward response execution. For example, the typist begins to group letters or even words together to be typed as a single unit. As this integration process continues, the information processing load appears to become reduced. The performer seems less rushed and better able to attend to other stimuli not related to the task.

Autonomous Stage.   This nearly automatic kind of performance is indicative of the final stage of learning, the **autonomous stage**. It is always amazing to see a typist, pianist, or even someone playing a difficult video game who can say hello to a friend without apparent interruption to the primary task. This person's performance as well as his or her information processing activities have changed as a result of practice.

Movement Time

In many situations, one of our objectives is to complete the movements required in as little time as possible. However, a special problem for information processing arises when the **movement time (MT)**—the time required to complete a movement—is reduced. This problem relates to the processing of feedback from the movement itself. Consider threading a needle. As you move the thread toward the needle, you move very slowly. Why? You must continually adjust the movement of your hands based on the discrepancy between the posi-

tion of the thread and the eye of the needle. This type of control (see Chapter 7) is called **closed-loop control** because the response-produced feedback "loops" back into the information processing channel (Figure 4.10, bottom). The entire movement is not planned in advance, but information processing activities are utilized to continually guide the movement to conclusion.

When circumstances dictate that a movement is to be completed very quickly, the movement may be over before response-produced feedback can be processed. Even simple proprioceptive and exteroceptive feedback require approximately 160 and 190 milliseconds, respectively, to be processed. Thus, in **open loop control** situations, the feedback loop is left "open" (Figure 4.10, top). All information processing must be completed before the movement is begun. Schmidt (1975) states that very rapid movements must be preprogrammed. The notion of a motor program, which is similar to a record or tape recording that can be played over and over, has gained wide acceptance in recent years.

The concept of a motor program implies that a set of prestructured commands capable of controlling a movement from beginning to end are stored in memory. These memories (programs) can be retrieved and run off, suggesting that active information processing related to the construction of an action plan does not have to occur if a motor program is available in memory. This has the potential to greatly reduce the information processing load.

Preparation Time and Anticipation

The previous section was concerned with the time available for movement execution or movement time. The concern now is with the time available for information processing before movement execution begins. What happens when the time available for information processing prior to the beginning of the movement is reduced? Consider a batter in baseball

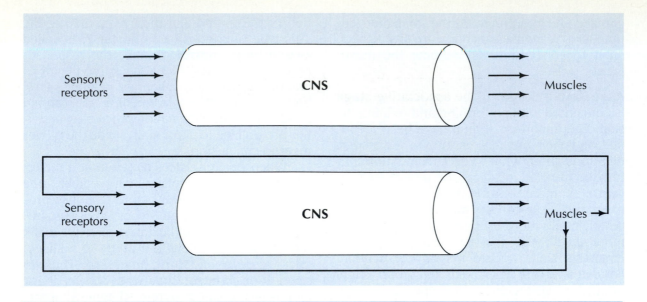

Figure 4.10 *Simplified diagram illustrating open-loop control (top) and closed-loop control (bottom). Closed-loop control utilizes feedback to guide the movement and open-loop control relies on prestructured motor programs to control movements.*

who must face Nolan Ryan's 100 mph fastball. A ball traveling 100 mph takes only about 400 milliseconds to get to home plate. However, only approximately 200 milliseconds elapse between the release of the ball and the point at which the batter must decide on a response. Sensation-perception, response selection, and action planning may require more time to process the available information completely.

In rushed situations, the solutions are only compromises. The options are to act on incomplete information and/or anticipate. Anticipation involves using past and/or current information to speculate on what will happen and when. Anticipation allows us to circumvent the long and sometimes critical delays in information processing. When guarding someone in basketball, does the defensive player wait until the opponent makes a move to the basket or is it important to use past and present information to anticipate when the move will occur? In baseball, does a batter wait until the ball is over the plate to swing or is it important to anticipate the arrival of the ball so as to initiate the swing well in advance? Antic-

ipation is a very important tool to the skilled performer.

Environment

Poulton (1957), in an attempt to characterize motor skills, classified movement environments on a continuum (Figure 4.11). **Closed environments** are relatively stable—conditions do not change from moment to moment. For example, the environmental conditions that you encounter in bowling are relatively fixed. The pins do not move without your displacing them and the conditions of the lane remain somewhat constant from frame to frame. Closed environments may place demands on sensation-perception and response selection processing but typically offer plenty of time for the processing to be completed. However, the tasks required in closed environments often involve very precise movements. This places demands on processing related to response execution. Consider bowling: very minor variations in the response production can result in poor performance. The same is

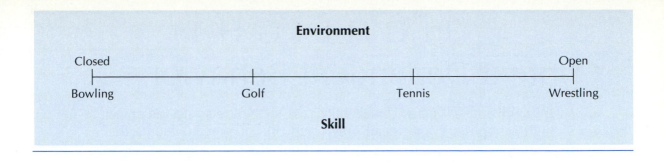

Environment

Closed   Open

Bowling   Golf   Tennis   Wrestling

Skill

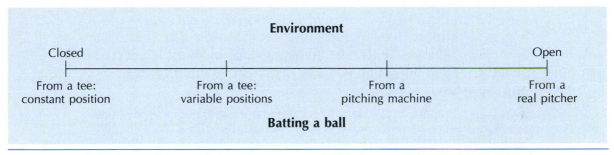

Environment

Closed   Open

From a tee: From a tee: From a   From a
constant position   variable positions   pitching machine   real pitcher

Batting a ball

Figure 4.12 *Diagram illustrating how batting a baseball can be adapted from a closed environment to an open environment. Gentile et al. (1975) suggest that adapting a skill from a closed to an open environment provides a good progression for skill development.*

true for golf, archery, and target shooting. In these latter examples, the environment is somewhat less stable than the environment in bowling. For example, changes in weather (gusty winds or rain) may vary from instant to instant such that a response prepared under one set of conditions may not be appropriate for the conditions a few minutes or even a few seconds later.

In **open environments**, the conditions are continually changing. Responses cannot be planned very long in advance because the conditions under which the response is planned have the potential to change very rapidly. In most cases, open environments are created because an opponent is involved. Opponents in tennis, wrestling, basketball, and football attempt to make the skill environment unstable. They realize that by creating uncertainty about what is happening or will happen, they can gain an advantage. In football, the offensive team varies the snap count and the

It is difficult for a ball carrier in football to plan in advance exactly where he will run on a specific play because the defense is constantly changing positions. This type of unstable conditions is an example of an open environment.

HIGHLIGHT

Context Dependent Behavior

It is not unusual for an older individual to think back to his or her high school days and recall only fragments of specific events that were landmark occurrences from that era. However, on returning to the high school gymnasium for a class reunion, the individual often experiences a spontaneous flood of vivid memories that were apparently unavailable outside the present context. Smith (1988) refers to this phenomenon as *environmental context dependent memory*. What is more important to the present discussion is what is termed *context dependent behavior*. That is, behavior, just like memory, is affected in subtle but often important ways by the environmental context. Bjork and Richardson-Klavehn (1988) state:

> The environmental cues during sport competition, including body-state variables such as stress, anxiety, and level of adrenalin, differ markedly from those present during practice. Unless one has highly overlearned the new technique—and managed to associate the technique with competition type cues—actual competition will trigger the old form, or worse yet, something in between the old and the new form. . . . In actual combat, military personnel trained in the operation of new equipment will often regress to motor behavior appropriate to old equipment. (p. 314)

What seems to be happening is that information processing is affected by environmental context.

Wright & Shea (1991) examined the role of incidental context on motor skill acquisition and retention. They had subjects learn a number of different typing sequences that had a unique background context associated with each throughout practice. Wright and Shea demonstrated that subsequent performance of the sequences was disrupted if the background context was changed. An interesting finding from this study was that learners were unable to report what it was about the context that caused the disrupted performance. These data suggest that the environmental context influences motor behavior and should be considered by teachers and coaches when planning practices.

play in order to create uncertainty about what will happen and when. Disguise and misdirection are integral parts of many sports skills. Many plays in football are created to appear like some other play to disguise the true intention of the offensive team.

Gentile, Higgins, Miller, and Rosen (1975) have applied the concept of open and closed environments to a single skill (Figure 4.12). Using batting in baseball as an example, they suggest that a progression from T-ball to baseball could be used to gradually introduce information processing complexity to the skill of batting by reducing the information load that must be processed. T-ball presents fewer demands on sensation-perception and response selection processing than normal baseball. Progressions like this are used extensively in youth sports programs and elementary school physical education programs.

Task

Motor skills are very difficult to categorize because they are so diverse. They range from speaking to walking, a gymnastics routine to yawning, threading a needle to writing your name . . . the list could go on and on. In terms of information processing, it is useful to describe motor skills on two somewhat independent continuums. The first involves the extent to which the movement termination is known prior to movement initiation. **Discrete movements** have a distinct beginning and a distinct ending. Motor skills such as serving in tennis, driving in golf, shooting in basketball, or writing your name are discrete motor skills. The majority if not all of the information processing activities for these movements can occur prior to movement initiation. On the other hand, **continuous movements** have no distinct ending. Attempting to catch a parakeet in a cage, running or tackling in football, or guarding an opponent in basketball are examples of continuous motor skills. These skills cannot be completely preplanned. Changes in the environment dictate that information processing activities must be utilized throughout the movement. It should be apparent that continuous skills are demanded more often in open environments and are less likely to be controlled in an open loop manner than discrete motor skills.

FINAL COMMENT

We actively and selectively process information. We choose what to do and what not to do. Under different circumstances or when we have more experience, we perceive things differently and choose different ways to react and respond. However, if a single link in the sequence of information processing fails, the end product, our movements, suffers. Jan Berry suffered damage to the part of his brain that processed the motor commands to the muscles and he could no longer write, sing, or dance as he once did. He could still feel and think but could not control his muscles very well. His world was changed forever.

KEY TERMS

behaviorism
classical conditioning
operant conditioning
information
   processing
central processes
peripheral processes
exteroceptors
proprioceptors

sensation-perception
sensation
perception
response selection
decision
translation
response execution
action plan
serial processing

parallel processing
parallel-distributed
   processing
cross-talk
reflexes
cognitive stage
associative stage
autonomous stage
movement time (MT)

closed-loop control
open-loop control
open and closed
   environments
discrete movements
continuous
   movements
context dependent
   behavior

5

Sensation and Perception

Angeline AND WOLF HOUSE BAY
  • *Sensorimotor Coordination*

Measuring Sensations
  • *The Method of Adjustment*
  • *The Method of Limits*
  • *The Method of Constant Stimuli*
  • *The Method of Signal Detection*

Methods for Measuring Psychophysical Functions
  • *Weber's Law*

Exteroception
  • *Vision*
  • *Hearing*
  • *Cutaneous Senses*

Proprioception and Kinesthesis
  • *Proprioception and Sensorimotor Control*

HIGHLIGHT: Dart Throwing and Visual-Motor Coordination
FINAL COMMENT
KEY TERMS

Angeline AND WOLF HOUSE BAY

Farley Mowat, a researcher for the Canadian Wildlife Services, pitched his tent on a hill overlooking a den of wolves, his study species. He called their home, "Wolf House Bay." For the next several weeks, he observed a playful family of wolves consisting of four pups, a father, a mother, and an uncle. His assignment was to determine the extent to which the wolves were slaughtering Arctic caribou. Because the caribou had migrated 200 or 300 miles from Wolf House Bay, Farley's first goal was to learn what wolves eat when the caribou are away. His first clue came when he saw the tail and feet of a mouse hanging from the mouth of the mother wolf. Angeline, as Farley called her, gobbled up the mouse. Then, as he watched, she proceeded to catch and devour 22 more mice.

Ootek, an elderly Eskimo medicine man, assured Farley that the mice had sufficient nutritional value to sustain the wolves. Farley's job, however, was to provide unmistakable evidence of that fact. He therefore decided to test the nutritional value of mice on himself. For the next several weeks, he ate little else besides mice. Each meal consisted of a dozen fat mice. They were skinned, marinated in ethyl alcohol for two hours, rolled in flour, salt, pepper, and cloves, fried about five minutes in a greased pan, and simmered slowly for 15 minutes in alcohol. He suffered no ill effects and he remained vigorous. At the same time, he determined that the mice population was large enough to sustain the wolves, and

Hunting engaged the wolves' senses of sight, hearing, smell, taste, and touch. After the sensations were received they had to be perceived. Perception involves using memory to interpret the sensory information.

- To understand the methods available to measure sensation and perception.

- To examine the relationship between the physical properties of sensory stimulation and perceptions of the stimuli.

- To appericate the diversity of the sensations provided by the many varied sensory receptors.

- To develop an appreciation of the roles sensation and perception play in performance and learning of motor skills.

he found mice remains in 48 percent of the excrement samples that he collected from the wolves. Clearly, mice were a main part of the wolves' diet.

After the caribou returned, Farley also had a chance to watch the wolves hunt a prey more worthy of their reputation as the Arctic's most feared carnivores. The hunting seemed to follow an Eskimo legend according to which Kailia, the god of the sky, sent wolves to "eat the sick, weak, and small caribou, so that the land will be left for the fat and the good ones" (Mowat, 1963, p. 85). The wolves were indeed skilled hunters, and part of their skill was in selecting only those caribou that were the easiest to catch.

The wolves' hunting style contrasted sharply with that of trappers who killed caribou to feed themselves and the dogs that pulled their sleds. The trappers aimed for the biggest, fattest, and strongest animals.

Farley reported his results to the Canadian Wildlife Service, but he did little to change the belief that trappers had spread about wolves' being bloodthirsty killers.

■ ■ ■

Hunting for mice engaged Angeline's sense of sight, hearing, smell, taste, and touch. She saw, heard, and smelled her tiny prey scurrying through tall grass. After snapping them up, she tasted her quarry as she felt

their bones crush in her teeth. Scientists observing these events would distinguish between **sensations**, the detection of information through the senses, and **perceptions**, the interpretation of sensory information. For example, Angeline might have sensed something brown and fuzzy. These sensations had no meaning until the brain interpreted them as the perception "mouse." Scientists also distinguish **exteroception**, the perception of things in the environment, and **proprioception**, the perception of body part positions. Angeline used exteroception to detect, identify, and locate the mouse. She used proprioception to coordinate her actions as she chased, lunged, and snapped up her game.

Sensorimotor Coordination

Motor control almost always involves exteroception, proprioception, or both. We therefore must attempt to understand **sensorimotor coordination**, the dual ability to guide motor actions by means of sensory information and to take into account motor actions when interpreting sensory information that is changed by those actions. A simple experiment might help you understand the dual nature of sensorimotor coordination.

Lay this book on the desk in front of you. Now close your eyes and lay your right hand lightly on the center of it. Sensory information will be used both to stop your hand when it comes in contact with the book and to find the center of the book. Close your eyes again and hold the book with your left hand. Move the book back and forth while your right hand is just slightly touching the surface of the book. Your perceptions are quite different depending upon which direction the book is moved. Now ask a friend to move the book while holding your wrist. Notice that the touch sensations on the palm of your hand are very similar in either case. Yet, you will easily distinguish between movements of your hand and movements of the book. This experiment demonstrates the two parts of sensorimotor control. The first part is that you can use sensory information from one hand to control the movement of the other hand. The second is that you can take into account your own movements when you interpret the sensations on your palm. These two parts often work together when we and objects in our environment move at the same time. One example of such simultaneous action is walking with a friend who moves while we move. Another instance is driving a car in traffic. The car next to us appears not to be moving even though both cars may be traveling quite fast.

In this chapter, we will (1) discuss methods for measuring sensations and perceptions, (2) introduce some general principles revealed by those methods, (3) study the physics, physiology, and psychology of each sense separately, and (4) review principles and applications of sensorimotor coordination in each sense.

Measuring Sensations

Let's imagine joining Farley on his mission. As he studies his environment, we will study him. Our first question is: What is the dimmest star that Farley can see from Wolf House Bay?

This is the kind of question asked in **psychophysics**, the study of relationships between physical energies (e.g., light from a star) and psychological responses (e.g., seeing the star). There are three kinds of psychophysical questions:

1. What is the **absolute threshold**, or the least amount of stimulus energy that can be detected? An example is the question just asked: What is the dimmest star that Farley can see from Wolf House Bay?

2. What is the **difference threshold**, or the smallest difference in intensity between two stimuli that can be detected? We could ask: How different do two stars have to be in brightness before the difference can be detected?

3. How do the intensity and other qualities of a stimulus relate to the intensity and other qualities of our sensations and perceptions. One question is: How would the apparent brightness of a just barely visible star change as we continued to make it brighter and brighter?

We could use many different methods for answering these questions, but we will limit our discussion to four: the methods of adjustment, limits, constant stimuli, and signal detection. We could also use all of these methods to measure both absolute and difference thresholds. But we will only consider our original question about Farley's absolute threshold for seeing a star, an artificial, adjustable star.

The Method of Adjustment

We would let Farley adjust the star using the **method of adjustment**. The star would be off or very bright at the beginning of an equal number of trials. Farley would increase or decrease the intensity until he could just barely see the star. The average of all his settings would define his absolute threshold.

The Method of Limits

We would control the intensity in the **method of limits**. We would alternate between trials starting with the star turned off (ascending trials) or bright (descending trials). We would ask: Do you see the star? When he said "no" on ascending trials, we would increase the brightness and ask again. We would stop and record the intensity the first time he said "yes." In contrast, he would say "yes" at first on descending trials. We would decrease the intensity and ask again until he said "no." The absolute threshold would be defined by the average of the settings at the end of all ascending and descending trials.

The Method of Constant Stimuli

We would present intensities in random order in the **method of constant stimuli**. We would choose an intensity that is almost never seen, one that is almost always seen, and about seven intensities equally spaced in between. We would then present all of these stimuli about 50 times in random order. The absolute threshold is defined as the intensity seen 50 percent of the time. Often, none of the presented intensities will equal exactly 50 percent. In this case, the intensity corresponding to 50 percent can be estimated from a graph of the data as shown in Figure 5.1.

The Method of Signal Detection

The method of signal detection is based on the assumption that absolute thresholds are not absolute. For example, the least amount of light that you can detect will vary from moment to moment because of fluctuations in the spontaneous flashes you see. Signal detection theory defines spontaneous sensory signals as **noise**. The distribution of the amount of noise present at any given moment is defined as the *noise distribution*. All sensory systems have

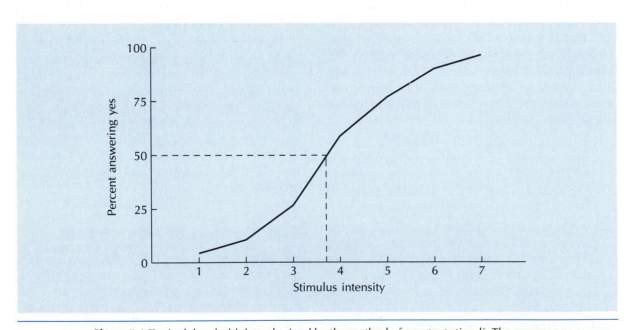

Figure 5.1 *Typical threshold data obtained by the method of constant stimuli. The curve crosses the 50 percent yes point at a stimulus intensity of 3.7, which is thus considered the threshold for these data.*

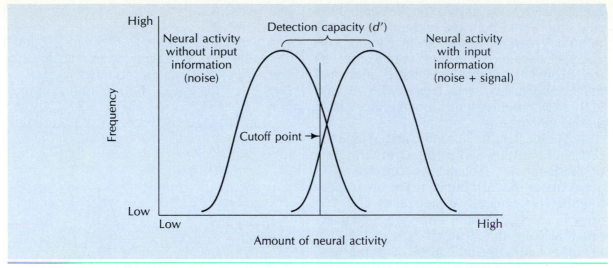

Figure 5.2 *Signal detection theory. The curve on the left is the noise distribution; the curve on the right is the noise + signal distribution. The noise distribution represents random neural activity (noise) that occurs when a stimulus is not present. Note that the distribution is shifted to the right when the signal (stimulus) is presented.*

noise distributions because all sensations are based upon neural impulses that spontaneously vary from moment to moment. When a sensory system responds to a signal in the environment, it adds to the neural activity. This addition creates a new distribution, the *signal plus noise distribution*.

The signal detection method measures the noise distribution by giving trials with no signal present. The method measures the signal plus noise distribution by giving trials with a signal present. Subjects score a **false alarm** every time they say "yes" when no signal is presented, and a **miss** when they say "no" and the signal is presented. Subjects score a **hit** whenever they say "yes" when a signal is present.

As shown in Figure 5.2, the noise and signal plus noise distributions overlap and subjects usually choose a response criterion that cuts through both distributions. Subjects respond "yes" whenever the neural activity in a sensory system is above the response criterion; subjects respond "no" whenever sensory activity is below the response criterion. Figure 5.3 indicates that d' corresponds to the dis-

tance between the mean of the noise distribution and the mean of the signal plus noise distribution. It is important to understand that this distance represents sensory sensitivity. Imagine two systems responding to the same signal. The more sensitive system would add more neural activity to the noise distribution. Therefore, it would move the signal plus noise distribution farther away from the noise distribution. For example, in Figure 5.3, the curves on the left might represent the sensitivity of a person with poor vision and the curves on the right might represent the sensitivity of a person with normal vision. For a given visual stimulus, the poor visual system shows little response, creating a small d'; the normal visual system shows a greater response, creating a larger d'.

Figures 5.3A and 5.3B each show a decision criterion that cuts through the point where the noise and signal plus noise distributions intersect. This is a neutral point used by people who have no response bias for saying "yes" or "no." People who have a response bias for saying "yes" set their decision criterion to the left of the neutral point (a lax criterion), as in Figures 5.3C and 5.3D. People who have a response bias for saying "no" set their decision criterion to the right of the neutral point (a strict criterion) as shown in Figures 5.3E and 5.3F. People who respond with a strict criterion tend to miss stimuli more often and make fewer false alarms. People who respond with a lax criterion tend to make more false alarms than misses.

It is especially important to understand the probability of hits and false alarms in terms of these figures. Probabilities correspond to areas under the distributions. The area under a whole distribution is a probability of 1. The area on each side of the mean is a probability of 0.5 because the mean cuts the distribution in half. Hit rates, the probability of saying "yes" when a signal is present, must be found under the signal plus noise distribution because that is the distribution created when a signal is present (see Figure 5.3G). They must also be found to the right of the decision criterion because people say "yes" only when the level of a signal is to the right of the decision criterion. Thus, hit rates correspond to the area under the signal plus noise distribution to the right of the decision criterion. Similarly, false alarm rates, the probability of saying "yes" when a signal is not present, must be found under the noise distribution because that is the distribution created when no signal is present (Figure 5.3H). They must also be found to the right of the decision criterion because people say "yes" only when the level of a signal is to the right of the decision criterion. Thus, false alarm rates correspond to the area under the noise distribution to the right of the decision criterion.

John A. Swets (1964) developed the signal detection method to test radar operators. Green and Swets (1966) promoted its use in research. Today, the method has many applications, including some in rehabilitation training. In one application, Gordon-Salant (1986) tested elderly persons listening to a speech. Lower d' scores indicated that the subjects had less sensitive hearing. A lower d' indicated that they had a lower criterion for saying they understood the speech. That is, they often

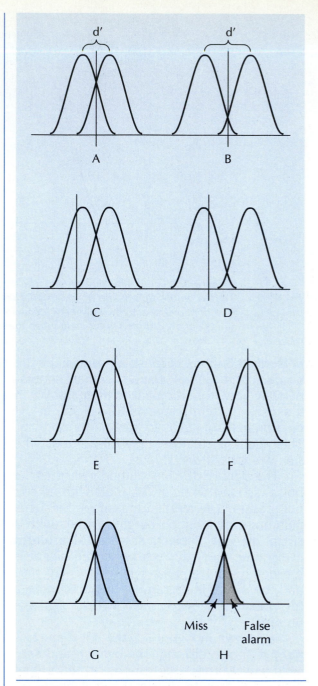

Figure 5.3 Distributions of signal and signal + noise for various decisions and stimuli conditions. Note that the vertical line indicates the subject's decision criterion. When neural activity increases above the criterion, the subject judges a stimulus to be present. Note also that the distance between the two distributions (d') indicates the sensitivity of the sensation/reception system.

Signal detection theory emerged from efforts to develop tests for radar operators. This theory has greatly improved our ability to measure the sensitivity of the sensory system.

said they understood when they did not. This response bias hinders communication because it provides false feedback to speakers.

Gordon-Salant recommends the use of the signal detection method during rehabilitation training to overcome this problem.

Methods for Measuring Psychophysical Functions

Psychophysical functions specify relationships between physical energies and psychological experiences over a wide range of physical magnitudes. Scientists measure them by having subjects behave like measuring instruments. Subjects make responses that are translated into numbers representing the psychophysical function. For example, we might ask Farley Mowat to compare the brightness of many pairs of stars. We would then translate his responses into a psychophysical function relating increases in stimulus intensity to perceived increases in brightness.

Scientists have developed special methods to constrain how people respond to psychophysical questions. Three of these methods follow.

1. The method of *magnitude estimation* asks subjects to assign any numbers that are proportional to their experience. In one study, subjects were told: "Your task is to assign a number proportional to the brightness as you see it. Use any number you find necessary—fraction, whole number or decimal—but try to keep the numbers proportional to brightness. If one stimulus looks twice as bright as another, the number you assign to one should be twice as large as the number you assign to the other" (Stevens & Galanter, 1957).

2. The method of *category judgment* asks subjects to match their experience to a small set of numbers. For example, subjects might be asked to tell how bright each light is on a scale of 1 (very dim) to 10 (very bright).

3. The method of *cross-modality matching* asks subjects to match one sensory quality with another. The instructions might be to indicate how bright each light is by adjusting the loudness of a tone to match the brightness.

All three methods have been used to develop general principles about psychophysical functions.

Weber's Law

The German scientist Ernst H. Weber (pronounced VAY-ber), was one of the first to state the general psychophysical principle that now bears his name. **Weber's law** states that a **just-noticeable difference (jnd)** in a stimulus is proportional to the original stimulus intensity. This law is often expressed as an equation, $JND/I = K$, in which JND is the least amount that must be added to detect a difference, I is the original intensity, and K is a constant. Table 5.1 shows K for various senses.

TABLE 5.1

Sensation	Weber Fraction
Electric Shock	0.013
Saturation, red	0.019
Heaviness	0.020
Finger span	0.022
Length	0.029
Vibration, 60 Hz	0.036
Loudness	0.048
Brightness	0.079
Taste, NaCl	0.083

Source: Teghtsoonian, 1971.

Let's use Weber's law and Table 5.1 to make some predictions. Suppose 100 candles provided the only light in Farley's tent at Wolf House Bay. How many candles would have to be added before the tent would be just noticeably brighter? We are given I (100 candles) and K (0.08). We find JND by multiplying $I \times K$ (100 × 0.08 = 8). Starting with 100 candles, we would need to add 8 more candles before we would see a just-noticeable difference. Now suppose the original light came from 200 candles. We are given I (200) and K (0.08). We find JND by multiplying 200 × 0.08 = 16. Starting with 200 candles, we would have to add 16 before we would see a just-noticeable difference. When the original intensity is twice as bright, we must add twice as much light before we will see a just-noticeable difference.

Table 5.1 indicates that Weber's law applies to many different kinds of sensations. All sensations to which the law applies are said to follow a quantitative or **prothetic** continuum. Sensations that do not follow Weber's Law are said to follow a qualitative or **metathetic** continuum (Stevens & Galanter, 1957). Prothetic sensations usually follow Weber's Law precisely except at extremely low or extremely high intensities. That is, K usually remains constant as predicted by Weber's Law unless the original intensity is extremely low or high. Let's turn now to some details about specific senses.

Exteroception

We noted earlier that Angeline used exteroception to detect, identify, and locate the mice. At the same time, Farley Mowat used exteroception to observe Angeline and the rest of her family. He watched them, listened to their distant howls, sampled the aroma and taste of their mice meals, and felt the crisp Arctic air that surrounded Wolf House Bay. Farley's senses are similar to our own. So let's think about his and ours as we take up each sense.

Vision

Figure 5.4 shows the human eye and its parts:

1. The *sclera* is the white opaque outer wall of the eye.

2. The *cornea* is a transparent curved surface on the front of the eye. It bends light to focus it as the light enters the eye.

3. The *aqueous humor* is the clear fluid in a chamber directly behind the cornea. It nourishes the cornea.

4. The *iris* is a doughnut-shaped muscle and the pupil is the opening in the middle of the iris. The iris opens and closes the pupil to regulate the amount of light that enters the eye.

5. The *lens* is a transparent structure directly behind the iris. The lens is held in place by ciliary muscles that stretch between the sclera and lens. The muscles change the shape of the lens in order to make find adjustments in focus. The lens gets rounder to focus closer objects and flatter to focus farther ones. These fine adjustments are called *accommodation.*

6. The *vitreous humor* is the transparent gel that fills the eye's main chamber and keeps it from collapsing.

7. The *retina* covers most of the eye's inner wall and contains tissue, blood vessels, receptors that respond to light, neurons that process information from receptors, and nerve fibers that carry information to the brain. Most blood vessels and nerve fibers are routed around the *fovea,* a very sensitive area of the retina.

Light Receptors: Rods and Cones. The retina contains two kinds of receptors: (1) cones located mostly in the fovea, and (2) rods located everywhere except the fovea. Cones in the fovea serve central vision, which is the center of the total area that we see at any one time. When we look at an object, we move our eyes so that the image of the object falls on the fovea. We see that object in the center of everything else that we focus our vision upon. The area of central vision covers about 3.35 inches. This area corresponds to the fovea and some of the retina immediately surrounding it (about eight degrees). Everything seen outside of central vision is defined as peripheral vision.

Pathways to the Brain. The importance of vision in motor control is reflected in the structure of the pathways between the eye and the brain. For example, Figure 5.5 shows that visual information that is to the right or left of where you are looking is sent to the side of the brain where it is needed most for motor control. Everything to the right of central vision is sent to the left hemisphere of the brain and everything to the left of central vision is sent to the right hemisphere. This division is important in motor control because the right side of the brain controls movements on the left side of the body and vice versa.

The structure of the pathways also reveals a division between focal and ambient vision (Owens, 1985). **Focal vision** (1) is limited to

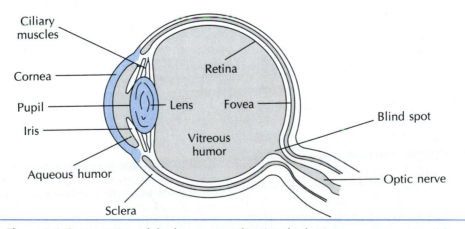

Figure 5.4 *Cross section of the human eye showing the basic structures: cornea, iris, pupil, lens, vitreous humor, retina, fovea, and optic nerve.*

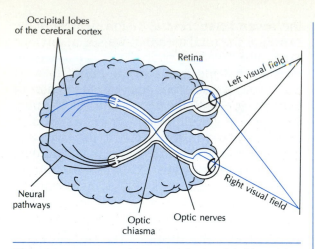

Figure 5.5 *Messages from the left visual field travel to the right occipital lobe; messages from the right visual field go the left occipital lobe. The place where they cross is called the optic chiasma.*

central vision, (2) has the function of determining what something is, and (3) is badly degraded by low illumination. **Ambient vision** (1) is served by the entire retina, (2) has the function of determining where something is, and (3) is not badly degraded by low illumination. If you want to know what the world would be like without focal vision, look at a flashbulb while someone takes your picture. For the next several minutes, almost all you will see in central vision is a silver spot. Try reading while you are still seeing this spot and you will find out how difficult it is to recognize letters and words without focal vision.

Other simple experiments will help you understand that ambient vision tells our motor system where objects are located. Try reading while walking around a classroom. The reading will occupy central vision. Since ambient vision is not limited to central vision, you still should be able to locate objects and avoid obstacles. You should find it relatively easy, for example, to walk up and down aisles between desks. If you gradually dim the lights during this experiment, you will be able to see that low illumination degrades focal vision much more than ambient vision. With low illumination, you will find it impossible to recognize letters while it is still relatively easy to walk up

and down aisles. If you raise the illumination again, you should be able to see that ambient vision is not limited to peripheral vision. You should be able to walk around the classroom while looking through a pinhole that restricts what you see to central vision. Your walking will be much slower, however. This makes the point that ambient vision is important. You will be much more hesitant when looking through a pinhole. In fact, it will be so hesitant that it should be easy for you to appreciate the important role that ambient vision plays in distinguishing objects in the periphery.

These demonstrations help us understand the unique characteristics of focal and ambient vision. We can understand these characteristics even better if we study the visual pathways. Starting in the retina, we see that cone and rod receptor cells are connected to ganglion cells that send signals out of the retina to the brain (Figure 5.6). In addition, signals travel laterally across interneurons. Thus, signals originating in receptor cells are modified before they leave the retina. A close look at this initial part of the pathway to the brain reveals why focal vision is good for recognizing details and poor for seeing in dim light. Focal vision is limited to central vision, which is served by cones. Cones are best for seeing

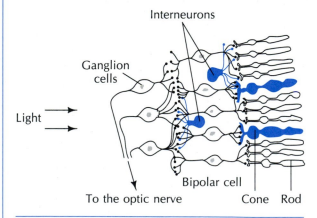

Figure 5.6 *The visual pathways go from the retina to other brain structures. Messages first go from receptor cells to bipolar cells. Each cone sends a message to a separate bipolar cell. Messages go from bipolar cells to ganglion cells, and then exit from the retina as part of the optic nerve.*

detail because almost every cone in the fovea reports to its own bipolar cell. Consider what happens when different light patterns fall on adjacent cones. Each cone can use its own one-to-one connection to report a different message to its own bipolar cell. These separate messages enable us to discern small differences or details in what we see. Cones do not function in dim light because each cone's message is too weak for bipolar cells to receive it.

The pathways between receptor cells and bipolar cells also explain why ambient vision in the periphery is good for seeing in dim light but poor for seeing details. Whereas each cone has its own bipolar cell, many rods in the periphery share the same bipolar cell. These many-to-one connections allow rods to add their messages together to make a signal strong enough for a bipolar cell to receive in dim light. But the addition of signals across different rods reduces our ability to discern details with rods in peripheral vision.

When we follow the pathways out of the retina back to the brain, we find additional reasons for the unique characteristics of focal and ambient vision. For instance, the retina sends 80 percent of its fibers to the lateral geniculate nucleus (LGN), a relay station that processes visual signals and sends them on to the visual cortex. The remaining 20 percent of its fibers are processed by the superior colliculus, a brain center that treats information from vision, hearing, touch, as well as muscle movements and coordinates postural adjustments. The general structure of these two pathways suggests that the former is concerned with focal vision and the latter is concerned with ambient vision. This possibility is supported by research on hamsters (Schneider, 1969) and primates (Trevarthen, 1968). For example, Schneider's research on hamsters indicated that elimination of the visual cortex has different effects than removal of the superior colliculus. Without a visual cortex, hamsters can locate objects but they cannot recognize them. Without a superior colliculus, hamsters can recognize objects, but they cannot localize them.

Vision and Sensorimotor Coordination.
Angeline's survival depended upon the sensorimotor skills that enabled her to pounce on mice and other game. Sensorimotor coordination was also vital to our prehistoric ancestors. It is easy to imagine their survival depending upon a deft spear toss or a quick leap away from a stalking beast. Today, athletes, pilots, and astronauts are among the few who push the limits of the high-fidelity sensorimotor system that we inherited from those prehistoric ancestors. All infants struggle to achieve sensorimotor coordination. It takes about five months before infants can accurately reach for and grasp objects (Bruner & Koslowski, 1972). Yet many adults take for granted their inherited abilities to coordinate sensorimotor actions until these skills are reduced by aging or disease. When that happens we again appreciate the central role that sensorimotor coordination plays in our lives.

Rock (1975) distinguished two major classes of sensorimotor coordination theories: stimulus theories and constructive theories. The dominant stimulus theorists advocate an ecological approach (Gibson, 1966). They postulate that our movements create invariant patterns in light-based information and we use these patterns to guide our movements. When people and animals move through their environment, they encounter obstacles and opportunity (see Figure 5.7). The choices they make depend on their ability to move to gain appropriate perspectives on the environment. According to ecological theory of perception, the relationship between a moving animal and its environment is such that moving patterns of light uniquely determine our perceptions of substances, places, objects, and events. The visual image of this book will expand in all directions, for example, if you move your head toward the book. The point of maximum rate of expansion indicates the point at which you will collide with the book if you stay on the same course (Regan, 1986). The expansion rate also indicates the collision time. Specifically, 1 divided by the expansion rate (an invariant called *tau)* equals time to contact. Lee and Reddish argue that birds use tau to time

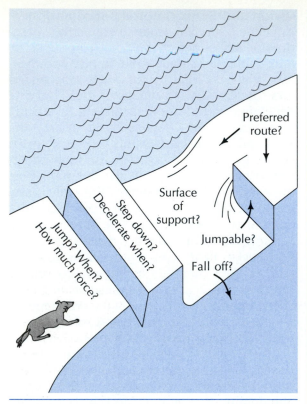

Figure 5.7 *Schematic adapted from Turvey and Carello illustrating that what animals perceive are the substances, places, and events of the environment instead of isolated objects in space.*

their dives to catch prey. Similarly, Wagner (1982) maintains that flies use tau to time soft landings. Unlike birds and flies, humans converge their eyes as an object approaches. We could therefore use eye movement information to judge place and time to contact. We do not do so, however, according to ecological theorists who hypothesize that light-based information is sufficient.

In contrast, constructivists theorize that oculomotor signals are critical in visual-motor coordination. Nemire, Bridgeman, and Massaro (under review) hypothesized, for example, that people use oculomotor information when hitting a table tennis ball. They built an automatic table tennis server to test their idea. One of their tests took advantage of the fact that tau is fully present when we close one eye. In contrast, oculomotor information is re-

duced when one eye is closed. If tau is sufficient to control the timing of the swing, then timing should be the same in both viewing conditions. The results did not support this prediction. Subjects swung later when viewing with one eye. The late swing resulted in hitting the ball with the paddle's leading edge instead of its center. When viewing with two eyes, people hit about an inch closer to the center.

Another line of investigation concerns *minor motor anomalies* (MMAs), which are dysfunctional states of slight misalignment or misregistration of body part positions (Shebilske, 1984, 1987). These motor states are abnormal in the sense that they are dysfunctional rather than rare. They are minor as opposed to major errors such as paralysis. An example of a dysfunctional alignment of body parts occurs when people view far targets in a dark or empty environment. They experience reduced acuity, anomalous myopia, because an increased tension in the ciliary muscles sets accommodation for a viewing distance shorter than the actual target distance (Liebowitz, Shiina, & Hennesey, (1972).

Another example of a dysfunctional registration of body part positions occurs after people maintain an eccentric direction of gaze for about 30 seconds or longer. The biased gaze direction causes a misregistration of eye position, which in turn causes observers to misjudge visual direction (Park, 1969; Levy, 1973; Craske, Cranshaw, & Heron, 1975; Ebenholtz, 1976; Paap & Ebenholtz, 1976). For instance, when the eyes are held to the right, they tend to drift to the right. You can create a similar drift in your arms. First, stand in a doorway and push the back of your hands outward against the door frame. Next, try to relax your arms at your side. Your arms will tend to drift outward away from your body. That is, they will drift in the direction you had pushed. The eyes will also drift in the direction that they are pushed or held. However, you do not have joint receptors in your eye muscles so your brain does not register the drift. Consider what an unregistered drift will do to perceived direction. Your eyes make an unregistered drift to the right. Then a light flashes on straight ahead. Where will you see it? The light will come on to the left of where your drifted eyes are looking. Since you think you are looking straight ahead, you will see the light to the left of straight ahead. This illusion of straight ahead is one of many that are caused by MMAs. This MMA illusion and others have been shown to influence visual-motor coordination during natural events such as throwing a dart or hitting a baseball (see Highlight: Dart Throwing and Visual-Motor Coordination).

Researchers have developed instruments for the blind that substitute other senses for vision. A cane can be equipped with a sonar device that emits high frequency sounds that hit objects in the environment and are reflected back to a receiver in the cane. The returning signals are converted to audible sounds or vibrations that can be used to locate objects and hazards.

Hearing

Wolves can hear the howls of other wolves over five miles away. Ootek, an Eskimo who lived his whole life in the Arctic, could also hear the howls at that distance whereas Farley Mowat, who was often exposed to the loud noises of modern civilization, could not. In one incident, Ootek cupped his hands to his ears while one of the wolves turned his ears and head toward some hills about five miles away. A minute or two later, the wolf threw his head back and let out a long howl that started low and ended on the highest note that Farley could hear. Ootek grinned and told Farley that the wolf had just announced that the caribou were coming. This incident reminds us of the role of hearing in communication, which is one of the ways that hearing guides actions. The incident also raises other questions: In what other ways does hearing guide action? How does sound travel from one point to another? Why do animals turn their ears and humans cup their hands to their ears? What is the difference between the lowest and highest notes in wolves' howls? Does the lowness or highness of a note affect the probability of our hearing it? This section answers these and other questions about hearing.

Characteristics of Sound. A wolf's howl travels through air in waves that are similar to waves in water. Objects vibrating in air send out invisible waves in all directions. Although they are invisible, you can imagine them by thinking of a twig vibrating on the surface of a pond. Scientists study sounds by converting them to visible waves, as illustrated in Figure 5.8. Let's imagine having a device for studying visible sound waves as we listen to the howls at Wolf House Bay.

Frequency and Pitch. What is the difference between low notes and high notes? This difference is called a change in **pitch**. Figure 5.9A shows that pitch corresponds to variations in a sound's **frequency**, which is the number of wave crests that occur in a second. The distance between two wave crests is called a

Dart Throwing and Visual–Motor Coordination

Dart throwers combine visual and oculomotor information to localize the bull's-eye, according to an experiment by Shebilske (1984). The experiment induced changes in the oculomotor information that indicate where the eyes are positioned. These changes were induced by having dart throwers hold their eyes to the extreme left for one minute. The visual effect of this manipulation was measured during dart throwing. The dart throwers sat on a stool that was 58 cm high and 146 cm from the target, which was a 1 cm circular center on polar coordinate paper. After practicing several dart tosses, subjects threw three darts after each of six 1-minute intervals. Two of these intervals required the subjects to hold their eyes to the extreme left. These were called *probe trials*. The other four required the subjects to hold their eyes straight ahead. These were called *baseline trials*. The trials for an experimental group of subjects were baseline, probe, baseline, probe, baseline, baseline; trials for a control group of subjects were all baseline.

The dart throwing error for each trial was the average perpendicular distance of three dart tosses from the target's vertical midline. This error was less than 5 mm on all trials for the control group. For the experimental group, the error was also less than 5 mm on baseline trials, but it was slightly greater than 15 mm on probe trails. This difference between groups was statistically significant. Although this 10 mm shift is only about 1 degree of visual angle, it was very reliable. In fact, 17 out of 18 experimental subjects shifted to the right on probe trials relative to baseline trials.

The obtained shift on probe trials is consistent with the hypothesis that maintaining a leftward eye position alters oculomotor information about direction. Furthermore, there is no reason to think that the induction procedure altered the proximal light information. Accordingly, responses to equivalent ambient light information depended upon the state of oculomotor information.

A related set of experiments suggests further that the visual consequences of changes in oculomotor information depend upon the state of ambient light information. Shebilske (1977) manipulated oculomotor information by procedures that were identical to those used in the dart throwing experiment. He measured the visual effect of this manipulation by asking subjects to point at targets with one hand which was hidden from their view by a partition located at neck level. He found that changes in oculomotor information caused errors in pointing and that the magnitude of these illusions depended on the state of ambient light information. The illusory shift in visual direction was 8.3 degrees while pointing with an unseen hand in darkroom conditions, and only 4.3 degrees while pointing with an unseen hand in a fully illuminated, structured condition. Both of these magnitudes were high in comparison to the 1-degree errors during dart throwing in an illuminated environment with the throwing hand visible.

In summary, the pointing and dart throwing experiments show that the perceived direction of objects in a given light pattern depends upon the state of oculomotor information, and the visual consequences of changes in oculomotor information depend upon the state of visual information. This pattern of results is exactly what would be expected if visual information and oculomotor information interact to determine perception of direction. Similar experiments support the same conclusions for direction perception during baseball hitting (Shebilske, 1986), and for distance perception (Ebenholtz, 1981; Shebilske, Karmiohl, & Proffitt, 1983).

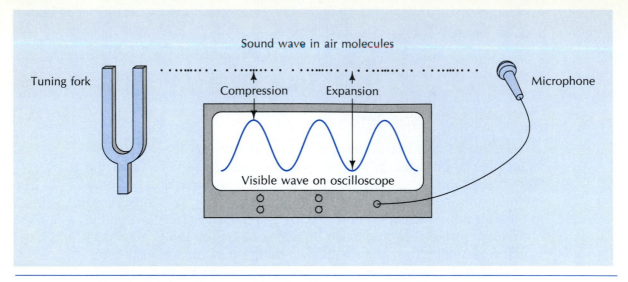

Figure 5.8 *The device shown here, an oscilloscope, makes pictures out of sound waves. A tuning fork makes a sound wave, which consists of compressions and expansions of air molecules. A microphone makes an electrical response to these compressions and expansions. The oscilloscope changes the electrical response into a moving picture on a screen similar to a TV screen. The picture is a wave with high and low points. A high point represents a compression of air molecules; a low point represents an expansion of air molecules.*

wavelength or **cycle**. Frequency is often measured in cycles per second, also called **Hertz** (Hz) after the man who initiated the cycles-per-second measure. Humans hear sounds ranging from 10 to 20,000 Hz, and wolves are capable of pushing the top end of that range. This is quite a feat when you consider that the highest note sung by a human soprano is about 1,046.5 Hz and the highest note on a piano is 4,186 Hz. The lowest note sung by a human bass singer is about 82.4 Hz and the lowest note on a piano is 27.5 Hz. Most music contains very few notes in the lowest extreme of this range. Accordingly, many moderately priced audio speakers only reproduce sounds down to about 35 Hz. But the few lower notes are very important to some people who will pay over a thousand dollars extra to buy speakers that go down to 25 Hz.

Amplitude and Loudness. Figure 5.9B shows that changes in loudness coincide with changes in **amplitude**, which is the distance between the top and bottom of a wave. This distance gets larger as the sound gets louder. One unit for measuring loudness is the bel, named after Alexander Graham Bell. The most frequently used unit is the **decibel**, which is one-tenth of a bel. A tenfold increase in sound level adds 10 decibels. A normal conversation is about 60 decibels. Live rock music is about 100 decibels, which is also about the level of a power lawn mower. A sonic boom is almost 130 decibels.

Waveform and Tone Quality. All the visible waves that we have considered so far are pure tones, which contain one frequency. Most natural sound sources, such as wolf howls, human voices, or musical instruments, produce complex tones, which contain many frequencies. These frequencies combine to give the sound wave a unique shape or *waveform*. Figure 5.9C shows visible complex tones from a trumpet and a clarinet playing the same note at the same loudness. The two instruments produce quite different waveforms, and therefore their unique sounds.

112

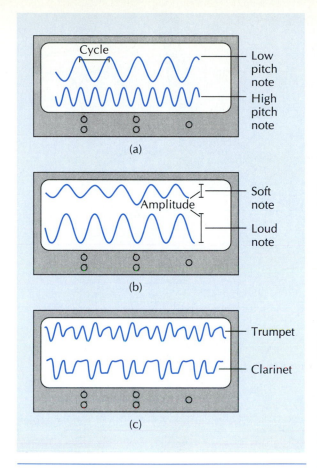

Figure 5.9 Each oscilloscope shows 1/100 of a second (0.01 second) from two sound waves: (A) a low pitch sound, with 600 cycles per second, and a higher pitched sound, with 1200 cycles per second; (B) a soft note and a loud note; (C) a note played on a trumpet and on a clarinet.

The Ear. Ootek could hear sounds that Farley could not because sound affected their ears differently. Let's consider some normal and abnormal ways that sound affects human ears.

Figure 5.10 shows that the ear has three subdivisions: the external ear, the middle ear, and the inner ear. Each of these plays a role in hearing.

The parts of the external ear include the pinna, which is the elastic flap we usually refer to as the ear. The ear canal is a tubular passage that funnels sound from the pinna in-ward. The eardrum is a thin membrane stretched over the innermost end of the ear canal. Sound waves strike the pinna and are funneled through the ear canal to the ear-drum. Turning the ears toward a sound source and cupping the hands around the ears help to catch more sound waves. The ear drum converts the sound from waves in air to waves in a membrane.

The middle ear is a small air cavity containing a chain of three bones: hammer, anvil, and stirrup. The hammer is connected to the ear drum so that waves in the ear drum move the bones, which carry the waves inward.

The inner ear looks like a snail and is called the cochlea, the Latin word for snail. The cochlea has an oval window which is an opening covered by a membrane that is connected to the stirrup. Thus, sound crossing the bones in the middle ear creates waves in the oval window. These vibrations then make waves in the fluid inside the cochlea. The fluid carries the waves to the basilar membrane, which stretches from one end of the cochlea to the other. Finally, the basilar membrane carries the wave to hair cells, which are receptor cells on the basilar membrane. These receptors generate neural impulses when their hairs are bent (Figure 5.11).

Continual exposure to loud noises damages these receptor cells and causes *boilermaker's deafness*, a permanent hearing loss from loud noise exposure. No worker should be exposed to noises above 85 decibels (about the loudness of a vacuum cleaner) for more than five hours without wearing ear protection. College students who frequently listen to live rock bands suffer hearing loss (Lipscomb, 1974). Similarly, Mowat was exposed to noisy battles for several years during World War II and suffered hearing loss. His loss was obvious when he compared his hearing to that of Ootek, who lived his life in a quiet environment.

Hearing and Sensorimotor Coordination. Angeline used her hearing during her hunts. One sound from her prey would launch Angeline in its direction. Similarly, a snapping twig

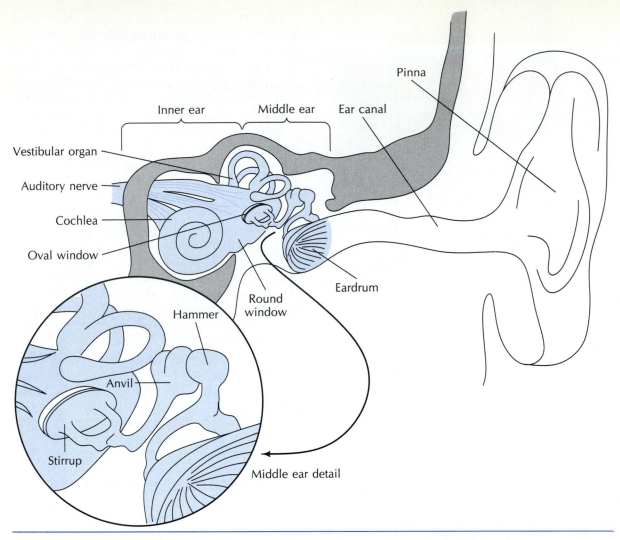

Figure 5.10 *The ear has three parts: the external ear or pinna, which includes the ear canal and the eardrum; the middle ear, which contains the hammer, the anvil, and the stirrup; and the inner ear, which contains the oval window and the cochlea.*

or any other sound from Angeline would set in motion her prey's escape. Thus, the ability to locate a sound (and guide actions accordingly) can be a matter of life or death. We have inherited this ability from our prehistoric ancestors whose lives depended on it. In fact, from the moment of our birth, we can turn our head in the direction of a sound (Castillo & Butterworth, 1981). How do we do it?

We localize sounds, in part, by unconsciously comparing small differences in sounds between the two ears. A sound that is straight ahead reaches both ears at the same time, is equally loud in both ears, and has the same waveform in both ears. All three of these factors change, however, when sound is off to the side so that it is farther from one ear. The sound in the farther ear arrives later, is softer, and has a different waveform. The timing and loudness differences are caused by the extra distance that the sound has to travel. The waveform differences are caused by the

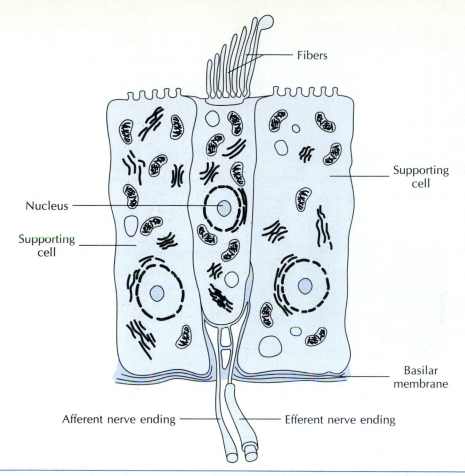

Fibers

Supporting cell

Nucleus

Supporting cell

Basilar membrane

Afferent nerve ending

Efferent nerve ending

Figure 5.11 Close-up of a small part of the cochlea, showing hair cells and the auditory nerve. If the fibers bend in the slightest amount, the cell transmits a sensory message to the brain.

waves' hitting the head before they get to the farther ear. Although these differences are too small for us to notice consciously, our brain detects the differences and uses them to compute sound locations. Information about sound localization is sent to the superior colliculus where it is used to coordinate our head movements and other actions.

Cutaneous Senses

Cutaneous senses refer to the sensations of the skin, which include temperature, pain, and pressure. Farley Mowat experienced all of these when he ran naked over rough ground after wolves had interrupted his sunbathing.

In this section we consider each cutaneous sense and the sense organs. Then we discuss examples of sensorimotor control and cutaneous senses.

Distribution of Cutaneous Sensitivity. The cutaneous senses are studied by stimulating the skin with warm or cold cylinders (temperature), needles (pain), and stiff fibers (pressure). Experimenters usually draw a grid on part of the skin, blindfold the subject, and stimulate areas within the grid. They find that the skin is not uniformly sensitive to all stimuli. For example, some spots are especially sensitive to cold (cold spots) and others are more sensitive to warm (warm spots). Figure 5.12 shows the results of exploring with a

Certain areas on the skin are especially sensitive to cold and others to warm. Likewise our sensitivity to pressures on the skin is also unevenly distributed.

1 millimeter cylinder the same square centimeter area of skin over several days. The spots change over the days, but the pattern of warm and cold spots is relatively stable. Sometimes when a cold spot is stimulated by a warm stimuli, it will feel cold. This experience is called *paradoxical cold*. Table 5.2

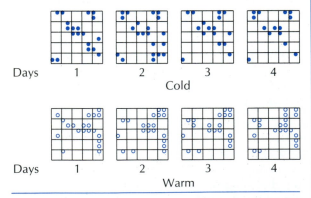

Figure 5.12 Mappings of cold and warm spots on the surface of the upper arm. Each cell corresponds to 1 square centimeter of surface.

shows that pain points are also unevenly distributed over the skin. Pain is tested in response to a sharp instrument applied with a constant force. Since the density of pain points tends to be less in the extremities of a limb in comparison to its base, the response to pain is correspondingly less.

TABLE 5.2   Pain Points for Selected Skin Regions

Skin Region	Pain "Points"/cm^2
Back of knee (popliteal fossa)	232
Neck region (jugular fossa)	228
Bend of elbow (cubital fossa)	224
Shoulder blade (interscapular region)	212
Volar side of forearm	203
Back of hand	188
Forehead	184
Buttocks	180
Eyelid	172
Scalp	144
Radial surface, middle finger	95
Ball of thumb	60
Sole of foot	48
Tip of nose	44

Pressure sensitivity also tends to be unevenly distributed. Figure 5.13 shows the least amount of pressure that can be detected in various body parts for females and males when nylon filaments are pushed against the skin. Females are more sensitive to pressure overall, but both males and females have the same order of relative sensitivity for various body parts. Beginning with the most sensitive, the order is face, trunk, fingers, arms, and lower extremities. The point localization values for different parts of the male body (top of Fig. 5.13) were obtained by measuring the distance between where a stimulation occurred and where subjects perceived the stimulus. The most mobile areas, the mouth, fingers, and feet, were the most accurate. Figure 5.14 shows the two-point threshold, the minimum distance between stimulations that can be perceived as separate stimuli. The pattern shown for males is almost identical to that for females and is very similar to the pattern for point localization.

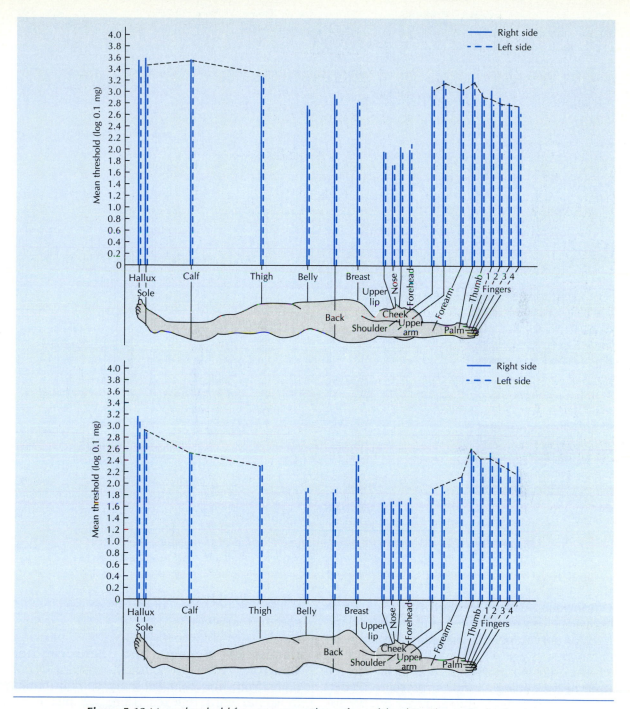

Figure 5.13 Mean threshold for pressure on the surface of the skin. The vertical axis represents the force necessary for perception of surface pressure. The top figure is for males and the bottom figure for females.

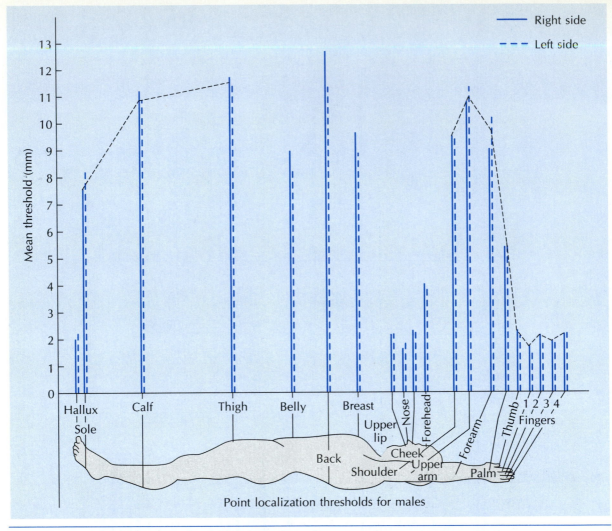

Figure 5.14 *Mean threshold for detection of the location of stimulation. The vertical axis represents the distance between the body point stimulated and the subject's perception of the location of the stimulation.*

Cutaneous Sensory Receptors. Figure 5.15 shows a cross section of skin. It contains a variety of nerve endings that play a role in the cutaneous senses: (1) cold (end bulbs of Krause), (2) warm (Ruffini endings), (3) pain (free nerve endings), and (4) pressure (Pacinian corpuscles, free nerve endings, and Meissner's corpuscles). This list does not account for all the data on cutaneous sensitivity. For example, cold spots are found in areas that have few or no end bulbs of Krause. The list is therefore only a simplified first approximation to the link between cutaneous sensitivity and specific receptors.

Cutaneous Senses and Sensorimotor Control. We can quickly withdraw our limbs from hot, cold, or sharp stimuli thanks to spinal cord reflexes. Here we discuss a more complex example of cutaneous sensorimotor control, "seeing with the skin." In the nineteenth century, Louis Braille used embossed dots to represent the alphabet, and he taught the blind to read by feeling the dots

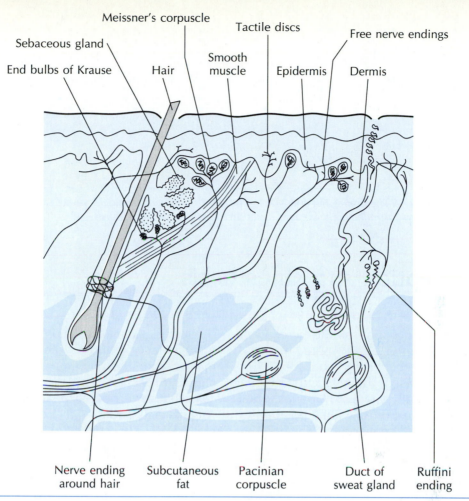

Sebaceous gland

Meissner's corpuscle

Tactile discs

Free nerve endings

End bulbs of Krause   Hair   Smooth muscle   Epidermis   Dermis

Nerve ending around hair   Subcutaneous fat   Pacinian corpuscle   Duct of sweat gland   Ruffini ending

Figure 5.15 *Cross section of the skin. Numerous sensory receptors are located in the three layers of skin: the epidermis (tactile discs, free nerve endings), dermis (Meissner's corpuscles, Krause end bulbs, Ruffini endings), and subcutaneous tissue (Pacinian corpuscles).*

with their fingers. Figure 5.16 shows the Braille alphabet. Today, experienced Braille readers enjoy many texts that have been translated into Braille (Foulke & Berla, 1978). In addition, most schools and institutes for the blind have Opticons, devices that optically scan normal print and translate letters into vibrations on the finger tips (Bliss, 1971).

Bach-Y-Rita and Hughes (1985) have also used the Opticon to teach the blind to recognize objects. Their goal is to develop a general Tactile Visual Substitution System (TVSS). Researchers at the Smith-Kettlewell Institute of Visual Science in San Francisco have been pursuing this goal for over a decade (Bach-Y-Rita, 1982). Their earlier versions stimulated the back or abdomen instead of the finger tips. In their laboratories, the blind have learned to use the TVSS to negotiate hallways and open doors, as well as recognize, localize, and pick up small objects. Success with the TVSS depends upon the blind person's being able to actively control the television camera. Such active control is also essential with other electronic aids for the blind (National Research Council, 1986).

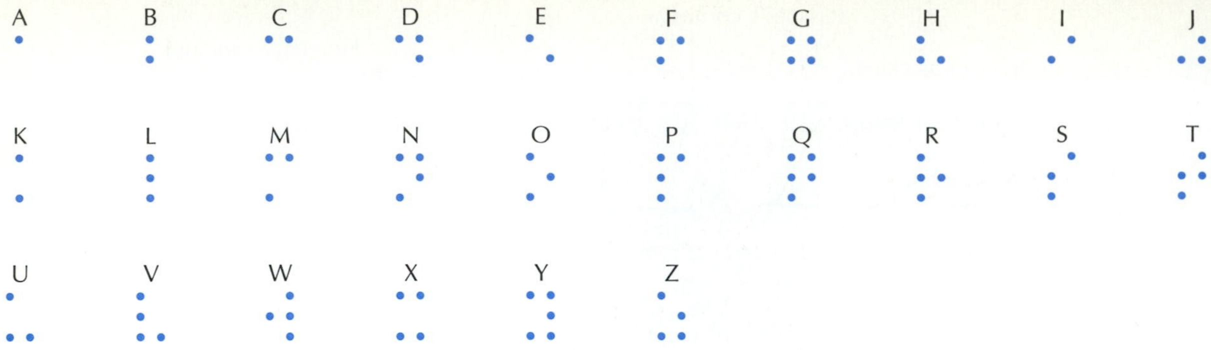

Figure 5.16 The Braille alphabet. Dots standing 1 millimeter above the surface and separated by 2.3 millimeters are used to represent letters and short words.

Proprioception and Kinesthesis

We defined proprioception as the perception of body part positions. We also noted that Angeline used proprioception to coordinate her actions as she chased, lunged, and snapped up mice. Traditionally, the term *proprioception* applies to perception of individual body parts or the whole body. It applies when the body or body parts are stationary or in motion. Another term, *kinesthesia* (from the Greek *Kinein,* to move and *aisthesia,* perception) refers to the sensations of position, tension, and movement of body parts. Originally, the term only applied to moving body parts, but today it is applied to both moving and stationary situations. Thus, the terms *proprioception* and *kinesthesis* are practically synonymous. Thus, we will use them interchangeably.

Later chapters in this book contain many discussions of people using sensory information to control body part positions. This section introduces the main sensory structures involved in proprioception.

Sense organs in the vestibular system determine our ability to perceive orientation and rotary acceleration. Figure 5.17 shows three major components of the vestibular system: the utricles, saccules, and semicircular canals. The utricles and saccules mediate perception of orientation with respect to gravity; the semicircular canals mediate the perception of angular accelerations. The pull of gravity moves stonelike calcium deposits in the utricles and saccules. This movement bends hair cells that send neural messages to the brain. Angular accelerations move fluid in the semicircular canals relative to hair cells, causing them to bend and to send messages to the brain. The vestibular system plays an important role in maintaining a particular orientation with respect to our surroundings.

Sensations of position, tension, and movement of body parts are perceived through receptors in joints, tendons, and muscles. Joints contain a variety of receptors (e.g., Ruffini, Golgi, Pacinian corpuscles, and free nerve endings). These receptors respond (1) to changes in joint angle and (2) to muscle forces in the absence of joint movement.

Tendons have simple receptors that are located between the muscle and the bone. Tendon receptors respond to changes in muscle force which can be created in three ways: (1) passively pulling the muscle, (2) actively changing the muscle length, or (3) actively contracting the muscle without changing its length, as in isometric exercises.

Muscles have receptors called **muscle spindles**, which contain not only stretch re-

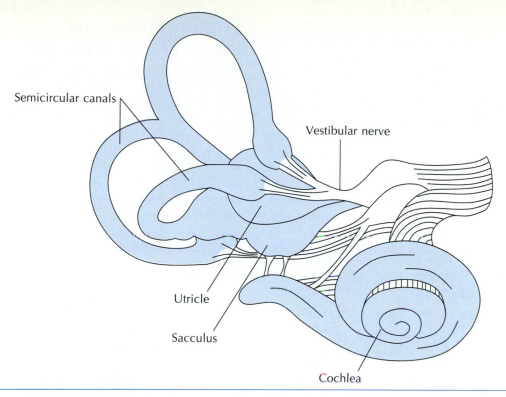

Semicircular canals

Vestibular nerve

Utricle

Sacculus

Cochlea

Figure 5.17 *The semicircular canals of the vestibular system are located in the inner ear. Fluids move in the canals when the head rotates in any direction, sending neural messages to the brain.*

ceptors that send information to the central nervous system, but also tiny fibers that receive information from the central nervous system (Figure 5.18). The spindles run parallel to the main muscle so that they are stretched when the main muscle is stretched. Stretching of the muscle spindle activates the receptors that send messages to the central nervous system. These receptors are in the middle of the spindle, and they can also be stretched by contracting the tiny muscles at the ends of the spindle. The spindle muscles are innervated whenever the main muscle is innervated. This dual innervation pattern causes the spindle to respond to changes in either muscle length or muscle force.

Notice that no single receptor can distinguish between changes in muscle force as opposed to changes in muscle length or joint angle. Thus, no single receptor can tell us the length of our muscles or the angle of our joints. This is an important puzzle, because we clearly know our muscle lengths and joint angles. We can demonstrate this knowledge by closing our eyes and using the distance between our palms to indicate the length of this

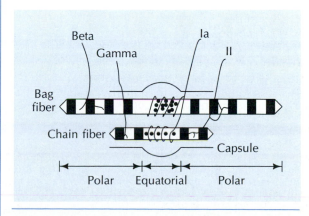

Figure 5.18 *A schematic drawing of a muscle spindle.*

book. Or we can try holding a rod to gravitational vertical or horizontal with our eyes closed. We can use our hands and arms in these and other ways that indicate precise information about muscle length and/or joint angle (e.g., Gibson, 1966). Many experts have suggested that we get this information by combining sensory signals from joints, tendons, muscle spindles, and skin (e.g., Wetzel & Stuart, 1976). It remains for future research to determine how this information is combined. In fact, an important goal for future research will be to determine how this proprioceptive information is combined with other information from the vestibular system, eyes, ears, and nose (Gibson, 1966).

Proprioception and Sensorimotor Control

Muscle spindles and **Golgi tendon organs** contribute to the control of flexor muscles. Suppose you are trying to hold your hand out straight with your arm bent at the elbow. Suddenly, someone drops a weight in you hand. The weight temporarily pulls your arm down which stretches the muscle holding your arm, as shown in Figure 5.19. This stretching starts a chain of events known as the stretch reflex (see Chapter 2). The stretch stimulates the muscle spindles which send sensory messages that excite motor neurons in the spinal cord. This excitation causes the flexor muscle to

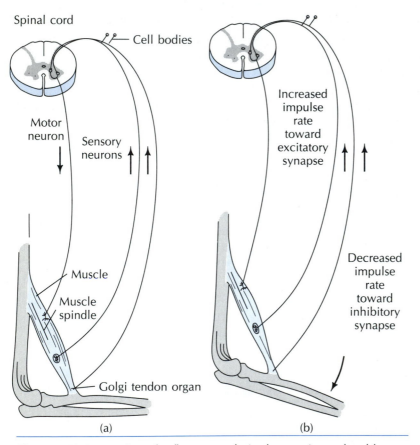

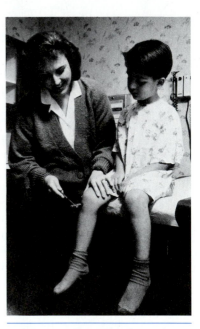

Contact of the hammer on the patellar tendon initiates a chain of events known as a stretch reflex, which causes the lower leg to jerk forward.

Figure 5.19 *Contraction of a flexor muscle in the arm is regulated by two types of receptors: the muscle spindle and the Golgi tendon organs. At rest (a) both receptors are somewhat active. However, flexion (b) leads to increased activity of the muscle spindles and decreased activity of the Golgi tendon organs.*

contract in opposition to the original stretch. Golgi tendon organs also help this opposing contraction. Ordinarily, Golgi tendon organs act as brakes against vigorous contractions. But during the stretch reflex, this braking action is released to aid the contraction. Their sensory messages inhibit motor neurons in the spinal cord and reduce contractions. Muscle contractions increase their sensory signals and muscle stretches decrease them. The original stretch, therefore, reduces the stimulation from Golgi tendon organs, which reduces the inhibition of motor neurons in the spinal cord.

This reduction of inhibition facilitates the contraction in opposition to the original stretch. The net result is that both muscle spindles and Golgi tendon organs help overcome an unintended muscle stretch. The action of both sensory receptors will oppose the unintended stretch.

Proprioception also plays an important role, of course, in more complex sensorimotor control skills, such as running down stairs without looking at your feet. The remaining chapters discuss many of these more interesting examples.

FINAL COMMENT

Our awareness and perception of the world around us come from our many sensory receptors. However, these receptors provide sensations that lack meaning until they interact with memory to provide perceptions. Indeed, the same set of sensations can be perceived quite differently depending on the context in which the sensations occur. For example, the sun or moon appears much larger when it is setting than when it is higher in the sky because its size is contrasted with the trees or buildings on the horizon. In each case, however, the sun or moon excites the same area of receptors on the eye.

KEY TERMS

sensation
perception
exteroception
proprioception
sensorimotor
   coordination
psychophysics
absolute threshold
difference threshold

method of
   adjustment
method of limits
method of constant
   stimuli
method of signal
   detection
noise
false alarm
hit

miss
opsychophysical
   functions
Weber's law
just-noticeable
   difference
prothetic
metathetic
focal vision
ambient vision

pitch
frequency
wave length
cycle
Hertz
amplitude
decibel
cutaneous senses
muscle spindles
Golgi tendon organs

6
Response Selection

Luke Skywalker: "STAR WARS"

Decisions and Translations

Uncertainty
- *Event Uncertainty and Hick's Law*
- *Temporal Uncertainty*
- *Perceptual Uncertainty*

Advance Information and Expectancies
- *Precuing*
- *Known Probabilities*
- *Sequential Dependencies*

Stimulus-Response Compatibility

Psychological Refractory Period
- *Refractory Theory*
- *Expectancy Theory*
- *Single Channel Theory*

HIGHLIGHT: Brain Work
FINAL COMMENT
KEY TERMS

Luke Skywalker: "STAR WARS"

In 1982, Twentieth Century Fox released a movie that was to become the biggest box office hit in the history of motion pictures. The movie *Star Wars,* was written and directed by George Lucas and starred Carrie Fisher, Harrison Ford, and Mark Hamill. This spectacular space fantasy involved adventure, romance, awesome special effects, and extraordinary space creatures. The story begins: "A long time ago in a galaxy far, far away . . . It is a period of civil war. Rebel spaceships, striking from a hidden base, have won their first victory against the evil galactic empire. During the battle, rebel spies managed to steal secret plans to the empire's ultimate weapon, the Death Star, an armored space station with enough fire power to destroy an entire planet. Pursued by the empire's sinister agents, Princess Leia races home aboard her starship, custodian of the stolen plans that can save her people and restore freedom to the galaxy."

As the movie begins Princess Leia is captured by the evil Imperial forces in their effort to take over the galactic empire. Venturesome Luke Skywalker and dashing ship captain Han Solo team together with the lovable droid duo, R2D2 and C-3PO, and the massive Wookiee named Chewbacca to help Princess Leia escape and crush the attack of the Imperial forces.

Darth Vader, the commander of the evil forces, appears to be closing in. They meet in the cargo bay. As Luke and Han fight to gain access to Han's ship, a distraction gives them the opportunity they need. Obi Wan Kenobe, an old Jedi warrior and the teacher of Luke Skywalker, engages Darth Vader in combat.

As the movie "Star Wars" begins, Luke Skywalker and a few unusual friends team up to help Princess Leia escape from the Imperial forces. In attempting to escape, Luke and the Princess have made a wrong turn that dead ends at a deep chasm in the death star.

CHAPTER OBJECTIVES

- To examine the role uncertainty plays in the process of determining what response to execute or not to execute.

- To understand the degree to which expectancies and/or advance information play in reducing the difficulty of decision making.

- To identify factors that affect the degree to which a stimulus nearly automatically elicits a response.

- To understand the conditions under which individuals may delay their processing of information.

As their light sabers clash, the evil warriors are distracted just long enough for Han, Luke, Princess Leia, Chewbacca, and the droids to move the few yards to the Han's ship, the Milenium Falcon.

Just as they enter the ship, Luke sees Darth Vader strike the mortal blow to Obi Wan. The old man is gone, but Luke hears him say "The force be with you." Obi Wan had attempted to teach Luke to rely on the force within himself in battle. Obi Wan said, "Don't think, trust yourself. . . . The force is what gives the Jedi warrior his power. It surrounds us and penetrates us and binds the galaxy together."

Once in Han's ship, they quickly enter hyperspace to travel to the fifth moon of the planet Alderaa where the leaders of the rebel forces impatiently await their return. It seems that C-3PO, while aboard the Death Star, was able to gain access to its main computer. The small droid holds the secret—the Death Star is vulnerable.

The rebel commander, Princess Leia's father, decides to mount an all-out attack on the Death Star. The evil forces have discovered the rebel's base and are preparing to destroy it as soon as it moves out from behind Alderaa. There are only minutes left. The plan is for one-pilot fighters to skim the surface of the Death Star and attempt to drop a proton torpedo down a small thermo exhaust port. It is their only hope—they can find no other vulnerability. Only seven minutes till the moon is exposed!

Fighter after fighter make runs at the exhaust port only to be destroyed by laser canons or turbo lasers. Only a group of three fighters makes it past the initial defenses. Two minutes left! The pilot of the first craft, aided by a computer guidance system, fails to hit the small port. The second pilot also fails. Only Luke Skywalker remains . . . 30 seconds left!

As Luke begins his run, he hears a voice—it's Obi Wan saying, "Trust yourself—the force is with you." Luke turns off his computer system and switches to manual control. At amazing speeds he navigates the narrow chasms leading to the exhaust port. Only a direct hit on the exhaust port will destroy the Death Star. Luke released the torpedo . . . a direct hit—the galaxy is saved.

■　■　■

Star Wars is a space fantasy that can only be played out in the minds of readers or movie viewers. Luke Skywalker, Princess Leia, Han Solo, as well as the other members of the rebel forces and the evil empire had scripts to follow in making the tough choices required in the midst of battle. The rest of us cannot rely on either a script writer or "the force" in choosing our course. If we were to skim the surface of the Death Star in a one-pilot fighter, events would occur too quickly and there would be too many options for us to make the right movements at the right time. Yet, experience may be able to assist us in much the same way that "the force" assisted Luke.

126

Decisions and Translations

Nearly every minute of every day, we make decisions. Our decisions may not be as important as those Luke Skywalker faced. In most cases our decisions are about simple everyday things, not ones that decide the fate of an entire galaxy. We decide to get up from our chair, change the channel on the TV, raid the refrigerator, or call a friend on the telephone. **Response selection** is the process of determining which movement to make or not to make given the current conditions. What we determine or decide in this stage of processing is a plan of action. The **action plan** can be considered a sketch or blueprint of the response to be made—a plan to write your name or a plan to fire the laser cannon at the approaching spacecraft.

It is easy to visualize the response selection stage as the intermediate step between sensation-perception and response execution processing (in serial processing). The sensation-perception processing stage provides information to the central nervous system that prompts us to engage in response selection processing. This processing is required before movements can be planned and executed. However, it is possible that the motivation for response selection can arise from an ongoing response or from internal thought processes.

Many times the process of response selection can be characterized as a conscious decision; at other times the process seems to be a much more automatic one, more like Luke's force, than the term *decision* implies. For the purposes of this text, a **decision** is the process of actively choosing one response or action from among a group of viable alternatives. This process often involves assigning weight to the alternatives or somehow factoring one response from the other possible choices (see Payne, 1976, for review). A **translation**, on the other hand, will be defined as an assignment of a response alternative to a specific stimulus condition based on past experiences. Greenwald's (1970) ideomotor theory suggests that with experience the stimulus arouses an image of the response that leads to action.

Translations can be relatively economical from an information processing standpoint. The time required to translate perception into action may be reduced and the attention demands normally required in the response selection process can be greatly reduced. The response selection processes involved in shifting gears on a standard transmission auto for experienced drivers and the process of typing a word or phrase for an experienced typist are examples of translation processes. Stimulus conditions prompt nearly automatic response selection processes. The experienced driver or the expert typist utilizes little attention to select the appropriate response. This is not the case for the beginning driver or typist. The process of response selection for the novice is a more attention demanding, conscious process.

We first discuss factors that increase the difficulty of the response selection process, namely uncertainty. A discussion of how advance information in used to reduce the difficulty of the response selection process follows. Finally, conditions that allow translation to occur and speed up the process of response selection and a special condition that has the potential to slow down the process of response selection are discussed.

Uncertainty

We increase difficulty by increasing uncertainty. **Uncertainty** is the extent to which an individual is required to process information in order to determine a course of action or inaction. Many factors increase the difficulty of processing in the response selection stage.

Just as Luke and Han Solo were faced with many options and were not sure which was the correct course to follow, we are often faced with uncertainty. Remember that factors that increase difficulty result in increases in reaction time and/or increases in response selection errors. In many sports, we purposefully attempt to increase the difficulty of the response selection process for our opponents. What could an offensive football team, the pitcher in baseball, a tennis player, or even Luke Skywalker do to increase the uncertainty of the response selection stage for an opponent (or enemy)? They can increase the uncertainty regarding which response will be required (event uncertainty) and when the response should be executed (temporal uncertainty). In addition, the offensive team or player can attempt to make two or more responses appear as much alike as possible (perceptual uncertainty). Increases in each form of uncertainty add to the delay in responding and/or probability of a response selection error.

Event Uncertainty and Hick's Law

Consider an offensive football team that only runs one play, a tennis player who always hits the same serve, a baseball pitcher who only throws one pitch, or a Jedi warrior who parries his light saber in only one way. In each case, the opponent has to deal with little uncertainty about what will happen. Thus, the problems associated with response selection are minimized.

In sports and games we quickly learn that it is not to our advantage to allow our opponent the luxury of knowing in advance what we will do. We want to create event uncertainty. **Event uncertainty** is increased as the number of equally likely alternatives is increased. Coaches teach more than one play, serve, or pitch to their players. They have learned from experience that this results in delays in responding and an increased likelihood of the opponent's responding inappropriately.

One of the earliest laboratory studies on this topic was described by Woodworth in 1938. Woodworth cited a set of reaction time experiments by Merkel in 1885. In the experiments, the digits 1 through 5 were assigned to the fingers of the right hand. Roman numerals I through V were assigned to the fingers of the left hand. On a given set of trials, the subject was informed how many possible alternatives (1 to 10) were active as well as the precise stimuli that were to be used. For example, on one set of trials three alternatives were active.

What can an offensive football team do to increase the uncertainty in the response selection stage for the defensive team?

Specifically, only the 2, 5, and III were to be used. On another set of trials, five alternatives (1, 2, I, IV, and V) were active. Throughout the experiment, various combinations of digits and number of alternatives were utilized.

The data from one of Merkel's experiments are given in Figure 6.1. The most obvious finding was that reaction time increased as the number of alternatives increased. Less obvious, but perhaps just as important, is that the line representing the increase in reaction time with increases in alternatives is not linear (straight). An increase in one stimulus alternative from 1 to 2 resulted in an increase in reaction time of about 120 milliseconds. However, an increase in one alternative from 9 to 10 resulted in an increase in reaction time of only a few milliseconds (approximately 5 milliseconds).

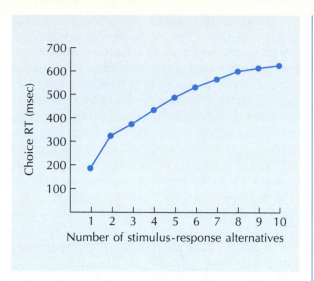

Figure 6.1 *Choice reaction time increases as the number of equally likely alternatives increases (Merkel, 1885 as cited by Woodworth, 1938).*

Number of Alternatives and Reaction Time. The discovery that increasing the number of alternatives resulted in smaller and smaller increases in reaction time has important practical and theoretical significance. Simply stated, increasing the number of stimulus alternative reaps initially large but rapidly diminishing reaction time returns. Coaches and players should be aware that increasing the number of possible plays, past some point, may only produce minimal delays in responding for the defensive team and may not be worth the time invested in learning new plays. This is not the case when the player or team is proficient in only one or two alternative responses. At this point, learning a new response may well be worth the effort.

Since Woodworth (1938) reported the findings of Merkel, event uncertainty has received much theoretical attention. The most widely cited attempts to account for the findings were presented by Hick in 1952 and Hymen in 1953. The experimental design and results of the Hick and Hymen experiments were similar to those of Merkel nearly 75 years earlier. What was important about these studies was the manner in which the researchers interpreted the data. Their theoretical notion has been variously termed **Hick's law** or the **Hick-Hymen law**.

Hick (1952) and Hymen (1953) noted that reaction time increased by a nearly constant amount each time the number of alternatives was doubled (1 to 2, 2 to 4, 4 to 8). This seemed to match up with the practice of expressing **information** in terms of bits or binary units. A **bit** is the amount of information obtained by learning which of two equally likely alternatives is present. Contemporary computer scientists (as well as some contemporary cognitive scientists) express information in a binary form such that 3 bits of information represent twice the information expressed in 2 bits and 2 bits contain twice the information contained in 1 bit. Three bits (2^3) of information are required to decide among 8 equally likely alternatives, 2 bits (2^2) to decide among 4 equally likely alternatives, 1 bit (2^1) for 2 alternatives and 0 bits (2^0) when only one alternative was possible.

The Shell Game. To illustrate the concept of information expressed as bits, consider a form of the shell game (Figure 6.2). In the shell game, the object is to guess which shell covers

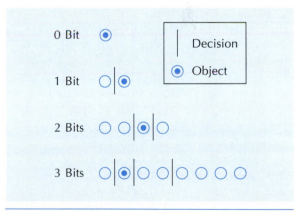

Figure 6.2 *Determining which shell hides a small object is made more difficult by increasing the number of shells. A logical person would not require a guess to determine the location of the object if only one shell were used; one guess would be needed for two shells, two guesses for four shells; and three guesses for eight shells. More information is required to find the object as the number of shells is increased.*

a small object. If there is only one shell, the game is very simple. There is no uncertainty regarding which shell covers the object. When two shells are used, a small amount of uncertainty exists as to which shell houses the object. If you guess the left side of the center and, you are wrong, do you have to guess again? No! You know the shell that houses the object is on the right side of center. If you guess the right shell first, you are correct. Do you need to guess again? No! One guess or one piece of information is all that has to be processed to locate the object.

Consider four shells. Over a set of trials, given that the object is randomly positioned, the most efficient way to locate the object is to halve the remaining alternatives. This always requires only two choices. First, is the object right of center? Second, is the object under the shell to the right side of center (of the remaining alternatives)? No matter what the responses are to the questions, you have located the hidden object. That reaction time increases by some constant as the number of bits increases suggests that the process of response selection may be similar.

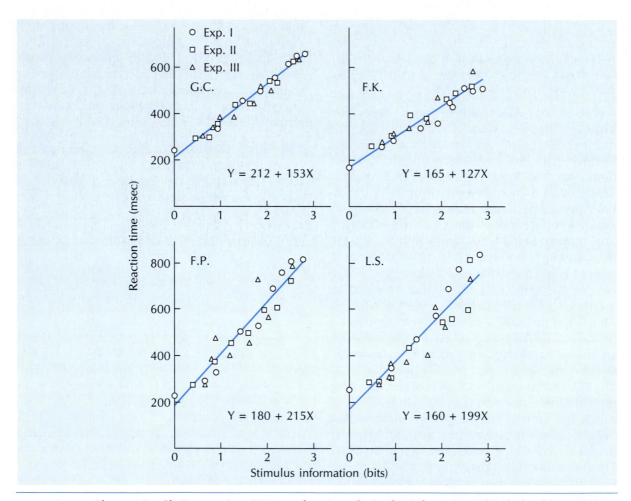

Figure 6.3 *Choice reaction time as a function of stimulus information. The slope of the line for each subject indicates the ease with which each subject responds to the stimulus conditions. A more gradual slope (F.K.) indicates that the subject's reaction time is affected less by increases in stimulus information than a steeper slope (F.P.).*

Data from four individual subjects in the Hymen (1953) experiments are presented in Figure 6.3. Note that the reaction times when plotted against bits of information roughly form a straight line. The slope of the line has been interpreted as indicating the difficulty the subject experiences in resolving event uncertainty (see section on Stimulus Response Compatibility in this chapter). Individual slopes indicate the efficiency with which the individual responds to event uncertainty. Figure 6.3 indicates that Subject F. K. was most efficient and Subject F. P. was least efficient. The cost, in terms of reaction time per bit of information, was 127 milliseconds for Subject F. K. and 215 milliseconds for Subject F. P. The reaction time value, when there is no event uncertainty (0 bits), is reflective of the information processing requirements unrelated to the resolution of event uncertainty.

Temporal Uncertainty

Consider an offensive football team that always runs its plays on the same snap count, a tennis player who serves at the same tempo and speed each time, a baseball pitcher who throws the ball at the same speed throughout a game, or a spaceship that always flies the same route at the same hyperspace speed. In each of these cases, an opponent is met with little uncertainty about when an event will occur. Coaches and players quickly learn that it is to their advantage to vary when the event will occur, thus creating temporal uncertainty that delays their opponents. **Temporal uncertainty** is increased as the predictability of when an event will occur decreases. Knowing when the ball will be snapped in football or when it will be in position to hit in tennis or baseball eliminates temporal uncertainty.

Temporal uncertainty can result from increases in the variability and length of the warning interval. The *warning interval* is the time between a readying or warning stimulus and the stimulus to move. For example, a starter in track provides two warning signals: "Take your mark" and "Set." The gunshot is the critical signal to move. Sprinters are interested in learning the tempo that a particular starter uses. They watch and listen to the starting of other races in order to reduce temporal uncertainty by being able to predict the time between the warning signal and the gun. In other activities, various stimuli provide a warning. The quarterback barks "Set;" the tennis player tosses the ball to serve; the pitcher begins the windup. These conditions ready the opponent for the impending critical stimulus.

Sprinters are interested in learning the tempo that a particular starter uses. They watch and listen to the start of other races in order to reduce temporal uncertainty.

Experiments by Klemmer (1956, 1957) found that reaction time increased as the average warning interval was increased. The data in Figure 6.4 are from Klemmer (1956). The warning interval varied from 1 to 12 seconds between blocks of trials but was fixed within blocks. Longer average warning intervals increased temporal uncertainty by reducing the predictability of when the critical stimulus would occur. However, this effect was relatively small. Factors that influence the expectancy of when the critical stimulus may occur in the warning interval seem to be more powerful.

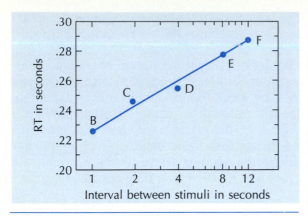

Figure 6.4 *Reaction time increases as the average warning interval increases. Longer warning intervals increase the subject's uncertainty as to when the stimulus will be presented because longer intervals are more difficult to judge.*

Mowrer (1940) asked subjects to respond to tones (critical stimulus) in a simple reaction time situation. In most cases the tone was presented at 12-second intervals. This resulted in an expectancy. However, on 10 percent of the trials the tone was presented before or after the 12-second mark. The data from the Mowrer (1940) experiment are given in Figure 6.5.

Reaction time was smallest at the 12-second interval but increased as the interval was either shortened or lengthened. Temporal uncertainty was increased because the predictability of when the critical stimulus would occur was decreased. Note that the increases

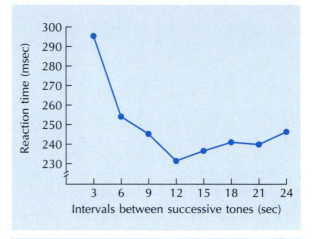

Figure 6.5 *Reaction time is lowest at intervals that are most probable. On 90 percent of the trials, the interval was 12 seconds, and on 10 percent of the trials the interval was 3, 6, 9, or 12 seconds shorter or longer than 12 seconds.*

As time elapses after the "ready" signal, the soap box derby drivers become increasingly expectant that the gun will go off. This may cause one of the drivers to false start if the starter waits too long to fire the gun.

in reaction time from the 12-second interval were greater for the shorter intervals than for the longer ones. Why? The answer appears to be related to another condition that results in decreased temporal uncertainty.

Aging Effect.   Consider your response to a stimulus light that will come on sometime in the next five seconds. The light could be activated anytime after the warning signal but before five seconds elapse. Where in the warning interval might you respond most quickly? An experiment by Drazin (1961) found that reaction time decreases as the time remaining approaches the longest possible interval length (Figure 6.6). Apparently, as the interval elapsed and the critical stimulus was not present, the expectancy for the stimulus increased. The range of times in which the stimulus could occur was functionally reduced. The subjects might think, "The stimulus has not occurred so it must be coming soon." Schmidt (1988) calls this an *aging effect* because "the subject has a basis for becoming increasingly expectant" as the warning interval "ages" p. 126. Thus, the offensive team in football loses the advantage of knowing the snap count as the 30-second clock counts down. The same is true as the shot clock winds down in basketball.

It should be noted that the aging effect (e.g., Drazin, 1961) is eliminated when catch trials are used. *Catch trials* are simply trials in which the stimulus is not presented at all. This negates the expectancy effects and therefore the aging effect.

Perceptual Uncertainty

Consider an offensive football team that lines up differently for each play it is going to run, a server in tennis who takes a different position for each serve, or a pitcher in baseball who winds up differently for each type of pitch. (Note that Darth Vader wore the same uniform as the other storm troopers but his was black instead of white. Did this make him easier to identify?) In each case, the opponent will readily be able to distinguish which event (play,

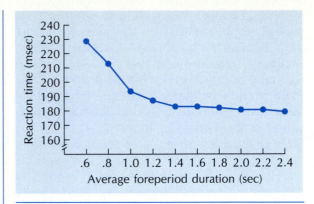

Figure 6.6   *When subjects know a stimuli will be presented sometime within a given interval, reaction time tends to decrease as the interval increases (ages). This effect is sometimes referred to as the aging foreperiod effect.*

serve, pitch) will occur. This simplifies the response selection process because perceptual uncertainty is reduced. **Perceptual uncertainty** is increased as a set of stimuli or events become less easily discriminated from each other (e.g., Vickers, 1970).

A simple laboratory example can illustrate this point. Subjects are presented with two visual stimuli for a brief period of time. The task is to depress a reaction time key when the stimuli are different. The difference in all stimuli is easily perceived given enough time. That is, with sufficient time, subjects will make the correct decision on all trials. Given the pairs of stimuli in Figure 6.7, which will

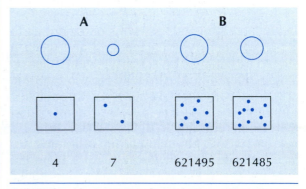

Figure 6.7   *As two stimuli are more similar, the reaction time to discriminate between them is increased. Note that Stimuli B are more similar than Stimuli A.*

result in the faster reaction time, set A or B? It should be obvious that in the case of the circles, A will be responded to more rapidly. Similarly, reaction to A will be faster for the dots and digits. Tversky (1977) proposes that the degree of similarity between two stimuli is based on a ratio scale rather than some absolute scale. Thus, the numbers 4 and 7 are quite distinct because 1 of 1 feature is different. The numbers 621495 and 621485 are relatively similar because only 1 of 6 features is different. The same is true for 1 and 2 dots versus 8 and 9 dots. Note that each is only one digit or one dot different and yet one is responded to more quickly than the other. This notion predicts that pairs with an equal number of features that are different would be responded to similarly.

Summing up, it is to the advantage of a player or team in many sports to attempt to increase the uncertainty for the opponent. There are three classes of uncertainty: event, temporal, and perceptual. An offensive football team varies the play (from a pool of plays) that is to be run (event uncertainty), varies the snap count (temporal uncertainty), and attempts to make quite different plays appear similar (perceptual uncertainty). Each factor that increases uncertainty has the potential to add to the opponent's delay in responding.

What happens when event, temporal, and perceptual uncertainty are greatly reduced or eliminated? Reaction time dramatically decreases! Little uncertainty, in some situations, allows the performer to carry out some of the processing in advance of the stimulus. Queseda and Schmidt (1970) demonstrated average reaction times of 22 milliseconds when uncertainty was greatly reduced. They argued that reaction time could potentially be zero if the stimulus and response demands were known in advance. Factors that decrease uncertainty are discussed in the next section.

It is also important to note that it is possible to create artificial situations that appear to have little uncertainty. In the first few games of the 1988 season, Joe Paterno, the legendary football coach and athletic director at Penn State, had his team use the same snap count on every play. He reasoned that his team was quick and strong enough to overcome the advantage gained by varying the snap count. His team did not jump offsides, but the opponents could get a jump on the ball too. But Joe Paterno was also very cagey. He gave up this advantage in order to assure his team of a 5-yard offsides penalty when he really needed it. In a critical situation, Paterno knew he could change the snap count and cash in on the penalty.

Advance Information and Expectancies

Many factors may tip off your opponent as to which response will be required and when it should be initiated: an offensive guard lines up a little differently, a team tends to run a certain play in a particular situation, or three inside running plays in a row have set up an option play. Upon returning to the rebel base, Princess Leia knew that her ship carried a homing device because the evil forces had let them escape too easily. Each of these clues may reduce or even eliminate event, temporal, or perceptual uncertainty. Coaches and players scout their opponents in order to reduce uncertainty.

They look for clues, chart tendencies, and plot sequences. Advance information, if reliable, will reduce the delays in responding normally associated with uncertainty.

Precuing

A **precue** is advance information that reduces the amount of processing required and thus reduces reaction time as well. For example, a precue may functionally reduce the number of alternatives that must be considered. The pitcher in baseball might position his elbow in

Brain Work

What is different about the information processing activities an individual engages in when first introduced to a new task and those engaged in after a great deal of practice on the task? After you learn to do something like touch type, sign your name, play a musical instrument, or play a video game it always seems that the demands of the task are less. That is, the performer appears to perform with less effort and the task appears to demand less attention. Researchers at the Brain Imaging Center at the University of California at Irvine recently studied this question (Haier et al., 1992).

Dr. Haier, professor of psychiatry and human behavior, injected subjects with a radioactive tracer that is absorbed in greater concentrations in the parts of the brain that are actively consuming glucose. The greater the brain activity (utilization of glucose) the greater the absorption of the radioactive tracer. This allowed the researchers, by means of a positron emission tomography (PET) scan, to determine the relative amounts of energy expended by subjects' brains. PET scans (see Fig. 2.21) result in a picture of the live functioning brain with the activity levels of the various parts of the brain color coded. For instance, blue indicates little brain activity and red indicates a high level of activity.

Subjects were asked to learn a complex video game. PET scans were completed during the first attempt of the game and after a good deal of practice. The results indicated that subjects expended less mental energy after they learned to play the computer game. However, the subjects' scores on the game after practice were seven times higher than on their first game. Apparently, the players were much more efficient, at least in terms of neural activity, after practice. Dr. Haier suggests:

> The implication is that we need to think about the different ways the brain can be efficient . . . what seems most likely is that the brain is efficient because it uses only certain important circuits rather than many extraneous circuits. It might be that the brain learns over time what circuits not to use to perform a task.

What is even more obvious is that subjects can functionally reduce the temporal, perceptual, and event uncertainty present in a task such as a video game. They learn what events are likely to occur, when events will occur, and how to distinguish between different cues. Thus, it seems that practice serves to provide the performers information that allows them to reduce the mental demands of a task. That is, practice allows better performance with less effort.

a unique way for a fastball. Knowing this serves as a precue because we are tipped off that a fastball is imminent. We also can reduce the alternatives that we will consider when we do not see the unique elbow position. A server in tennis may toss the ball higher or grip the racquet differently for a slice serve. Either action serves as a precue.

Special situations may also reduce the likelihood that a particular alternative should be considered. A pitcher in baseball has fewer options when the batter has a three balls–no strikes count and the bases are loaded than at the beginning of an inning. In the former situation, the pitcher is said to be "behind the batter" because the advantage has shifted from the pitcher to the batter. Fourth and one on the 5-yard line in football suggests that the repertoire of appropriate plays has been reduced. The number of alternatives that the defensive team must consider is also reduced. In these cases the constraints imposed by the situation can be considered precues.

Precuing has been studied extensively in the laboratory (Rosenbaum, 1980; Miller, 1982; Reeve & Proctor, 1984). Typically, during the warning interval, subjects are informed that one or more of the alternatives will be eliminated from consideration for that trial. For example, consider the two setups in Figure 6.8. In both situations only one of four stimu-

lus lights will be illuminated (e.g., light 2). The task is to respond by depressing the appropriate response key as quickly as possible when the light is illuminated. Response keys 1 and 2 are to be depressed with the index and middle fingers of the left hand. Response keys 3 and 4 are assigned to the index and middle fingers of the right hand. In the setup to the left, precues are not given. However, on the right, two of the alternatives are precued. An "X" above an alternative indicates the alternative is active and may be illuminated. Note that the precues in Figure 6.9A indicate that the left hand is to be used so that only the specification of the correct finger is transmitted by the critical stimulus. The precuing technique permits the specification of hand (left or right), finger (index or middle), or mixed precues to be given.

Does the precue affect reaction time? Yes, reaction time is reduced when the number of possible alternatives is reduced. If two of the four alternatives are eliminated, reaction time should be reduced as if only two alternatives were present in the first place (from 2 bits to 1 bit). Generally, this is true provided there is sufficient time for the precue to be processed. But would reaction time be influenced by which two alternatives were precued?

Miller (1982) provides evidence that precues that specify hand result in faster reaction

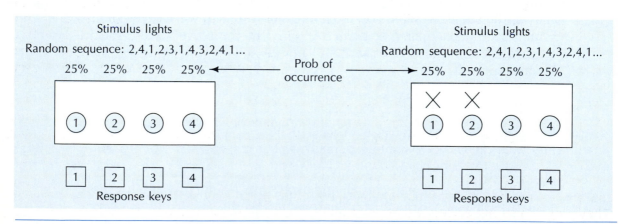

Figure 6.8 *Precuing is a method of indicating that one or more of the possible alternatives will or will not be used on that trial. In the setup on the right, the subject is informed (precued) that only stimuli-responses 1 and 2 will be used for that trial.*

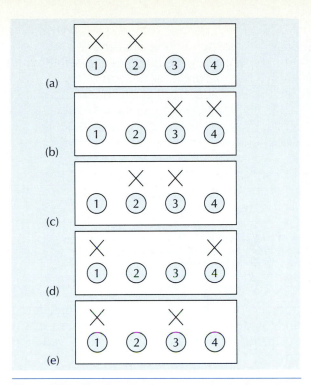

(a)

(b)

(c)

(d)

(e)

Figure 6.9 *Consider that responses 1 and 2 are to be made with the index and first finger of the left hand and responses 3 and 4 with the first and index finger of the right hand. The X's precue the left hand (A), right hand (B), first finger (C), index finger (D), or neither a specific hand or finger (E).*

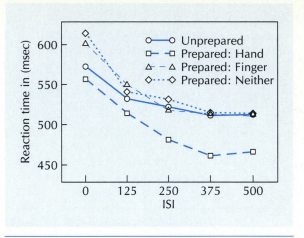

Figure 6.10 *Example from a precuing experiment using various interstimulus intervals. Reaction time was fastest for the prepared hand condition.*

Known Probabilities

In most situations, events do not occur with equal probability. A pitcher may throw a fastball 80 percent of the time; a football team may pass on only 10 percent of the plays or run to the wide side of the field 75 percent of the time. One thing that aided the rebel band's escape from the Death Star was the robotlike and predictable actions of the storm troopers. Knowledge concerning the likelihood of a stimulus occurring is termed **known probabilities**. This information may be valuable to the opponent because each stimulus does not convey the same amount of information. Consider the reaction time setup in Figure 6.11. On the left, each light will come on with equal probability in a random sequence. However, on the right, the probabilities are not equally distributed. Light 3 will occur 80 percent of the time. The remaining lights will be illuminated only 5 or 10 percent of the time. Which setup will be responded to more quickly on the average? Reaction times to the setup on the right will be faster (Hymen, 1953). But what about the reactions to lights 1, 2, and 4? Reaction times to these lights will be slower, with reaction times to the 5 percent lights somewhat slower than those to the 10 percent light. The average, however, is not greatly affected by

times than precues that specify finger or mixed precues (Figure 6.10). In fact, reaction times when the precue specified a finger were no faster than those to the mixed precue or when no precue was used. Miller suggested that the hand precue allowed the performer to plan the response for that hand in advance of the critical stimulus indicating the specific finger. Precues indicating the finger to be used were of little use because the commands for the finger cannot be prepared until the hand is specified. Miller argued that response selection is a fixed order process. For example, arm must be specified before hand and hand must be specified before finger, and so on. Reeve and Proctor (1984, 1985) questioned this view. They provided strong evidence that given sufficient time response selection can be a variable order process and all precues can be utilized with equal effectiveness.

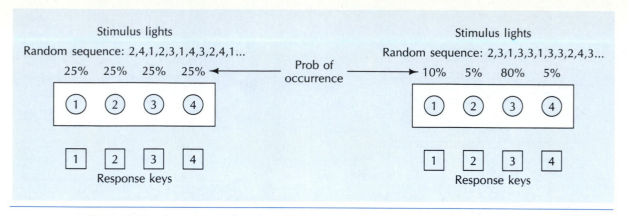

Figure 6.11 *Average reaction time decreases as subjects determine the probabilities with which particular stimulus will be presented. Reaction time is decreased because the subjects can anticipate that stimulus 3 (right) will occur most often.*

the few inflated reaction times to the lower probability lights.

Why would reaction times increase as the probability of occurrence for that event decreases? The amount of information conveyed by the occurrence of an alternative is increased as the probability of its occurrence is decreased. Earlier in this chapter we saw how information was quantified for event uncertainty. One bit of information had to be processed to decide between two equally likely alternatives (50 percent chance each) and two bits for four alternatives (25 percent chance each). Remember also that the average reaction time to two alternatives was less than to four alternatives. Per stimulus, the alternatives that have a 50 percent chance of occurrence require one-half the information to be processed that a 25 percent alternative requires.

Let's return to the example in Figure 6.11. Light 3 (80 percent) provides approximately one-eighth the information relative to light 1 and approximately one-sixteenth the information of lights 2 and 4. The less information (bits) that is required to resolve the choice, the faster the reaction time. Using a method developed by Hick (1952), an alternative that occurs 80 percent of the time yields 0.41 bits, 10 percent yields 3.32 bits, and 5 percent yields 4.32 bits. Thus, any factor that increases the

number of events that must be considered and/or decreases the probability of an event occurring will result in increased reaction time.

Sequential Dependencies

Even when events occur with equal probability, there may be a sequence in which the events occur. **Sequential dependencies** occur when an individual uses knowledge about a sequence with which alternatives occur to reduce reaction time. In some instances the sequence may be a repeating one. A pitcher may, with some regularity, throw two fastballs, a change-up, a curve, two fastballs, a change-up, and so on. Similarly, a football team may run plays in a particular sequence or a tennis player may hit shots in a sequence. Consider the reaction time example given in Figure 6.12. In both situations, each alternative will occur 25 percent of the time. However, in the example to the right, the stimulus lights follow a particular sequence. Will knowledge of the sequence affect reaction time? Yes, because event uncertainty is functionally reduced. The subject will know in advance which light will be illuminated. The illumination of the expected light holds little, if any, information and therefore requires little processing.

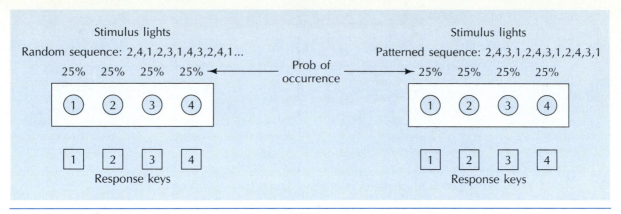

Figure 6.12 *Average reaction time decreases as subjects determine the sequence with which particular stimuli will be presented. Reaction time is decreased because the subject can anticipate which stimuli will occur next.*

In most situations, repeating sequences are seldom observed. However, it is sometimes possible to detect fragments of sequences. That is, baseball scouts may note that whenever a particular pitcher throws three fastballs in a row, a change-up will follow. The pitcher may seldom put himself in this position, but when the situation does arise the next pitch is predictable. A football team may never run the same play three times in a row. Therefore, when a play has been run twice, it can be eliminated as an option for the next play.

In sum, precues, known probabilities, and sequential dependencies are all established with experience. This knowledge is used collectively to combat uncertainty. Most of the examples given have related to event uncertainty, but the principles apply equally well to temporal and perceptual uncertainties.

Stimulus-Response Compatibility

Some stimulus-response situations seem to elicit an appropriate response more automatically than other situations. It is difficult to teach a beginning boxer to counter punch because the natural tendency is to move away when an opponent throws a punch. However, with practice a boxer can learn to respond nearly automatically in specific situations. Consider a beginning and a skilled typist. For the beginning typist, a specific letter (stimulus) does not elicit a specific response, and numerous information processing activities are required to type. This is not the case for the skilled typist. Letters to be typed are nearly automatically translated into a response. Luke Skywalker had been flying the one-pilot fighters since he was very young. He became so skilled that flying a fighter plane was nearly automatic. Luke did not have to think about how to control his plane any more than a skilled driver has to think about shifting gears in a car.

Figure 6.13 depicts a continuum from decision to translation using typing as an example. In order for a beginning typist to type a word or series of characters, the typist must actively decide which finger should be used and where the appropriate key is located. At this stage, the decision is attention demanding and involves conscious processing. After con-

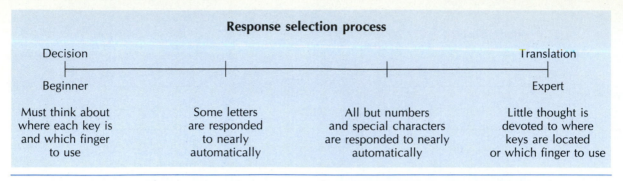

Response selection process

Decision ——————————————————————————————— Translation

Beginner | | | Expert

| Must think about where each key is and which finger to use | Some letters are responded to nearly automatically | All but numbers and special characters are responded to nearly automatically | Little thought is devoted to where keys are located or which finger to use |

Figure 6.13 *Continuum from decision to translation for typing.*

siderable practice the process becomes much more automatic and there is a shift from decision to translation. A compatibility between the stimulus and response has been developed. **Stimulus-response compatibility** is the degree of natural or learned correspondence between a stimulus and associated response.

Because of past experiences we have developed many stimulus-response compatibilities or stereotypes (Loveless, 1963). Green lights mean go. Red lights mean stop. Up or to the right means more and down or to the left means less. Clockwise turns of a dial indicate increases or tightening, and counterclockwise turns mean decreases or loosening. Which control knob would you use to turn on the top right burner of the two stoves depicted in Figure 6.14? Why? Note that there is a stronger correspondence between the control knobs and the burner for the stove on the left. However, most of you would pick the "A" control knob and the back left burner, the "B" control knob and the front left burner, etc. These compatibilities play a large role in establishing controls for our cars, appliances, and work equipment.

In the reaction time setups illustrated in Figure 6.15, which response key arrangement best corresponds with the arrangement of the stimulus lights? Subjects would respond more quickly if the response keys were adjacent to the corresponding stimulus lights. Other arrangements would initially require additional decision processing. In fact, the arrangement to the left (A) would elicit faster reaction times

than the one in the middle (B), and the arrangement to the right (C) would be responded to most slowly.

Engineers involved in the design of instrument panels and other displays pay particular attention to the compatibility issue. In a review by Fitts and Posner (1967), the power of stimulus-response compatibility is well illustrated (see Figure 6.16). As you examine this figure, remember that 1 bit indicates that two choices were used, 2 bits indicate four alternatives, and 3 bits involve eight alternatives. Remember, also, that the slope of the line indi-

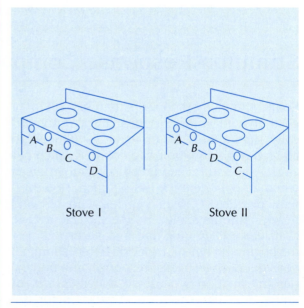

Figure 6.14 *Which knobs would you use to turn on the different burners?*

140

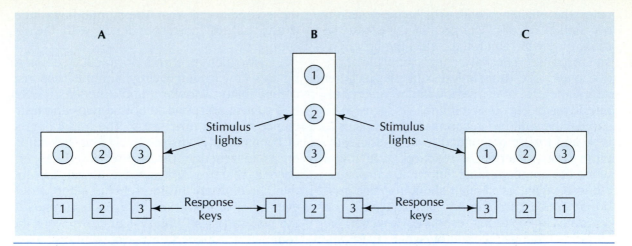

Figure 6.15 *Examples of three-choice reaction time setups: (a) represents high stimulus-response compatibility, (b) represents moderate compatibility, and (c) represents low compatibility.*

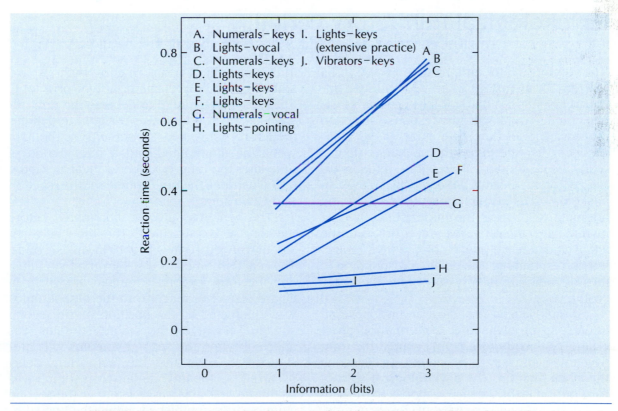

Figure 6.16 *Reaction time data from a number of experiments. A flatter slope indicates that the stimuli-responses were more highly compatible than those with steeper slopes.*

cates the efficiency with which the decision-translation occurs. The greater the slope the more time was required to select the appropriate response. The flatter the slope the more automatic the translations. In these latter cases, the cost of increasing the number of alternatives or events is minimal. As Figure 6.16 shows, the stimulus-response conditions in G, H, I, and J were responded to very efficiently. Little cost, in terms of reaction, was found when the number of bits (information) was increased. What is similar about these conditions? Yes! The stimuli are, maybe even naturally, linked to the response. However, the stimulus-response conditions A–F were responded to less efficiently. Increases in the number of bits resulted in substantial increases in reaction time. What is unique about these conditions? Yes! The stimuli have little, if any, natural correspondence with the response.

Past experience and/or practice seems to be the key to improving stimulus-response compatibility. Mowbry and Rhoades (1959) had subjects respond to both a two- and four-choice reaction time setup. The initial degree of compatibility was relatively low, but differences in reaction time were noted. As expected, reaction times were lower for the two-choice than the four-choice setup. However, after 42,000 trials, the reaction times to the two- and four-choice situations were the same. Event uncertainty was diminished or eliminated by the development of a high degree of stimulus-response compatibility.

Psychological Refractory Period

It is not unusual for an athlete to appear to be "frozen" for an instant when attempting to initiate a response. A batter thinks he sees a fastball coming and begins the response selection process. A brief time later (maybe 100 milliseconds), he determines that a change-up has really been thrown. The batter appears to freeze for an instant. A defensive player in basketball sees his man move to the right and attempts to process the information. A brief instant later, the offensive player drives to the left. The defensive man "took the fake" and is late in responding. The delay in responding in these conditions is very short but often very costly.

Stimuli spaced very close in time pose an interesting problem to the information processing system. Telford (1931) coined the term psychological refractory period to describe this phenomenon. The **psychological refractory period** is the delay in response to the second of two stimuli spaced very closely in time.

This phenomenon can be illustrated with reaction time. Karlin and Kestenbaum (1968) informed subjects that one or both of two stimuli could be presented: a light or a tone. The light was a signal to depress the right response key. The tone was a signal to depress the left response key. On some trials the light would be illuminated and a brief period of time later the tone would be activated. Figure 6.17 illustrates the time course for the reaction to the two stimuli.

The light was always illuminated before the tone was presented. The time between stimuli ranged from 90 to 1090 milliseconds. The reaction times to the light (first stimulus) and the tone (second stimulus) are given in Figure 6.18. The reaction to the first stimulus was unaffected by the position of the second stimulus. However, the second stimulus was affected. When the second stimulus was presented very soon after the first, a long delay occurred. As the interval between stimuli was increased, the delay in reacting to the second stimulus was diminished. When the two stimuli are separated by a sufficient amount of time, the reaction time to the second stimulus

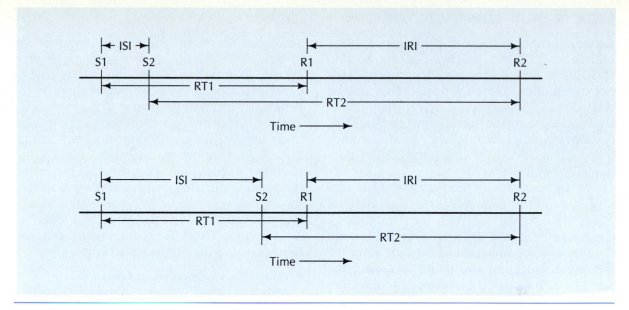

Figure 6.17 *The time course for the psychological refractory period. When the second stimulus is presented determines how long the subject is delayed in responding to the second stimulus.*

is the same as if the first stimulus had not been presented. There is no significance to the

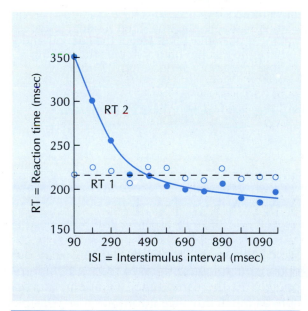

Figure 6.18 *Reaction time to both the first and second stimuli as a function of the interstimulus interval (ISI). Note that reaction time is delayed to the second stimulus when the interval is short.*

finding that the auditory reaction times for the longer interval are less than those for the visual stimuli. As we noted in Chapter 4, this is typically the case.

Why is the response to the second stimulus delayed? This is a difficult question that does not have a simple answer. However, three theoretical explanations for the psychological refractory period follow: a refractory theory, an expectancy theory, and a single channel theory.

Refractory Theory

Refractory theory seems to be borrowed from the field of neurophysiology. When a nerve fiber is electrically stimulated twice in rapid succession, a response to the second stimulation is not evoked—the nerve is not receptive to a second stimulation. This has been termed a *refractory period*. Telford (1931) suggested that the nervous system was briefly made somewhat less sensitive by processing the first stimulus. However, there is little support for this position.

Expectancy Theory

Expectancy theory (Eithorn & Lawrence, 1955) maintains that the reaction to the second stimulus is delayed because the subject does not expect it to follow so rapidly. This may be related to findings concerning very short warning signals (see section on Temporal Uncertainty in this chapter). Very brief warnings that a stimulus was imminent resulted in drastically delayed reactions.

Expectancy theory predicts that if the second stimulus is expected, the psychological refractory period should be eliminated. Creamer (1963) held the time interval between the first and second stimuli constant. Over trials, the subjects should come to expect the rapid occurrence of the second stimulus. The psychological refractory period was diminished over trials, but not eliminated. This finding suggests other factors contribute to the delay.

Single Channel Theory

A widely accepted theory to account for the psychological refractory period is the single channel theory first proposed by Craik (1947). The single channel theory proposes that subjects can attend to only one decision process at a time. Attention to a second stimulus has to be delayed until the first stimulus is processed. This notion is analogous to a pair of gates that opens to allow information in for response selection purposes. The gates close during response selection processing and open only when a selection has been made. The single channel theory predicts that if the response selection requirements are increased for the first stimulus, the psychological refractory period will also be increased. This prediction has been confirmed (Reynolds, 1966).

Wickens (1984) likened the delay to a bottleneck, using the following analogy:

> Imagine a kindergarten teacher (the bottleneck) who must get two children ready for recess (stimuli 1 and 2). Both are able to put on their coats by themselves (this is the automatic "early" processing that does not require the teacher-attention-to function), but both need the teacher to zip or button the coats. Therefore, how long Child 2 will have to wait is a joint function of how soon she arrives after Child 1 and how long it takes the teacher to button Child 1. The total time required for Child 2 to get the coat on (analogous to reaction time) is equal to the time it normally takes to put the coat on and have the teacher button it, plus the waiting time (refractory period). (pp. 379-380)

FINAL COMMENT

In many competitive sports, we attempt to increase the uncertainty for our opponent. We do this by varying in an unpredictable way as many factors as possible. We vary what we are going to do (event uncertainty) and when we are going to do it (temporal uncertainty), and we attempt to make one movement sequence appear like another (perceptual uncertainty). We do this in the hope that we can delay our opponents or cause them to respond inappropriately. At the same time, we attempt to secure as much advance information as possible from our opponent. We look for sequences, tendencies, and/or probabilities that may allow us to respond more quickly and efficiently.

KEY TERMS

response selection
action plan
decision
translation
event uncertainty

information
Hick's law (Hick-
   Hymen law)
bit
temporal uncertainty

perceptual
   uncertainty
precuing
known probabilities
sequential
   dependencies

stimulus-response
   compatibility
psychological
   refractory period

7

Response Execution

Mary Lou Retton: A VAULT WITHOUT A FAULT

Introduction
Role of Feedback in Motor Control
   • *Closed-loop Control*
   • *Open-loop Control*
   • *A Closed/Open Loop Continuum*
   • *Hierarchical Control*

Factors Contributing to Motor Control
   • *Mechanical Factors*
   • *Neurological-Reflexive Factors*
   • *Synergies*

Factors Influencing Movement Production
   • *After-Contraction Phenomenon*
   • *Tonic Neck Response*

HIGHLIGHT: Walking Machines
FINAL COMMENT
KEY TERMS

Mary Lou Retton: A VAULT WITHOUT A FAULT

She was 16 years old, small and stocky, with a big grin and bubbly disposition. On this Friday night in 1984, the Pauley Pavillion in Los Angeles was charged with excitement and the eyes of the United States were on her. Mary Lou Retton was poised to do what no American woman had ever done—win the gold in Olympic gymnastics. Not just the gold in one event, but a gold medal in the all-around. Retton was the reigning American all-around champ and had not lost a meet in the past year and a half, but she had very little international experience.

The evening had begun with the entrance of Retton and two other U.S. female competitors before a crowd of 9000 excited spectators. In the photographers' pit was her coach, Bela Karolyi. He was there unofficially, but every time he yelled instructions, Retton nodded and punched at the air—a sign that she was "fired up."

Based on the compulsory and optional rounds, Mary Lou had a 0.15 lead (39.525 to 39.375) over Romania's Ecaterin Szabo, but the experts gave her little chance to hold the lead. In the first rotation, Szabo drew the balance beam and Retton the uneven bars. As the crowd watched amazed, Szabo performed four back handsprings in a row—something no other elite woman gymnast had ever attempted. The score: a 10. The best Retton could do was 9.85. They were tied at 49.375.

Mary Lou Retton did something that no other American woman had ever done. She won the gold medal in Olympic gymnastics.

CHAPTER OBJECTIVES

- To understand the role of feedback in the execution of movement.

- To compare and contrast closed and open loop control.

- To understand the advantages and disadvantages of closed and open loop control.

- To appreciate the role that mechanical and reflexive factors play in the control of movement.

- To identify factors that bias the control of movement.

The second rotation sent Retton to the beam and Szabo to the floor exercise. Szabo's performance, nearly flawless—scored 9.95. Retton managed a respectable 9.80. The score was 59.325 to 59.175 in Szabo's favor. The experts' prediction that Szabo would win seemed about to come true.

But Retton and Bela Karolyi were not about to quit. Earlier in the day, Mary Lou had said, "Well, at least she's [Szabo] about my size. But what she doesn't know about me is that I'm tougher than she is." Mary Lou knew she was behind, but she also knew that she had the floor exercise and the vault coming up—her best events. As she moved to the floor exercise, she stopped, looked toward Bela, threw her fists into the air, then squared her shoulders to begin. The mighty mite began with a stunt that only she could perform, an unbelievable double-back somersault in the layout position. Three more versions of double-backs led to a spectacular dismount. Could it be a 10? Yes! Szabo's vaults earned a 9.90.

Szabo led 69.225 to 69.175, but the stage was set for the final event. Retton planned a layout-back somersault vault with a double twist. No other woman could do it! She looked at Bela, threw her fists into the air, squared her shoulders, and ran down the runway into history. Score: 10. Even though the score would not count, she was required to make another vault. Perfect again! The final scores were 79.125 for Szabo and 79.175 for Retton. On that night, the United States gained a bona fide Olympic heroine we could all look down to.

■ ■ ■

Mary Lou Retton's gymnastic success did not come overnight. At age 12 she had moved from her hometown of Fairmont, West Virginia, to Houston, Texas, to train with Bela Karolyi, the former national coach of Romania. Karolyi, who had trained Nadia Comaneci, winner of three Olympic gold medals in the 1976 Games, had defected to this country in 1981.

Retton stressed that "Bela can really teach, I've learned so much from him. Many long hours were spent in the gymnasium . . . repetition, feedback, repetition, and experimentation. Somehow, after a lot of bumps and bruises, it got easier as if I could float." Retton could execute extremely difficult stunts and routines flawlessly. How was this possible? How could she so skillfully control her muscles?

Introduction

After Retton decided to perform a routine on the floor exercise, vault, uneven bars, or balance beam, she had to rely on information processing to execute her routine. The **response execution** stage of information processing involves the formulation of the specific commands to the musculature. To execute a vault, for instance, the appropriate musculature must be turned on and off in an exact sequence. Changes in posture must be effected to maintain balance prior to changes in limb position. Force is regulated by increasing the number and/or synchronization of the motor units contributing to the movement, and commands must be sent to the individual muscles. One small mistake—a command out of sequence or occurring too soon—and the judges would deduct points from Retton's score.

The planning that occurs in the response execution stage required to execute a gymnastics routine or a simple everyday task can be likened to the process of composing a musical score for a piano. The result of the act of composing is the musical score that specifies the unique features of the music. For the purpose of the analogy, consider each piano key as a motor unit and the pedals as a method of altering the excitability of the motor system. Remember that the pedals on a piano are used to dampen or heighten the resonance of the note (key) being played. The musical score is a plan that contains information about not only which keys are to be played, but also the sequence, timing, intensity, and/or resonance of the notes. Action plans must be specified similarly. Motor units must be innervated in the proper sequence, and the commands must be metered out at appropriate time intervals. Intensity, in the case of motor commands, refers to the force or number of motor units. Notes (keys) are the building blocks of a musical composition just as motor units are the fundamental units from which movements are composed. The end result, if you are a Mozart, is an ageless musical score or, if you are a Mary Lou Retton, an olympic gold medal.

Role of Feedback in Motor Control

The central nervous system is continually receiving feedback from the various sensory receptors. Consider the information Retton's senses were relaying to her brain. The feedback is unquestionably used in the selection of a response and the formulation of the action plan. The question that remains, however, is the extent to which this feedback is or can be utilized in the control of an ongoing movement. Was Retton actively processing information during her floor exercise routine or had she practiced the routine to the extent that it could be executed automatically? This question has been debated in the literature for years (see Adams, 1971, and Schmidt, 1976, for reviews).

Closed-Loop Control

According to closed-loop theory (Adams, 1971), feedback can be used not only to plan and initiate movements but also to adjust the progress of an ongoing movement. In threading a needle, for example, as you move the needle and the thread closer together, it may become necessary to engage in additional information-processing activities to complete the task. On the basis of feedback, it may become apparent that the thread is not moving on a trajectory to meet the eye of the needle. This information is then processed and a corrected trajectory is effected. The sequence may be repeated until the thread successfully passes through the eye of the needle. In a sense, Retton had to "thread the needle" in her beam exercise. If she sensed the slightest imbalance during her performance, she would have to make an adjustment, and hope the judges would not detect it. Adams (1971) states:

> A closed-loop system has feedback, error detection, and error correction as key elements. There is a reference that specifies the desired value for the system, and the output of the system is fed back and compared to the reference for error detection and, if necessary, corrected. The automatic home furnace is a common example. The thermostat setting is the desired value, and the heat output of the furnace is fed back and compared against this reference. If there is a discrepancy the furnace cuts in or out until the error is zero. A closed-loop system is self-regulating by compensating for deviations from the reference. (p. 116)

Closed-loop control does not require detailed initial movement commands. Adjustments based on response produced feedback are used to adjust the progress of the movement. Thus, movement control is regulated by an error nulling process and the movement is completed only when all perceptible error has been eliminated.

Evidence for Closed-Loop Control. A large body of research has demonstrated that under certain conditions, subjects utilize sensory information for the control of movement. In general, the experiments designed to test the extent to which feedback is utilized to control movement degrade or eliminate the sensory information normally available. If motor performance suffers when one or more sources of sensory information are reduced or eliminated, then it can be argued that the information was utilized in the control of movement. Experiments that have manipulated exteroceptive information will be discussed first, followed by experiments related to proprioceptive information.

Keele and Posner (1968b) trained subjects to move a hand-held stylus to a small target (Figure 7.1). After substantial practice at a particular movement time, the room lights were

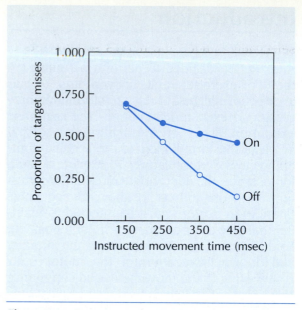

Figure 7.1 *Proportion of target misses as a function of instructed movement time and lighting condition. Whether the lights were on or off did not influence performance at the shorter movement time, but subjects made fewer errors with the lights on when the movement time was longer.*

turned off at the instant the subject left the starting position during 50 percent of the test trials. When movement time was sufficient to allow visual information to be processed (approximately 350 milliseconds), subjects missed the target twice as often when the lights were turned off than when the lights remained on. The proportion of misses for the lights out condition increased to three times that of the lights on condition when movement time was 450 milliseconds. Responses with movement times of 250 milliseconds or less did not appear to be influenced by the elimination of visual information. However, more recent findings (e.g., Zelaznik, Hawkins, & Kisselburgh, 1983) indicate that anticipated visual information can influence responses with movements times as low as 130 milliseconds.

Experimentally manipulating proprioceptive information is not as easy as manipulating exteroceptive information. Attempts to degrade or eliminate proprioceptive information in intact humans have not been totally successful. Sensory feedback has been experimentally reduced by injecting anesthesia to selectively deaden the nerves serving sets of sensory receptors (Smith, 1978) or by applying a blood pressure cuff to the arm to cut off the oxygen supply to the sensory nerves (Laszlo, 1967). The compression block technique (see Laszlo & Bairstow, 1971) involves the application of a sphygmomanometer (blood pressure cuff) to the upper arm. The pressure in the cuff is maintained above that of the systolic blood pressure. This amount of pressure is thought to be sufficient to cause the afferent (sensory) nerves below the cuff not to respond. Proprioception below the cuff is gradually lost as a result of the lack of oxygen. Evidence from a number of studies (Laszlo, 1967; Dahlback, Edstedt, & Stalberg, 1970) has indicated that the application of the cuff selectively affects the sensory receptors and nerves, leaving the efferent fibers (motor) operational. Motor performance while the compression block was applied was, in general, degraded. However, it was not clear whether performance suffered as a result of the degraded feedback or if the efferent nerves were also affected by the cuff.

Advantages and Disadvantages. Closed-loop control has three major advantages and two significant disadvantages. The first advantage is that closed-loop control can be utilized to produce unpracticed movements. As long as the performer can determine the discrepancy between his or her current position and the desired position, a correction can be executed. Second, a great deal of movement flexibility can be exhibited under closed-loop control. This is because movement control is not dependent on specifying in advance the exact movement path required to achieve a movement goal, but rather involves nulling the error between a current movement state and a desired state. Consider the problem of catching a fish in an aquarium or a pet mouse in a cage. The desired outcome is to catch the pet in your hand or in a net. The movement required to achieve this goal may require a very flexible execution plan that is determined by the pet's movement. Last, closed-loop control

can be used to produce very accurate movement outcomes such as threading a needle or removing a splinter from your finger. Movements of this kind require a great deal of precision and are clearly controlled by closed-loop processes.

The price the performer pays for closed-loop control may be significant in some situations. First, the execution of corrections in closed-loop control appears to be attention demanding (Figure 7.2). Moving toward a small target is more attention demanding than moving toward a larger target (Posner & Keele, 1969). This is so presumably because more corrections are required as greater accuracy is required. However, the greater disadvantage of closed-loop control is the time required to execute successive corrections. Keele and Posner (1968) suggest that it takes approximately 200 milliseconds to produce visually based corrections. Later research sug-

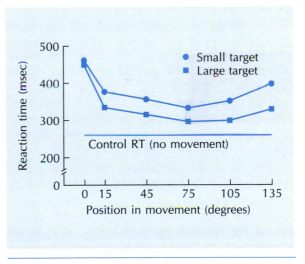

Figure 7.2 *Reaction time to a tone presented at various positions in the movement to small and large targets. When the tone was presented, the subject depressed a response key as quickly as possible with the hand not used to produce the movement to the target. The increase in reaction time over the control condition is thought to represent the amount of attention required at that specific point in the production of the movement to the target. Note that reaction time increases (attention demands increase) for movements to a small target relative to a large target.*

gests that correction can be effected more quickly than 200 milliseconds, but the visual feedback loop is certainly not less than 100 milliseconds (Carlton, 1981; Zelaznik et al., 1983). Thus, closed-loop control may be limited to relatively slow movements.

Open-Loop Control

Open-loop control is based on the concept of a motor program. The motor program concept has a long history (James, 1890; Lashley, 1917) in explaining behavior that cannot be easily explained by closed-loop principles. A **motor program** was defined in 1968 as a "set of muscle commands that are structured before a movement sequence begins, and that allows the sequence to be carried out uninfluenced by peripheral feedback" (Keele, 1968, p. 387). This definition suggested that a motor program was the biological analog to a computer program. This analogy may be unfortunate, because the nervous system is quite different from a computer and a motor program may be quite different from the simple computer programs with which most of us are familiar. However, one useful aspect of the analogy is that more sophisticated computer programs can be designed to be somewhat flexible in their operation and can be instructed to receive input from the operator or some sensing device.

Consider the many movements you execute each day that appear to be controlled almost automatically. These movements may be controlled by a motor program. Many experts believe that at least parts of Mary Lou Retton's gymnastics routines would have to be controlled by a motor program. The routines are extremely well practiced and consistently performed. Indeed, many coaches tell their advanced gymnasts not to think about the routine—just do it, let it flow. Could it be that these athletes have developed motor programs? Here is how Bela Karolyi expressed it:

> Someone should be able to sneak up and drag you out at midnight and push you out on some strange floor, and you should be able to do your entire routine sound asleep in your pajamas. Without a mistake. That's the secret. It's got to be a natural reaction.

Evidence for Open-Loop Control. The evidence of motor programs in animals is rather convincing. For example, Wilson (1961) demonstrated that locusts, after surgical preparation to deprive them of sensory feedback, exhibited relatively complex wing movements that closely resembled the wing movements of intact locusts in flight. Although substantial evidence exists for motor programlike activity in animals (also see Nottebohm, 1970), including monkeys (Taub & Berman, 1968), it is not clear to what extent this evidence may be extrapolated to humans. In fact, Schmidt (1975) suggests that the arguments for a motor program are generally default or anecdotal in nature. Schmidt (1975) explains:

> There is really no direct human evidence of a motor program; centralists reason that there is no other known means of producing movements; thus programs must be the explanation. Actually, it should be shown either (a) that feedback is present in movement but not used, or (b) that feedback is not present and movement can still occur. Strictly, neither of these possibilities has been shown experimentally. (p. 231)

In fact, Schmidt (1975) acknowledges that it may be impossible to prove the existence of motor programs.

However, three lines of research have resulted in findings that can be interpreted to be consistent with the motor program concept. One tack is to attempt to observe motor control when feedback is eliminated or reduced. If controlled movement is exhibited in the absence of feedback, some form of program must be responsible for the motor commands. Lashley (1917) describes a patient who lost sensory information from his lower limbs after an accidental gunshot. Yet, the patient could position his limbs relatively well in the absence of feedback. Similarly, a man affected by a disease that eliminated sensory feedback could sequentially touch his thumb to each finger of his hand and touch his finger to his nose with his eyes shut (Marsden, Rothwell, & Dell, 1984).

The second line of research consistent with the motor program notion utilizes a more behavioral approach. These researchers manipulate the demands of the task (number of movement segments) and record the time required to initiate the movement. Henry and Rogers (1960) reasoned that increasing the "complexity" of the movement should not affect reaction time if closed loop processes were responsible for the production of the movement. However, if the movement was preplanned, increased difficulty should be reflected in increased reaction time. Henry and Rogers (1960) found reaction time to systematically increase as the number of segments in the movement was increased (Figure 7.3). The simplest movement only required the subject to release the reaction time key. The more complex movements required the subject to release the key and strike either one or two suspended tennis balls. A large number of experiments have yielded similar results and have generally been interpreted as evidence of increased preplanning of the response (see Klapp, 1980).

Perhaps the most convincing evidence (also the most debated) for motor programs arises from the simple demonstration that skilled movements can be executed too rapidly for feedback to intervene in the control process. It seems quite unlikely that a movement could be initiated, sensory information processed, errors detected, and corrections initiated in very short movement times (less than 200 milliseconds). Although researchers continue to debate the time required to process feedback, it appears that something more than 100 milliseconds is required to process proprioceptive information (Chernikoff & Taylor, 1952) and visual information (Carlton, 1981). Yet, subjects can initiate, carry out, and terminate movements in less than 100 milliseconds.

Similarly, what would happen if the demands of a task were changed after a motor program was initiated? If an initiated motor program carries a movement sequence to completion without the aid of feedback, the program should not be influenced by demands introduced after the program was initiated and before the movement was completed. Slater-Hammel (1960) asked subjects to depress a response key while watching the hand of a clock that moved at one revolution per second. The task was to lift the finger (this stopped the clock hand) from the response key such that the clock hand would stop at the target position (the "8" or 800 milliseconds after starting). Subjects were told not to respond if the clock hand stopped before reaching the target. On a few trials the clock hand was stopped before reaching the target position. Figure 7.4 illustrates the probability of the subjects' lifting their fingers before the clock hand reached the target position. These data suggest that the action was set into motion about 150 milliseconds before the actual response occurred and that it could not be inhibited once triggered.

Advantages and Disadvantages. Open-loop control has two major advantages and two disadvantages. The first advantage is so obvious that it could easily be overlooked. Open-loop control can produce very rapid movement or movements under conditions in which normal feedback sources have been

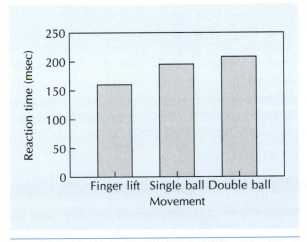

Figure 7.3 *Reaction time to movements of differing complexity. Note that reaction time increases as movement complexity increases.*

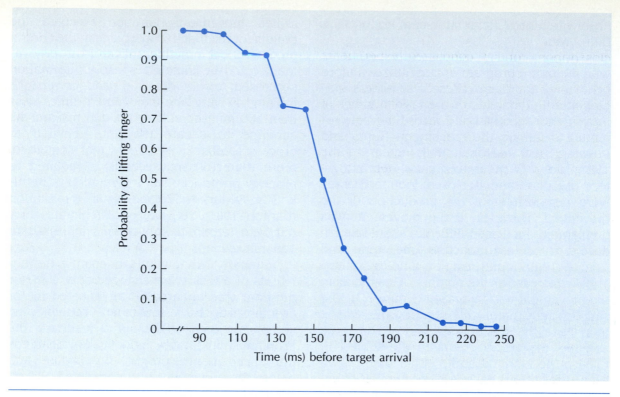

Figure 7.4 *Probability of lifting the finger even though the clock hand has stopped (Slater-Hammel, 1960).*

eliminated or disrupted. Second, because open-loop control is prestructured, feedback does not have to be processed during the movement, and attention normally allocated to making corrections (and presumably other information processing resources) is not tied up. This permits the performer to engage in other strategic processing that would not be possible if closed-loop control were employed.

The disadvantages of open-loop control are also somewhat obvious. As Adams (1976) states:

> An open-loop system has no feedback or mechanism for error regulation. The input events for a system exert their influence, the system effects its transformation on the input, and the system has an output. . . . A traffic light with fixed timing snarls traffic when the load is heavy and impedes the flow when traffic is light. The system has no compensatory capability. (p. 89)

Open-loop control is not effective when the environmental conditions are constantly changing such that the demands of the movement cannot be determined in advance. Likewise, movements that require a great deal of precision may require extensive amounts of practice for an efficient motor program to be developed.

A Closed/Open Loop Continuum

In the 1970s, particularly as a result of theoretical proposals put forward by Adams (1971) who argued for closed-loop control and by Schmidt (1975) who favored open-loop control, researchers debated the viability of closed- and open-loop principles for explaining motor control. Initially, the debate tended

154

to focus on providing evidence for one mode of control over the other. Those arguing for closed-loop control conducted experiments that utilized slow, self-paced tasks and/or tracking tasks that required the subjects to compensate for changes in the target position. Researchers defending the open-loop position tended to use discrete, rapid tasks that could be preplanned. In the late 1970s and early 1980s, the split began to narrow. Researchers tended to discuss motor control in terms of the relative contributions of feedback. This led to the view that closed- and open-loop control defined a continuum of feedback utilization during the progress of the movement (see Chapter 5). MacNeilage and MacNeilage (1973) state:

> The need for peripheral sensory feedback can be thought of as inversely proportional to the ability of the central nervous system to predictively determine . . . every essential aspect of the following act. (p. 424)

Thus, feedback was thought to be relatively more important for control purposes for continuous, slow, and unpracticed movements. Alternatively, reliance on feedback was thought to diminish for discrete, rapid, and well-learned movements.

Hierarchical Control

The **hierarchical control** model proposes that some higher level in the system is responsible for monitoring feedback and making adjustments, and that lower levels are responsible for carrying out those decisions. It may be useful to think of hierarchical control as the motor equivalent to a military command center. A general (or other high-level officer) receives intelligence reports concerning the progress of the troops in achieving some objective. At periodic intervals, the command center has enough information indicating that the original orders must be adjusted. A new order is issued. The troops receive the new command and are expected to comply. The troops continue the original course until new orders are received. In this analogy the troops execute their orders in an open-loop mode and the general issues commands in a closed-loop mode. Thus, hierarchical control can be considered a hybrid of open- and closed-loop control.

Consider an experiment conducted by Pew (1966). Subjects attempted to control the movement of a trace dot displayed on an oscilloscope by alternately pressing two control buttons. One button caused the dot to accelerate to the right and the other resulted in acceleration to the left. The object was to keep the dot centered on the screen. Early in practice (Figure 7.5), subjects appeared to press a button, observe the result, then press the other button (closed-loop control). Later in practice, subjects began to string together very rapid sequences of button presses (open-loop control), interrupting the sequence only when the dot "drifted" away from the center of the screen. Even though errors were constantly present (because the dot could never be main-

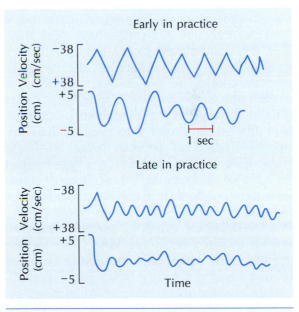

Figure 7.5 *Performance tracing from a button-pressing task in which subjects alternated pressing two buttons in an attempt to keep a dot centered on an oscilloscope. Early in practice (top), subjects pressed a button approximately 2 to 3 times per second, while late in practice (bottom), the buttons were pressed approximately 5 to 8 times per second.*

tained on the center line), corrective action was not issued until the dot began to move away from the center consistently. Thus, each button press was not controlled on the basis of feedback, but rather by open-loop processes with occasional intervention of closed-loop control (hierarchical control).

Kohl and Shea (1990) found evidence that suggested that hierarchical control was a strategic decision made by the subject. Pew (1966), and later Martiniuk (1976), had suggested that practice experiences were required to move from closed-loop to open-loop control and then to hierarchical control. Kohl and Shea allowed a group of subjects to observe other subjects performing a variation of the "Pew task." While the subjects performing the task responded initially using closed-loop control, they eventually executed control indicative of hierarchical control. However, the observers controlled the movement of the dot in a hierarchical fashion on their first attempt of actual practice.

Factors Contributing to Motor Control

The control of human movement is assisted in very subtle but often important ways by a number of mechanical and neurological factors that potentially reduce the complexity of the control process. For many years motor learning and control theorists have been troubled by accounts of motor control that requires the higher centers of the brain to directly control all the muscles involved in movement. Bernstein (1967) noted that it was difficult to imagine the mental work (information processing) required to elicit all the commands needed to produce even a simple movement. He reasoned that the system must be capable of reducing the number of direct commands required of the higher centers of the brain.

Consider, for example, the processes involved in locomotion (walking). The turning on and off of motor units needed for walking requires a script many times more complicated than the most intricate musical score. However, McMahon (1984) demonstrates that the swing phase of walking can be achieved without higher level control of muscle activation. That is, the swing phase need not be specifically controlled. Rather, the system can rely on the mechanical properties of the leg, gravity, and neurological reflexes to accomplish the swing phase. This is particularly important because it suggests that we can take advantage of factors that are available and produce a coordinated movement that requires less physical and/or mental effort. The next sections highlight some of the factors that may be exploited to reduce the complexity of movement control.

Mechanical Factors

The forces exerted in movement can be classified in two general categories: (1) forces attributable to contraction of the muscle fibers and (2) those attributable to the elastic properties of the muscle-tendons. The potential force resulting from contraction is greatest when the muscle is at an optimal length. However, the potential forces decrease as the muscle is lengthened or shortened (Figure 7.6). At optimal length a maximum number of cross-bridges between the muscle filaments are available, and maximum tension can be produced. The filaments are pulled apart as the muscle lengthens, and the tension that can be generated via contraction decreases. Likewise, the cross-bridges overlap as the muscle is shortened, which interferes with the production of force.

HIGHLIGHT

Walking Machines

Most children learn to walk at about one year of age. Within a few years, walking becomes completely automatic, requiring little or no conscious thought or attention. From a motor control standpoint, however, walking is anything but simple. This point is emphasized by the fascination people have had with building walking machines.

To build a walking machine, it is important to identify the essential characteristics of walking. Raibert and Sutherland (1983) list the following five conditions as basic for a walking machine:

1. It must regulate the sequence of footfalls.
2. It must not tip over.
3. It must distribute load and lateral forces among its legs.
4. It must ensure that the legs do not move beyond their travel limits or bump into each other.
5. It must ensure that chosen footholds provide adequate support.

This list of conditions is not easy to fulfill. For many years, engineers attempted the task without success, until 1966, when a four-legged walking machine was built at the University of Southern California (McMahon, 1984). This machine required a human driver but was too small to support a person. A larger version, built by General Electric in 1968, was servo driven such that the front legs moved when the driver's arms moved and the back legs moved when the driver's legs moved. This type of control was depicted in the loaders used in the science fiction movie *Alien*. The contraption was very awkward and difficult to maneuver.

A six-legged machine was built in the early 1980s. Each leg had a pair of hydraulic actuators controlled by a computer. The computer shifted the flow of hydraulic fluid from one leg to the contralateral leg. This resulted in a process much like reciprocal inhibition so important to human locomotion. In addition, the hydraulic system made many adjustments automatically based on the forces acting on the machine. Thus, the machine, like a human, exploited the physical characteristics of the system.

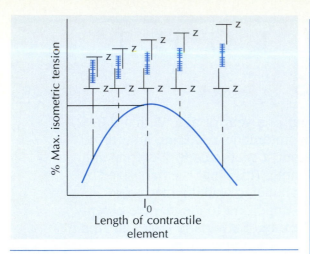

Figure 7.6 *Tension produced by the contractile elements of the muscle at different lengths. Relationships of the contractile elements of the muscle at the various lengths are illustrated at points on the length tension curve.*

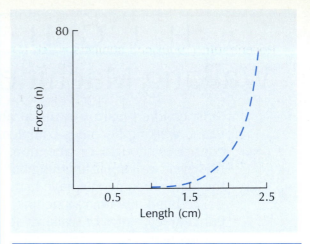

Figure 7.7 *Tension derived from the elastic qualities of the muscle-tendon as a function of muscle length.*

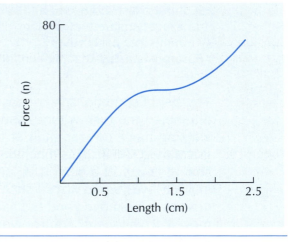

Figure 7.8 *Tension derived from contracion elements and elastic qualities of the muscle-ligament.*

Muscles and tendons also have elastic qualities that can be exploited in the control of movement. These elastic qualities can be classified as serial or as parallel elastic components. Muscles have a substantial amount of connective tissues in series with the contractile components; these are called *serial elastic components.* The connective tissues that surround the contractile element are called *parallel elastic components.* These elastic tissues probably dampen or "smooth out" the process of shortening or lengthening the muscle. The parallel elastic components, which behave something like a spring or elastic band, are involved in the stretching of the muscles, tendons, and ligaments. When stretched, these connective tissues exert passive forces (Figure 7.7). Winter (1990) suggests that "during most human movement the presence of elastic elements is not too significant, but during high-performance movements such as jumping it is responsible for storage of energy as a muscle lengthens immediately prior to rapid shortening" (p. 175).

These mechanical forces can be used alone or in conjunction with forces derived from muscle contraction to produce a controlled result. The resulting force available to the performer (Figure 7.8) is the sum of the active (contraction) and passive (elastic) compo-

nents (Ralston, Inman, Strait, & Shaffrath, 1947). It is interesting to note that children will rapidly lower themselves after completing a pull-up in an attempt to "bounce-up" for the next attempt. Apparently, they have learned that a certain amount of force can be generated by stretching the muscle-tendon. Children find a pull-up much harder to do if the instructor requires them to come to rest at the bottom. It is also interesting that children often get "stuck" just before their chin gets to the bar. This is the point at which the muscle is so shortened that the force generated via contraction is reduced.

Rosenbaum (1990) had subjects reach for a handle in order to turn it from a starting position to a target position (Figure 7.9A). A number of starting and target positions were utilized. Rosenbaum states:

> We found that a simple 'rule of thumb' accounted for their behavior. Subjects adopted relatively awkward arm postures when first grabbing the handle, but these postures ensured that by the end of the handle rotation the subject's arms were always at or close to the resting position. (p. 10)

Apparently the subjects were taking advantage of their limbs' mechanical properties (Figure 7.9B). They essentially "wound up" their arm in an attempt to move the handle to the target position. It is not only significant that subjects chose this strategy, but that the strategy was effective in reducing the variability in their responses. Increasingly, researchers are discovering the extent to which the physical properties of the body and the environment enhance movement efficiency and facilitate movement control (see Thelen, Kelso, & Fogel, 1987; Bizzi & Mussa-Ivaldi, 1989). Why does a golf stroke involve a back swing before a down swing? Perhaps golfers have learned that to "coil up" dynamically before the downward phase of the swing is important to consistent movement production. Newspaper writers described Mary Lou Retton as "a coiled spring." Clearly, athletes utilize the elastic qualities of their muscles.

Neurological-Reflexive Factors

Neurological-reflexive factors contribute to movement control efficiency because these automatic processes reduce the number of commands that have to be formulated to produce controlled movement. For example, **reciprocal inhibition** is a genetically defined reflex that tends to inhibit the flexors of a joint when the extensors are activated. This reflex, coupled with the **crossed-extensor reflex**,

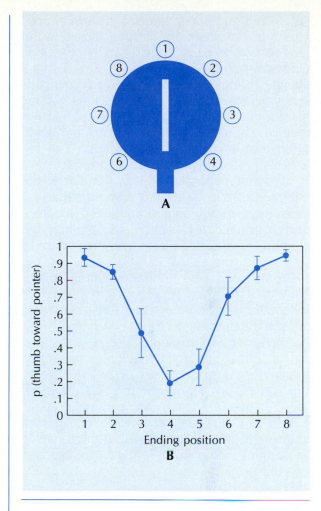

Figure 7.9 (A) Apparatus used in a handle-turning experiment. The subjects' task was to grasp the handle and turn the pointer to cover up setting #1. The starting position was varied to include all positions (2–8). (B) The graph indicates the probability of the subjects' grasping the handle with the thumb toward the pointer. For many conditions this required that the subject start in an awkward position but end up in a comfortable position.

where-by the extensors of one limb are activated when the flexors of the contralateral limb are activated, is thought to reduce greatly the number of central commands required in such actions as walking.

The control of locomotion in animals and humans has been proposed to involve what has come to be known as a **central pattern generator**. This neural circuit, when activated, is thought to produce a rhythm of activation of extensors and flexors, including the associated reflexes previously cited. Shik, Orlovskii, and Severin (1968) severed the spinal cord of a cat, separating the higher centers where perception and consciousness reside from the lower levels. The cat could not receive stimulation from the limbs and could not execute voluntary movements. The cat was supported as pictured in Figure 7.10.

When the spinal cord was stimulated, the cat produced a patterned response that resembled normal locomotion. Indeed, locomotion continued for a short while when the stimulus was turned off. In fact, the pattern of movement increased as the speed of the treadmill increased. Apparently, the higher centers of the brain are required to initiate the locomotor sequence but are not required to control the process.

Reflexive adjustments also simplify the motor control process. Consider the monosynaptic reflex termed the stretch reflex. This reflex relies on **alpha-gamma coactivation** (see Chapter 2). This reflex can very rapidly (30–40 milliseconds) respond to unexpected changes in muscle length. Adjustments made to stepping into a shallow hole or in response to picking up an object that is heavier than expected probably involve this process. However, this reflex plays a much more common role in smoothing out our movements. If this reflexive process was not available, smooth graded responses would be much more difficult to execute. It is interesting to note that some muscle types have a higher proportion of muscle spindles to muscle fibers than other muscle types. In fact, muscles that are typically used for slow, refined movements tend to have a greater number of spindles than muscles generally responsible for higher force, more ballistic responses.

Many other reflexes are present in humans and are thought by many motor control experts to play a vital role in motor control. Reviews by Easton (1972, 1978) and Stein (1982) detail the possible role of reflexes in movement control.

Synergies

Muscle-tendon groups are functionally combined to support movement across joints and neurologically linked as a result of the neural circuits in the spinal cord. The functional

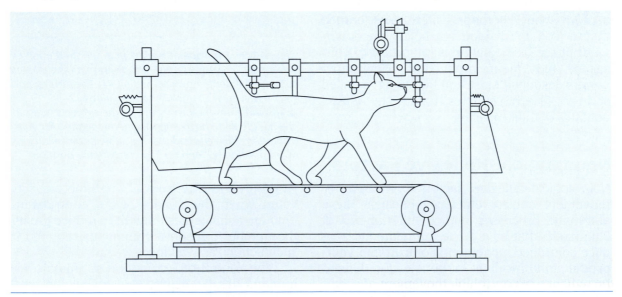

Figure 7.10 *Cat supported on a treadmill in the study of spinal mechanisms by Shik, Orlovskii, and Severin (1966).*

ing to control the movement of a marionette. Each joint or body part of the marionette is connected by a string that the puppeteer can use to control the movement. Does the puppeteer attempt to control each string independently or have these artists learned that they can link the strings together to decrease the difficulty but still achieve relatively complex movements? Yes, these artists can configure the strings so that relatively complex movements such as walking (including not only leg movements but also head and arm movements) can be realistically created by simply tilting the paddle to which the strings are attached back and forth.

Engineers use synergic principles in designing machinery. Consider an airplane control example provided by Tuller, Turvey, and Fitch (1982). They noted that the ailerons on the wings, the elevators on the tail, and the rudder on the tailfin of an airplane must be coordinated to achieve efficient flight control.

Each joint or body part of the marionette is attached to a string that the puppeteer can use to control the movement. Puppeteers do not try to control each string independently, rather they link the strings together in a manner that decreases the difficulty of controlling so many strings but still allows them to achieve relatively complex movements.

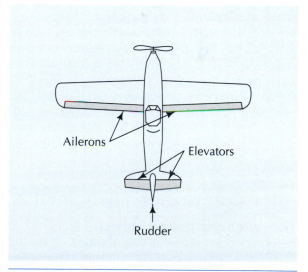

The ailerons on the wings, the elevators on the tail, and the rudder on the tailfin of an airplane are not controlled independently by the pilot. Engineers have found that they can reduce the load on the pilot without sacrificing maneuverability by linking these systems together (Tuller, Turvey, & Finch, 1982).

group formed by this linkage between muscle groups is termed a **synergy**. What does this mean? The activation of one muscle group is related in subtle but potentially important ways to other muscle groups. Bernstein (1967) and later Turvey (1977) noted that these linkages may play an important role in reducing the difficulty of controlling movement.

To understand the concept of synergies, consider the example of a puppeteer attempt-

Would it be effective for the engineers to design the control system so that the pilot had to control the ailerons, elevators, and rudder independently? No! This would overload the pilot. Evasive maneuvers would be almost impossible. As Tuller et al. (1982) point out:

> What is needed is a way of organizing the parts of an airplane so as to simplify its control without losing its desirable maneuverability. One way to do this is to link parts of the system together. First, the aileron and the rudder can be linked into a functional relationship; when the aileron on the left goes up by one position, the rudder goes to the right by one position. . . . Next, the right aileron can be linked to the rudder so that when the right aileron moves up the rudder moves to the left. . . . Think of what we are attempting to do. We are trying to make the airplane manageable. (p. 257)

The point of this discussion is not to explain how marionettes or airplanes work but to describe efficient control systems. There is every reason to believe that the human control system is the most elegant system ever assembled and that synergies are an integral part of this system. Chapter 8 continues the discussion of coordinative structures.

Factors Influencing Movement Production

What happens when you play a record or tape on different stereo systems? Small but significant changes in the music may be detected even though the stored music has not changed. Similar effects may be noted for movements produced when the neuromotor system is changed in very small ways. Motor program theories suggest that well-learned rapid movements are generated from a set of prestructured commands (Keele, 1968; Schmidt, 1975). The motor program concept suggests that movements are executed with little or no feedback. Therefore, if the performer's neuromotor system is changed, the resultant performance may be biased accordingly. The following section discusses two sources of biases that appear to influence the execution of learned responses.

After-Contraction Phenomenon

The **after-contraction effect** refers to a heightened motor response thought to be the result of a change in the excitatory state of the neuromuscular system (Hutton, Enoka, & Suzuki, 1984). The effect is typically observed as an increase in the force elicited by a voluntary contraction. By the late nineteenth century, there existed a number of documented demonstrations of prior neuromuscular activity that influenced subsequent responding. Salmon (1916) and independently Kohnstamm (1915) reported an involuntary repetition of an original movement and correlated sensations of lightness or floating of a relaxed limb following contraction. Their demonstrations are easily replicated by having a standing subject exert force with the arm outward against a wall for a brief period of time. The after-contraction effect is elicited by having the naive subject relax and close his or her eyes. This procedure results in an involuntary upward (abduction) movement accompanied by a feeling of lightness in the affected limb.

There are numerous examples of a previous contraction and/or limb movement influencing subsequent movement of the same limb. In a timing task, Weeks and Shea (1984) found that subjects responded either too quickly or too slowly depending on the previous response. When the previous response required a fast movement, subjects tended to respond too fast in the attempted production of a slower movement. Likewise, when the previous response required a slow movement, subjects tended to respond too slowly to the production of a faster response.

Shea, Shebilske, Kohl, and Guadagnoli (1991) conducted two experiments to investigate the direct influence of a prior contraction on the execution of a learned dynamic force production task. The results indicated that as the intensity of the precontraction increased, the magnitude of the induced bias increased (see Figure 7.11). The results of the Shea et al. (1991) experiments indicate that a simple contraction temporarily biases subsequent learned responding with the intensity of the previous contraction related to the magnitude of the bias.

From a practical standpoint, it is important to note that the duration of the precontraction used in the Shea et al. (1991) experiments was only 20 seconds and that even an intensity as

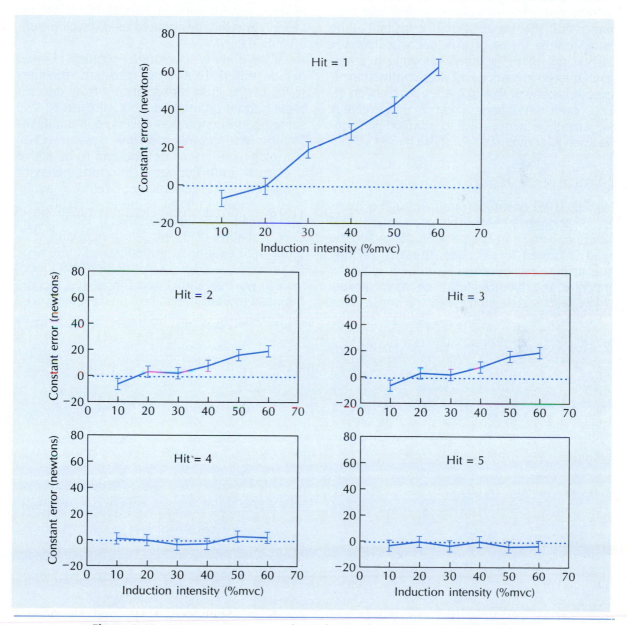

Figure 7.11 *Mean constant errors by induction force (Shea, Shebilske, Kohl, & Guadagnoli, 1991).*

low as 30 percent MVC produced substantial biases. Indeed, Hutton et al. (1984) found precontractions of 5 seconds duration to produce strong after-contraction effects. Contractions of this duration and intensity may be experienced on many occasions in sports, work, and everyday life. For example, the hitting of a batter who has just used a weighted bat or donut to "warm-up," the gentle toss of a pitcher to first base on a bunted ball after the delivery of a fastball to the batter, or the throw of a fielder who has just pushed up off the ground following a diving catch may be influenced by after-contraction effects. It is conceivable that after-contraction effects exert an influence on many everyday movement sequences and that skilled performers learn to compensate for these biases.

Tonic Neck Response

Fukuda (1961) demonstrated through a number of photographs of athletes, dancers, and other performers in competition that when the head is turned to one side, the arm on that side (ipsilateral) becomes extended while the opposite arm (contralateral) becomes flexed. This effect is consistent with the **tonic neck reflex** exhibited by infants and has been labeled the **tonic neck response** in adults. Motor development researchers have noted that reflexive behavior such as the tonic neck reflex signifies a relative immaturity of the nervous system (Gesell, 1952). As the nervous system matures, the reflex is thought to be gradually phased out or counteracted by other reflexes and/or volition. Persistence of the reflex is generally designated as a developmental enigma.

In the early twentieth century, it was demonstrated that head position modifies tonus of the limb musculature of the decerebrate animal (Mangus & de Kleijn, 1912). The same phenomenon was observed in adults affected with central nervous system (CNS) pathology, but it was not thought to be active in normal adult humans. Therefore, behavior consistent with the tonic neck reflex in adults was generally thought to be an indication of widespread CNS disease (Byers, 1938). However, Hellebrandt, Houtz, Partridge, and Walters (1956) examined the effects of tonic neck response on maximal wrist flexion and extension in normal adults and found that turning the head toward the limb of interest enhanced

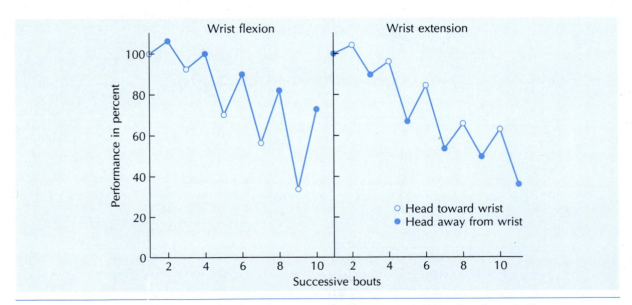

Figure 7.12 *Maximal force exerted over trials as a function of head position (Hellebrandt, Houtz, Partridge, & Walters, 1956). MVC = maximum voluntary contraction.*

maximal wrist extension and diminished wrist flexion of that limb (Figure 7.12)

More recently Shea, Guadagnoli, and Dean (1993) documented the effect of changing head position on the production of learned forces. The forces used in their experiments were more indicative of those utilized in everyday movements. The results indicated that head position does affect the production of a learned force. The analysis revealed that subjects tended to produce more force when their heads were turned toward the limb relative to the center head position and less force when their heads were turned away from the limb. This effect was relatively consistent at each force requirement. The findings of the Shea et al. (1991) experiments using submaximal force production tasks as well as those of Hellebrandt et al. (1956) for maximal force production clearly demonstrate the effect of head position. Presumably performers are able to compensate for the changes in internal state resulting from changes in head position. This may be due in part to the performer's not being able to perceive the subtle changes in internal states.

The tonic neck reflex was demonstrated by Fukuda (1961) through a number of photographs of athletes, dancers, and other performers in competition.

FINAL COMMENT

The degree to which feedback is utilized in the control of movement may be dependent on a number of factors including the time available, the degree of accuracy required, the stability of conditions, and the degree of practice. When a great deal of accuracy is required, the conditions are constantly changing, and the task is unpracticed, relatively more feedback is required (closed loop), and the movement tends to be slower and graded. On the other hand, rapid well-learned movements in stable environments are likely to be performed relatively feedback free (open loop).

KEY TERMS

response execution
closed-loop control
open-loop control
motor program
hierarchical control

reciprocal inhibition
crossed-extensor
    reflex
central pattern
    generator

alpha-gamma
    coactivation
synergy
after-contraction
    effect

tonic neck reflex
tonic neck response

8
Theoretical Perspectives on Motor Control

Nan Davis' Story: OVERCOMING PARALYSIS

Closed-loop Theory: Adams, 1971
- *Memory States*
- *Criticisms of Adams' Theory*

Schema Theory: Schmidt, 1975
- *Sources of Schema Information*
- *Invariant and Variant Features*
- *Temporal and Spatial Demands of Movement*

Mass-Spring Hypothesis

Coordinative Structures and Multilimb Control

HIGHLIGHT: Training the Deaf to Speak
FINAL COMMENT
KEY TERMS

Nan Davis' Story: OVERCOMING PARALYSIS

Nan Davis was a healthy, active young woman with an exciting future until the accident. What happened to Nan happens at least twenty times a day, roughly 8000 times a year, to someone in the United States. Nan suffered a spinal cord injury and was paralyzed. She would never walk again—or would she?

In 1983, the 22-year-old paraplegic Nan Davis accomplished a seemingly impossible task—she walked across the stage to receive her college diploma. Although Nan was heavily supported by professors on each side, the computer-controlled electrodes and accompanying devices that controlled the stimulation and coordination of her leg muscles gave Nan a temporary sense of autonomy previously unheard of for paralytics. Nan had been the subject of many grueling hours of research in functional neuromuscular stimulation (FNS), a process in which paralyzed limbs are electrically stimulated in order to provide signals that mimic missing neural impulses.

Nan and other carefully selected individuals who have suffered spinal cord injuries have accomplished feats such as walking or riding a bicycle ergometer with the aid of FNS. Others have attained the control required to brush their teeth or feed themselves. For both quadriplegics and paraplegics, these devices can artificially restore function in paralyzed limbs. This promises new and exciting possibilities for independence for these individuals. However, it is most important to realize that

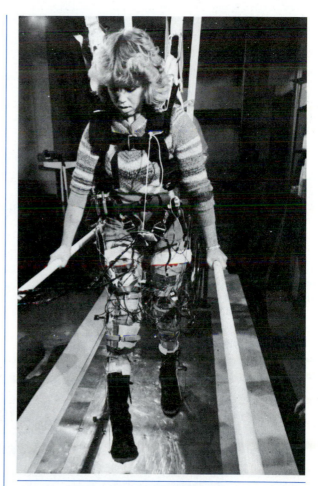

Nan Davis, paralyzed Wright State University student, attracted international attention when she used her own muscles to walk with the assistance of a computer-controlled electrical stimulation system.

- To understand the historical context in which motor learning and control theories were proposed.

- To appreciate the evidence for and against the principles proposed in recent motor learning and control theories.

- To identify experimental evidence in support of or inconsistent with the principles proposed in recent motor learning and control theories.

these techniques are only experimental. A great deal more must be known before such devices can leave the laboratory.

■ ■ ■

Howard Chizeck (1985) reports a tendency for public reports of the technique to exaggerate the accounts and capabilities of FNS devices (also see Rosen, 1985). It is clear that the process of walking, one that most of us take for granted, is a very complex one that is not easily reproduced by computers and electrical stimulation devices.

One reason scientists are not more successful at devising electronic means of control is that we do not fully understand the natural processes involved in control and learning. We understand how individual motor units are controlled and some of the processes involved in the regulation of force, but scientists have yet to get the big picture.

Four contemporary theories of motor control are the subject of this chapter. The theories are presented in chronological order. This progression helps highlight the development of theoretical thought relative to motor control. In many cases, the "new" theoretical formulations were proposed in order to satisfy criticisms or inadequacies of the prevailing theory. The specifics of one theory that held up under scrutiny were retained while those that did not were rejected. In most respects, the first two theoretical proposals can be considered true theories of motor learning and control. The second two proposals are more appropriately termed motor control hypotheses (the distinction between a theory and hypothesis is outlined in Chapter 1). However, these latter proposals offer hope that the processes that govern movement control can someday be understood well enough to help the many paralyzed people like Nan Davis walk again.

Closed-loop Theory: Adams, 1971

At the time that Adams proposed his closed-loop theory of motor learning (Adams, 1971), much of the motor learning research involved slow, linear positioning responses. In order to ground his theorizing upon solid experimental evidence and the laws derived from this evidence, Adams' formal theory was limited to slow positioning responses. However, it is clear from his writings that he believed that the principles of performance and learning that applied to the linear positioning response would hold for the learning of a wide range of movements.

Memory States

The theory proposes two memory states (termed *traces* by Adams). Adams recognized that in order for a system to be capable of detecting its own errors, two memory states would be required. The term *trace* was selected because Adams felt that repeated utilization of the memory left traces in the central nervous system such that learning involved the continued development and strengthening of the correct trace. The theory proposes that the **memory trace** is a modest motor program responsible for initiating a movement in the correct direction. The theory does not indicate that the memory state is developed as a result of practice and therefore is assigned only a modest role in the process of movement control and learning.

The major responsibility for movement control and learning is given a separate, independent memory state. The **perceptual trace** is a reference of correctness representing the feedback qualities of the correct response. After the memory trace is used to initiate a movement, the perceptual trace is continually compared to the response-produced feedback. If the current feedback does not match the perceptual trace, an error is detected, a subsequent discrete correction is executed, a subsequent error analysis is conducted, and this continues until no differences are detected between the response-produced feedback and the perceptual trace. Thus, movement control is regulated by an error nulling process and limited by the quality of the perceptual trace.

Knowledge of results was proposed to play an important role in the development of the perceptual trace. The perceptual trace is thought to represent the collection of traces accumulated with repeated exposures to a task. Since knowledge of results tends to drive the movement closer to the target, the collection of traces laid down when knowledge of

The Suzuki method of learning to play the violin has the student listen to a piece of music repeatedly to establish a reference of correctness for the music before attempting to play. When the student begins to play, he or she should have a reference to evaluate the music they play.

results is provided should represent a closer approximation of the correction response than when knowledge of results is not present. Likewise, any factor that results in inaccurate movement should retard learning. That is, errors are viewed as detrimental to learning and any factor that correctly guides the movement should be beneficial to learning. (Remember this point because it will be important later in this book.) In addition, Adams proposed that a sufficiently developed perceptual trace should be capable of sustaining accurate performance after knowledge of results is withdrawn.

Criticisms of Adams' Theory

Adams' theory was widely questioned on three major points. First, the theory proposes that for each movement, a perceptual trace is developed that is responsible for movement control. Movements that differ even slightly would require different perceptual traces. This poses problems in terms of the storage and retrieval of the large number of perceptual traces that would be required to be accessible for daily life. Second, the theory does not propose how movements that are attempted for the first time would be controlled. Without a perceptual trace, movement control comes to a halt. Last, the theory requires that sufficient time be available for feedback to be processed relative to the perceptual trace. Although estimates of this time required to process feedback vary widely, it is clear that we can execute skilled movements much too quickly for feedback to play the major role in movement control.

Schema Theory: Schmidt, 1975

Partially as a reaction to and result of Adams' closed loop theory of motor skill learning, Schmidt (1975) proposed the **schema theory** of discrete motor skill learning. Although borrowing from Adams' theory, Schmidt's schema theory attempted to respond more effectively to the major concerns that plagued Adams' theory—namely, (1) the production of novel movement, (2) the storage and retrieval of the memory states, and (3) the difficulty in handling the delay in the processing of feedback. Thus, schema theory is based on the concept of a schema and open loop or motor program principles.

As in Adams' theory, Schmidt proposed that two memory states, which he termed *schemata*, were required to control and evaluate movement. A **schema** (the singular of *schemata*) is an abstraction of a set of rules for determining a movement. Because the important features of a potentially large number of specific movements can be abstracted in a schema, memory and retrieval requirements are greatly reduced. In addition, Schmidt proposes that novel movements can be generated because the rules encapsulated in the schema can be applied to new movements within a class of movements. Thus, schema theory proposes that movements are controlled by a **generalizable motor program**.

Sources of Schema Information

Schmidt proposes that four sources of information can be abstracted to form the basis of the motor response schemata (Figure 8.1). The motor response schemata consists of two memory states termed recall and recognition schemata. The **recall schema** is responsible for organizing specific motor programs capable of initiating and controlling movements. After the completion of the movement, the **recognition schema** is responsible for evaluating the movement outcome and updating the recall schema if errors are detected. The evaluation process is accomplished by comparing the actual sensory consequences against the expected sensory consequences.

The first two types of information abstracted in the schemata are determined before the movement is produced and the second two are abstracted after the movement is in progress. The first, termed **initial conditions,** relates to the current status of the organism. It includes current posture, position of the limbs, and external forces acting to stabilize or perturb body position (gravity, wind, an opponent, etc.)—factors that must be considered before a movement can be effectively planned. Second, **response specifications** provide the unique requirements of the specific response to be made (see following discussion of invariant and variant features). The task may require the movement to be made in a specific direction, with a specific muscle group, and with carefully regulated force and/or speed. The response specification determines the manner in which a current response differs from other potential responses controlled by the same generalizable motor

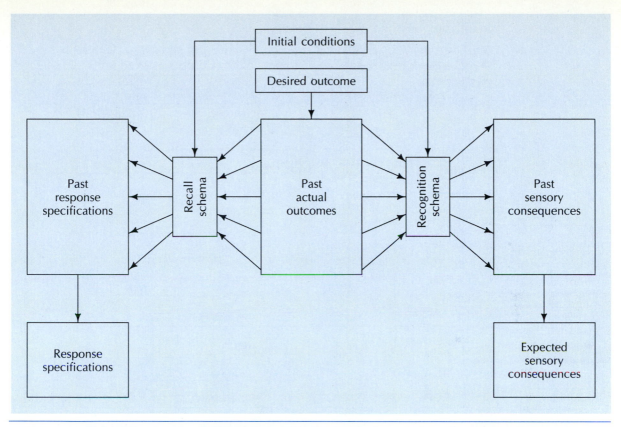

Figure 8.1 *Sources of information used by the recall schema to formulate the response specification and the recognition schema to generate the specific expected sensory consequences of the proposed movement.*

Before a golfer attempts a putt it is important to correctly determine the unique conditions that will influence the movement of the ball. These conditions will determine the variant features of the response.

program. Third, the **sensory consequences** of the movement, consisting of the information transmitted from the various sensory systems during the production of the response, are abstracted. Fourth, the **response outcome** provides information detailing the end result of the movement. This source of information may include knowledge of results. Figure 8.2 illustrates the sequence of events occurring during a trial.

Invariant and Variant Features

The product is a generalizable motor program that when provided with response specifications produces a unique response. The program is composed of **invariant features** that define the generalizable characteristics of the

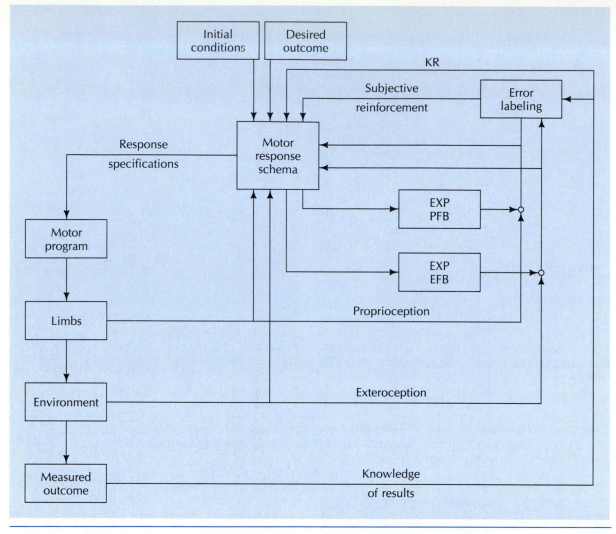

Figure 8.2 *Flow of information as conceptualized by schema theory (EXP PFB = expected proprioceptive feedback; EXP EFB = expected exteroceptive feedback).*

motor program. These features are thought to include the hierarchical characteristics of the movement (termed *order of elements* by Schmidt, 1975), the relative forces, and relative timing. Since the invariant features consist only of the relative characteristics of the movement, the program must be scaled or **parameterized** in order to produce a specific movement. Based on the specific requirements, the **variant features** of the program that must be specified are thought to include the specific muscles to be used, the actual force, and the actual timing of the movement.

Consider a handwriting example (Figure 8.3) first presented by Merton (1972). Assume for the sake of the example that the writing (in cursive) of your name is controlled by a generalizable motor program. As a result of practice experiences, the recall schema is well developed. The invariant features of the generalizable signature program consist of the hierarchical structure such that the order of

Figure 8.3 Invariant features in a handwriting sample are the characteristics that do not change form.

A Able was I ere I saw Elba

B Able was I ere I saw Elba

C Able was I ere I saw Elba

D Able was I ere I saw Elba

E Able was I ere I saw Elba

Figure 8.4 Note the invariances in the five examples of handwriting. Writing with the dominant hand (A), with the dominant arm (wrist immobilized) (B), with the non-dominant hand (C), with the pen held in the teeth (D), and with the pen taped to the foot (E).

the elements (letters) does not change from one execution to another. Likewise, our signature results in a consistent but relative pattern of innervations both in terms of time and force. Specific points in the production of the signature are consistently produced with more force relative to other points, and the flow of the pattern consistently maintains a relative timing or flow pattern.

By parameterizing your generalizable signature program, you can easily produce your signature with the light touch of a felt-tip pen within the lines of fine-lined paper or on an easel (specify muscle groups) or you can scratch your signature on a desk top with a pen knife or with a hard lead pencil (specify actual force). Similarly, your signature can be executed very quickly or very slowly (specify actual timing). Depending on the specific demands, you can produce your signature in many ways without violating the invariant features or basic structure derived from the recall schema.

Raibert (1977) offers an interesting example of his writing of a sentence that is consistent with the concept of a generalizable motor program (Figure 8.4). He drastically manipulated the muscle groups used to execute the movement by writing in five different ways: (1) normally, (2) with his wrist immobilized, (3) with his left hand, (4) with the pen in his teeth, and (5) with a pen attached to his foot. Although many differences are evident in the writing, there are also many similarities.

John Hancock and his famous signature.

Temporal and Spatial Demands of Movements

Another line of evidence that is consistent with the schema notion comes from experiments that have manipulated the temporal and/or spatial demands of movements. Consider, for example, an experiment by Shea et al. (1981). They asked subjects to move from a start button through a hinged barrier or to another button (Figure 8.5). The termination of the response was to be coincident with the illumination of the last light on a Bassin anticipation timer (see anticipation and timing section, Chapter 9 for more details). The subject's hand passed through a series of photocells while moving from the start button to the termination point. The Bassin timer presented sequences of lights that appeared to move at different speeds. Most interesting for this discussion was that the subjects' movements to the faster moving lights appeared to be speeded-up copies of their movements to the slower moving lights. Thus, it appeared from the structure of the responses that subjects used the same generalizable motor program and simply altered the speed parameter on the basis of the light sequence presented.

Hollerbach (1978) asked subjects to write the word *hell* in different sizes. The acceleration patterns were similar even though one example was half the size of the other (Figure 8.6). In this example it appears that the subject again used the same generalizable motor program and simply altered the force parameter and perhaps the specific muscles used. The result was two nearly identical movement patterns that were scaled differently.

Note that the acceleration pattern in writing is not solely determined by the word being written but also, at least to some extent, by the individual. Work in our laboratory for an electronics company that produces automatic banking machines has demonstrated that the acceleration pattern from an individual's signature is quite unique to that individual. Although a skilled forger could produce a signature almost perfectly, he or she could not replicate the acceleration patterns used. Someday we may find ourselves having to sign on a special pad at a bank machine to get our money. The machine would compare the acceleration pattern of the signature provided with the pattern stored on the bank's computer. If a match were determined, you would get your money.

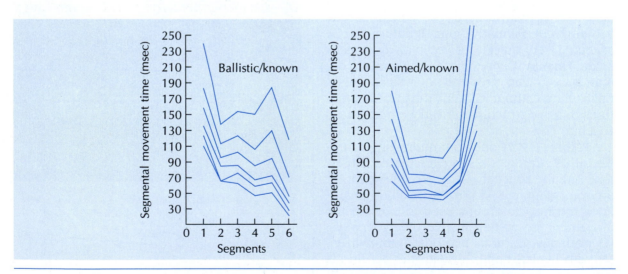

Figure 8.5 *Average segmental movement times for movements through a barrier (ballistic) and to a button (aimed) as a function of the apparent velocity produced on a Bassin timer.*

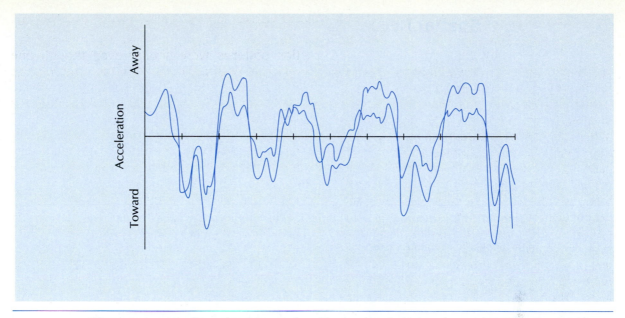

Figure 8.6 *Vertical accelerations produced by a subject's writing the word* hell *with one execution having half the amplitude of the other.*

Mass-Spring Hypothesis

Feldman (1966a) and later Polit and Bizzi (1978, 1979) noted that agonist and antagonist muscles act on limbs (bone) in some ways similar to those in which complex springs (or rubber bands) would act on a lever (Figure 8.7). Muscle-tendon groups for a given innervation rate tend to produce more tension as the length of the muscle is increased. Likewise, springs behave according to Hook's Law. Hook's Law states that for a given spring, increases in length result in a proportional increase in tension. The example illustrated in Figure 8.7, taken from Rosenbaum (1990), utilizes rubber bands rather than springs to illustrate the **mass-spring hypothesis**. Utilizing rubber bands may be an excellent choice because rubber bands generally act like springs but increases in length tend to produce nonlinear increases in tension. This is similar to the nonlinear relationship between muscle

tension, resting length, and activation level (Rack & Westbury, 1969).

When the resting length and stiffness of the rubber bands are equal, the lever achieves a 90 degree angle with the base. However, either a stiffer rubber band or a rubber band with a shorter resting length attached to the right side results in the lever's being displaced to the right. Note that the forces exerted by the rubber bands are equalized by the movement of the lever. A stiffer or shorter rubber band pulls the lever in its direction, reducing the tension that it exerts. While this is occurring, the other rubber band is stretched to the point that the tension it produces equals that of the stiffer or shorter rubber band. Thus, the lever moves to an equilibrium point defined by equal tension on each side of the lever. Note that the equilibrium point (joint angle) is defined by the ratio of forces acting on the lever.

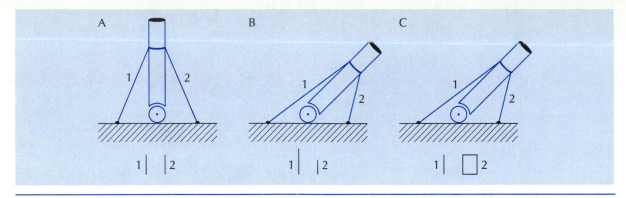

Figure 8.7 *Illustration of the mass-spring concept using rubber bands of different thicknesses and lengths rather than springs. Note what happens as the length or thickness of the rubber band is changed.*

Now consider that muscles act as variable tension springs or rubber bands with the level of activation and the resting length of the muscle defining the current length-tension relationship. Thus, a single muscle group behaves as a population of springs or rubber bands. For example, consider the flexor and extensor muscle groups that act on the elbow joint. The position of the lower arm relative to the upper arm is defined by the tension exerted by the two muscle groups. Increased activation to the flexors relative to the extensors creates more tension on the flexor side. To achieve an equilibrium point, the flexor reduces its length via contraction and the extensor increases its length via stretch until the two tensions balance out. Figure 8.8 illustrates hypothetical limb positions as a result of activation levels and resting length.

What was the most interesting to theorists about this view of motor control was that a single ratio of agonist and antagonist activation could be used to specify limb position. Thus, smaller demands would be placed on memory because only the relationship between the innervation ratios and limb position would have to be learned before accurate movements, even to novel positions, could be made. Indeed, important evidence from animal research (Polit & Bizzi, 1978, 1979), ocu-

lar motor research (Mays & Sparks, 1980), and limb movement research with intact humans (Schmidt, 1980; Schmidt & McGown, 1980) suggests reasonable support for mass-spring principles contributing to the control of simple movements.

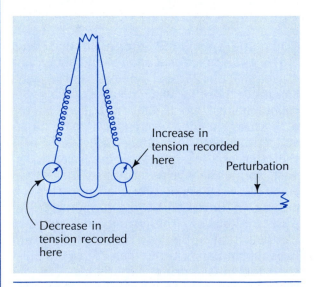

Increase in tension recorded here

Perturbation

Decrease in tension recorded here

Figure 8.8 *The mass-spring concept: position of the limb is determined by the forces exerted by the springs (muscles). The limb always moves to a position of equilibrium in which the forces on one side equal the forces on the other.*

Coordinative Structures and Multilimb Control

The notion of coordinative structures (Bernstein, 1967; Easton, 1972; Kugler, Kelso, & Turvey, 1982) proposes that the control system has the ability to temporarily constrain the many degrees of freedom to act as a single unit. This is quite different from the traditional view that individual muscles are directly controlled by a motor program or other control processes. Bernstein argued that groupings of muscles, termed **coordinative structures**, were controlled as functional units. He noted that this control process reduced the number of commands and decisions to a minimum and reduced the computational requirements necessary to achieve skilled movements.

Although the notion of coordinative structures potentially reduces the demands on the control system, it may pose difficulties under some conditions. Consider that your hands/arms are constrained to act as a functional unit. What happens when you wish to uncouple this functional unit? To answer this question, simply try rubbing your stomach and patting your head. This is difficult without practice because it requires you to undo a long established and coordinated structure between limbs. Even after practice on this task, you will find that your head patting is still linked in some subtle way to rubbing your stomach.

Kelso, Southard, and Goodman (1979) required subjects to make aiming movements with the left, right, and both hands. According to speed accuracy relationships (discussed in Chapter 9), subjects' movement time should be reduced when the target is closer or larger. This was the case for single hand/arm movements (Figure 8.9, Conditions 1–4). This was also the case for bimanual movements with the same requirements (Conditions 5 and 6). However, when the movement of one hand required a different distance to be traversed or a different size target to be contacted than the other hand, both hands/arms appeared to be constrained to act as a unit. This resulted in

Extremely skilled athletes appear to be able to uncouple the movements of their arms. As Michael Jordan uses one arm to gently tip the ball, he exerts a great deal of force with the other arm to fend off Croatia's Stojko Urankovic. Summer 1992 Olympics, Barcelona.

longer movement time for the shorter distance or larger target (Conditions 7 and 8) than that occurring when the limb was acting alone.

In a related experiment, subjects were asked to move both hands from a home position to adjacent targets (Kelso, Putnam, & Goodman, 1983). Distance and target size were the same for both hands, but a cardboard barrier was placed between the home position and the target for one hand but not the other. Trajectories for one subject are given in Figure 8.10. If the limbs were controlled independently, the limb without the barrier should take a direct route to the target and arrive before the other limb. This was not

Training the Deaf to Speak

In a review of motor control, Steven Keele (1986) points to an interesting motor control dilemma: teaching deaf people to speak. Deaf people have great difficulty learning to speak, not because they experience some fundamental problem with the motor control of speech but because they lack auditory feedback and a visual template to which feedback can be compared. Could the teaching of speech to the deaf be facilitated if some augmented feedback was provided? A review of what you learned about hearing in Chapter 5 may be helpful at this point.

Some years ago a training program developed by Nickerson, Kalikow, & Stevens (1976) used a transducer that was sensitive to throat vibrations and audio output to display visual representations of speech on a video screen. In one scheme, called "ball game" (Figure 8A), the deaf child's task was to control a parameter of speech such as pitch in order to get a ball displayed on the video screen to move through a hole in a partition and into the basket. At the beginning of an attempt, the ball moves from left to right, the height of the ball is controlled by the pitch vocalized by the child. If the voice pitch is nearly correct, a basket is made and a smiling face appears; if the pitch is not correct, the child can see what he or she did wrong. Note that the pattern on the right of Figure 8A is more complicated than that on the left.

Another video procedure used by Nickerson et al. (1976) involves comparing the teacher's utterance with the sounds produced by the student (Figure 8B). The image on the left represents the teacher's utterance of the word *be;* that on the right represents the student's reproduction attempt. In the display, voice frequency is portrayed on the vertical axis; the width of the image is controlled by voice intensity. The height of the teacher's and student's responses are determined by pitch. Pitch is the difference between low and high notes.

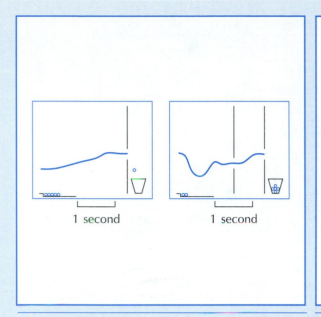

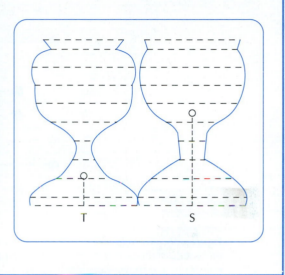

Figure 8A *Two video displays used by Nickerson et al. (1976) to train deaf children to speak. The height of the ball as it moves across the screen is controlled by voice pitch.*

Figure 8B *In this video display, the image on the left represents the teacher's utterance and the image on the right displays the student's attempted reproduction. Voice frequency is shown on the vertical axis and voice intensity on the horizontal axis. The dashed horizontal lines indicate that the consonant is voiced (Nickerson et al., 1976).*

Note that the teacher's response becomes a standard for the student to try to reproduce. Success for the student is rated by how closely he or she matches the teacher's performance. These researchers claim that speech is improved not only while the device is being used but also outside the classroom when the device is no longer available. Presumably, the students learn an internalized reference of correctness that can be used outside the laboratory.

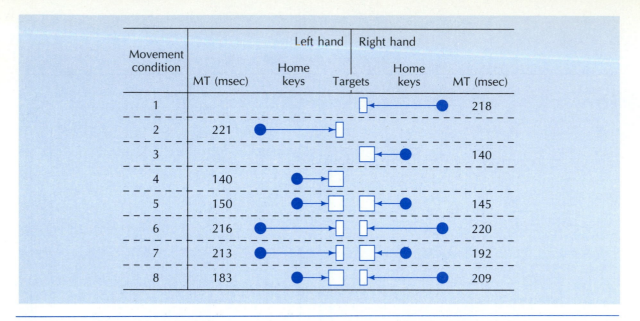

Movement condition	Left hand MT (msec)	Home keys	Targets	Right hand Home keys	MT (msec)
1					218
2	221				
3					140
4	140				
5	150				145
6	216				220
7	213				192
8	183				209

Figure 8.9 *Average movement times for one and two-handed movements to targets of different distances and sizes. Note that in two-handed movements, the two hands are constrained to move together.*

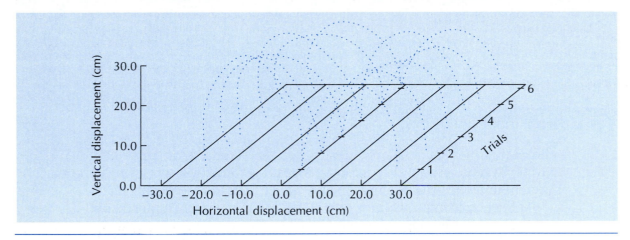

Figure 8.10 *Tracings of a subject producing two-handed movements. A barrier is placed between the starting point and the ending position for one hand and yet the other hand follows a similar trajectory.*

the case. Both limbs arrived at virtually the same time taking essentially the same route.

The uncoupling of limbs appears to be very difficult to achieve even with extended practice. Konzem (1987) asked subjects to rapidly write a "V" with one hand and a lower-case Greek letter gamma ("γ") with the other hand. Subjects practiced each letter individu-ally for 225 trials and then were asked to perform the tasks simultaneously. Figure 8.11 depicts performance on selected trials. Schmidt (1985) reports that the subjects generally found the dual task to be very difficult and that the hands did not appear to become uncoupled even after 1000 practice trials.

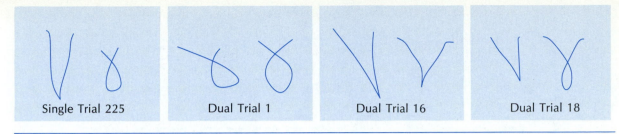

| Single Trial 225 | Dual Trial 1 | Dual Trial 16 | Dual Trial 18 |

Figure 8.11 *Tracing of a subject's attempt to simultaneously draw a V with the left hand and a gamma with the right hand. Even after a number of trials, the hands appear coupled or linked together.*

FINAL COMMENT

Adams' closed-loop theory and Schmidt's schema theory propose two memory states: one to get the movement started and one to evaluate the movement's success. The difference is that the closed-loop theory proposes that the evaluation takes place during the movement and the open-loop theory maintains that the evaluation occurs after the movement has run its course. Additional theoretical proposals (mass spring and coordinative structures) suggest more elegant (perhaps simplified) control schemes that reduce the demands on memory. These latter control notions represent the most promising avenues to understanding how we do the things we do.

KEY TERMS

memory trace
perceptual trace
schema theory
schema
generalizable motor
  program

recall schema
recognition schema
initial conditions
response
  specifications

sensory
  consequences
response outcome
invariant features
parameterize
variant features

parameter
mass-spring
  hypothesis
coordinative
  structures

9
Speed-Accuracy Principles

Nolan Ryan: ARM WITHOUT END

Speed-Accuracy Trade-off

Fitts' Law
- *Index of Difficulty*
- *Accounts for Fitts' Law*

Impulse Variability Theory
- *Effective Target Width and Movement Demands*
- *Force-Force Variability Relationship*
- *Accounts for the Force-Force Variability Relationship*

An Apparent Speed-Accuracy Paradox
- *Anticipation and Timing*
- *Factors Influencing Anticipation and Timing*
- *A Batting Example*

HIGHLIGHT: Speed and Accuracy in Controlling Machines
FINAL COMMENT
KEY TERMS

Nolan Ryan: ARM WITHOUT END

On June 11, 1990, baseball history was made in Oakland, California. The Athletics were hosting the Texas Rangers for a night game. An old man, the oldest in the major leagues at 44, was pitching for the Rangers. He had been on and off the disabled list since April and was still obviously suffering from stress fractures in his back. But that did not keep him from breaking a record he had begun almost nineteen years before by becoming the only baseball player in history to pitch a no-hitter in three consecutive decades.

It had not been uncommon for Nolan Ryan to pitch one hitless inning after another. In addition to his record of five no-hit games achieved by 1981, he had pitched 12 one-hitters (tying Bob Feller for the major league record). Ryan had also struck out 9.57 batters for every nine innings pitched since 1967, started 706 games (fifth in history), pitched 4990 innings in the major leagues, and had 293 victories under his belt. He has a fastball that is still predictably radared at 95 miles per hour and a change-up that is unmatched in the major leagues today, but a no-hitter had not been his goal at the beginning of this particular night—staying in for the entire game was.

By the seventh inning, the A's were still hitless and Ryan was not giving up. He realized a no-hitter was possible. He had been using his fastball consistently, but it was obvious he was slowing down. He went to a full

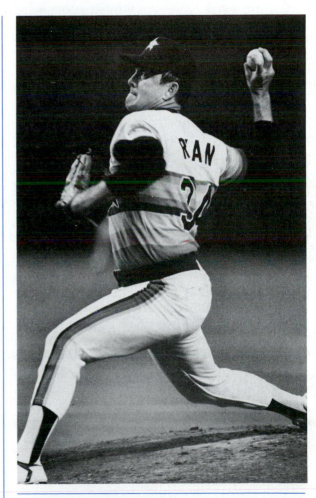

Nolan Ryan has a fastball that even at the age of 44 is predictably radared at 95 miles an hour and a change-up that is unmatched in the major leagues today.

- To understand the concepts of a speed accuracy trade-off and index of difficulty.

- To identify the similarities and differences between Fitts' Law and impulse variability theory.

- To identify different types of anticipation.

- To appreciate the impact of timing and spatial errors on tasks like hitting a baseball

count on each hitter. An Athletic connected with the ball and sent a soft fly to Ruben Sierra in right field, ending the inning with many of the 33,436 Athletics fans cheering Ryan.

The eighth inning continued in the same manner. Several of the A's players went to full counts but none got to first base. The tension filled the air in the ninth inning, but Nolan Ryan had been there before. He faced only three batters in the ninth inning and swiftly secured his sixth no-hitter—more than any player in the history of the major leagues. The old, aching pitcher was able to maintain consistency in his play and triumphed once again.

■   ■   ■

Nolan Ryan is not only an inspiration to old ball players but a truly gifted athlete by any scale of measurement. He was able to maintain the speed of his fastball without losing a great deal of control. This is no easy task for a pitcher or anyone else who wishes to do something quickly. Increased speed usually results in decreased accuracy. As you read this chapter, think about the speed accuracy trade-off from both the pitcher's and the batter's perspectives. Remember, the batter is faced with similar problems; a faster, more forceful swing is less accurate than a more graded response. This is why batters choke up on the bat or bunt when they want to make sure they contact the ball.

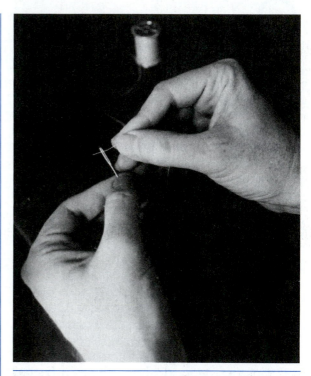

When attempting to thread a needle it is important to move slowly because the eye of the needle is very small. That is, we must sacrifice speed in order to gain accuracy.

Speed-Accuracy Trade-off

Nolan Ryan, like all baseball pitchers, is concerned with speed and accuracy. Nolan's fastball is legendary, but he also is the major league all-time leader in walks (2614). When we increase the speed with which we do something, we often increase the errors we make. To perform more accurately we must slow down. Surely Nolan Ryan could have "taken something off" his fastball to avoid walking so many batters, but would he have been as effective a pitcher? The reduced speed of the pitch could be more troublesome than the potential walks. This basic principle has come to be known as the **speed accuracy trade-off** because performers must trade off speed in order to increase accuracy or trade off accuracy to increase speed.

In 1899, Woodworth studied the relationship between the speed and accuracy of repetitive line drawing tasks. Subjects were required to draw lines with a pencil back and forth between two lines (targets). They were to attempt to stop each movement at the targets but were required to keep pace with a metronome. The speed of the movement was increased or decreased by varying the setting on the metronome. In one set of experiments, Woodworth had subjects perform with their eyes open or closed and movement velocity was manipulated by changing the setting on

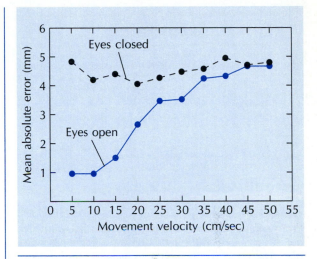

Figure 9.1 *Mean absolute error for hand movements by subjects with their eyes open or closed. Note that as the velocity of the movement increases (movement time decreases), the difference between the eyes open and closed conditions is reduced.*

the metronome (Figure 9.1). When subjects were permitted to view their movements, the average distance from the target increased as movement velocity increased. When eyes were closed, errors were even larger. The finding that accuracy decreases as movement speed increases forms the basis for some of the fundamental principles of motor control.

Fitts' Law

In 1954 Paul Fitts conducted a series of experiments on the relationship between the speed and accuracy of simple aiming movements. Fitts, an industrial engineer, attempted to apply mathematical and information processing concepts to the study of these simple movements. His findings are known as **Fitts' law**. Subjects attempted to tap back and forth as quickly as possible between two targets with a stylus (Figure 9.2). The amplitude (A) between targets and the width (W) of the targets were manipulated. The task was scored as the number of taps in 20 seconds. This score could be transformed into average movement time (MT) by dividing the number of taps into 20 seconds.

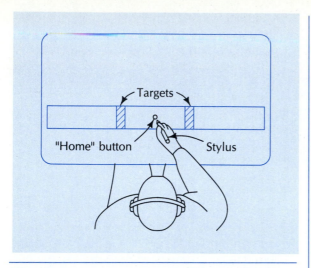

Figure 9.2 *Overhead view of a subject performing a Fitts' tapping task. This task requires the subject to alternately tap between the two targets as quickly as possible. The task is altered by changing the distance between and the width of the targets.*

This reciprocal tapping task was not thought to require control processes fundamentally different from single aiming movements or the reciprocal line drawing task used by Woodworth. The task simply allowed a rel-

atively large number of movements to be executed in a short period of time.

Index of Difficulty

Before presenting the findings from Fitts' (1954) experiments and what he proposed as an index of difficulty, let's make some predictions of our own. First, consider the effect of manipulations to target width on movement time (Figure 9.3A). What would happen to the speed of tapping when the width of the target is increased? A larger target area (right) would require a less precise movement than a smaller target (left). Would movement time increase or decrease as the target width is increased? Decrease, of course! Thus, movement time decreases as target width increases. Stated mathematically, MT varies with $1/W$.

Second, consider the effect of changes in the amplitude (distance between targets) on movement time (Figure 9.3B). What would happen to the speed of tapping when the amplitude is decreased? A shorter amplitude (right) with the same size target would require less precision than a longer amplitude (left). Would movement time increase or decrease

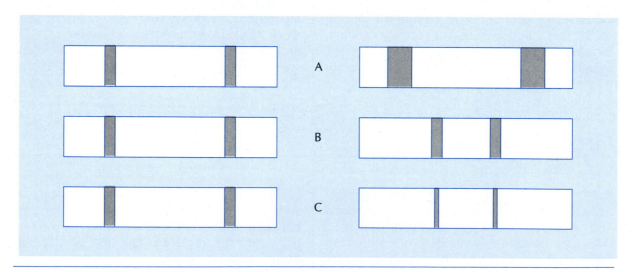

Figure 9.3 *Different requirements for the Fitts' tapping task. Compare the left layout with the right in each of the examples (A, B, and C). If subjects were instructed to tap as quickly as possible between the targets for 15 seconds, which pair of targets, (left or right) could be tapped most often? The answers are: A—right pair, B—right pair, C— number of taps would be approximately equal.*

as the amplitude is decreased? Decrease, of course! Thus, movement time decreases as the amplitude decreases. Stated mathematically, MT varies with A.

Now consider the combined effects of manipulating both target width and amplitude (Figure 9.3C). A shorter amplitude with a smaller target (right) would require demands similar to a greater amplitude and larger target. Could the effects of target width and amplitude be combined in some way to ensure similar movement times? The answer is yes! Mathematically, we could state that MT varies with A/W. This relationship, however, suggests that the influence of amplitude and target width are comparable such that a one-unit change in amplitude has a similar effect as a one-unit change in target width.

Fitts (1954) carried out experiments aimed at further examining the relationships we have just derived. Thus, he systematically manipulated target width and amplitude. His experiments suggest two fundamental points in addition to those we have already discussed.

First, subjects' performances are more sensitive to changes in target width than amplitude. Thus, target width must be weighted more heavily than target amplitude. Second, Fitts found it useful to characterize the relationship as a linear function or straight line. To do this he multiplied the factors by $\log_2$. Fitts' data is illustrated in Figure 9.4 after it is transformed by the log function. Thus, Fitts proposed an **index of difficulty** (**ID**) as the following expression:

$$\log_2(2A/W).$$

The index of difficulty can be used to describe an individual's or group's average movement time with the following equation:

$$MT = a + b[\log_2(2A/W)].$$

The constant a is the intercept and represents movement time when the index of difficulty is zero. Note that an index of difficulty of zero results when the amplitude is one-half the target width. For example, an amplitude of 2 units and a target width of 4 units would result in an

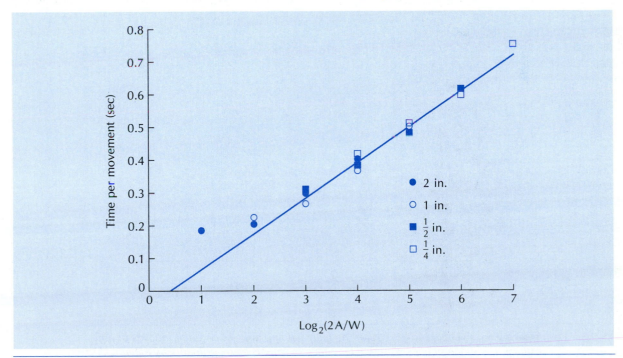

Figure 9.4 *Average movement time for the Fitts' tapping tasks of different difficulties.*

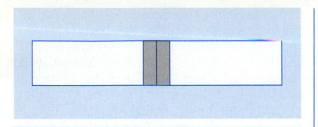

Figure 9.5 *According to Fitts' law, this task would have no difficulty (ID = 0) and thus no movement time because the subject would not have to move the stylus to achieve the targets.*

index of difficulty of zero [ID = $\log_2(2 \times 2/4)$]. It makes sense that the index of difficulty be zero because there is no movement difficulty. Indeed, subjects do not even need to move, because under these conditions the two targets overlap (Figure 9.5).

The constant b is the slope and represents the change in movement time associated with a one-unit change in the index of difficulty. Thus, a set of conditions that results in a

smaller slope would be said to involve a more sensitive limb system than a condition that results in a larger slope.

Langolf, Chaffin, & Foulke (1976) tested tapping responses involving primarily finger, wrist, or arm movements across a wide range of the index of difficulty (Figure 9.6). As we might suspect, the results suggested that finger movements are more sensitive than wrist movements which, in turn, are more sensitive than whole arm movements. This interpretation is made because an increase in slope *(b)* indicates a less sensitive limb system and a corresponding greater difficulty managing increased amplitudes and decreased target size. However, it is important to note that each limb system studied by Langolf et al. (1976) seems to follow Fitts' law very closely.

Perhaps the most remarkable aspect of this relationship is the wide range of tasks that appear to follow Fitts' law. The relationship seems to hold for single aiming movements in air (Fitts & Peterson, 1964) or water (Kerr,

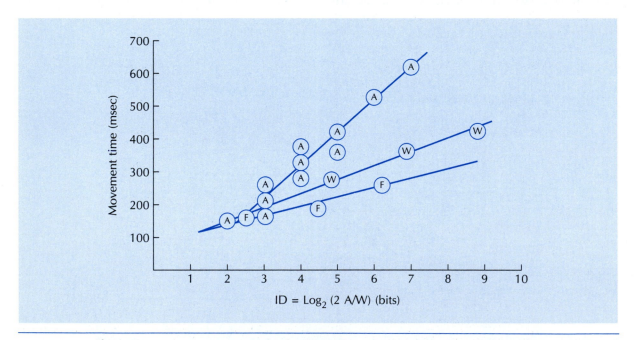

Figure 9.6 *Average movement for the Fitts' tapping tasks of different indexes of difficulties. The different lines represent tapping movements made primarily by the arm (A), the wrist (W), and the fingers (F).*

1973); moving a joystick, handle, or cursor (Jagacinski, Repperger, Moran, Ward, & Glass, 1980; Meyer, Smith & Wright, 1982); throwing darts (Kerr & Langolf, 1977); and even for eye movements.

Accounts for Fitts' Law

Fitts was clearly influenced by information processing accounts of human motor control. This led to the notion that movement time represented the time required to process a sufficient amount of information to achieve the movement goal. Movements with higher indices of difficulty required more information to be processed than movements with smaller indices of difficulty and therefore required more time to attain the target.

An account for Fitts' law that was not based on information was proposed by Crossman and Goodeve in 1983. This account, which was similar to Woodworth's (1899), proposed that movements to targets are composed of two alternating phases: a relatively open-loop phase that resulted in a movement toward the target and a closed-loop correcting phase that adjusted the trajectory of the movement when an error was detected. The open-loop phase is used to initiate a movement toward the target until the closed-loop processes detected an error, at which time a second adjusted open-loop phase is initiated. Crossman and Goodeve suggested that the number of open-loop phases required to achieve the target depended on the amplitude and target width. Longer amplitudes and smaller targets require more corrections than shorter amplitudes and larger targets. Movement time is affected because each correction was thought to require a fixed amount of time.

To illustrate the Crossman & Goodeve (1963) notion, consider the following example. The task is to move a pencil from a starting point to a circle as quickly as possible without lifting the pencil from the paper (see Figure 9.7). Assume, for the sake of the example, that your movements have a 5-degree error (the dotted line in the figure is the correct trajec-

tory). If the target is very close or very large, the number of corrections (if required at all) is reduced. Example A results in hitting the target without needing to make a correction. However, when the amplitude is increased (Example B), the same trajectory would not hit the target without initiating a correction. Longer amplitudes (Example C) may require even more corrections. If the target width is increased in proportion to the increase in amplitude (Examples D and E), no additional corrections should be required.

It is important to note that the accounts for Fitts' law involve closed-loop processes that require a sufficient amount of time for feedback to be processed. What happens when the movements are very rapid and the influence of feedback is reduced? Are performers still required to trade off speed for accuracy even when the movements are relatively short in duration? Schmidt et al., (1978, 1979), relying on principles derived from schema theory, proposed an interesting answer to this question.

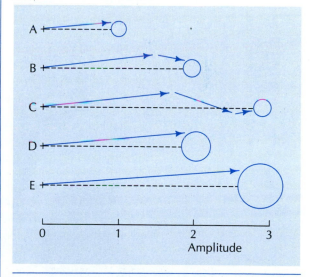

Figure 9.7 *Hypothetical examples of corrections required to contact targets of different amplitudes and widths. As a small target is moved farther away, the more corrections may be required. However, if the target is moved farther away and increased proportionally in size, an increase in the number of corrections may not be required.*

Speed and Accuracy in Controlling Machines

Can the principles of Fitts' law be applied to humans' control of machines? Earlier in this chapter we presented an example of aiming tasks requiring primarily finger, wrist, or whole arm movements. When movement time was plotted against the index of difficulty (ID) the slope for the finger movements was flatter than for the wrist or arm movements (see Figure 9.6). The interpretation was that the flatter the slope the more sensitive the control system, that is, the same increases in difficulty resulted in smaller changes in movement time for the finger movements than for those involving wrist movements. Can this principle be applied to human control of machines (see Keele, 1986 for review)?

Consider how we control the movement of a cursor on a computer screen. We might use a mouse, light pen, joystick, or keyboard. How does an engineer decide which device is best? To test the devices we could ask subjects to move the cursor to targets presented on the

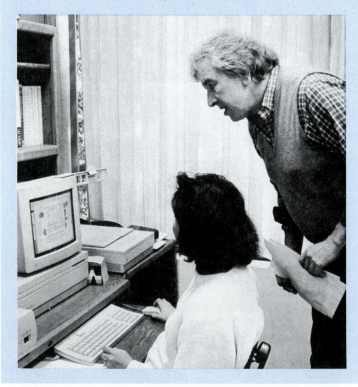

Researchers have found that a mouse is a very effective pointing device.

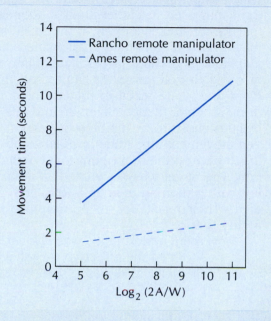

Movement time for different amplitude/target widths ratios (indices of difficulty) for the Rancho and Ames remote manipulators (McGovern, 1974).

computer screen with a variety of devices available. The targets would appear at different distances from the cursor and be of varying sizes. Remember, the index of difficulty (ID) for each movement would be calculated based on the width and amplitude of the target from the cursor. If we plotted movement time for each of the control devices tested versus the ID for the different targets, we could determine the most efficient system. The system that results in the flattest slope is the most efficient control device. Card, English, and Burr (1978) found the slope for the mouse to be about half that of the joystick.

Consider the application of Fitts' law to a more complicated control system. McGovern (1974) evaluated two remote manipulators (robotic arms). For both systems the operators inserted their arm in a master sleeve that was jointed at the shoulder, elbow, wrist, and fingers. When the operators moved their arm, the master sleeve transmitted the movement pattern to a robotic arm situated in front of the operator. The operators' task was to move their arm (and thus the sleeve) in such a way that the robotic arm moved to pick up objects of different sizes. The results showed clearly that the control system for the Ames remote manipulator was better than for the Rancho.

Impulse Variability Theory

As noted in Chapter 8, schema theory (Schmidt, 1975) proposes a generalizable motor program that could be parameterized to carry out a variety of movements with the same invariant features. The question of interest in this chapter concerns whether or not the execution of a generalizable motor program parameterized to meet different movement goals would result in a speed/accuracy trade-off.

Effective Target Width (W_e) and Movement Demands

Schmidt and his colleagues (Schmidt, Zelaznik, & Frank, 1978; Schmidt, Zelaznik, Hawkins, Frank, & Quinn, 1979) attempted to answer this question. However, the way in which data were collected had to be adjusted from that used in earlier studies. Remember that earlier studies looking at the speed accuracy trade-off generally manipulated target amplitude and width (accuracy requirements) in order to determine the impact on movement time. As a result of predictions derived from schema theory, Schmidt and his colleagues chose to manipulate movement time and movement amplitude in order to observe the impact on the movement to a target position. The target was designated as a point or line rather than an area as in the Fitts' paradigm. Their results led to the **impulse variability theory.**

Movement performance was evaluated by what was termed the **effective target width**, or **W_e**. This measure represents the spread of

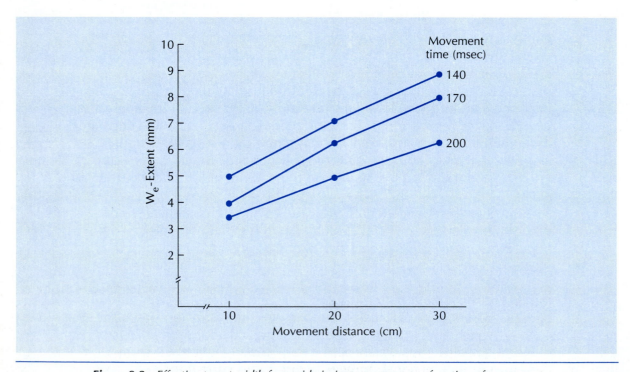

Figure 9.8 *Effective target width for rapid aiming responses as a function of movement time and movement distance. Effective target width increases as movement distance increases and decreases as movement time decreases.*

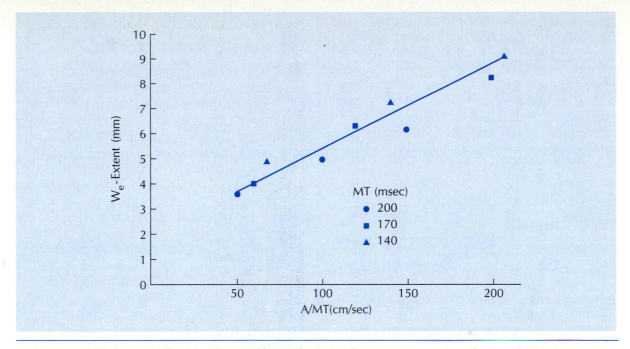

Figure 9.9 *Effective target width as a function of average movement velocity (A/MT).*
As A/MT increases, there is a nearly linear increase in effective target width.

the movement endpoints in the direction of the movement about the target position (Figure 9.8). W_e was calculated as the within-subjects standard deviation of the endpoints.

Subjects were required to move a stylus from a starting point to a target of fixed distance. For different sets of trials, the movement distance and the movement time could be changed. During initial training, subjects were taught to terminate the movements in specific movement times through movement time feedback. During the actual testing only movements that were within ± 10 percent of the goal movement time were used in the analysis.

The results indicated that the functional target width varied directly with movement amplitude and inversely with movement time. That is, longer movements resulted in larger functional target widths than did shorter movements. Stated mathematically, W_e varies with $1/A$. In addition, decreasing movement time resulted in larger functional targets widths. Stated mathematically, W_e varies with MT.

A speed accuracy trade-off was observed for rapid aiming movements. Note that movement speed was increased holding movement time constant and varying movement amplitude. Alternatively, movement speed could be increased by holding movement amplitude constant and decreasing movement time. The speed-accuracy trade-off is even more evident when the data are plotted as a function of average movement velocity (Figure 9.9). Interestingly, average movement velocity is calculated as movement amplitude divided by movement time. This is precisely the relationship previously described; W_e varies with A/MT.

The question of utmost importance is why does a speed accuracy trade-off occur for rapid movements? It is clear that information (Fitts, 1954) or feedback accounts used to explain the speed accuracy trade-off in slower movements cannot be utilized. The movements utilized by Schmidt et al. (1979) were thought to be motor program controlled with little if any opportunity for feedback to intervene in the control of the movement. If the centrally stored motor program is stable and the response specifications are not changed from trial to trial, the source of variability must exist in either the motor program or in the neuromuscular system that executes the commands elicited by the program. In an attempt to answer this question, Schmidt et al. (1979) determined the within-subjects relationship between force and force variability resulting from motor program execution.

Force-Force Variability Relationship

Why did rapid programmed movements produce a speed accuracy trade-off? Schmidt et al. (1979) reasoned that both decreasing movement time (holding movement amplitude constant) and increasing movement amplitude (holding movement time constant) required the subjects to generate greater forces to produce the velocities required to achieve the target. Could there be a systematic relationship between the amount of force produced by programmed responses and the variability in that force over trials?

In a series of experiments conducted by Schmidt et al. (1979), subjects were asked to produce forces against an immovable handle. The forces exerted were displayed on an oscilloscope positioned in plain view of the subject. Increases in force were simultaneously registered as an elevation of a trace dot on the oscilloscope. Over a series of trials, the subjects attempted to have the trace dot "shoot up" to a target position marked on the oscilloscope. After some initial practice, within-subjects standard deviations of the forces were calculated and then a different target force was learned.

The results indicate that increases in force result in corresponding increases in force variability, at least at moderate levels of force (Figure 9.10). Sherwood and Schmidt (1980) found a similar linear relationship, although force variability was somewhat elevated for dynamic force production tasks (Figure 9.11).

Accounts for the Force-Force Variability Relationship

What characteristic(s) of the motor system could account for this relationship? Schmidt et al. (1979) proposed that in simple aiming movements, an agonist burst propels the limb toward the target. After the initial burst, the limb simply falls or coasts toward the target. Thus, the endpoint of a movement is determined by the magnitude and duration of the agonist burst. The ability of both the motor system and the motor program driving the response to accurately innervate the musculature will determine the movement accuracy.

It is fairly clear that the motor system is relatively faithful in executing consistent responses to central commands except under extreme conditions (fatigue, extreme temperature, etc.). This is known from studies in which the motor neuron or muscle has been electrically stimulated repetitively and the variability in the responses has been observed. This should not be interpreted to mean that the motor system does not have some degree of "noise" but that this source of variability cannot account for the largest portion of variability in simple aiming movements. This leaves the motor program and its translation into motor commands as the prime suspect.

Consider the following hypothetical motor program. The program is designed to produce f amount of force for t amount of time. To accomplish this, the motor program contains a set of rules for determining the population of motor units to be called on and the rules for determining frequency characteristics of the neural volleys to summate and maintain the force for the appropriate amount of time. Each execution of the response requires that the rules be translated into motor commands (even assuming the same response specifications). If the rules are not well specified (the motor program not well developed), then the translation should be somewhat variable. This type of variability could contribute to the magnitude of W_e.

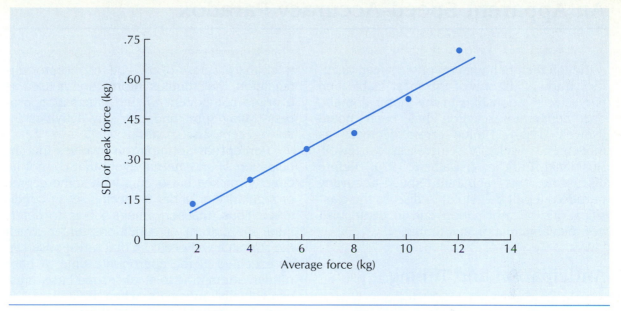

Figure 9.10 *Variability in force (statically produced) as a function of average force. As force increases, subjects become more variable in producing the force.*

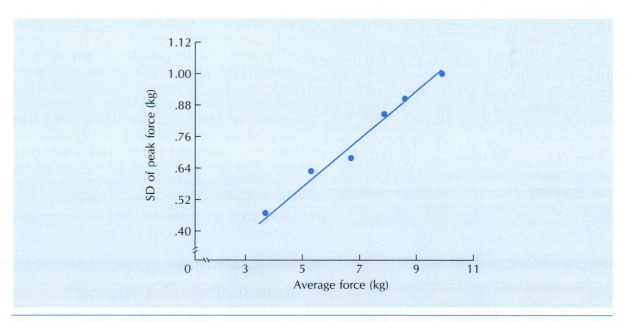

Figure 9.11 *Variability in force (dynamically produced) as a function of average force.*

An Apparent Speed-Accuracy Paradox

Although the phenomenon of the speed-accuracy trade-off is one of the most stable and pervasive relationships in the motor domain, one apparent exception has been noted (Newell, 1980). Timing errors decrease as movement velocity increases (Newell, Hoshizaki, Carlton, & Halbert, 1979). Before discussing this apparent **speed-accuracy paradox**, it will be helpful to discuss the classifications of anticipation and to distinguish between anticipation and timing.

Anticipation and Timing

Anticipation and timing are extremely important to many motor skills. **Anticipation** requires that performers coordinate or in some way synchronize their motor responses to an external event. Hitting a baseball, timing the snap count in football, keeping the beat in dancing, and even guessing when the bell signaling the end of class will ring are all examples of anticipation. **Timing** generally is taken to involve the timekeeping responsible for the duration of internal events such as the timing of an agonist burst or the internal timing of responses as a whole. It is important to understand, however, that in some literatures the terms are used almost interchangeably. The important point is to recognize the relevance of anticipation and timing behaviors to skilled performance.

Poulton (1957), a British psychologist, proposed three types of anticipation. The first two, receptor and perceptual anticipation, fit our definition of anticipation because both involve anticipating the occurrence of an external event.

Receptor anticipation involves the anticipation of the arrival of an external event when some aspect of the event can be tracked in some manner. Determining when a baseball will arrive at home plate involves reception anticipation because the batter can visually track the progress of the ball. In receptor anticipation, the stimulus information is used as a prime component in the anticipation process. Many sport and everyday activities involve receptor anticipation.

Perceptual anticipation involves the anticipation of an external event that cannot be directly tracked but occurs with some degree of regularity or under a specific set of conditions. Thus, the performer's job is to determine the pattern or conditions under which the stimulus will occur so that a response can be executed at the appropriate time. A base runner, attempting to steal second base, must perceptually anticipate when to initiate the steal. The runner must use the regularity of the pitcher's move to home plate, along with tendencies of the pitcher, to get a "jump." Likewise, a defensive player in football attempts to perceptually anticipate the snap count (movement) of the offensive team. Regularity and prior knowledge of the team's or quarterback's tendencies are helpful in making this judgment.

Effector anticipation is described by Poulton (1957), although it probably fits better under our classification of timing than anticipation. Effector anticipation involves the process of determining how long one's own movements or movement component will take to initiate and execute. This is extremely important to all aspects of skilled performance. To correctly anticipate when an event will occur but misjudge either how long it will take to get a movement initiated or executed can lead to performance errors.

Factors Influencing Anticipation and Timing

Anticipation and timing are very important parts of our motor performance repertoire, but this type of performance is influenced by a number of factors. Receptor/effector anticipation tasks appear to be particularly influenced by the duration and uncertainty of stimuli as well as the type of movement involved.

Shea et al. (1981) examined the effects of stimulus velocity, stimulus duration, and stimulus uncertainty on both the structure of the response and timing performance. The task required subjects to move from a start button through a hinged barrier (10 centimeters square) or to a button (4 centimeters in diameter). The termination of the response was to be coincident with the illumination of the last light on a Bassin anticipation timer. The Bassin timer consists of a row of lights that can be sequentially illuminated to give the appearance of movement. The lights can be illuminated in sequence at various intervals to give the appearance of different speeds and the number of lights can be varied to change the duration of the stimulus presentation for a particular velocity. In this study, stimulus uncertainty was manipulated either by informing or not informing the subject in advance regarding the stimulus velocity.

The progress of the movement was monitored by five photocells (PC) that were mounted along the movement path. As the subject's hand left the start button, the Bassin timer was initiated and as the subject's hand passed under the various photocells, the progress of the movement was monitored (Figure 9.12). This allowed the experimenters to determine the progress of the movement by plot-ting the time required to traverse from one photocell to the next. The total time was used to determine timing error.

Stimulus Velocity, Duration, and Uncertainty. The results of the first experiment indicated that when the stimulus velocity was known in advance (known condition), timing errors decreased as the stimulus velocity increased (also see Wrisberg, Hardy, & Beitel, 1982). Note that, as previously stated, this appears to be contrary to the speed accuracy trade-off. However, when the stimulus velocity was not known in advance, timing errors increased as the stimulus velocity increased. These findings were consistent for both aimed (button) and ballistic (barrier) movements. A hint as to why this occurred can be taken from the structure of the arm movements (Figure 9.13).

When information concerning the stimulus velocity was provided prior to ballistic movements, the responses to faster stimuli appeared to be "speeded-up" copies of responses to slower stimuli. That is, the segmental movement times looked similar, only elevated when the stimulus speed was reduced. When information concerning the stimulus velocity was not provided, subjects initiated a common response for approximately 260 milliseconds before adjustments were made to the specific stimulus. The differences in response structure were taken to in-

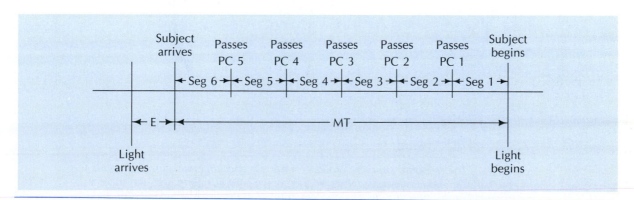

Figure 9.12 *Temporal events in a hypothetical trial during which the subject terminated the movement too early.*

dicate differences in the level of feedback utilization during the progress of the response.

It is important to note that in Experiment 1 of the Shea et al. (1981) paper, the length of the stimulus array was kept constant. Thus, as stimulus velocity increased, stimulus duration decreased and the effects that could not be attributed to stimulus velocity were suspect. In Experiment 2, the confound was eliminated by varying the length of the stimulus array and the stimulus velocity. This experiment found that response structure and timing errors were independent of stimulus velocity and dependent on stimulus duration (Figure 9.14).

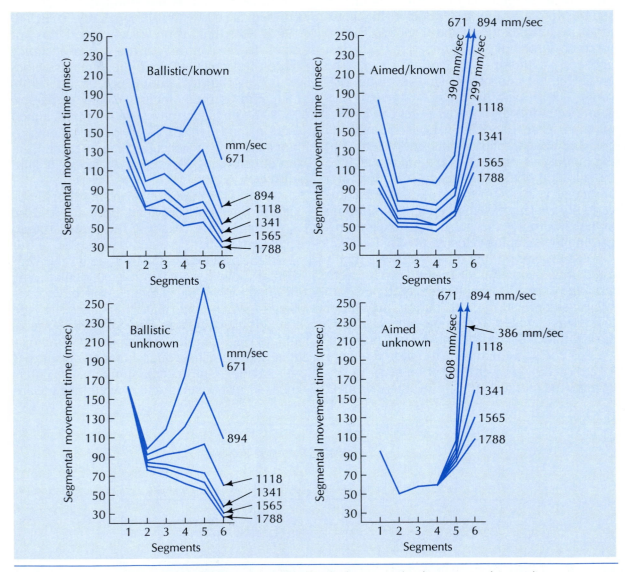

Figure 9.13 The response structure profiles for known and unknown stimulus conditions for ballistic and aimed movements. In the known stimulus condition, the subject was informed of the stimulus velocity and uninformed in the unknown condition. Ballistic movements required the subject to knock over a hinged barrier; aimed movements required subjects to depress a button.

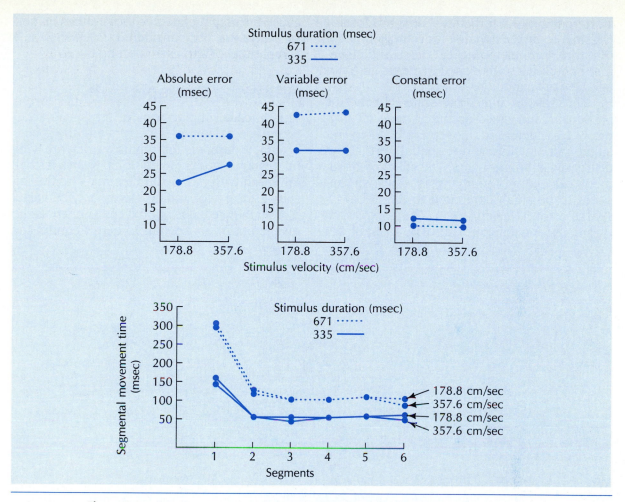

Figure 9.14 *Mean errors scores (top) and response structures (bottom) for movements in which the duration of the stimulus preview and apparent velocity of the stimulus were varied. The data suggest that the duration of the viewing time is the primary determiner of response accuracy and variability.*

Timing Behavior. Perhaps the most interesting and telling experiment concerning timing behavior (effector anticipation) was conducted by Newell (1980). Newell's earlier work (Newell et al., 1979; Newell, Carlton, Carlton, & Halbert, 1980) had suggested that a speed accuracy trade-off did not exist for timing responses. Timing errors decrease as movement velocity increases. It is important to note that this finding is different from the work utilizing receptor-effector anticipation tasks that had demonstrated that stimulus velocity did not trade off with timing errors. More in keeping with the notions pertaining to Fitts' law, movement speed did not necessarily trade off with timing accuracy. The basic thrust of Newell's experiment was to determine if increases in movement velocity lead not only to decreased timing errors but also to simultaneous increases in spatial errors.

In the experiment by Newell (1980), subjects were instructed to move a stylus from a start position to a target in a time as close as possible to the designated movement time for that trial. Various movement times and movement amplitudes were used to create six average velocity conditions.

The results indicated quite clearly the paradox of the speed-accuracy trade-off (Figure 9.15). Increased movement velocity resulted in increases in spatial error but decreases in timing errors. The effect of movement velocity on timing errors, however, appears to be small compared to the effect on spatial errors (Newell, 1980). The comparison of spatial and temporal error is difficult be-

cause the actual effects of these errors on performance are not considered. In effect, it is a comparison of apples and oranges.

A Batting Example

The practical implications of the speed-accuracy trade-off for spatial errors and the speed-accuracy paradox for timing errors are very interesting. Batters facing Nolan Ryan's fastball are faced with a difficult dilemma—trading off spatial errors for timing errors or vice versa. Should they reduce their bat speed or choke up on the bat in an attempt to better control the

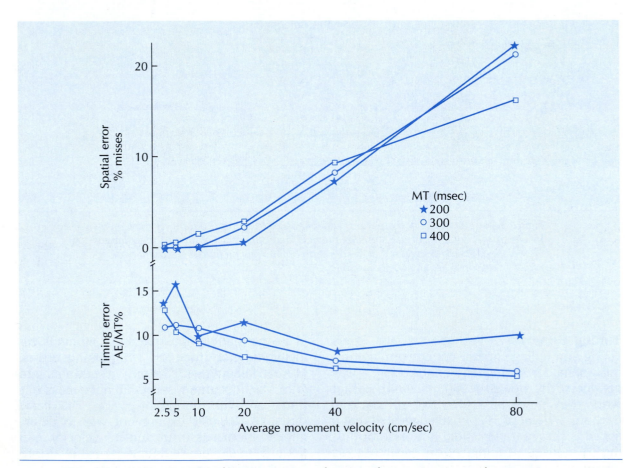

Figure 9.15 *Spatial and timing errors as a function of movement time and movement velocity. Note that spatial error increases and timing error decreases as movement velocity increases.*

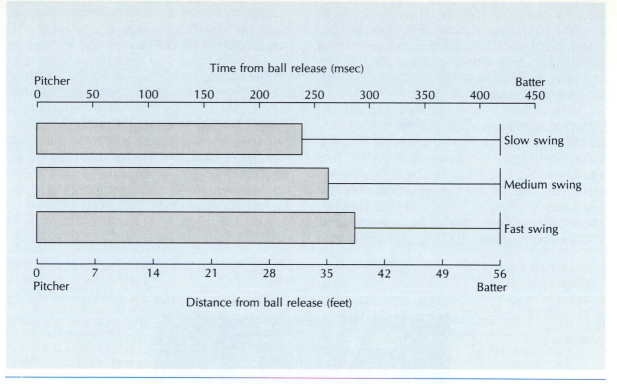

Figure 9.16 *The hatched area indicates the amount of time available for information processing prior to the initiation of the bat swing for a pitch of approximately 89 mph. As the speed of the swing increases (middle and bottom), more time is available for processing and the ball is closer to the plate when the bat swing must be initiated.*

bat (reduce spatial error) and at the same time increase their timing error? It would seem that batters would need to find a movement (bat) speed that minimizes the dual and opposing effects of spatial and timing errors. This may be quite difficult. If the problem were trivial, more of us would be able to hit a baseball well enough to play in the major leagues.

A few facts concerning hitting a baseball are provided in an attempt to illustrate the difficulties faced by batters. First, Hubbard and Seng (1954) found that a ball traveling at 89 mph took approximately 460 milliseconds to reach home plate. A typical, if there is such a thing, bat swing from initiation until the bat was in hitting position above the plate took about 160 milliseconds. This means that the bat swing must begin 160 milliseconds before the ball reaches the plate or when the ball is

21 feet from the plate. However, a whole sequence of information processing events is required to initiate the bat swing. How long do these processes take? It is very difficult to judge how long these processes would require, but certainly a significant portion of the 300 milliseconds that remain.

Consider the following examples involving two different bat speeds (Figure 9.16). What are the effects of swinging faster or slower on the events involved in hitting a baseball? Any increase in bat speed results in more time to carry out information processing. This and other factors related to the impact of the ball and bat make it important for the batter to swing as quickly as possible. Thus, the dilemma. One choice is to swing fast in order to increase the processing time, decrease timing error, and hit the ball harder but suffer increased spatial errors. The other choice is to slow the bat swing in order to position the bat more accurately (reduce spatial error); but this will result in less time to process information and increased timing error, and the ball will be struck with less force!

Now consider some options available to batters that may relate to the speed-accuracy relationships. A batter has a choice of bats. Longer or heavier bats may require more force and time to swing. This can be compensated for by choking up on the bat or bunting the ball when contact with the ball is important. These factors can generally reduce errors arising from both spatial and temporal sources.

Last, consider an observation commonly made by baseball coaches and players. The ball tends to be popped up or hit on the ground more often and the ball tends to be hit up the middle of the infield when a fastball pitcher is on the mound. This suggests small timing error and variable spatial performance. However, when a pitcher throws more slowly, the batters tend to hit the ball more solidly all over the field. This suggests small spatial errors but variable timing performance. Do coaches use this type of information to position their fielders more appropriately?

Batters are faced with two opposing problems: timing the bat swing in order to get the bat over the plate when the ball arrives and moving the bat through the same plane as the ball. Swinging faster seems to decrease timing errors but increase spatial errors.

FINAL COMMENT

The speed-accuracy trade-off is one of the earliest and most stable relationships in the motor domain. The speed-accuracy trade-off holds for a wide variety of tasks, conditions, and subjects. This relationship was first studied systematically by Woodworth (1899) nearly 100 years ago. Formal mathematical statements of the speed-accuracy relationship have been proposed by Fitts (1954) and Schmidt et al. (1979). An exception, termed a speed-accuracy paradox by Newell (1980), has been noted for timing errors. Timing errors tend to decrease as movement velocity or stimulus velocity increases. Thus, performers must trade off not only speed and accuracy but spatial and temporal errors.

KEY TERMS

speed-accuracy
    trade-off
Fitts' law
index of difficulty

impulse variability
    theory
effective target width
    (W_e)

speed-accuracy
    paradox
anticipation
timing

receptor anticipation
perceptual
    anticipation
effector anticipation

10

Information Feedback

Super Cockpit: THE VIRTUAL DISPLAY

Classifications of Information Feedback

Distinction Between Learning and Performance

Theoretical Issues
- *Reward, Motivation, and Information*
- *Guidance Hypothesis and the Processing of Feedback*

Knowledge of Results
- *Absolute and Relative Frequency of KR*
- *Bandwidth KR*
- *KR Delay and Post KR Delay*
- *Summary KR*
- *Precision of KR*

Considerations Related to the Error Measure Used

Knowledge of Performance

HIGHLIGHT: A New Generation of Feedback
FINAL COMMENT
KEY TERMS

Super Cockpit: THE VIRTUAL DISPLAY

In the early spring of 1987, an Air Force program was unveiled that may change the entire concept of a cockpit as we know it today. This program, estimated to cost $100 to $120 million, has as its goal the development of a prototype cockpit system that will remove all conventional instrumentation from an airplane and replace it with a multitude of high-tech pilot accessories. Pilots will be more in command of their surroundings because they will be in a computer-generated world of their own. This computer world, called a *virtual environment*, is based on a person's interacting with perceived images and sounds representative of the actual environment but presented in such a way that information can be more quickly and efficiently processed.

The most amazing, and yet fundamental, aspect of the Super Cockpit may be the pilot's helmet. Its special design includes a faceplate that presents the pilot with a panoramic, three-dimensional, color representation of the view outside the plane. This pictograph is based on complicated data retrieved by onboard sensors and intricate terrain data maps. This information may be presented by tiny one-inch diameter cathode ray tubes or possibly using holographic techniques. In daylight the pilot will be able to see the actual world, but the computer-displayed scene will be superimposed over it. At night and in bad weather the pilot may rely totally on the images provided by the helmet.

The "copilot" (also referred to as a "pilot-intent inference engine") is an artificially intelligent electronic device that will be able to interact with the pilot through voice commands, eye movements, head and hand gestures, and touch. The copilot will be able to respond to these signals and assist the pilot in setting up and firing weapons, monitoring and organizing the pilot's work load, clustering ap-

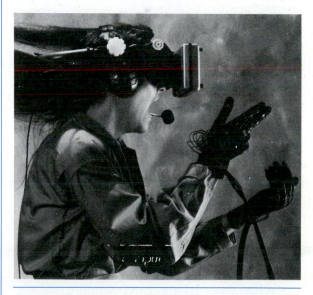

Wearing fiberoptic gloves and a computerized visual display, a NASA researcher experiences the electronic world of "virtual reality." The device allows a pilot not only to see and hear a computer-generated environment but to interact with it.

- To appreciate the diversity of information sources available to performers.

- To clarify the distinction between performance and learning.

- To understand the roles information feedback plays in the performance and learning of motor skills.

- To identify the ways in which knowledge of results can be manipulated to facilitate performance and/or retention.

- To understand the roles knowledge of performance plays in the performance and learning of motor skills.

propriate display information, and providing speech-synthesized three-dimensional directional warnings of enemy threats. The copilot also will monitor the pilot's physiological state and will be able to take control of the plane's functions in case of loss of consciousness or other physical or mental ailment.

■ ■ ■

The presentation of feedback is important to the learning and performance of everyday tasks, not only to very complicated tasks such as flying advance aircraft or spacecraft. NASA and the U.S. Air Force are investing a great deal of time, energy, and money in developing helmets that display information about the environment and instruments. Since this information is available to them no matter where their head is turned, it is called a "heads-up" display. The information displayed about the environment is called a virtual display because it incorporates the important features of the environment in an easily comprehendable form. Clearly the Air Force recognizes the importance of enhanced information to performance and learning.

What applications could virtual world displays have for teaching? A quarterback in football could practice reading defenses while the coach directed the computer to generate different defensive options. The quarterback

The helmet cam designed by Charles Shea at Texas A&M University is built into a standard football helmet. The device relays the view from the player's perspective and the exact position the player is looking at to the sideline and a recording device.

could throw a simulated ball and view the ball's flight and see the responses of the receiver and defensive backs. Such a device would be valuable for training just about anyone who would benefit from experiences in simulated situations (e.g., pilots, emergency personnel, police officers, athletes, or even college students).

A device designed to be used by football players with one of the features of the Super Cockpit helmet was tested at Texas A&M University in the spring of 1990. The device, built into a standard football helmet, consists of eye sensors and a miniaturized, high-resolution camera. The device relays the view from the player's perspective to the sidelines and to a recording device. The coach could view and later review with the player not only the player's field of view but the specific point the player was fixating on (looking at). This allows the coach to see the sequence of events (termed *keys* in football lingo) the player was using to decide what to do. The device seems to be particularly well suited for use with quarterbacks and defensive backs. Other applications of this kind of high-tech gadgetry are being used in drivers' training simulators, golf simulators, and special devices for the visually impaired.

What applications can you envision? Forget for a moment what you think can be done and concentrate on what would be useful. The advanced technology available today is well ahead of the applications. If you can conceive of something, you can almost bet that the technology is available now or will be developed in the near future.

■ ■ ■

Feedback is important for all aspects of motor behavior. Feedback, in one form or another, is our brain's only link to the body and to the environment. Feedback indicates that we are hungry, tired, fatigued; that we should do something; that we should do nothing; that we are in danger; that we are embarrassed; or that we are comfortable. Right now innumerable sensory receptors are communicating with various centers of the brain. Stop for a second and pay attention to the sensations. What do you feel? What you consciously feel is feedback, but many other sources of feedback that you are not conscious of play important roles in your life, in your control of movement, and in the process of learning.

Classifications of Information Feedback

In this chapter, we will be concerned with the feedback sources that most impact the performance and learning of motor skills. We do not mean to suggest that the many other sources of feedback that contribute to the regulation of bodily function and homeostasis are not important to life or even movement behavior. However, we are eliminating from our discussion the many sources of sensory feedback that are not directly related to skill learning. We also do not concentrate on sensory feedback available prior to the initiation of movement even though this information is critical to the decision and planning process.

Our focus is on feedback sources that can be manipulated to improve performance and learning. Such feedback can take many forms in learning environments, but it generally serves the role of providing information to performers about the proficiency with which they move.

For our purposes, it is helpful to classify information into two categories: knowledge of results and knowledge of performance. **Knowledge of results (KR)** is information received concerning the extent to which a response accomplished the intended movement goal. If you attempt to kick a football through the center of the goal posts, knowledge of results is that information you receive concerning your success. In a later section, we discuss the many sources of this information and the many forms it can take. **Knowledge of performance (KP)** is information received about the actual performance and execution of the movement. Was the movement performed correctly or the way it was intended to be performed? This information provides a basis on which to assess the correctness of the movement pattern. Thus, it is possible for the performer to receive positive KP and negative KR or vice versa. The movement can be performed correctly or the way it was intended but still not achieve its goal.

It is important to note that either KR or KP can arise from intrinsic or extrinsic sources. **Intrinsic feedback** is internal feedback normally received during and after the execution of a task. The normal sensory information received during and after hitting a baseball is intrinsic feedback. You feel the bat strike the ball and see where the ball goes without any special assistance. **Extrinsic feedback** is external feedback received during and/or after the response from some additional source. Coaches, teachers, experimenters, and even some special devices are capable of providing additional, augmented information to the performer. This information is considered extrinsic feedback because it may not always be available.

Distinction Between Learning and Performance

Before taking a closer look at the role information feedback plays in performance and learning, it is important to review the distinction between performance and learning (see Chapter 1). It will be especially important in the remaining chapters to distinguish between temporary factors that affect performance and the factors that contribute to the relatively permanent changes in performance, termed **learning**.

For example, a teacher could have a group of beginning bowlers wear a special visor that would not permit them to see the pins but would allow them to see the lane marks near the scratch line. Another group would not be required to wear the visor. Would there be a difference in the performance of the two groups? Would you expect differences in learning? Surely, the visor would at least temporarily affect performance; thus, it would be considered a **performance variable**. It is not

so clear, however, whether the use of the visor would affect learning. To assess the influence on learning, it is not appropriate to simply look at the scores at the end of the bowling unit. The two groups are performing under different conditions. The performance of the two groups must be assessed under the same conditions—probably without the visor. What prediction would you make concerning temporary performance effects and more stable changes related to learning?

If differences are observed during practice, performance effects are indicated. If differences are observed during a retention or transfer test under common conditions, learning effects are indicated. Variables that affect learning are termed **learning variables**. This distinction is critical to the interpretation of the experiments conducted on information feedback (see Salmoni, Schmidt, & Walter, 1984, for review).

Theoretical Issues

Most of the researchers in motor learning consider information feedback to be a very important, if not the most important, variable affecting performance and learning. This is evident by the role information feedback plays in Adams' closed-loop theory (1971) and Schmidt's schema theory (1975). However, the important question for most theorists is why and how information feedback influences performance and learning. Several theoretical attempts to answer this question are discussed, but the reader should be warned that a comprehensive theory of information feedback has not yet been proposed.

Reward, Motivation, and Information

The study of information feedback, particularly KR, has its roots in the work of Thorndike (1927). Thorndike's **Law of Effect** states that organisms tend to repeat responses that are rewarded and avoid responses that are not rewarded or are punished (see Adams, 1978, 1987 for reviews). If a rat pushes a bar and food is presented, the food is regarded as a reward. The reward-task relationship results in the rat's pushing the bar more often than if food were not presented.

All parents are quite familiar with this process. Reward the good behaviors of your children with a few kind words, a smile, or hug; ignore or punish the inappropriate behaviors. If it works, good behaviors are repeated and inappropriate behaviors occur less often. (We have not been very successful with this strategy, but our lack of success could be attributed to our hard-headed children rather than our behavior modification techniques.)

In terms of motor skill performance and learning, how could information feedback like KR serve as a reward or increase motivation? Consider, for example, that you are learning to bowl (no visor this time). If you throw a strike, it is possible for you to interpret your success as a form of reward or as a factor that may increase your motivation. You will want to repeat the performance and you tend to feel better. Visit a bowling alley and watch for beginners who throw a strike. What kind of reaction do you see? Certainly not a negative one! More probably you will view an almost ridiculous display of excitement. What about the response you see after a gutter ball? Certainly

"I DON'T *WANTA* GO OUTSIDE AN' PLAY ... ...UNLESS SHE SAYS I *CAN'T.*"

Our uses of rewards and punishments don't always elicit the response we want. "Dennis the Menace" used by permission of Hank Ketcham Enterprises, Inc. and © by North America Syndicate.

the bowler does not wish to repeat the response and you typically will not see outward evidences of increased motivation. This kind of anecdotal evidence is difficult to understand and dangerous to interpret.

The question remains: Does this notion apply to the learning of motor skills? To answer this question, we turn to research on KR. The data from KR research suggest that subjects tend to change their behavior when they are provided error information. When this information is not presented, they tend to repeat their original behavior. This appears directly opposite to the predictions of the Law of Effect. However, when you consider the subjects' interpretations of error information, a different picture emerges. When large errors result, subjects tend to make larger changes in their behavior than when smaller errors are observed. This is consistent with Thorndike's proposals. Large errors are interpreted as punishment and small errors as rewards.

Clearly, the reward and motivational effects of feedback are not well understood and should not be ruled out as playing a role in the performance and learning effects observed. What is better understood is that feedback plays an important informational role in performance and learning.

Do feedback sources such as KR and KP provide performers with usable information? Most certainly! For example, subjects use KR to make adjustments in their performance in the direction of the movement goal. In fact, only when error information is provided do subjects consistently make corrections in the right direction. Simply saying "good job"/"bad job" or "right"/"wrong" may be sufficient to act as a reward or provide motivation, but it is not sufficient to promote learning.

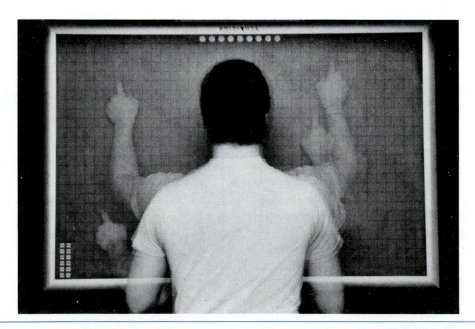

"Acuvision" is a vision training system designed to improve eye/hand coordination. This device, which is being used at the Olympic Training Center in Colorado Springs, provides immediate feedback to the athlete.

Guidance Hypothesis and the Processing of Feedback

Feedback can provide the performer with information on how to correct a movement or attain a target. That is, feedback can be used almost like a guide to follow to the correct movement and/or the target. To get a feeling for the basis of the **guidance hypothesis**, consider the following personal experience.

During my first few years at Texas A&M University, I visited Houston on various occasions. On most trips I was driven or accompanied by someone who knew the way around that big, confusing city. When I did the driving, my passenger would navigate, telling me when and where to turn to reach our destination. After five or so years and dozens of trips to Houston, I finally made the trip alone. Confident that I would have no trouble finding my way around because I knew many landmarks and had never gotten lost, I started out. Guess what happened. I got miserably lost! I kept seeing places I knew but was not able to get my bearings. On previous trips my navigators

had done all the work for me. I had not learned my way around Houston; I only thought I had. . . . Even skills that have been learned can be forgotten. Think about how your math skills deteriorate as you come to rely on a pocket calculator or what happens to your spelling skills as you depend more and more on your word processor's spellcheck.

But does feedback that guides the performer toward the target result in better performance and learning? It is relatively clear that the guidance features of feedback can be used to positively influence performance when this source of feedback is present. However, as we discuss later in this chapter, the effects may be present only as long as the feedback is present. Indeed, evidence suggests that subjects may become overly dependent on the guidance. A number of KR paradigms are discussed that suggest that when guidance is available, subjects fail to seek out other sources of feedback, develop relationships between errors and responses, and they do not test alternative strategies that do not rely on guidance information.

Knowledge of Results

For nearly a century, researchers have been concerned with the role that knowledge of results (KR) plays in the learning of motor skills. (Remember, KR is information received concerning the extent to which the response accomplished the intended movement goal.) For the most part, however, this experimental work did not involve a test of retention. Unfortunately, the lack of a common retention test clouds any interpretation of the results in terms of assessing the influence on learning. Thus, many aspects of the so-called "laws of KR" found in older textbooks are now thought to be incorrect.

The early work conducted without retention tests is very interesting from a historical viewpoint and perhaps provides a theoretical perspective from which we can interpret the

theories of the day. This work is carefully chronicled in several excellent review papers (Newell, 1977; Salmoni, Schmidt, & Walter, 1984; Adams, 1987). Our attention is primarily directed toward KR research that includes some method of assessing the relatively stable changes in behavior indicative of learning. For the purposes of this text, KR experiments are divided into sections based on the information provided and the schedule of KR presentation.

Absolute and Relative Frequency of KR

The most obvious, and perhaps the most used, manipulation of KR relates to the number of trials for which KR is available. For many years this question appeared to have a relatively direct answer: the more trials with KR the better the performance. But recently this conclusion has been questioned by theorists.

Salmoni et al. (1984) suggested that KR may have both detrimental and beneficial effects on learning. The detrimental effect involves a type of dependency on KR that the learner seems to develop when provided KR (see previous section). Accompanying this dependence is a tendency for the learner not to process other sources of feedback or attempt alternative strategies when KR is provided. Subjects are virtually "spoon fed" when KR is available but have to scavenge for information when it is not. Apparently, the process of scavenging has at least some positive effects on learning. Scavenging causes the subject to try new strategies, seek out available sources of information, and, in general, be more resourceful and less reliant on KR.

The determination of an optimum schedule of providing KR is left with dual and opposing considerations. Too much KR results in a guidance effect; too little KR and subjects are potentially left with little assurance that they are achieving the response goal. Several experimental KR schedules have been tested. **Absolute frequency** refers to the actual number of KR trials without consideration for the total number of trials. **Relative frequency** refers to the percentage of total trials for which KR is provided. Note that manipulations of absolute frequency can change relative frequency and vice versa. At their extremes, absolute and relative frequencies can involve a manipulation in which KR is provided on all trials or KR is not provided on all trials. This would result in 0 and 100 absolute frequency and 0 percent and 100 percent relative frequency.

Number of KR Presentations Versus Number of Trials. In a classic study, Bilodeau, Bilodeau, & Shumsky (1959) asked four groups of subjects to move a lever on a linear slide to an unknown target for 20 trials. The groups were differentiated in terms of the number of trials in which the subjects received experimenter-provided KR after the trial. Groups received KR after the first 19 of 20 trials, the first 6 of 20 trials, the first 2 of 20 trials, or 0 of 20 trials. In addition, the 0 group received 5 additional trials with KR.

The results, in terms of absolute error, are depicted in Figure 10.1. Subjects tended to improve their performance, particularly early in practice, only after trials in which KR was provided. When KR was withdrawn, performance deteriorated; and when KR was not provided, improvements in performance were not observed. Perhaps the most interesting feature of the figure is the section on the right that plots the first 5 trials for the 19 group against the performance of the 0 group on trials 20–24. It appears that the 20-trial experience without KR did not increment performance even after KR was provided.

Similar results have been found in a number of studies (Trowbridge & Cason, 1932; Newell, 1974; Bennett & Simmons, 1984). Apparently, KR does affect performance and learning; in fact, learning does not appear to occur in the absence of KR. These findings have traditionally led to the conclusion that the absolute frequency of KR is an important performance and learning variable, but the influence of relative frequencies is less well understood.

Relative Frequency. Bilodeau and Bilodeau (1958) assigned subjects to four different relative frequency conditions: 10 percent (10 of 100 trials), 25 percent (10 of 40 trials), 33 percent (10 of 30 trials), and 100 percent (10 of 10 trials). Absolute frequency of KR was constant across groups. Each group received experimenter-provided KR after 10 trials that was distributed uniformly across the total number of trials.

The trials following the KR presentation are plotted in Figure 10.2. The results indicate that there was no performance effect due to the relative frequency of KR. Essentially, the trials without KR were neutral with respect to improving performance. The authors con-

212

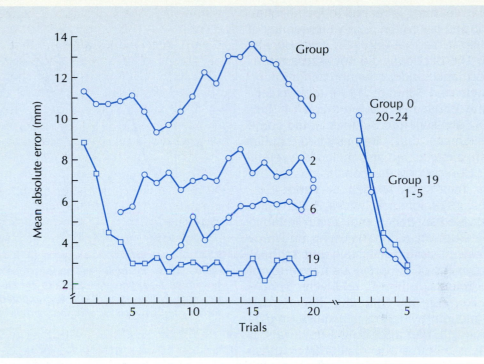

Figure 10.1 *Absolute error for linear positioning responses under different knowledge of results conditions. The group numbers indicate the number of trials for which knowledge of results was provided. The graph segment to the right compares the zero group on five additional trials in which knowledge of results was provided with the first five trials of the 19 group.*

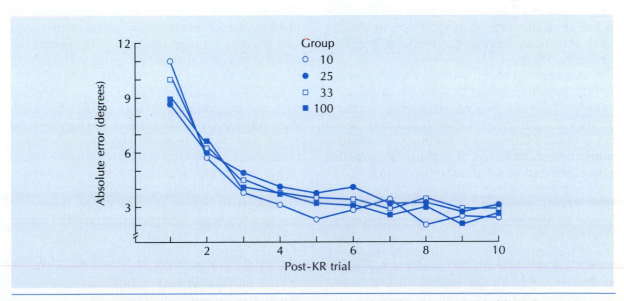

Figure 10.2 *Absolute error for a positioning task in which subjects received knowledge of results after 10, 25, 33, or 100 percent of the trials of practice. Only trials immediately following knowledge of results are plotted.*

cluded that "learning is related to the absolute frequency, and not to the relative frequency of KR" (p. 382). Note that only performance was assessed. The Bilodeaus did not assess retention performance under common conditions.

Winstein and Schmidt (1990) took exception to the Bilodeau's interpretation of their 1958 data. Winstein and Schmidt noted some limited evidence that demonstrated similar performance effects but also included a retention test. Contrary to the conclusions of the Bilodeaus, their study as well as others (e.g., Ho & Shea, 1978; Johnson, Wicks, & Ben-Sira, 1981) provided evidence that lower relative frequencies do not reduce learning and may even enhance learning. Winstein and Schmidt noted that most of the previous frequency of KR experiments utilized relatively simple motor tasks (e.g., line drawing, linear positioning), and improvements in acquisition performance leveled off after only a few trials. It was unclear whether the results from these tasks could be generalized to more complex tasks. In addition, they were concerned that even a no KR retention test might not truly reflect the extent to which the task was learned. A no KR retention test is more similar to lower relative frequency than to higher relative frequency conditions. Thus, subjects provided lower frequency conditions during acquisition have an advantage during retention testing (see Specificity Versus Variability of Practice, Chapter 11).

In Experiment 1, Winstein and Schmidt (1990) provided subjects with 99 acquisition trials on two consecutive days under either a 100 or 33 percent relative frequency of KR condition. Retention was assessed 10 minutes after the second day of acquisition practice and consisted of 27 trials under 0, 33, 66, or 100 percent relative frequency of KR condition. The task was to move a lever in an attempt to produce a goal movement pattern (Figure 10.3). The goal movement pattern and the actual movement pattern were displayed to the subject on a computer monitor along with a measure of the discrepancy between the two patterns (RMS—see Appendix A). This

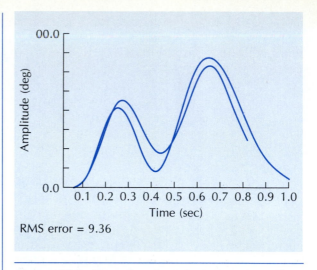

Figure 10.3 Example of performance on a lever movement task. The standard and actual performance are plotted. The error (RMS) is computed as the area (force-time) between the standard and the performance.

type of KR has been called *kinematic KR* by Adams (1987) and might be considered KP because the movement pattern is evaluated (see later section on Knowledge of Performance).

The results indicated that improvements in acquisition performance occurred throughout practice. There was a tendency of the subjects provided 33 percent relative frequency to produce larger errors than subjects provided 100 percent relative frequency. However, the effect was not statistically significant. Subjects under the 33 percent condition during acquisition tended to perform better on the retention test, but this difference was also not significant (Figure 10.4). This trend was evidenced regardless of the relative frequency condition utilized during retention. Contrary to the traditional viewpoint, the results suggest that increasing the relative frequency of KR presentation does not facilitate learning. Rather, Winstein and Schmidt (1990) report that their data, although not statistically significant, suggest that lower relative frequencies might enhance learning. This conclusion should be viewed with caution without additional experimental evidence.

214

Fading and Reverse Fading of KR. Winstein and Schmidt (1990, Experiment 2) manipulated the distribution of KR trials in a 50 percent relative frequency condition to produce what they called a fading schedule. A **fading schedule** provides KR more frequently early in practice and then gradually reduces the number of trials for which KR is presented later in practice. These researchers suggested that the guidance hypothesis predicts that error information should be more useful early in practice when a greater degree of guidance is required but relatively less useful later in practice. (A **reverse fading** condition could be constructed by providing fewer KR trials early in practice and increasing the number of KR trials as acquisition progresses [see Nicholson & Schmidt, 1990].)

Using generally the same procedures and tasks previously described, but with a delayed retention test, Winstein and Schmidt (1990, Experiment 3) tested a fading schedule within a 50 percent relative frequency. A 100 percent relative frequency condition was included. The acquisition and delayed retention performances are provided in Figure 10.5. No differences in performance were found during acquisition but the 50 percent fading relative frequency condition resulted in superior retention regardless of the type of retention test administered. Contrary to traditional views of KR and intuition, fewer KR presentations, when the presentations were faded, resulted in superior retention. Less information resulted in smaller errors! How could this be?

Winstein and Schmidt (1990) propose that the lower relative frequency may be beneficial because the subject is required on no KR trials to attend to response-produced feedback associated with the movement. Likewise, no KR trials may cause the subject to engage other cognitive processes such as those related to error detection. Alternatively, a 100 percent relative frequency condition readily provides the subject with the information required to generate response adjustments from trial to

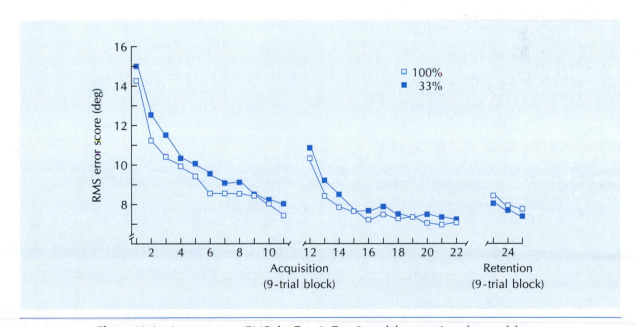

Figure 10.4 *Average error (RMS) for Day 1, Day 2, and the retention phases of the experiment. The 33 percent group received knowledge of results on one-third of the trials and the 100 percent group received knowledge of results on every trial.*

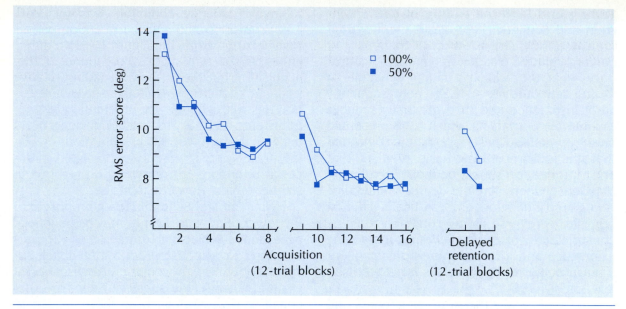

Figure 10.5 *Average error (RMS) for Day 1, Day 2, and the retention phases of the experiment. The 50 percent group received knowledge of results on half of the trials in a fading schedule. That is, knowledge of results was presented on more trials early in practice and gradually reduced over acquisition. The 100 percent group received knowledge of results after each trial.*

trial, reducing the need to seek out additional information. This may result in a dependency on the KR because the KR actually becomes part of the task. Perhaps, 100 percent relative frequencies are really detrimental to learning and reduced frequencies are beneficial.

Bandwidth KR

Another frequency of KR manipulation involves using the subject's actual performance errors to determine whether or not KR is provided. The **bandwidth of KR** procedure (Sherwood, 1988) involves setting some criterion range of errors within which KR is not provided and outside of which KR is provided. The rationale for this manipulation involves the argument that KR is not productive on trials in which the subject produces a movement with small error. This is particularly the case when the error may simply represent an inherent variability in the motor system (see Im-

pulse Variability Theory, Chapter 9). When the errors are small, subjects tend to continue to use the error information to make adjustments on the next response. Winstein and Schmidt (1990) cite a personal communication with Robert Bjork, who labeled these adjustments **maladaptive short-term corrections**. If KR is not provided on these trials, the subject will likely repeat the relatively correct response and performance stability will be encouraged. It should be noted that the wider the bandwidth, the lower the relative frequency of KR that results. Bandwidth schedules may also produce a fading schedule of presentation because as practice progresses, the subject's performance approaches the goal and KR is provided less often.

Sherwood (1988) tested three groups of subjects on a rapid elbow flexion task with a goal movement time of 200 milliseconds. The groups were differentiated in terms of the size of the bandwidth around the 200 milliseconds goal. A control group (0 percent bandwidth) was provided with KR after every trial. A 5 percent bandwidth group was provided KR if the error exceeded 10 milliseconds and a 10 percent bandwidth group was supplied KR when the error was greater than 20 milliseconds. The results indicated that response variability decreased as the bandwidth increased. Response accuracy, however, was not influenced by the bandwidth manipulation. The fact that a bandwidth manipulation affects response variability but not response accuracy may be important (see Considerations Related to the Error Measure Used later in this chapter).

Bandwidth and Relative Frequency.   Lee and Carnahan (1990) attempted to separate the bandwidth from the relative frequency effect. (Remember that as the bandwidth is decreased, a corresponding increase results in relative frequency. At the extreme, a 0 percent bandwidth results in 100 percent relative frequency and a 100 percent bandwidth results in 0 percent relative frequency.) To accomplish this, Lee and Carnahan asked subjects to knock down a series of three barriers in 500 milliseconds. Two groups of subjects were tested under a 5 percent and 10 percent bandwidth. This produced a fading relative frequency schedule that was used to determine the KR presentations of two additional groups. These groups received KR using the same schedule as the first two groups, but the presentation was not dependent on their actual score. For example, if a subject in one of the bandwidth groups received KR on trials 3, 5, 6, and 9 in a specific block, a subject in a parallel group received KR on trials 3, 5, 6, and 9 regardless of his or her actual error. These subjects are said to be yoked to bandwidth subjects.

As in previous bandwidth experiments, the retention results indicated that larger bandwidths (less frequent KR) resulted in enhanced response stability during retention. The analysis of response accuracy did not indicate any significant effects, although there was a slight tendency for 10 percent bandwidth subjects to perform more accurately than other subjects. The findings also suggest that the bandwidth effect is not totally attributable to a relative frequency effect. It seemed important not only to reduce the number of KR trials but also to reduce them selectively on the basis of actual performance.

KR and Response Stability.   Lee and Carnahan (1990) made another, potentially important, observation relative to the effect of KR on response stability. To do this they replotted their acquisition data in order to separate out the trials following KR and the trials following no KR. The results of this recalculation are given in Figure 10.6. Subjects under all conditions tended to change their response following the presentation of KR and tended to repeat their previous response on trials in which KR was not presented. Surely, repeating a relatively correct trial (bandwidth groups) rather than just any trial (yoked groups) is contributing to the bandwidth effect.

Lee and Carnahan (1990) point out that it may be important to note that the retention advantage of the larger bandwidth over the smaller bandwidth and yoked relative frequency conditions was in terms of movement consistency. The more stable performance may have come from the fact that nearly correct responses in which KR was not provided were rewarded with the statement "correct response" causing the subject to attempt to repeat the previous response. Repeating nearly correct responses may help stabilize performance.

It is also important to note that in the search for optimal learning conditions, larger bandwidths contribute to only half of the goal. Lee and Carnahan (1990) note that motor learning entails both acquiring the capability to adapt performance as necessary and acquiring the capacity to stabilize performance as necessary. The ultimate goal is the production of consistent and accurate performance. It may be that an "optimum" set of conditions will be found to involve features of the bandwidth procedures to produce response stability with features of other KR manipulations that increment response accuracy.

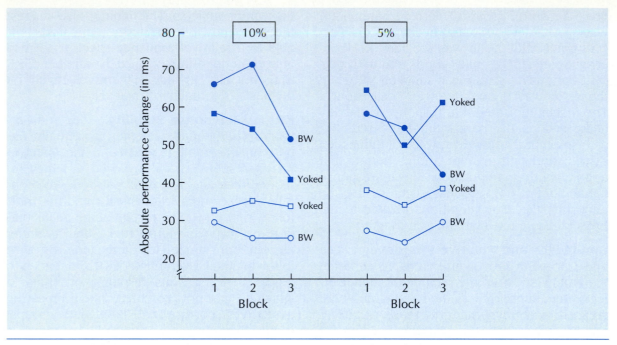

Figure 10.6 *Average absolute change in performance for subjects on trials that were followed by knowledge of results (closed symbols) and trials that were not followed by knowledge of results (open symbols).*

KR Delay and Post KR Delay

In typical sports skills, KR is available almost immediately after the performance. You hit, throw, or kick a ball and observe the result. In other activities, you may perform a motor skill and have to wait to be informed of the degree of success or failure of your response. A gymnast or diver does not receive KR from the judges until a minute or two after the routine or dive is completed. What are the implications of altering the time when KR is presented? This question is very complex and probably not very well understood.

Two intervals can be manipulated when varying the temporal location of KR (Figure 10.7). The **KR delay interval** is the time that elapses between the completion of the response and the presentation of KR. The **post KR delay interval** is the time that elapses between the presentation of KR and the beginning of the next response. Together these intervals comprise the **interresponse interval**.

KR Delay Interval. Based primarily on animal studies, early theorists considered the KR delay interval important to learning (e.g., Hamilton, 1929; Roberts, 1930). Animals learned to do simple tasks more quickly when food was dispensed immediately after correct responses. As the interval between the response and reward was increased even a few seconds, learning progressed more slowly. However, this does not appear to be the case for the learning of motor skills in humans.

Lorge and Thorndike (1935) asked subjects to toss balls to an unseen target. Following delays of one to six seconds or even a trial later, subjects were informed of their response error. No performance effects were observed. Similarly, Bilodeau and Bilodeau (1958), in a series of experiments, manipulated the KR delay interval (seconds to one week) during the learning of a variety of tasks. No effects were observed during acquisition. Note that retention tests were not used. This precludes the interpretation of the data in terms of learn-

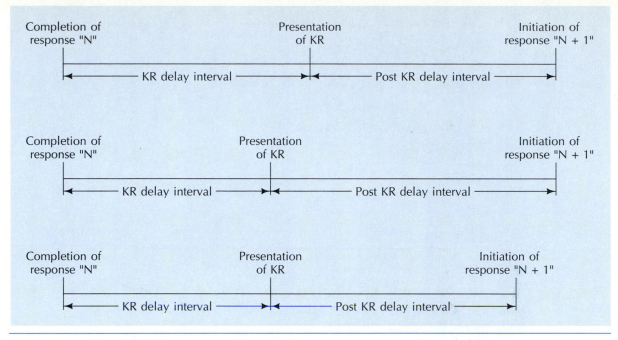

Figure 10.7 *Temporal events that determine the knowledge of results delay interval and the post knowledge of results interval. Note that lengthening or shortening one of the intervals affects the other interval.*

ing. Thus, we are left with the need for further research on this interval (see Salmoni et al., 1984, for further comments).

One experiment related to the KR delay interval did include a no KR retention test (the authors referred to the test as a *transfer test*). Shea and Upton (1976) asked two groups of subjects to learn two linear positioning responses on each of 20 trials. Both groups received KR for both trials 30 seconds after the completion of the second response. For one group, the interval between the completion of the second response and the presentation of KR for the first response was unfilled. The interval was filled with the performance of additional movements for the other group.

The results (Figure 10.8) indicate that the additional interpolated tasks were detrimental to performance and learning. Apparently, these tasks created interference that negatively affected the processing of the KR when it was finally presented (see Marteniuk, 1986).

Post KR Delay Interval. What is the effect of varying the post KR delay interval? Just as with the KR delay interval, most of the early experiments did not include a common retention test. There are some indications, however, that severe decreases in the post KR delay interval have detrimental effects on performance and learning. However, Salmoni et al. (1984) caution that manipulations to either of the intervals change the interresponse interval and this interval may be important (see Practice Distribution, Chapter 11). McGuigan (1959b) and Dees and Grindley (1951) have demonstrated that increasing the intertrial interval increased learning.

What if the post KR delay interval is filled with additional activity? Shea and Upton (1976) found activity introduced in the KR delay interval to negatively affect performance and learning. What about the post KR delay interval? Magill (1973, 1977) did not include a retention test but did present data that suggest

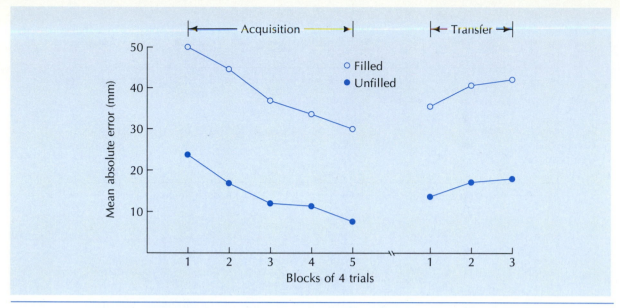

Figure 10.8 *Absolute errors for a positioning task as a function of the processing demands imposed during the knowledge of results delay interval.*

that interpolated activity in the post KR delay interval negatively affects performance.

In an experiment that did include a common retention test, Lee and Magill (1983) asked three groups of subjects to learn to "knock down" a series of three barriers in 1050 milliseconds. The groups were differentiated in terms of the activity they were required to perform during the post KR delay interval: rest, nonmotor guessing task, or the same movement pattern in 1350 milliseconds (see Figure 10.9). Activity during the post KR delay interval once again negatively influenced acquisition performance but did not appear to influence learning (see Benedetti & McCullagh, 1987, for slightly different results).

The general conclusion, although not stated with much confidence, is that manipulations to the post KR interval do not significantly affect learning. (Magill, 1988, reported some findings that suggest that related motor tasks interpolated in the post KR delay interval did increase transfer.) It should be noted that when alternate tasks are placed in the post KR

delay interval, a sort of variable practice schedule is created (see Specificity Versus Variability of Practice, Chapter 11). The variability of practice literature suggests that related tasks interpolated between criterion tasks (in the post KR delay interval) positively affect learning. The Lee and Magill (1983) findings do not support this contention.

Summary KR

In a little different manipulation, the KR delay interval can be filled with additional trials of the task to be learned. **Summary KR** is used when a set of trials is completed before KR is presented for that set. The use of the term *summary* may be unfortunate because typical summary presentations do not summarize the results of a set of trials in a statistical way (e.g., mean, median, etc.), although this manipulation is possible. Rather, KR for each individual trial is presented although the presentation is delayed.

Bilodeau (1956), using a linear positioning

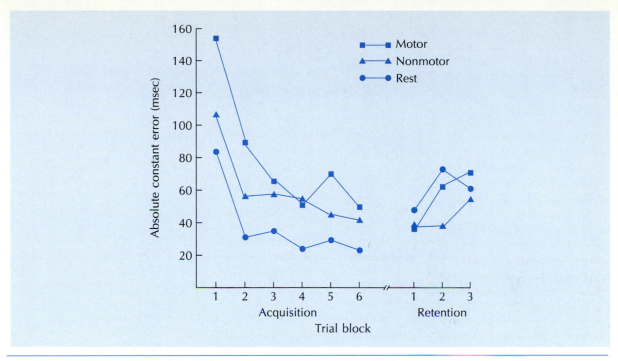

Figure 10.9 *Absolute constant errors for a barrier knockdown task as a function of the activity imposed during the post knowledge of results delay interval.*

task, and later Annett (1959), using a force production task, challenged the necessity of presenting KR immediately after each trial. Both investigations demonstrated that performance did not differ at the end of acquisition for conditions receiving immediate KR and KR summarized over a block of trials (no retention test was used).

Lavery (1962) tested summary conditions and utilized retention tests (Figure 10.10). Lavery's subjects demonstrated improved performance on a delayed retention test for a group that received summary KR, as opposed to groups provided KR immediately after each trial and a group experiencing a combination of both immediate and summary KR. Lavery, relying on an argument proposed earlier by Miller (1953), stated that:

> If the artificial (experimenter supplied) feedback makes the correct response more accessible, then it is liable to encourage

subjects to try for high scores instead of learning the cues inherent in the task which they must perceive in order to make the right type of response. (p. 108)

Schmidt, Young, Swinnen, & Shapiro (1989), using a linear slide reversal task, demonstrated that as the KR summary length increased (at least up to 15 trials), acquisition decrements were greater. However, as the number of trials over which KR was summarized increased, retention performance improved relative to shorter summaries and immediate KR conditions (see Figure 10.11A). In a similar experiment, Schmidt, Lange, and Young (1990) utilized a relatively more complex task. They found retention did not improve as the length of the summary increased. Rather, they found an optimal summary length of 5 trials compared to 1, 10, and 15 trials. On the basis of these findings, Schmidt et al. (1990) suggested that the optimal (in terms of

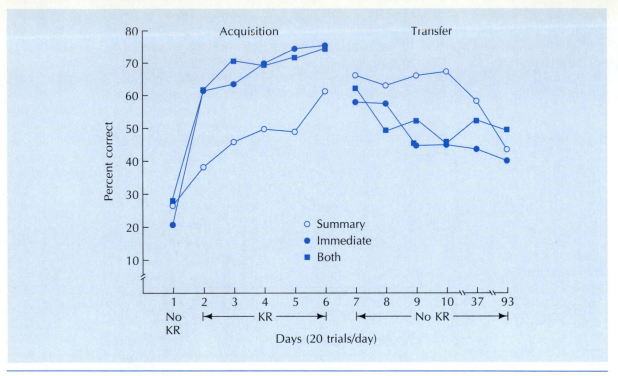

Figure 10.10 *Percent correct response as a function of immediate, summary, and both (immediate and summary) knowledge of results conditions.*

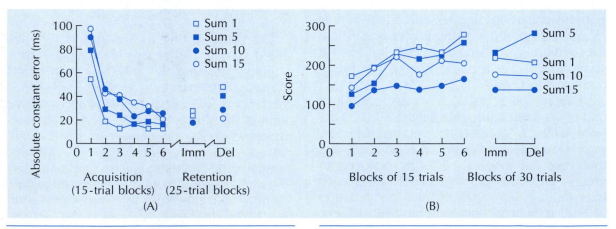

Figure 10.11A *Average absolute constant error for a timing task as a function of summary knowledge of results length. Retention was measured after 10 minutes (Imm) and after two days (Del). Knowledge of results was not provided on the retention test.*

Figure 10.11B *Average score for a timing task as a function of summary knowledge of results length. Retention was measured after 10 minutes (Imm) and after two days (Del). Knowledge of results was not provided on the retention test.*

retention) summary length may decrease as the task complexity increases. In both Schmidt et al. (1989, 1990) experiments, significant differences were observed for response bias. Response variability was unaffected by changes in summary length.

Gable, Shea, and Wright (1991) tested subjects on a simple force production task. They found (Experiment 1), as predicted by Schmidt et al. (1990), a summary length of 16 trials to result in retention superior to that of summary lengths of 1 or 8 trials. Gable et al. also found summary length to influence response bias but not response variability.

Apparently, summary manipulations are an effective way to provide the informational content inherent in KR without incurring the negative effects of guidance. When the strong guidance properties of immediate KR are removed through the presentation of a string of trials without KR (as in summary conditions), additional information processing activities may occur. Schmidt et al. (1989, 1990) indicate that in the absence of immediate KR, the subject is encouraged to engage other information processing activities that might focus on additional important task or environmental cues and/or response-produced feedback important to long-term retention. In doing so, Schmidt et al. (1989) speculate that subjects may become more sensitive to the errors they produce during practice and from this develop an intrinsic capability to detect them. This ability may reduce their dependency on other forms of information. Such an ability becomes extremely useful should the learner experience a series of no KR trials during retention.

Note that the summary manipulation as well as the KR delay manipulations with interpolated tasks are forms of a trials delay procedure popularized by Bilodeau (1956, 1966, 1969) and Lavery and Suddon (1962).

Precision of KR

The informational content of feedback depends on the form the feedback takes and the extent to which the subject is able to interpret it. **Precision of KR** refers to the level of accuracy with which KR is presented. Both qualitative and quantitative KR are possible. **Qualitative KR** can take two forms, depending on the task requirements; it can inform subjects that their performance was correct/incorrect or it can provide information that the performance was too fast/slow, too hard/soft, too long/short, and so on. In either case, the subjects have access to information on the quality of their performance without additional quantification. **Quantitative KR** not only indicates the direction of an error but the magnitude of that error in some units. Quantitative KR can be presented with varying precision.

Smoll (1972) asked three groups of subjects to learn to roll a ball at 70 percent of each subject's maximum velocity. KR was provided in either qualitative form (too slow or too fast) or quantitative form (1/100 or 1/10 of second units). A retention test was not used (Figure 10.12). The results indicated that the quantitative conditions resulted in acquisition performance superior to the qualitative condition. It could be concluded that quantitative KR results in performance superior to qualitative KR, although Rogers (1974) has demonstrated that quantitative KR can be too precise.

Incorporating a common retention test, Magill and Wood (1986) asked subjects to learn a six-segment movement task. Subjects were provided either qualitative or quantitative KR. The results indicated that early in practice, KR conditions produced little differences in performance. However, later in practice the quantitative KR resulted in superior acquisition performance. The superiority of the quantitative KR carried over to the retention test.

Reeve, Dornier, and Weeks (1990) investigated the qualitative versus quantitative KR distinction. The task was to make an 80-centimeter movement from a start button to a target in 500 milliseconds. Qualitative KR was varied by using a small (±10 milliseconds) or large (±50 milliseconds) criterion for determining whether a trial was performed cor-

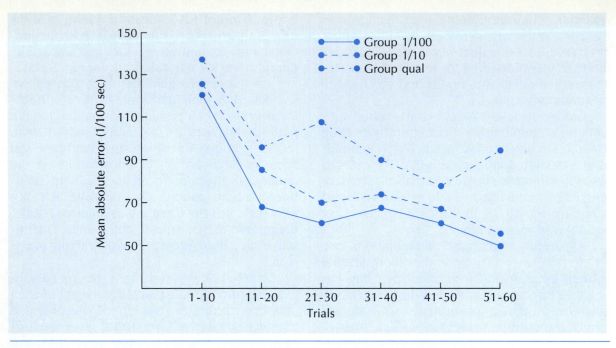

Figure 10.12 *Average absolute error for a bowling task as a function of the precision of knowledge of results.*

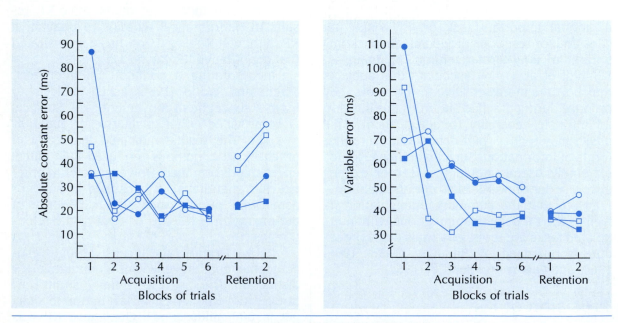

Figure 10.13 *Average absolute constant (left) and variable (right) errors for a timing task as a function of knowledge of results (qualitative = unfilled symbols and quantitative = filled symbols) and size of the bandwidth (broad = square symbols and narrow = circle symbols).*

rectly or not. Quantitative KR involved providing KR in milliseconds when the performance exceeded the small or large criterion. Thus, a kind of bandwidth was formed that was used to provide either qualitative or quantitative KR.

The results, which are consistent with the bandwidth studies, found more stable performance for the larger bandwidths during acquisition (Figure 10.13). However, bandwidth of this type did not influence retention. Consis-

tent with other KR precision studies, quantitative KR resulted in retention superior to qualitative KR.

These collective results suggest, tentatively at least, that quantitative KR results in superior performance and learning, provided that the KR is not too precise and that sufficient practice is provided. However, the number of experiments that have utilized retention tests is limited.

Considerations Related to the Error Measure Used

It is interesting for theoretical and practical reasons to note that particular KR manipulations produce results in different error measures. For example, the bandwidth KR manipulations have generally been observed in response variability (variable error). That is, the retention performance of subjects under narrow bandwidth conditions during acquisition is more variable than that of subjects who had learned under wider bandwidths. Bandwidth manipulations have resulted in little or no effect on response bias. On the other hand, the summary KR manipulations are generally observed in response bias (absolute constant error). An optimal summary length results in smaller tendencies to produce negative or positive errors. Little or no effect is observed in response variability.

This finding may be very important to our understanding of the processes the subjects engage in as a result of a particular KR manipulation. Schmidt et al. (1989) have suggested that absolute constant error is sensitive to the subjects' capability to accurately parameterize a motor program. It seems reasonable that optimal summary length conditions might con-

tribute to this process. In summary conditions, the subjects are forced to seek out alternative bases for parameterizing responses during the trial set. After a set of trials is completed and KR is provided, the subjects can evaluate the degree of their success on each trial.

Schmidt et al. (1990) also suggest that response variability indexes motor program development. If this is the case, larger bandwidth conditions appear to promote motor program development. On trials with small errors that fall within the bandwidth, KR is not presented. This should be interpreted by the subjects as a signal not to change response specifications in order to duplicate the previous response. What corrective action should a subject take if after a trial or two with no KR, KR from the next trial indicates an error has been produced? There is no reason to suspect that the response specifications were incorrect because the subject had no reason to change them. Presumably, this signals the subject to update the program. The program that has been supplied the same parameter values has produced unstable responses.

A New Generation of Feedback

Imagine being able to see Carl Lewis sprint his way to a new world record from a totally different perspective—from the inside out! What if you could see each of his muscles stretch and tighten? What if you could watch his adrenaline skyrocket as he learns of his feat? How would you like to see his joints compress under the impact of his steps? These may seem like ridiculous concepts to most people but, thanks to *virtual environments,* they may be a reality in the not too distant future.

Virtual environments, or *virtual realities* as they are sometimes called, already exist in laboratories across the nation (see Super Cockpit at beginning of this chapter). They have been used to investigate topics as diverse as insects' eyes and mathematical equations, and other uses for virtual realities are being actively pursued in medical and technological fields.

Some virtual environments go beyond simulating only the visual sense by using gloves with fiber-optics. The glove is used to relay information to the computer. The movement of the hand can be displayed in the virtual display and/or can be used to command the computer. In the not too distant future, it is possible that a microsurgery device could be controlled by the movement of the surgeon's hand via the fiber-optic glove while the surgeon views a realistic display of the inside of the heart. At the University of North Carolina, a research team has been using virtual world technology to help physicians position the beams of radiation used in cancer therapy and to aid biochemists searching for targets on protein molecules where they can attach drugs.

In the current version of virtual reality technology, the user wears a set of goggles or a helmet that generates images on a liquid crystal display. The picture appearing before each eye is slightly different, giving the illusion of three dimensions. An electromagnetic field is generated so that a magnet mounted on the top of the helmet can be used to locate the wearer's exact head position. Thus, the computer adjusts the wearer's view that is projected on the goggles depending on his or her head position.

Can you image the potential for the study of human movement and the development of sport skills?

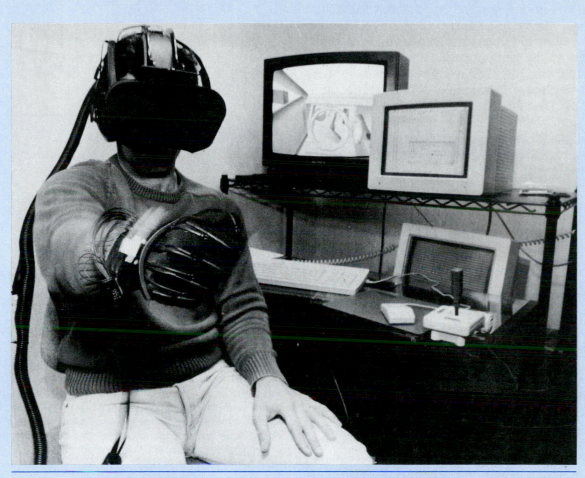

VPL Research in Redwood City, California have developed a virtual reality system that simulates driving a car.

Knowledge of Performance

Remember that knowledge of performance (KP) is information received about the actual performance and execution of the movement. The question that is asked pertaining to KP is: Was the movement performed correctly or the way it was intended to be performed? KP may be important in teaching and coaching situations. The instructor's objective may be to change the movement pattern not because the subject cannot produce a relatively accurate response but because flaws in the response structure may ultimately limit the subject's ability to progress to higher levels. We are all familiar with a tennis or basketball player who is relatively capable at achieving the goal of the task (hitting or shooting the ball) but has terrible form. Teachers and coaches may want to concentrate on changing the response structure and, at least for a while, not pay attention to the outcome of the response. This is done with the hope that the changes in the response structure will ultimately allow the performer to advance to higher levels of skill.

However, when the goal of the practice session is to change the response structure, the differences between KR and KP become clouded. KR relates to the degree to which the goal is achieved, which is now the performance structure. This has led researchers to call this kind of KP *kinematic KR* (see Winstein & Schmidt, 1990, this chapter; Kohl & Shea, 1990, Chapter 11). Many studies provide graphic displays of performance from which the subjects can determine their response errors and this is termed *information KR*.

Lindahl (1945) presented a group of workers with tracings from a strip chart that depicted the pattern of their foot movements on a shop task (Figure 10.14, top). Typical workers had only been provided with information about how many tasks were completed and the quality of the work. Lindahl's subjects were provided a strip illustrating the correct

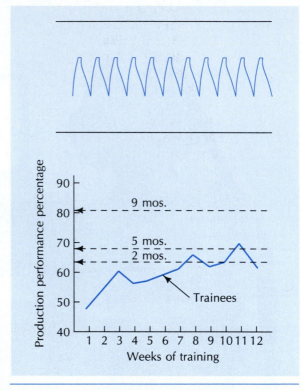

Figure 10.14 *Ideal pattern of foot action required by the operator to complete a disc cut (top). The graph (bottom) illustrates the performance of workers using the graphic information during 12 weeks of training. The dotted lines indicate performance standards achieved by workers trained under other methods after 2, 5, and 9 months of work experience.*

foot pattern and periodically supplied tracings of their performance. The results indicated that the workers provided with the kinematic information achieved levels of performance in 11 weeks that took the typical worker 5 months to achieve.

In a more recent study Newell, Quinn, Sparrow, and Walter (1983) provided subjects with either no information, movement times,

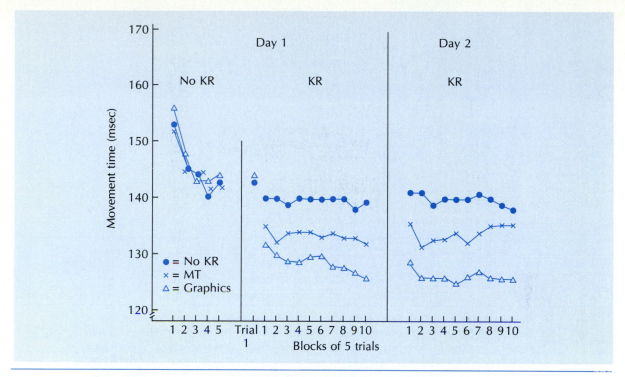

Figure 10.15 *Average movement time for a speed of movement task as a function of the type of knowledge of performance provided. The graphics condition consisted of a graphic display on a computer monitor of the velocity-time tracing.*

or a velocity-time trace on a computer monitor (Figure 10.15). The task was to move a lever from a start position to a target as quickly as possible. All subjects were provided movement times on the first 25 trials and then were given 2 days of practice (50 trials/day). The results indicated that the kinematic information group outperformed the other groups. Note that a common retention test was not administered, and therefore it is difficult to infer the effects this manipulation may have had on learning.

Newell and Carlton (1987) evaluated kinematic feedback in an experiment that included a no feedback retention test (Figure 10.16). The task required three groups of subjects to apply isometric force to a transducer with the index finger of their dominant hand. The goal was to produce a criterion force-time tracing. The groups were differentiated in terms of the post response information provided. One group was told the total amount of force exerted (impulse). A second group was provided a computer-generated force-time trace superimposed over the criterion trace. The third group was provided the force-time trace without the criterion and was also supplied the oral information that was provided to the first group. The results indicated that the kinematic information resulted in better acquisition and retention performance than the orally presented information. The presentation of the criterion response on the kinematic display did not appear to enhance the effect. However

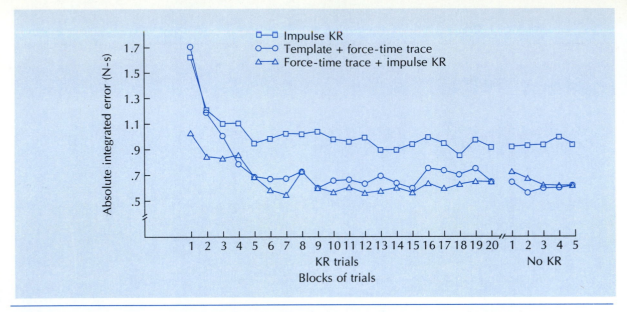

Figure 10.16 *Absolute integrated error (RMS) for an isometric force production task in which the goal was to produce a given force-time impulse. The impulse group was told the total amount of force produced, the template + force time trace group was given a display in which their force-time trace was overlaid on the goal trace, and the force-time + impulse group received both trace and the impulse.*

in Experiment 2, Newell and Carlton found the inclusion of the criterion trace to be beneficial to both acquisition performance and retention. They concluded that the criterion display was important when the response trace was unfamiliar or asymmetrical in shape.

With the increases in the capabilities to provide nearly immediate kinematic or kinetic feedback, an increase in the number of experiments testing the influence of different types of KP is expected. These techniques may, in the future, change the way skills are taught.

FINAL COMMENT

This chapter summarizes the influence of two types of information (KR and KP) provided during the acquisition of motor tasks. Even subtle manipulations (e.g., bandwidth KR, summary KR, kinematic KR/KP) of this information have been shown to have dramatic effects on performance and learning. Although the mechanisms responsible for these effects are still unclear, it appears that when information is consistently available during acquisition, subjects become dependent on it (guidance hypothesis). This dependence appears to reduce the likelihood that subjects seek out intrinsic sources of feedback and new strategies that may ultimately be important for learning. It is also noted that alternative forms of information (e.g., kinematic displays) may enhance learning.

KEY TERMS

knowledge of results (KR)

knowledge of performance (KP)

intrinsic feedback

extrinsic feedback

learning

performance variable

Law of Effect

guidance hypothesis

absolute frequency

relative frequency

learning variable

fading schedule

reverse fading

bandwidth of KR

maladaptive short-term corrections

KR delay interval

post KR delay interval

interresponse interval

summary KR

precision of KR

qualitative KR

quantitative KR

11
Practice Scheduling and Composition

Alex Rogan: THE LAST STARFIGHTER

Designing Effective Practice

Retention and Transfer

Scheduling of Practice
- *Practice Distribution*
- *Contextual Interference*

Composition of Practice
- *Specificity Versus Variability of Practice*
- *Part-Whole Practice*
- *Mental and Observational Practice*

HIGHLIGHT: The Men and Women Behind the Patriot Missiles
FINAL COMMENT
KEY TERMS

Alex Rogan: THE LAST STARFIGHTER

The movie *The Last Starfighter* is about Alex Rogan, a young man with special abilities that launch him on an incredible adventure. Alex lives in a rundown rural trailer court, the Starlite Starbrite, in Crooms County, USA, and he is trying every way he knows how to get away from home and "be something." His favorite diversion in this lonely place has been perfecting his skills at a video game called "The Starfighter." One starry night, the game salutes him as usual: "Greetings, Starfighter, you have been recruited by the Star League to defend the frontier against Xur and the Ko-Dan Armada." With a small audience that includes a big yellow cat sprawled on the game's case, Alex blasts enemy ships and incoming rockets; on and on he fights without defeat. Finally, breaking every previous record, he blasts the Command Ship.

Later that night, a strange man named Centari drives up in an ultra modern "car" and introduces himself as the inventor of the video game. He entices Alex into his car with a proposition and leaves a clone in Alex's place. Much to Alex's horror, they fly to a planet called Rylos where Alex is immediately prepared to become a starfighter against the real Xur and his Ko-Dan Armada, which are threatening to take over the entire galaxy and its frontier, including Earth. And so begins a futuristic fairy tale of excitement and adventure.

Alex Rogan concentrates on mastering the Starfighter video game, unaware that it was placed on Earth to recruit actual Starfighters for the Star League of Planets.

- To clarify the distinction between retention and transfer.
- To identify ways to manipulate practice schedules in order to enhance retention and/or transfer.
- To identify ways to manipulate practice composition in order to enhance retention and/or transfer.

■ ■ ■

Children spend millions of hours every year in front of video and television game monitors, honing "video skills" that were unheard of twenty years ago. Is the time spent in front of those monitors wasted? Can these games build skills that will be important in the high-tech world of the future?

In fact, a video game called "Space Fortress" is being evaluated by the U.S. Air Force and by scientists around the world as a possible tool for selecting pilots for their new generation aircraft. An entire issue of the international psychology journal *Acta Psychologica* was devoted recently to the scientific study of the video game. Some newscasters even called the 1991 war with Iraq the Nintendo war because some of the video released by the U.S. military showing pilots' using their "smart weapons" looked more like a Nintendo game than real combat. Video images projected onto the pilot's visor displayed the targets, weapons systems, and other information much like a video game.

Computer instruction often involving gamelike features is used from the primary grades to the college level on a regular basis. This type instruction is capable of very precisely controlling the subject's exposure to the material to be learned. As you read this chapter, it will become apparent that simple manipulations to practice composition and practice schedule may result in profound effects on performance and learning.

Designing Effective Practice

The purpose of practice, at least as it relates to learning, is to improve the performer's capability to perform under game or test conditions. But what practice conditions will best improve these capabilities? Obviously, there are a great number of ways in which we can spend our practice time. The important question, however, is: How can we best maximize this time to improve learning? The focus of this chapter is on two facets of this question: practice scheduling and practice composition, which are two interrelated characteristics of practice. **Practice scheduling** is concerned with manipulations that cause the conditions under which, or the context within which, a specific task is executed to change. Manipulating the order in which tasks are learned and manipulating practice/rest intervals are examples of practice scheduling. **Practice composition** is manipulated by varying the task or task variations that are practiced or the manner in which tasks are practiced. Manipulations that vary the number of tasks or task variations intermingled in a practice session or vary the manner in which a task is practiced (physical, mental, observational, or simulated practice) involve practice composition.

Retention and Transfer

One of the prime objectives in motor learning is to determine the acquisition conditions under which motor skills will be best learned. **Acquisition** refers to experiences provided to a learner that are thought to enhance learning. It will be helpful to view acquisition as the stage in which the concern is primarily with providing experiences that improve learning and not with demonstrating how well the player, student, or subject can perform. This is an important concept because some manipulations that ultimately improve learning result in poor acquisition performance. In this regard, it is useful to distinguish between two related learning objectives, retention and transfer. **Retention** refers to delayed practice experiences (test or game) on a task that was experienced during acquisition, even if the conditions under which the performance is measured are altered from those of acquisition. If we practice a task and then are tested at a later time on that task, the test would be considered a retention test. **Transfer**, on the other hand, refers to practice experiences on a variation of the task or on another task that was not experienced during acquisition.

As noted in Chapter 1, acquisition, retention, and transfer performance are evaluated in what is commonly termed a **transfer paradigm**. This paradigm involves two distinct phases (see Salmoni, Schmidt, & Walters, 1984). In the acquisition phase the independent variable of interest is manipulated (Figure 11.1). That is, different groups receive different treatments. After the acquisition phase is completed, the retention or transfer phase is conducted. Prior to this phase, a period of time is allowed to elapse so that any temporary effects of the acquisition conditions (fatigue, frustration, etc.) will dissipate. Then the groups are assessed under a common level of the independent variable. This permits evaluation of the relatively permanent effects of acquisition manipulations that are

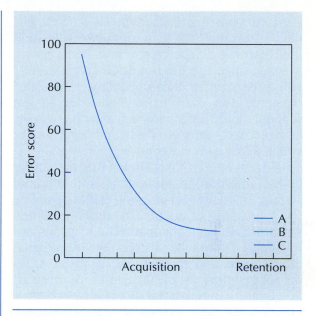

Figure 11.1 *Possible outcomes of an experiment involving acquisition and retention tests. Retention A indicates a performance decrement over the retention interval; Retention B indicates that performance was maintained over the retention interval; and Retention C indicates an improvement over the retention interval.*

relatively uninfluenced by other, more temporary, effects specific to the acquisition manipulations. An important consideration for the experimenter is to determine under what common condition(s) retention and/or transfer should be assessed. This is a difficult question because a group(s) switched to a new condition may perform more poorly just because the condition is new. Likewise, if subjects under one condition are tested under that condition, they may have an advantage simply because they are familiar with the conditions. The use of this paradigm is very important to the study of learning.

Scheduling of Practice

How can practice be scheduled to best enhance learning? This is a formidable question that learning psychologists have been asking at least since the time of Ebbinghaus (1885/1964). Remember the scheduling of practice concerns how the practice/rest intervals are scheduled, the order in which a series of tasks is practiced, and/or the conditions under which a task(s) is experienced.

Recent research has shown that the nature of the information processing and memory states responsible for learning is influenced by the scheduling of practice. Three interrelated types of practice schedule manipulations are highlighted: practice distribution, contextual interference, and context effects. These areas do not comprise an exhaustive list of research involving manipulations of practice schedule but do represent classifications of research typical of recent research efforts.

Practice Distribution

Practice distribution concerns manipulations to the practice-rest intervals (see Adams, 1987; Lee & Genovese, 1988, for reviews and theoretical perspectives). Generally, this involves changing the ratio of practice time to rest time within blocks of trials but also includes manipulations to the time between practice sessions. **Massed practice** is defined as ratios of rest intervals to practice intervals of less than one. If practice intervals, perhaps practice trials, are packed together such that the time between practices is no longer than the time involved in actual practice, the session is said to be massed. **Distributed practice** is defined as ratios of rest intervals to practice intervals of greater than one. That is, more time is devoted to the rest interval than to actual practice. Although the cutoff of "one" to distinguish between massed and distributed practice schedules has been used historically, it may be useful to think of massed and distributed practice as the ends of a practice/rest continuum.

In an analysis of the practice distribution literature, Lee and Genovese (1988) found that massed practice, relative to distributed practice, tended to depress acquisition performance. However, there was a tendency for distributed practice, particularly on continuous tasks, to result in better retention.

Discrete and Continuous Tasks. Bourne and Archer (1956) asked subjects to perform 21 acquisition and 9 retention trials on a pursuit rotor task. In this task, subjects attempt to keep a stylus on a moving light source. The light source is mounted in a record player-like device with a cut-out pattern on the top so that the light appears to move in a particular pattern (circle, triangle, etc.). The speed of the light's movement can be changed, and the stylus contains a sensing device that closes a contact when the stylus is positioned over the light. Each trial was 30 seconds and the time between trials was 0, 15, 30, 45, or 60 seconds. All subjects performed retention trials with 0 seconds between trials. The results indicated that distributed practice positively influenced both acquisition and retention performance. Similar results have been found for continuous tasks (Denny, Frisbey, & Weaver, 1955). However, the effects of practice distribution on discrete tasks are less clear.

Stelmach (1969) asked subjects to attempt a discrete ladder climbing task for 16 acquisition trials and 6 retention trials. Retention was assessed for both massed and distributed practice groups under distributed practice conditions. The results indicated that massed practice exerted a strong negative influence on acquisition but little if any influence on retention (Figure 11.2).

Carron (1969), using a discrete peg-turn task, found little difference between distribution conditions during acquisition and a slight advantage of massed condition during reten-

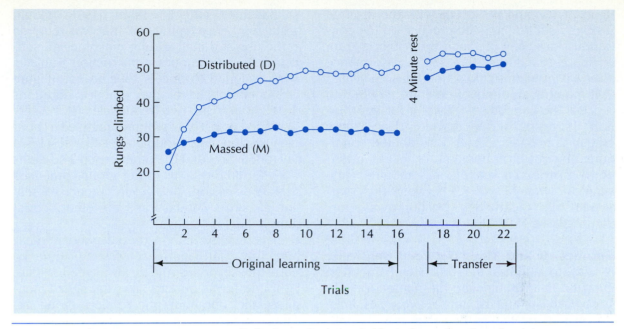

Figure 11.2 *Average rungs climbed on a Bachman ladder task as a function of practice distribution. Transfer was tested under distributed practice conditions.*

tion. These kinds of discrepant results prompted Lee and Genovese (1989) to study the interaction of task and practice distribution.

Interaction of Task and Practice Distribution. To study the proposed interaction between task and practice distribution, Lee and Genovese (1989) created a discrete and continuous version of a single task. The task was a movement timing task that involved either one timing estimate per trial (discrete) or 20 timing estimates per trial (continuous). The intertrial intervals of 25 seconds or 0.5 seconds were used for both acquisition and retention. The results demonstrated differential results across tasks. Acquisition and retention benefited from distributed practice conditions for the continuous task. However, only a slight acquisition and retention benefit was observed for discrete tasks.

It is difficult to isolate the reason(s) why distributed practice facilitates acquisition and

retention while massed practice appears to enhance performance and learning of discrete tasks. Historically, Hull (1943) suggested that practice distribution is influenced by a kind of fatigue related to the task termed *reactive inhibition*. Adams (1987), in recounting Hull's notion, states:

> Whenever an organism makes a response, there is an increment of reactive inhibition that works in opposition to the reaction potentiality for the ongoing response and lowers performance. Reactive inhibition is a positive function of the amount of work involved in making the response and of the number of response evocations, and it spontaneously dissipates as a function of time between responses. (p. 49)

Although Hull's notions related to reactive inhibition are probably wrong, the influence of practice distributions appears to be related to the amount of work or boredom of the task. Massed practice on Lee and Genovese's (1988) continuous task may prompt some sort of fatigue that would not occur with the discrete task. In addition, massed practice on the continuous task may preclude the subjects from evaluating and updating their performance after each attempt. Research has indicated that minimal amounts of time are required to process the various sources of error information. In terms of the discrete task, where fatigue is not the problem, distributed conditions may result in boredom or loss of attention. Distributed conditions required the subject to wait 25 seconds between each one-second trial. Clearly this question awaits further research.

Number of and Time Between Sessions. A way to address the practice distribution question is to manipulate the number of sessions each day and the time between sessions. This technique has particular practical applications. Given that only a certain amount of practice can be allotted to a unit of instruction, teachers and coaches must decide whether to plan more but shorter sessions or fewer longer sessions.

Baddeley and Longman (1978) taught postal workers a typing task that was required in the use of a mail sorting machine. All subjects received 60 hours of instruction. Subjects were assigned to one of four groups (Figure 11.3A) comprised of two practice durations (1 or 2 hours) and two frequencies (1 or 2 sessions per day). Two groups practiced 1 hour each session. One group practiced 1 session a day for 60 days and the other group 2 sessions a day for 30 days. Two other groups practiced 2 hours a session. One group practiced 1 session a day for 30 days and the other, 2 sessions a day for 15 days.

The results related to two dependent measures are particularly interesting—time to learn the keyboard and typing speed (Figure 11.3B). In terms of both time and speed measures, the one-hour/one-session group attained the criterion performance levels first. The two-hour/two-session group required the most time to attain the performance goals. Perhaps most interesting was that subjects tended to prefer the two-hour/two-session schedule better than the one-hour/one-ses-

Baddeley and Longman (1978) found that postal workers learned a typing task used on a mail-sorting machine more quickly when taught one hour/one session a day than a group taught in two hours/two sessions a day.

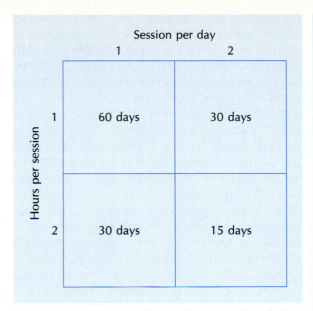

Figure 11.3A *Design of the experiment by Baddeley and Longman (1978). Subjects practiced a typing task either one or two hours a session either one or two times a day.*

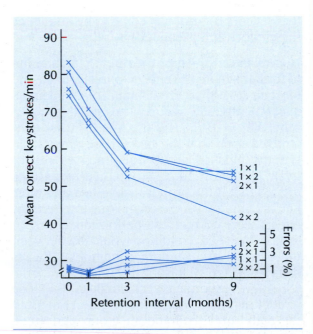

Figure 11.3B *Retention of the typing skill over a nine-month interval as a function of practice schedule. Both mean correct keystrokes per minute and percent errors are presented.*

sion schedule. That is, the subjects tended to prefer the condition that resulted in the poorer performance!

The Baddely and Longman (1978) experiment may have direct application for teachers and coaches. It appears that students and athletes may benefit from shorter practice sessions distributed over more days. However, a number of important questions remain for researchers to address. It is not clear whether the negative effect of longer sessions could be diminished or eliminated by organizing the practice sessions differently. For example, a practice session could be organized so that a number of tasks are practiced in a random order during a single session. Each task is presented for a single trial at a time, but the entire session is relatively long.

Contextual Interference

When a number of tasks or task variations are experienced within practice sessions, the manner in which those tasks are organized may influence acquisition, retention, and transfer performances. At the extreme, practice schedules can be organized such that the tasks to be learned are practiced in a random (C-A-B, B-C-A, B-A-C) or blocked (A-A-A, B-B-B, C-C-C) order. Note that both groups receive the same number of trials, spaced at the same intertrial interval. Which group would perform better during acquisition, retention, or transfer?

Shea and Morgan (1979) had subjects attempt 54 acquisition trials (6 blocks of 9 trials) on 3 variations of a task in either a blocked or random sequence. The task variations were similar in that each variation started (picking up a ball) and ended (placing the ball in a slot) in the same way but varied in terms of the combinations and/or order in which 3 of the 6 barriers were to be "knocked down" (Figure 11.4). The movement time of subjects performing under random conditions decreased more slowly, but eventually (by block 6) approached that of subjects in the blocked condition. After 10 minutes rest, retention and transfer were measured for one-half of the subjects under

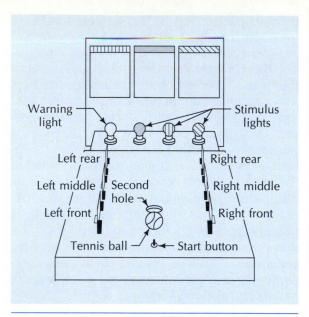

Figure 11.4 *Barrier knockdown task used by Shea and Morgan (1979). The stimulus lights indicated which pattern hung above the lights was to be performed. The pattern indicated the order in which three of the six hinged barriers were to be knocked down. After the warning light was illuminated, one of the three stimulus lights was turned on. This indicated that the subject was to leave the start button, pick up the tennis ball, and knock the barriers down in the prescribed order.*

blocked or random conditions. The other half of the subjects performed the retention and transfer tests after 10 days. Retention and transfer performance after both 10-minute and 10-day delays, when collapsed across both retention conditions, was significantly better for subjects who learned the task variations under random conditions (Figure 11.5).

Shea and his colleagues (Shea & Morgan, 1979; Shea & Zimny, 1983, 1985) utilized Battig's (1979) conceptualization to suggest that the dramatic reversal of the random group from acquisition to retention and transfer arises as a result of the multiple and variable processing strategies adopted by subjects when faced with random conditions. Central to this theoretical position is the concept of

contextual interference. Blocked conditions are thought to promote low contextual interference because the context remains relatively stable from trial to trial. Random schedules, on the other hand, generate high contextual interference because the context within which a given task is executed changes from trial to trial. Under blocked schedules the subject is more likely to invoke similar strategies from attempt to attempt, and the conditions under which memory operations occur are more likely to remain stable. This results in relatively good acquisition performance but does not enhance retention or transfer. Retention is facilitated under random schedules because the acquisition schedule induces the subject to engage in more varied processing strategies under more varied contexts than blocked schedules. Integral to these differences in processing strategies is the notion that under blocked practice there is a tendency for the subject to engage only in intratask (within task) elaboration. Random practice schedules are thought to promote both intratask and intertask (between task) elaboration. Thus, this theoretical proposal has come to be known as the **elaboration perspective**.

Reconstruction Hypothesis. In an attempt to further isolate the effects found by Shea and Morgan (1979), Lee and Magill (1983) included a serial practice group. The serial practice schedule (A-B-C, A-B-C, A-B-C) was constructed such that the tasks were predictable like the blocked group but practiced repetitively like the random group. Lee and Magill argued that if the proposals by Shea and Morgan accounting for the contextual interference effects were correct, the performance of subjects in the serial condition would fall between the blocked and random conditions. The results indicated that subjects under the serial condition responded very similarly to those under the random condition (Figure 11.6). Both the serial and the random group performed more poorly than the block group during acquisition but performed significantly better on the retention test.

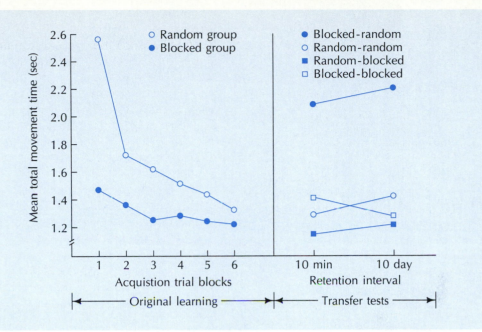

Figure 11.5 *Mean total movement time on the barrier knockdown task as a function of practice conditions. Subjects in the blocked conditions practiced 18 trials on one task before practicing the next task. Subjects in the random condition practiced the tasks in a random order. Retention was assessed without knowledge of results.*

Both the elaboration perspective and the reconstruction hypothesis used to account for contextual interference effects suggest that football teams should practice offensive plays in a random order. However, the majority of coaches practice one play until the team gets it right before moving on to the next play.

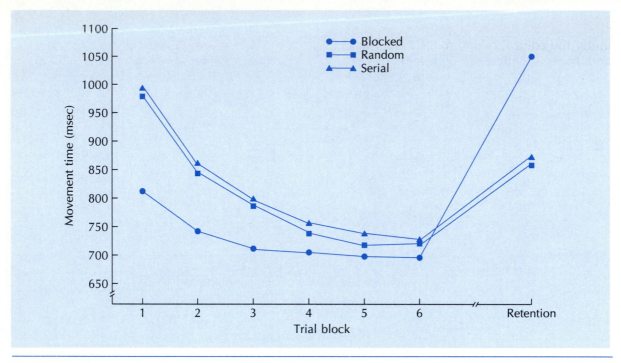

Figure 11.6 *Average movement time on three segment movements as a function of practice schedule. The serial condition involved performing the tasks in sequence (A-B-C, A-B-C, . . .). Retention was assessed without knowledge of results.*

On the basis of their results, Lee and Magill (1985) formulated what has come to be known as the **reconstruction hypothesis**. They suggest that on each trial under random or serial conditions, subjects tend to reconstruct the response from memory because the interpolated responses interfere with the short-term memory for a particular response. Thus, subjects store (code in memory) varied retrieval channel/strategies to prepare for the demands of the next response. However, under blocked conditions the memory representation(s) responsible for the present response is not forgotten and can be utilized to accomplish the subsequent response. Thus, permanent memory stores may be updated and/or accessed less frequently under blocked conditions. Retention is facilitated for the random and serial conditions because the processes of "forgetting" and "reconstruction" are thought to promote better qualitative and quantitative analyses of the response and thus more varied interactions with long-term memory stores.

Contextual Interference: Same Versus Different Motor Program. In a review of contextual interference, Magill and Hall (1990) argued that contextual interference did not influence the learning of all types of tasks. In particular, they presented evidence and a rationale for stating that blocked and random manipulations result in the contextual interference effect when movements are controlled by different motor programs but not when the movements are controlled by the same motor program. For the purposes of their review, movements were considered to be controlled by the same motor program if the variations of the movements shared the same relative timing, sequence of events, and/or spatial configuration. The multisegment tasks used by Shea

242

and Morgan (1979) and Lee and Magill (1983) were considered by Magill and Hall to be under the control of different motor programs and thus susceptible to the beneficial effects of contextual interference. Their rationale is based on the notion that when task variations that are controlled by different motor programs are presented in a random order, higher levels of contextual interference are created. Randomly manipulating variations of the same motor program results in only minimal levels of contextual interference, levels not sufficient to invoke the effect.

This is an interesting argument that appears to have some support in the related literature (Turnbull & Dickinson, 1986; Wood & Ging, 1991). However, the proposal is contingent on demonstrating null effects (no differences) and this is always problematic for science. One example that provides some sup-port for the position of Magill and Hall (that contextual interference is reduced when the same motor program is utilized) comes from evidence by Shea, Kohl, and Indermill (1990). They found that contextual interference effects may require substantially more practice to surface when the task variations are controlled by the same motor program.

Contextual Interference: Extended Practice. Shea, Kohl, and Indermill (1990) manipulated blocked and random practice schedules on a rapid force production task. Subjects practiced the task variations for 50, 200, or 400 trials, and retention was assessed under either blocked or random conditions. The task required subjects to strike the padded arm of a force transducer with the medial surface of their dominant hand with varying amounts of force (Figure 11.7) Because the

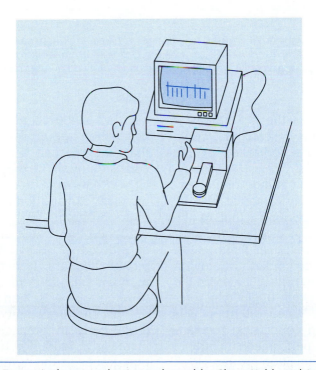

Figure 11.7 *Dynamic force production task used by Shea, Kohl, and Indermill (1990). The subject contacted the padded arm of the force transducer with the medial surface of the dominant hand in an attempt to produce a criterion force. The actual force of impact and criterion force (horizontal line) were displayed on the computer monitor.*

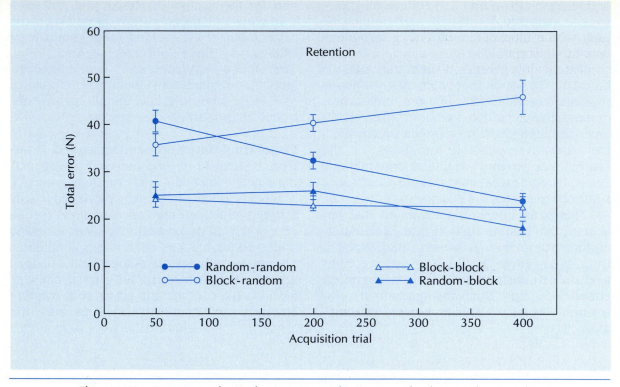

Figure 11.8 *Average total error for retention performance on the dynamic force production task. Subjects received 50, 200, or 400 acquisition trials under either blocked or random schedules prior to retention being assessed under blocked or random conditions.*

variations simply required the generation of more or less force, many researchers would consider the tasks to be controlled by the same motor program.

As in previous contextual interference experiments, acquisition performance of the blocked groups was superior to that of the random groups. Results of blocked and random retention are presented in Figure 11.8. Retention performance depended not only on the number of acquisition trials but also on the context (random or blocked) under which retention was measured. When retention was assessed under blocked conditions, the random acquisition groups performed similarly to those of the blocked acquisition groups. How-

ever, after 400 acquisition trials, the random acquisition group performed with less error than the blocked acquisition group. This is consistent with the proposal of Magill and Hall (1990) that contextual interference effects are reduced for variations controlled by the same motor program.

When the results of random retention are considered, a very different and interesting picture appears. Generally, retention performance under random conditions was inferior to retention performance under blocked conditions. The random acquisition group was inferior early in practice (after 50 trials) but increasingly superior to the blocked acquisition groups as the number of acquisition trials increased. In fact, with 400 acquisition trials, the random acquisition group performed similarly to the blocked acquisition group under blocked retention.

The practical implications of the retention data are somewhat paradoxical. Random practice schedules will promote the learning of a rapid motor task better (or at least equally well) as blocked practice. In fact, increasing the amount (number of practice trials) of blocked practice had no effect on retention assessed under blocked conditions and had a negative effect when retention was measured under random conditions. Apparently the benefits of blocked practice occur very early in practice with the response strategy becoming increasingly more rigid and inflexible. On the other hand, the benefits of random practice surface after initial practice, presumably as a result of a more flexible response/control strategy.

One notable exception was found where the random acquisition group performed less accurately on random retention after 50 trials than did the blocked acquisition group. This suggests that very early in practice it is difficult for subjects to determine the appropriate strategies when faced with random conditions. Fitts (1964) and Fitts and Posner (1967) termed this early stage the *cognitive phase* of learning and Adams (1971) labeled it the *verbal-motor stage* (see Chapter 4). They suggest that the subject's primary concern early in practice is to understand what is to be done and how performance is to be evaluated, rather than to determine the most efficient way of meeting the task demands. The increased interference, and perhaps increased task complexity induced by random schedules, may retard this process. Consistent with the findings of DelRey, Wughalter, and Whitehurst (1982), the data suggest that a blocked, then random schedule may benefit the retention of the task, particularly if retention is to be assessed under random conditions.

Internal Context Manipulation. A quite different example of what appears to be contextual interference effect was presented by Shea, Shebilske, Kohl, and Guadagnoli (1991). They noted that changes in the processing context from trial to trial seemed to be important to the contextual interference effect. They reasoned that if the internal conditions under which the movement was performed could be varied, a form of contextual interference may be created. Experiments 1 and 2 demonstrated the impact of an after contraction effect on the performance of basically the same rapid force production task used by Shea et al. (1990). The effect was created by asking the subjects to statically exert a specified amount of force against a load cell for 20 seconds prior to performing the criterion task. The results indicated that as the intensity of the static contraction increased, a bias was introduced to the subsequent movement. The greater the precontraction, the greater was the bias. Clearly, the precontraction resulted in a change in the excitability of the neural network responsible for the movement and thus a change in the internal processing context. Experiment 3 involved a constant condition in which the precontraction intensity was held constant during acquisition. In a random context condition, the precontraction intensity was varied (higher and lower) during acquisition. Retention was assessed under conditions identical to those of the constant condition.

The results indicated that the acquisition performance of subjects experiencing varying precontraction intensities during acquisition was inferior to that of the subjects experiencing constant conditions (Figure 11.9). However, the reversal of the random group from acquisition to retention commonly seen in contextual interference studies was observed. An important question that remains unanswered is the extent to which these manipulations arise from similar mechanisms.

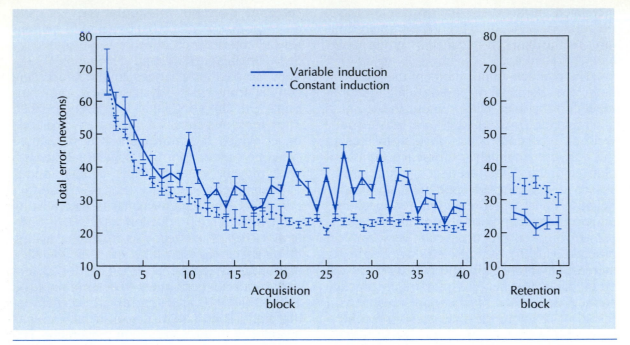

Figure 11.9 *Average total error for acquisition and retention performance on a static force production task. The induction involved exerting a static force for 20 seconds between trials on the criterion task. The induction force for the variable group was varied from trial to trial and for the constant group was the same across trials. Retention was assessed under constant induction conditions.*

Composition of Practice

Another way in which practice can be manipulated is by varying the composition of practice. Remember, practice composition is manipulated by varying the tasks or task variations that are practiced or the manner in which these tasks are practiced. Teachers and coaches must be concerned with the tasks that they include in practice sessions. The question is: What should be practiced?

Specificity Versus Variability of Practice

Historically the question of practice composition has been discussed in terms of the speci-

ficity of learning principle, which appears to have been borrowed from the specificity of training principle in exercise physiology (Barnett, Ross, Schmidt, & Todd, 1973) and is best articulated in the work of Henry (1960) and Adams (1971). Henry's **specificity hypothesis** proposes that motor skills are specific and only superficially resemble other similar motor skills. This implies that changing the motor task only slightly produces a new motor task for which a new motor program must be developed. Adams (1971) also takes a specificity position in the formulation of the closed-loop theory of motor skill acquisition (see Chapter 8). Adams emphasizes the use of sensory feedback and knowledge of results to build the perceptual trace of a specific movement. Adams (1987) reemphasizes the specificity notion and attributes the principle to the identical elements theory developed by Thorndike and Woodworth (1901a, 1901b). The central prediction of the specificity principle is that practice should be specific to the task and condition to be learned. This notion has received limited support for both gross motor (Bachman, 1961; Singer, 1966) and fine motor performance (Henry, 1960).

An alternative viewpoint is the **variability of practice hypothesis**, which states that variable but related practice experiences enhance the memory states responsible for motor control. This hypothesis was derived from schema theory (see Chapter 8). The variability of practice position, for the most part,

The variability of practice hypothesis derived from schema theory suggests that practice under a variety of conditions enables athletes to perform well in new and unique game situations.

has been discussed in terms of transfer to a novel variation of a task rather than the retention' of a specific motor task. Schmidt (1975, 1976) proposes that the subject does not store in memory the specific characteristics of each movement but, rather, abstracts the information along with knowledge of results to form a rule or schema that is capable of governing motor control for that class of movements. The schema notion postulates that the strength of the schema is directly related to the variability of practice that the subject receives within a particular schema class. The greater the variety of experiences, the more generalizable are the response capabilities. Thus, the prediction from schema theory is that increasing the variety of practice experiences leads to increased schema strength.

Studies prompted by the predictions of schema theory and the variability of practice hypothesis generally were designed to determine the extent to which practice experiences contributed to transfer performance. Much more recently, studies have investigated the variability of practice hypothesis in terms of retention.

Transfer and Variability of Practice. A number of studies (Newell & Shapiro, 1976; Gerson & Thomas, 1977; Carson & Wiegand, 1979; Moxley, 1979; Wrisberg & Ragsdale, 1979) have found that variable practice enhances the ability to transfer to a novel task variation. The typical paradigm used in the study of schema and variability of practice notions requires subjects to practice either one (constant practice) or a variety (variable practice) of task variations and then assesses transfer to a novel variation. According to the variability of practice hypothesis, the variable practice group should perform better on a transfer test than the constant practice group. Variable practice experiences increment the memory states responsible for generating the new response to a greater extent than constant practice.

McCracken and Stelmach (1977) asked subjects to learn to move from a start key to a hinged barrier. The object was to knock down the barrier in precisely 200 milliseconds. The distances from the start key to the barrier could be changed (15, 35, 50, 60, and 65 centimeters). Groups were either constant practice (15, 35, 60, or 65 centimeters only) or variable (15, 35, 60, and 65 centimeters in a random order). After 300 acquisition trials, all groups were tested under a 50-centimeter transfer condition. This represented a novel condition that was not experienced by any group during acquisition. The goal movement time for acquisition and retention was 300 milliseconds.

The results indicated that the variable practice group performed more poorly at the end of acquisition than the constant practice group (Figure 11.10). However, the variable practice group performed better on the novel task than the constant practice group. Similar results have been reported for other timing tasks (Wrisberg & Ragsdale, 1979; Catalano &

Kleiner, 1984). As predicted by schema theory, variable practice seems to be important to the ability to generate novel variations of movement.

Retention and Variability of Practice. In general, teachers and coaches, preparing their students for a specific test, competition, or game, appear to opt to provide experiences as specific as possible to the game or test conditions. However, when the purpose is to develop a more general skill (e.g., throwing, jumping, hitting), variable practice is often prescribed. As previously discussed, the variable practice scheme is thought to equip the performer better to produce novel task variations than specific practice. But what type of practice composition results in the best retention? Intuition and limited experimental evidence might suggest specific practice.

Shea and Kohl (1990) investigated the im-

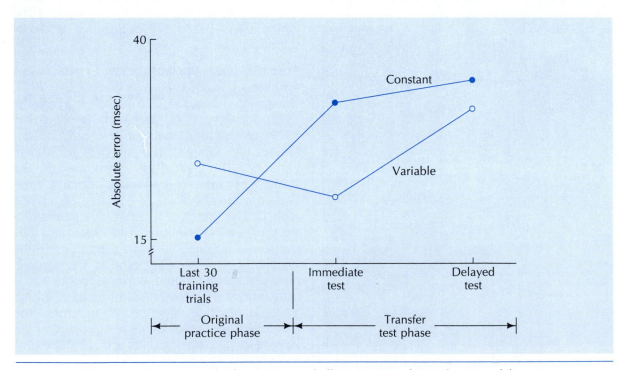

Figure 11.10 *Average absolute error on a ballistic timing task as a function of the variability of practice conditions. The distance the subject was required to move in 200 milliseconds was kept the same for the constant group and varied for the variable group.*

pact of variable versus constant practice on retention performance. The task was to exert an impulsive force against a force transducer in an attempt to produce a criterion force. The desired force was displayed on a computer monitor and feedback was provided immediately after each attempt. Figure 11.11 illustrates the experimental design and feedback displays. In Experiment 2, subjects were assigned to either a specific + space, specific + variable, or specific + specific acquisition condition. The specific + space acquisition group received five trials per block on a criterion target force spaced at 16-second intervals. The specific + variable group also received five trials per block on the criterion target force,

but the intervals between each attempt at the criterion were filled with three intervening trials at variable forces for a total of 17 trials per block. The specific + specific group received 17 trials per block at the criterion force. Retention was assessed under the same conditions as those experienced by the specific + space condition during acquisition.

The results clearly indicate that acquisition practice with variations of the criterion task in conjunction with practice on the criterion task leads to better retention than practice with the criterion task alone (Figure 11.12). Perhaps most startling was the finding that additional practice on the criterion task (practice time held constant) resulted in ex-

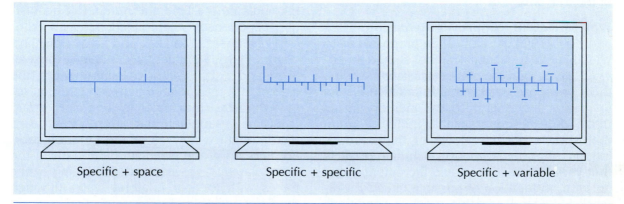

Group	Acquisition		Retention
Specific + space	C C C C C		C C C C C
Specific + specific	C C C C C C C C C C C C C C C C C		C C C C C
Specific + variable	C A B E C D B E C B E A C D B E C		C C C C C

Figure 11.11 *Schedule and composition of practice for acquisition and retention (top). The C task represents a task goal of 150 newtons while the A, B, D, and E tasks represent 100, 125, 175, and 200 newtons, respectively. The display on the monitor at the conclusion of a block of trials for the specific + space (left), specific + specific (middle), and specific + variable (right) conditions (bottom).*

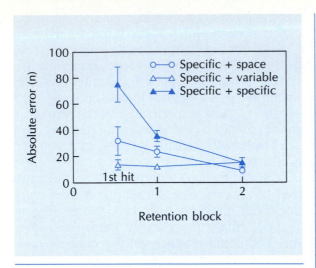

Figure 11.12 *Average absolute error for a static force production task as a function of the schedule and composition of practice. Retention was assessed under the same conditions that were experienced by the specific + space group during acquisition.*

tremely poor retention performance. These findings suggest that practice on a discrete task such as shooting a foul shot in basketball may benefit from practice on task variations even though the requirements during the test of retention (game) will never be altered. Variations can be introduced by increasing or decreasing the weight of the ball or the position of the foul line.

Why Variability Improves Retention. Shea and Kohl (1990) present three proposals as to why this effect occurs. The first should be obvious given our previous discussion: schema theory proposes that variable practice results in greater increments to the memory states underlying the generalizable motor program than specific practice. However, in the formulations of schema theory, Schmidt predicts that variable practice should increment transfer with no mention of possible effects on retention. Second, variable practice conditions may create a form of contextual interference. Variable practice conditions are in many ways similar to random practice conditions. Likewise, specific practice could be considered

blocked practice even though only one task is practiced.

Last, variable practice creates a form of spacing or lagged practice. A good deal of literature in the verbal domain (Peterson, Wampler, Kirkpatrick, & Saltzman, 1963; Young & Bellezza, 1982) suggests that two presentations spaced in time or lagged between other presentations benefit retention compared to two massed presentations. Similarly, Jacoby, Glenberg, and their colleagues (Glenberg, 1977; Cuddy & Jacoby, 1982; Glenberg & Smith, 1981) argue that when two items are spaced very closely in time, subjects tend to bypass much of the processing of the repetition that would otherwise be required on a later repetition. On an immediate repetition, or to a lesser degree on a repetition spaced across a short rest interval, any processes or problem-solving operations used on the previous repetition can be remembered and reemployed. On spaced or distributed repetitions, more complete processing is required, enhancing the strength of the memory representation responsible for the event. This position has much in common with the reconstruction hypothesis (Lee & Magill, 1983) discussed in relation to contextual interference.

Additional Experiments. In two related experiments, Shea and Kohl (1991) further manipulated the type and number of acquisition experiences interpolated between criterion responses. The task and screen displays (Figure 11.13) were nearly identical to those of Shea and Kohl (1990). In Experiment 1, the type of task interpolated between criterion responses was manipulated. For one group (specific + variable), the interpolated tasks were simply variations of the criterion task. For another group (specific + alternative), the interpolated task involved producing static forces with the contralateral limb. Although the demands of the two classes of tasks could not be equated, the alternative task was sufficiently difficult to anticipate that its execution would require substantial cognitive resources and produce considerable interference. If the

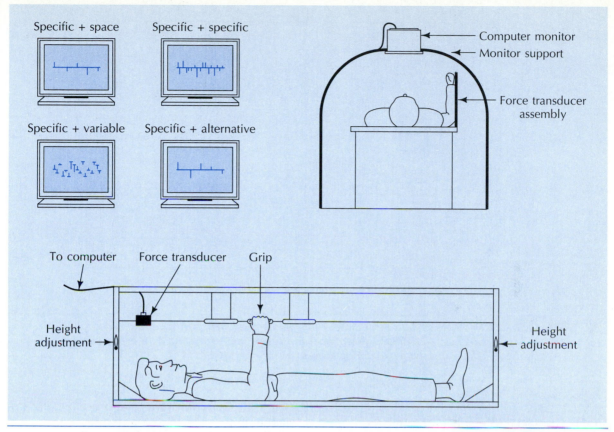

Figure 11.13 *The display on the monitors at the conclusion of a block of trials for the various acquisition conditions (top-left). End view (top-right) and side view (bottom) of the static force production task used by Shea and Kohl (1990). The subject exerted force on the grip in line with the force transducer in an attempt to produce a criterion force. The actual force and criterion force were displayed on the computer monitor.*

locus of the effect noted by Shea and Kohl (1990) were due primarily to lag/spacing or reconstructive processing (Lee & Magill, 1985), then the specific + variable and the specific + alternative conditions should result in similar retention benefits, and both conditions should exhibit better retention than the specific + space condition. However, if the related movements were involved either in schema development (Schmidt, 1975) or in promoting interitem elaborative and distinctive processing (Shea & Zimny, 1983), the specific + variable condition should result in superior retention.

The specific + variable condition resulted in retention superior to the specific + space condition which in turn was superior to the specific + specific condition (Figure 11.14). More important, the specific + space and the specific + alternative conditions resulted in similar retention performance. Apparently the interpolated tasks must be related to the criterion task in order for their use to benefit retention. Similar findings have been noted by Shea and Wright (1991) in a short-term memory paradigm.

In Experiment 2, Shea and Kohl (1991) assessed the impact of increasing the number of

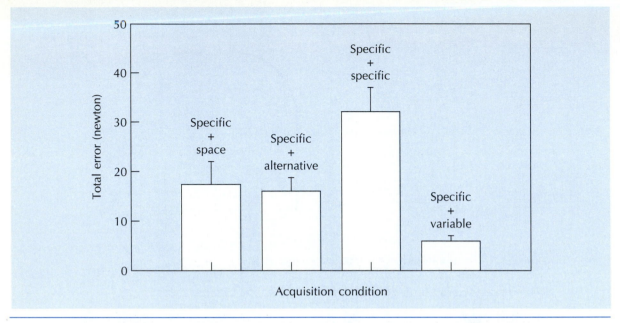

Figure 11.14 *Average total error for retention testing as a function of acquisition scheduling and composition conditions. Retention was assessed under the conditions experienced by the specific + specific group during acquisition.*

related tasks interpolated between criterion trials. The specific + space condition required subjects to attempt the criterion force five times per block at 16-second intervals. The specific + 1-variable condition required one variable trial between criterion trials and the specific + 3-variable condition required three variable trials between criterion trials. The results indicated that interpolating one related motor task between criterion trials resulted in significant retention benefits while three interpolated tasks further incremented retention (Figure 11.15).

The results of the experiments conducted by Shea and Kohl (1990, 1991) suggest that even subtle manipulations to the composition of practice can be important to the retention of a simple discrete motor task. Retention can be enhanced by altering the composition of practice, by interpolating related motor tasks between criterion experiences, and by increasing the number of interpolated related tasks. These manipulations appear to increase the potential for interitem elaboration and enhancement to the motor schema.

Part-Whole Practice

Many motor skills, particularly complex skills, can be partitioned into relatively independent components. The question of interest is whether it is effective to design practice to include independent practice on the various components of the overall skill, that is, **part-whole practice** (see Wightman & Lintern, 1985; Chamberlin & Lee, in press, for reviews).

Wightman and Lintern (1985) identified three methods for constructing part practice: fractionation, simplification, and segmentation.

Fractionation. When practice is variously composed of one or more parts, the practice is said to be fractionated. Thus, the partitioning of the components to be practiced changes from practice session to practice session. A tennis coach may have his or her players prac-

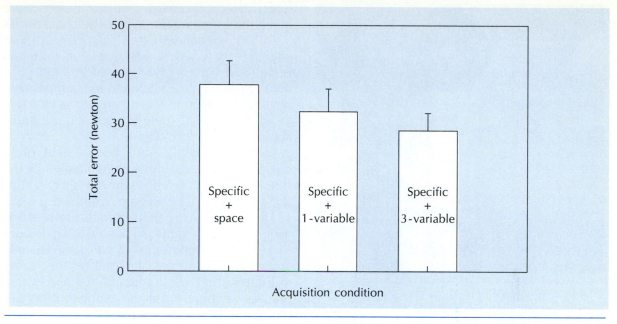

Figure 11.15 *Average total error for retention testing as a function of acquisition scheduling and composition conditions. Retention was assessed under the conditions experienced by the specific + space group during acquisition.*

tice cross court shots (forehand then backhand, etc.) or practice serve and volley segments. That is, the components are practiced in various combinations at subsequent practices.

Simplification. Simplification involves reducing the demands of one or more of the task components so as to reduce the overall difficulty or complexity of the skill. In tennis an instructor may simplify the demands by using a ball machine to practice the forehand or backhand stroke. The machine projects the ball to the same place at the same speed trial after trial. A similar tactic is often used in little league baseball. The younger children play T-ball before progressing to a game in which the ball is consistently projected by a pitching machine. Eventually the little leaguers are introduced to the real game (see Chapter 4).

Mané, Adams, and Donchin (1989) found no clear advantage of adapting the level of difficulty of a complex task (video game) by slowing the task down and then speeding it up as the subjects became more proficient. They also found substantial negative effects of practicing a simplified version when a higher level of difficulty was attempted. This negative effect, termed *negative transfer,* suggests that beginners develop habits and/or strategies as a result of practicing a simplified version of the task that are ineffective for more difficult versions.

Segmentation. Segmentation involves partitioning the skill along spatial or temporal dimensions. Segmentation strategies can be classified as *pure part* or *progressive part.* In pure part practice, the segments of the task are practiced to criterion before moving to another part without regard to temporal or spatial progression. Progressive part involves either a forward or backward chaining. For example, in forward chaining the first part of a skill is practiced to some criterion before introducing the second part and so on. In back-

T-ball is an example of a part-whole practice method termed simplification. Simplification involves reducing the demands of one or more of the task components so as to reduce the overall difficulty or complexity of the skill.

ward chaining the last segment is learned first. Tennis instructors often teach students the serve by having them practice the ball toss first and then the racquet motion before putting the whole skill together. This teaching method is used by many physical education teachers and coaches to teach sequential tasks. Sequential tasks, such as a tumbling, dance, or skating routine, are composed of a set of tasks that are linked together to form a single performance.

Effectiveness of Part-Whole Practice. Chamberlin and Lee (in press) suggest that the answer to this question of whether part-whole practice is more effective than whole practice hinges on the degree to which the components of the skill are independent. They maintain that as the degree of interdependence of the components decreases, the value of part training increases. Naylor and Briggs (1963) asked subjects to predict the appearance of images on a computer screen. They manipulated the interdependence of the type, number, and location of the images. Whole practice was more effective than part practice

when the characteristics of the images were highly interdependent. When the characteristics were independent, part practice was more effective than whole practice. For example, Briggs and Waters (1958) found that independent practice on the pitch and roll components of a flight simulator was not nearly as effective as whole practice. Clearly, pitch and roll interact to maintain level flight.

Similar benefits have been found on a computer game currently being studied by the U.S. Air Force (Newell, Carlton, Fisher, & Rutter, 1989; Shebilske, Regain, Arthur, & Jordan, 1991). The game, called "Space Fortress," is like many video games available today (Figure 11.16). The components of the game include ship control, ship velocity, and response rate to friends and foes. It appears that part-whole practice is effective for this game, but only to the extent that subjects are effective in "seeing" the connections between parts (Frederiksen & White, 1989; Mané et al., 1989).

Shebilske et al. (1991) devised a modified part-whole practice scheme for the "Space Fortress" game that attempts to facilitate the learning of the connections between components. The method, termed *active interlocked modeling* (AIM), requires individuals to work in pairs. One subject controls half of the task while interlocked with a partner who controls the other half. Actions of one require reactions of the other and vice versa. Subjects learn the whole task by alternately practicing one-half of the task and then the other half. This method facilitates the learning of the connections between the halves by viewing and responding to the actions and reactions of the partner. The AIM protocol can therefore be viewed as a part-whole learning method that is modified to establish connections between parts.

Mental and Observational Practice

Remember that practice composition is concerned with what and how we practice. Constant and variable practice represent only one

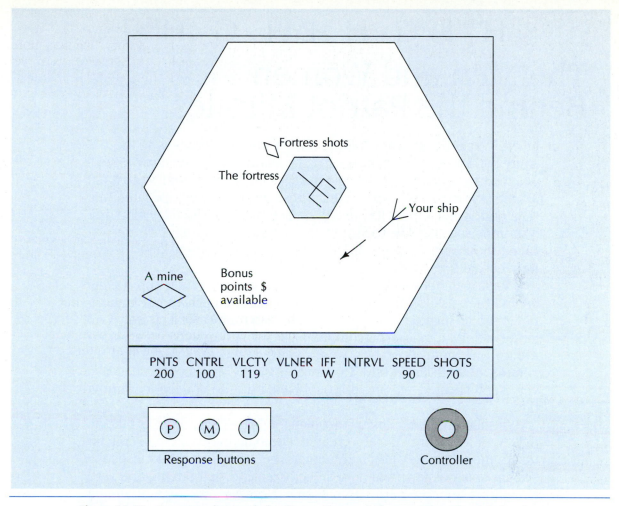

Figure 11.16 *Screen and controls for "Space Fortress." The control on the right is a joystick used to control the ship and shoot missiles. The buttons on the left are used to collect bonuses by pushing either the points (P) or missiles (M) button at the appropriate time. The "I" button is used to identify whether a ship is friend or foe.*

dimension of practice composition, that related to physical practice. Another dimension of practice concerns mental and observational practice in which the subject engages cognitive operations related to the task but does not physically practice. Occasions arise in which it is not feasible to engage in physical practice. Physical practice may increase the likelihood of injury, or conditions (i.e., inclement weather, lack of available facilities) may require that other forms of practice be used, provided

those methods are productive in incrementing skill.

Mental Practice.   **Mental practice** refers to the processes associated with mentally rehearsing the performance of a skill in the absence of any overt physical practice. Often mental practice is associated with mental imagery, but this is not always the case. What appears to be important is that mental and physical practice share the same cognitive

HIGHLIGHT

The Men and Women Behind the Patriot Missiles

In the Persian Gulf War of 1991, one of the big heroes was the U.S. Army patriot missile. Night after night millions of viewers worldwide watched as Scud and Al-Hussein missiles launched from Iraq to Saudi Arabia or Israel were intercepted. These amazingly complicated missiles performed almost flawlessly. In fact, many of the television analysts reported that the patriot missiles hastened the end of the war, saved thousands of lives, and perhaps more important kept the war from escalating.

What was not mentioned on the news were the men and women behind the missiles. Although the patriot can be operated in an automatic mode, it could not be in this war. Too many allied aircraft were in the vicinity to allow the computer control systems to operate automatically. Human operators were required, and they performed this complicated job flawlessly. This level of skill was accomplished by a very sophisticated training protocol based on the concept of simulation.

Simulation is a technique in which the perceived context of the activity of interest is artificially created. Football and basketball coaches utilize modest simulation techniques when they use the loudspeaker system to simulate crowd noises. Fairly realistic golf driving and flight simulators are commercially available. However, the type of simulation used in training the operators of patriot missiles is so realistic that the operator cannot determine real incoming missiles and firing from simulated ones. The army used a number of Lockheed Sanders' Patriot Operator Tactics Trainers (OTT). It took 34 weeks to train a basic console operator for the patriot system. The training involved realistic real-time engagements that were recorded for detailed review and analysis. In fact, the simulator system kept track of the strengths and weaknesses of each trainee on the various scenarios in order to tailor the training sessions.

Trainees were provided detailed descriptions of their errors after each scenario. The device prescribed practice that was aimed at developing the specific deficits of each individual. Practice was perfected because even a small mistake could mean life or death.

operations (MacKay, 1987; Kohl, 1990; Kohl, Ellis, & Roenker, 1992). Roland, Larsen, Lassen, and Shinhoj (1980) reported that when subjects mentally rehearsed learned finger sequences, blood flow to the supplementary motor cortex was similar to that during actual practice. However, mental practice did not increase blood flow to the motor cortex as did actual practice. The supplementary motor cortex is thought to be a site for high-level movement planning and/or the site of already developed movement plans (Wiesendanger, 1987).

An interesting experiment involving mental practice was conducted by Kohl and Roenker (1980). In their second experiment, three practice groups were used. A physical practice group attempted 18 trials on a pursuit rotor task with their right hand. The pursuit rotor was set at 60 revolutions per minute and trials were 30 seconds. The mental practice group held the stylus with their right hand and rehearsed performing the task for 18 trials. The mental practice subjects had only seen the experimenter perform the task for one trial but had never physically practiced the task. A control group was not permitted to physically or mentally practice the task. Following the acquisition period all subjects were given six trials on the task using their left hand.

The results are given in Figure 11.17. The mental and physical practice groups performed similarly, and both were superior to the control group. The results suggest that the cognitive activities associated with mental and physical practice are similar because similar benefits were observed.

The bilateral paradigm used by Kohl and Roenker (1980) is not typical of that used to investigate the influence of mental practice. Most experiments have simply contrasted mental, physical, and some combination of mental/physical practice. These experiments generally find some benefits of mental practice and larger benefits for a combination of mental/physical practice (see Richardson, 1967a & b; Corbin, 1972; Feltz & Landers, 1983, for reviews). However, almost without

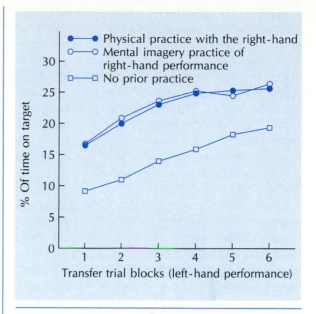

Figure 11.17 *Percent time on target for the transfer trials on a pursuit rotor task as a function of practice condition. During acquisition subjects practiced with their right hand, imaged using their right hand, or did not practice. Retention was performed with the left hand.*

exception physical practice has been shown to result in better retention than any combination of mental and physical practice. These experiments have been concerned with the actual benefits of mental practice rather than determining the mechanisms that are responsible for those benefits.

Observational Practice. Much can be learned through **observational practice**—observing others as they engage in motor tasks. Note the number of observers who mass around a new video game in the arcade. Can they learn by observing others perform the video game? What about sports skills? What kind of information is gained by observing other players perform a task?

It has been argued by many theorists and researchers (Bandura, 1969, 1977; Carroll & Bandura, 1982, 1985, 1989; Adams, 1986, 1987; Scully & Newell, 1985; McCullach, Weiss, & Ross, 1989) that the cognitive activities associated with observational practice are similar to the cognitive activities associated with actual practice. It has been proposed that as the performer (demonstrator) utilizes feedback, the observer can also observe some aspects of the available feedback. Although subjects involved in actual and observational practice may perform similar cognitive operations, their perspectives on the feedback are clearly different.

After an extensive review of the literature on observational practice, Newell, Morris, and Scully (1985) concluded that actual practice or a first-person perspective on feedback was a more effective practice method than observational practice when the processing of feedback was a critical factor for performance and learning. They noted that observational practice or a third-person perspective on feedback was particularly valuable either when the subject had to execute previously learned skills under new conditions or when internal sensory feedback was not critical to the control of the movement.

Scully and Newell (1985) proposed that the most useful information conveyed by the demonstrator to the observer were the relative features of the movement pattern. They proposed that "the problem for the learner of motor skills appears to be one of coordinating the body to reproduce the observed relative motion and scaling the relative motion appropriately" (Scully & Newell, 1985, p. 181). Therefore, it may be important to distinguish between error scores and the patterns of movement in interpreting the effect of demonstrations. Researchers who have measured error scores and movement patterns have provided evidence consistent with the Newell and Scully proposal (Martens, Burwitz, & Zuckermen, 1976; McCullagh, 1987; Whiting, Bijlard, & den Brinker, 1987).

Martens et al. (1976) performed four experiments to determine the effects of observing a task demonstration on subsequent retention. In Experiment 3, the performer (demonstrator) organized response patterns that were described as slow and gradient. Gradually as practice progressed, the per-

former's method of responding was described as ballistic. On the test of retention, observational subjects, performing for the first time, were able to mimic this pattern of movement but their errors were higher than those of a control.

Kohl and Shea (1991) asked subjects to perform a response that required them to alternately press two buttons in an attempt to keep an accelerating dot on a target line that appeared on a computer monitor. The dot ac-

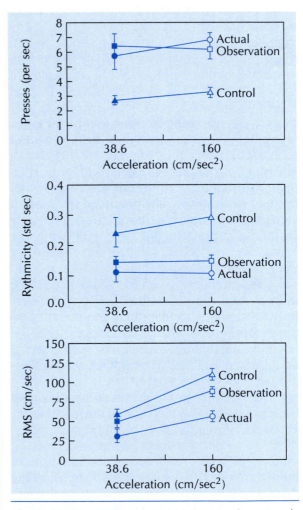

Figure 11.18 *Average presses per second (top), rythmicity (middle), and root mean square error (bottom) for retention trials on the more difficult reciprocal button pressing task as a function of practice condition.*

258

celerated to the right when the right button was pressed and moved to the left when the left button was pressed. In a series of experiments, the difficulty of the task was manipulated by changing the movement of the target and the speed with which the dot accelerated. Figure 11.18 depicts the method of responding (number of presses and rythmicity) and error score (RMS—root mean square error, see Appendix A). In each experiment the rate and the rythmicity of responding for both the subjects actually performing the task and the observational subjects were indistinguishable. In fact, there were no differences between the actual and observational practice subjects on the retention test of the easier task. However, actual practice subjects performed with less error than the observational subjects when the difficulty of the task was increased.

In summary, observational practice appears to be a viable practice method to improve particular characteristics of movement strategies and scaling relative features of movements. Observational practice, like mental practice, may also be important because physical injuries and/or fatigue are not experienced, and actual practice environments are not required.

FINAL COMMENT

Even subtle changes in the structure of practice sessions may impact acquisition, retention, and transfer performance. Practices can be structured to consider the schedule of practice trials and the composition of practice. Practice schedule manipulations that have been shown to impact performance include the distribution of practice trials and contextual interference manipulations. Practice composition manipulations that influence performance and learning include variability of practice and mental/observational practice conditions.

KEY TERMS

practice schedule
practice composition
acquisition
retention
transfer

transfer paradigm
practice distribution
massed practice
distributed practice
contextual
    interference

elaboration
    perspective
reconstruction
    hypothesis
specificity hypothesis

variability of practice
    hypothesis
part-whole practice
mental practice
observational
    practice

12
Human Performance in a Social Context

Muhammed Ali: "I AM THE GREATEST"

Why Study Social Influences?

The Social Nature of Some Basic Concepts
- *Arousal*
- *Social Comparison*

Goal Setting: The Influence of Social Context
- *Group Polarization*

Social Learning Theory

Performing Alone or With Others
- *Social Facilitation Versus Social Inhibition*
- *Social Loafing: Robbing Individual Motivation*
- *Home-Court Advantage: Where We Perform*

The Power of the Group
- *Focus of Attention*
- *Concern With Evaluation*
- *Social Identity*

HIGHLIGHT: Men and Women in Groups
FINAL COMMENT
KEY TERMS

Muhammed Ali: "I AM THE GREATEST"

Throughout history heavyweight boxing has been thought of as a sport involving little grace, but much strength. Fighters adopted such names as "The Brawler" or "The Mauler." Winners were those who could absorb the most punishment and throw the hardest punch. But all this changed in the 1960 Olympics when a brash young fighter showed the world a new style; instead of engaging in a slugfest, this fighter "floated like a butterfly, and stung like a bee." With the grace of an accomplished dancer, this fighter glided around the ring, searched for an opening, and then darted in to pepper his opponent with crisp jabs. Cassius Marcellus Clay not only brought a new style to boxing, he also revived a sport that had been languishing since the days of Joe Louis and Sugar Ray Robinson.

Clay grew up in Louisville, Kentucky, in a world that told blacks that they were inferior and only fit for the most menial jobs. At times Clay resented the color of his skin that closed so many opportunities to him. But the resentment only isolated him. His boyhood hero was Joe Louis, a black heavyweight boxing champion. In an effort to feel a sense of purpose, a sense of belonging, Clay spent time at a local gymnasium watching fighters train. He watched their every move and rehearsed in his mind how he would fight. By age twelve, the skinny 112-pound boy convinced Joe Martin, a white policeman, to teach him to box. Clay trained almost every evening and spent hours on conditioning exercises. The other boxers

In 1959 Cassius Clay won the Golden Gloves championship, and in 1960 he dazzled the world, winning the Olympic gold medal in boxing.

- To understand the impact of social variables on arousal, motivation, and performance.

- To appreciate the different ways in which models affect performance and learning.

- To identify the conditions under which the presence of others facilitates (or inhibits) performance and learning.

- To examine the process through which group membership and concern with social evaluation affect self-identity.

- To understand the basis from which groups derive power to influence members.

helped him, giving him tips and building up his self-image both as a boxer and as a black person. Clay's coordination and quickness developed as did his strength. His self-confidence also grew and he became such a braggart that some people dubbed him "Gaseous Cassius."

In 1959 Clay won the Golden Gloves championship. Then in 1960 he dazzled the world as he won the Olympic gold medal. The Olympic experience was a unique one. On one hand Clay was part of the U.S. team where the members helped and cheered each other. On the other hand, Clay was locked in combat in front of an audience of millions. The excitement and attention lifted Clay's boxing skills to new heights of excellence. This context also increased Clay's boastfulness and set the stage for his taunting cry of "I am the greatest!"

After the Olympics, Clay began to fight professionally. His fame grew as his boxing skills improved. He was a beautiful fighter to watch as he glided around the ring flicking lightening-like jabs. As his audience grew, so did his taunting style and bragging. Clay was on his way to becoming one of the greatest boxers in history. But with success and atten-

tion, a new side of Clay emerged. Throughout his life he had been deeply hurt by the unfair treatment of blacks in the United States. Prejudice and discrimination hurt Clay more than any punch he had ever taken. He had won the Olympic gold medal for his country, but he was not allowed to enter many restaurants in that country.

In 1964, Cassius Clay joined the Black Muslims and changed his name to Muhammad Ali, which means "one who is worthy of praise." The public reacted with anger, and promoters threatened to cancel his fights. In an ironic twist, others viewed the Black Muslims as a "race-hate-sect." Ali remained loyal to his new religion, arguing that he was not anti-white, but pro-black. His boxing skills had made him a symbol for blacks, and he felt compelled to stand by his convictions and beliefs. Ali beat Sonny Liston to become the world heavyweight champion.

But the turmoil surrounding his life increased. The United States was involved in the Vietnam War, and Ali was a vocal critic of that war. He felt it was a "white man's war" and a violation of his religious principles. On April 28, 1967, when his name was called by the induction board, he walked slowly to the table and signed a statement refusing induction. He was branded a traitor, and his boxing license and title were stripped from him. He was sentenced to five years in prison and a $10,000 fine. For three-and-a-half years he was exiled from the ring as he fought the conviction in court.

But Ali did return. A heavier and somewhat out-of-shape Ali rose to chants and jeers of a wild crowd to defeat Jerry Quarry. In 1971 Ali was defeated by Joe Frazier. But he won a major victory that year when the Supreme Court overturned his conviction for draft evasion. Ali could now fight as a free man. The years of inactivity had taken their toll on Ali, but he challenged Frazier for a rematch. Although it seemed that Ali was physically outclassed by the younger Frazier, Ali again rose to the occasion and regained his title. Each time he fought, Ali seemed to come to life with the roar of the crowd. He lost and then regained his title for the third time in the 1978 fight with Leon Spinks. Ali retired a champ, but he could not stay retired. He longed for just one more time in the limelight. But he went down in final defeat to Larry Holmes in his last attempt to regain his world crown.

■ ■ ■

Why Study Social Influences?

Ali was a wonderfully skilled fighter, a joy to watch. He combined graceful footwork, quick and powerful movement of the upper body and arms, and an elusive, bobbing head to escape punishment and deliver a beating to his opponent. Ali's actions embody the field of motor learning and human performance—the acquisition of motor skills and the performance of those skills. To understand Ali's ability, we are tempted to narrow our focus to the man, to the individual's actions. But let's pause a moment before taking this focus.

Let's begin with one of the most basic human motor skills involving learning and performance: a baby (we'll call her Susan) learning to walk. Let's watch Susan as she sits alone in a room playing with her toys. She seems content to play for hours, until her mother or father enters the room. Suddenly Susan drops her toys and turns her attention to the intruder. There is verbal and nonverbal communication between the two. Susan gets very excited and begins crawling toward the parent. The parent laughs and exclaims, "Let's see if you can walk to me. Remember how you did it yesterday." The parent stands Susan up, steps back a bit, and asks Susan to walk. Susan immediately sits down; the parent frowns and drags Susan to her feet again. This time Susan takes a faltering step and our parent begins a celebration, similar to Christmas morning; there are laughs, hugs, kisses, and Susan becomes a star.

Susan's activities involved motor movement, coordination, motivation, and performance. But each of these events involved something else: a social setting and social influence. So too did the social setting and social influence play a central role in developing Ali's boxing skills. And so too do social factors affect the way you learn motor skills and the process of teaching skills to others. Indeed, most learning and teaching can be viewed as a social interaction between two or more people. Therefore, in order to truly understand motor learning and performance, it is important to consider the role of social factors in the process. And it is to these social factors that we now turn our attention.

The Social Nature of Some Basic Concepts

Throughout this book we have discussed some basic concepts that relate to learning and performance. We have seen the central role arousal plays in both processes and the importance of rewards, motivation, and feedback. There is often a tendency to view these concepts as relating only to the individual, even as being internal processes within the individual. Yet each of these concepts has a distinct social aspect.

Arousal

Arousal refers to the physiological activity of the individual. We measure arousal by examining such functions as blood pressure, heart rate, breathing rate, and galvanic skin response (GSR). Arousal is clearly affected by individual and environmental factors such as predictability (Glass & Singer, 1972), control (Bandura & Wood, 1989), and physical stress to the body. A solid blow from an opponent's right hand sent Ali's physiological functions to higher levels.

But arousal also has a social component. At the most basic level, **competition** has been shown to create greater arousal than cooperation (Forsyth, 1990). Trying to beat another person or knowing that person is trying to beat you causes greater arousal than cooperating with that person. Even the mere presence of a person in the room or the knowledge that someone is watching us leads to arousal. At a more complex level, the reactions of others influence our level of arousal and the way we interpret that arousal. For example, Lazarus (1982) argued that the way other people react to an event influences how aroused we will become. A child who cuts himself or herself may hardly react to the slight flow of blood if other people ignore it. However, this same child will become very agitated and pierce the air with shrieks if others look alarmed.

In an interesting experiment, Schachter and Singer (1962) aroused subjects with an injection of epinephrine. Subjects who did not know the arousing properties of the drug were then placed in a room with an experimental accomplice who acted either euphoric or angry. Even though the arousal experienced by the subjects was the same, those with the happy confederate reported experiencing happiness and elation, while those with the angry confederate reported feeling angry. Therefore, the actions (and presence) of others influence when we will become aroused, the degree of our arousal, and the interpretation we place on that arousal.

Social Comparison

Numerous investigators have argued that knowledge of results or feedback is vitally important to motor learning (Ammons, 1956; Holding, 1965; Smoll, 1972). For the most part, their concerns focused on receiving information about the effects of our actions: when I follow through on my golf swing, will the ball go straight down the fairway? An important aspect of feedback concerns the quality of an action. In some cases, this can be determined by a simple physical measure such as the degree of slice on the golf ball. But in other cases, the issue is a social one. Ali brashly boasted, "I am the greatest!" and at other times, "I am the most beautiful boxer that ever lived!" How did he arrive at these conclusions? How do you determine how good a golfer or tennis player you are or even how beautiful or handsome you are?

According to Leon Festinger (1954), we determine the answers to these and many other questions by comparing ourselves with others, in other words, through **social comparison**. Our movements and actions are designed to achieve certain results, but the quality of these results can only be determined by comparison with others. When you hit a golf ball, you not only want feedback about whether it goes down the fairway, but does it go as far as other golfers' balls? Depending on the answer to this latter question, you will be satisfied (or dissatisfied) with your performance and alter your motor activity as needed.

According to the theory of social comparison, we do not compare with just anyone; rather we attempt to make comparisons with others who are similar to us (Goethals & Darley, 1987). Ali could not conclude that he was the greatest boxer by finding that he could beat children or amateur boxers. He wanted feedback from other professional boxers, the best boxers he could find. But this is not the whole story. Although we want accurate feedback, we also want to find that we are good; we want to develop a positive self-image. Therefore, on important dimensions we are tempted to get positive feedback by engaging in downward comparison (Tesser, 1985). We seek others who are slightly inferior to us so that the comparison we make will be a positive one.

We could continue along this line by discussing the social nature of rewards, motivation, and punishment. However, the point should be clear: many of the central concepts for understanding learning and performance involve a social component. And it is important to consider this social component when studying learning and performance, or teaching motor skills to others. With these points in mind, let's examine some of the social theories and research related to learning and performance.

Goal Setting: The Influence of Social Context

In discussing his career, Ali argued that a driving force for him was the high goal he set for himself. He wanted to be the best fighter of all time. This goal motivated him to spend thousands of hours working on his techniques in the gym. This goal drove him to pick the best opponents available. And this goal was behind his desire to make a comeback after each defeat. **Goal setting**, or **level of aspiration**, is the level of performance that a person desires to achieve. It gives purpose to learning and direction to performance. There is considerable evidence that having a goal improves learning and performance.

For example, subjects in one study were required to use foot and hand control to match a set of display lights (Locke & Bryan, 1966). Some subjects were simply told to do their best to learn the task as quickly as possible. A second group was given a specific goal (speed of learning) to strive for. As can be seen from the results in Figure 12.1, the group with the specific goal learned the task more quickly. In another study involving performance on a strength task (elbow flexion), subjects were given either a goal in the form of norms for performance or no norms. Those subjects with a norm (goal) performed significantly better than the group with no standard goal.

Although we often view setting goals as an individual activity, Ali relates an interesting story that shows its social nature. Early in his career, his managers and coaches wanted Ali to develop slowly, taking on opponents who were rated similarly to him. Ali, on the other hand, was anxious "to get the show on the road" and wanted to take the more risky approach of boxing much higher-rated opponents. After considerable individual disagreements, they all met to discuss the issue. During the group discussion, the managers' and coaches' opinions shifted. The result was

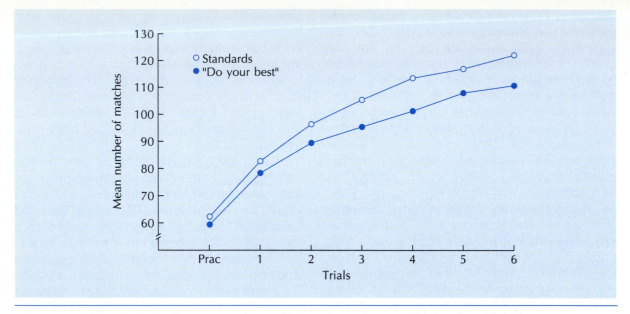

Figure 12.1 *Performance on the Mashburn task as a function of the goal established prior to practice.*

a decision to follow the riskier course of action and set the high goal of a quick title fight.

This incident raises the issue of how groups affect our attitudes and goals. The early view was that groups would have a conservative effect on people, causing them to be cautious in their approach (Whyte, 1956). But a study by Stoner (1961) found the opposite. Stoner had subjects set their own level of risk for a number of situations. The subjects then discussed their choices in a group, and to Stoner's surprise, the recommendations coming out of the group were riskier than the individual decisions.

Group Polarization

Numerous studies followed and the picture that emerged was that groups tend to polarize people's attitudes (Wallach, Kogan, & Bem, 1962; Knox & Stafford, 1972). If people are inclined to follow a conservative course of action (set low-risk goals), group discussion leads them to become even more conserva-

tive; but if the general individual tendency is toward risky goals, the group discussion leads to taking a riskier position.

Numerous explanations have been suggested for this **group polarization** effect. One focuses on social comparison and argues that people want to appear at least as extreme as others on issues (Myers, 1982). The group discussion gives them a chance to compare their position with others and adjust this position. A second explanation suggests that the language available to support an extreme position is more forceful and convincing than that available to support a middle-of-the-road position. Therefore, within the group, the people with extreme positions are able to mount a more persuasive campaign (Burnstein, 1982).

Regardless of the process involved, we should remember that goals are important for performance and learning and that goals are often set in social settings. The social settings often push people to adopt more extreme goals than they would adopt on their own (Table 12.1).

TABLE 12.1   Examples of Risky-Shift Dilemmas

1. A captain of a college football team, in the final seconds of a game with the college's traditional rival, may choose a play that is almost certain to produce a tie score, or a riskier play that would lead to sure victory if successful, sure defeat if not.
2. The president of an American corporation that is about to expand may build a new plant in the United States where returns on the investment would be moderate, or may decide to build in a foreign country with an unstable political history where, however, returns on the investment would be very high.
3. A college senior planning graduate work in chemistry may enter university X where, because of rigorous standards, only a fraction of the graduate students manage to receive the Ph.D., or may enter university Y which has a poorer reputation but where almost every graduate student receives the Ph.D.
4. A low-ranked participant in a national chess tournament, playing an early match with the top-favored opponent, has the choice of attempting or not trying a deceptive but risky maneuver that might lead to quick victory if successful or almost certain defeat if it fails.

Source: Wallach et al. (1962), p. 77.

Social Learning Theory

Ali's discussion of his boxing career not only illustrates how our social setting influences our goal setting, but it also anticipates our discussion of social learning. As a boy, Ali watched films of Joe Louis, his hero. Louis was a graceful, cunning boxer who combined footwork with a lightening-fast jab to help him become a heavyweight champion. Ali watched Louis' technique and he saw the results; Louis not only beat his opponents but became a national figure. Also during his boyhood, Ali spent much of his free time in the gym watching other boxers train. Soon he got his chance to enter the ring and begin his own career, and everyone marveled at how quickly he learned boxing moves.

But did his learning begin when he started training? According to **social learning theory**, Ali's learning began long before he entered the ring (see also Observational Practice, Chapter 11). He began learning when he watched the first films of a boxer, possibly those of Joe Louis. Social learning theory argues that much of our learning takes place through our imitation of others (Bandura & Walters, 1963; Bandura, 1973). As we watch others perform, we rehearse their activities and learn the behaviors. We can learn from real-life models, televised models of real people, or cartoons (Bandura, Ross, & Ross, 1961, 1963). We are especially likely to learn from models who are of our same gender (Bandura et al., 1961) and from high status rather than low status models (Turner & Berkowitz, 1972). It is clear that Joe Louis fit these characteristics for young Cassius Clay.

Although we may learn a skill by watching others, we will not necessarily perform that activity. According to social learning theory, we will perform an activity when we receive positive **reinforcement** for doing so. Thus, even though Ali may have learned many boxing moves by watching others, he did not rush home to try out his new behaviors on his par-

According to social learning theory, people learn behaviors from models. Television often supplies those models.

an adult praised the model for the aggressive behavior. In another condition, the model was punished by the adult for the behavior. The children were then given the opportunity to play with a Bobo doll similar to the one they had seen in the film. The children who saw the model praised began to punch, kick, and hit the model with a hammer. Those who saw the model punished did not play aggressively with the Bobo doll. We might conclude that this latter group did not learn from the model. However, when these children were offered a reward if they could imitate the model, they carefully reproduced the behaviors they had observed. Therefore, they too learned from the model but did not imitate the behavior unless they felt they would be rewarded for doing so. Thus, learning does not take place only through shaping and reinforcement contingencies (see Chapter 10). We learn a great deal by observing others. We can, in fact, learn very complex movements through modeling. Reinforcement, however, is very important in determining when we will perform these learned behaviors. And again, we can see the importance of social influences on motor learning and performance.

ents. It was not until he entered the boxing ring where he was encouraged and rewarded for boxing that he actually performed. In demonstrating this process, Bandura (1965) had children observe a model beating a Bobo doll. The model punched, kicked, and hit the inflated doll with a hammer. In one condition

Performing Alone or With Others

Social Facilitation Versus Social Inhibition

Ali spent thousands of hours in the gym conditioning himself, practicing his footwork, jabbing a punching bag, and shadow boxing. This was how he learned boxing, but when it came time to perform, Ali stood in front of thousands of screaming fans. Was this program of training alone in order to perform in front of others a wise move, or would Ali have been better advised to train before an audience to simulate more closely the conditions under which he would have to box?

In order to answer this question, let's go back to the turn of the century. Norman Triplett (1897) was interested in helping bicyclists get their best performance (fastest time). Cycle racing took two forms at that time. In one case, a cyclist would race around the track alone trying to get the fastest time. A second method involved cyclists' competing together on the track for the fastest time. When Triplett examined the records associated with these two methods, he found cyclists who raced in the presence of others had approximately 20 percent faster times than cyclists who raced alone. Although this effect may have been due to the presence of others, it is also possible that it was caused by drafting (riding behind another cyclist to avoid wind resistance) or some other physical effect. So Triplett devised a rather simple experiment. He asked children to wind up a fishing reel as quickly as possible. Children performed this task either alone or in the presence of other children working on the same task. Once again, Triplett found that the faster times occurred when the children worked in the presence of others.

A flurry of studies followed Triplett's work; in general this research found that people performed better when they were in the presence of others. This result was found when there was competition or **coaction** with others, or when others served as an audience (Allport, 1924; Travis, 1925). One researcher (Chen, 1937) even found that an ant worked harder

In one of the earliest studies of social influences on performance, Triplett found that cyclists raced 20 percent faster in head-to-head competition than when trying to beat the clock.

(removed more balls of dirt from a tunnel) when in the presence of other ants than when working alone! From these data we might conclude that there is a **social facilitation** effect such that the presence of others aids learning and performance.

But the picture did not remain clear for long. Other research began to find the opposite effect, **social inhibition**. For example, Pessin and Husband (1933) found that an audience caused subjects to learn maze and nonsense-syllable tasks more slowly. Interestingly, once subjects had learned the tasks, they performed better in front of an audience than when alone.

Learning and Performance. How do we reconcile these seemingly contradictory results? Zajonc (1965, 1972) drew a clear distinction between the learning phase and the performance phase. He suggested that learning complex tasks requires developing new skills and suppressing older, ingrained tendencies. Performance of well-learned skills involves giving dominant responses. Zajonc suggested that the presence of other people increases our arousal. This increased arousal energizes us and facilitates the performance of dominant responses. At the same time, this increased arousal makes it more difficult to learn complex new skills, because of the tendency to emit dominant responses. Therefore, the presence of others inhibits learning new responses but facilitates performance of well-learned responses.

Numerous studies have shown that others do inhibit learning complex activities while facilitating performance of dominant behaviors (Guerin & Innes, 1982; Wilke & van Knippenberg, 1988). Some of the investigators, however, have suggested other explanations for social facilitation. For example, an audience may be distracting (Sanders, 1981). This distraction makes it difficult to concentrate on learning new skills. At the same time, it keeps the individual from concentrating too much on himself or herself, thereby reducing the tendency to "clutch" and allowing the body to perform well-learned behaviors smoothly.

Regardless of the reason for the effect, we can see that the presence of others can either facilitate or inhibit activity. The nature of the influence is dependent on the complexity of the task and whether the individual is learning a new skill or performing a previously learned behavior. Hence, Ali's program of learning in the relative isolation of the gym and performing before an audience was probably a wise strategy. Indeed, we might compare Ali's program with that of Mike Tyson, who after winning the heavyweight crown opened his training camp to reporters and many others. He was defeated by Buster Douglas, a relative unknown, in his next fight.

Social Loafing: Robbing Individual Motivation

The social facilitation literature suggests that the presence of others can help an individual achieve a personal performance goal. But what about the situation in which a group goal is at stake? Do we work harder for a group goal when alone or in the group? In order to answer this question, Ringelmann (1913) asked male subjects to pull on a rope as hard as they could. They pulled either alone or in groups of two, three, or eight. Ringelmann found that two-man groups pulled 1.9 times as hard as the single person, three-man groups pulled 2.5 times as hard, and eight-man groups pulled 4 times as hard. Thus, although adding additional people to the task resulted in an increase in overall effort, it was clear that each individual was performing less well. In the eight-man group, each subject was putting half as much effort into the task as in the case where they acted alone. This effect was found with other tasks. In one study people clapped alone and in a group (Latané, 1981). Although the group produced more noise than the individual, the average individual clapped less loudly in the group. This effect has been labeled **social loafing**.

Coordination Loss.   If we compare group performance with individual performance, we can see a number of causes for this effect. The first is coordination loss (Steiner, 1972). Group tasks such as rope pulling require that each person exert maximum effort at the same time to achieve the best performance. Achieving this timing is often difficult in groups, especially large groups.

Motivation Loss.   A second problem is motivation loss; individuals may lose motivation to perform at their peak in groups. It is on this effect that explanations for social loafing have concentrated. In groups, people are often anonymous, and it is difficult to determine who is performing well and who is not. Members lose their sense of responsibility for the outcome. Demonstrating this effect, investigators found that subjects performed as well in a group as when alone if they believed that their individual performance was being monitored in the group.

Sucker Effect.   Another explanation for social loafing is referred to as the **sucker effect** (Kerr, 1983). When in a group, you may look around and see some other members who are not putting in maximum effort. However, because the product is a group effort, all members will benefit equally from the outcome. You may ask yourself: Why should I work so hard for the benefit of these lazy members? They are, in a sense, playing you for a sucker. And you respond by reducing your effort.

Free Rider Effect.   Another possible explanation is the **free rider effect**. In this case, you examine your group and find that things are going pretty well and that the group is moving toward its goal. Given that all is well, you may decide that the group really does not need you to work to your potential, and therefore, you reduce your effort and loaf (Kerr & Brunn, 1983).

Commitment to Group.   Still another possible cause of social loafing concerns your feelings about the group. In many groups, we feel little commitment to the group goal or that we are not a central part of the group. For us, the group represents a collection of individuals rather than a unit of people who belong together and are committed to each other. These feelings have been found to reduce individual performance aimed at a group goal (Worchel, Hart, & Buttemeyer, 1989).

The bottom line is that individual performance can be inhibited by being in a group setting. This is especially likely when the individual feels anonymous, believes that others in the group are not giving their maximum performance, senses that the group does not need maximum performance from him or her, and feels little commitment or belonging to the group.

Home-Court Advantage: Where We Perform

We have been focusing on the issue of whom we perform with. Now let's turn our attention to where we perform. Ali publicly boasted that he would "fight anyone, anywhere." But despite this boast, his managers put a great deal of effort into choosing the place where Ali fought and ensuring that he became familiar with the ring. When possible, they wanted to have a "friendly" crowd, although this was difficult to achieve when Ali earned the scorn of the nation for his antiwar stance.

Anyone with even a passing interest in athletics is familiar with the term **home-court advantage**. Coaches attempt to schedule their most difficult games on their home court. Gamblers usually give better odds to the team playing on its home field. The assumption behind these activities is that we perform better in our home area than on foreign territory. Indeed, there seems to be some truth to the advantage of the home court; Worchel and Sigall (1976) found that Atlantic Coast Conference basketball teams won 88 percent of their games on their home court and 65 percent of their games on the road.

Given these beliefs and statistics, we can next ask why there is a home-court advantage. Let's first deal with the most obvious reasons. Teams have been known to make the physical environment most unpleasant for the

A home-court advantage exists in a variety of sporting contests. The home team wins a majority of the games. One important exception may be in important championship games.

visitors by placing their benches in the coldest area of a stadium or giving them inadequate locker room facilities. There is also the yet unsupported impression that referees, umpires, or judges will make decisions that benefit the home team and hurt the visitors. And there is the issue of familiarity with the environment. Players will know the soft spots on their own basketball court, how the wind affects the flight of a tennis ball, or how the grass affects the path of a bunt on the infield of a baseball diamond. In some cases, it is even possible to prepare the home court to help the home team's performance. For example, groundkeepers have been known to wet the infield to slow runners when the visiting team has a history of successful base stealing. All of these possibilities will influence the performance of players. Finally, there is the issue of fatigue; playing away from home often requires exhausting travel.

And there are some less obvious influences on performance. As we pointed out in Chapter 10, we tend to learn skills for which we receive positive rewards and inhibit activities that are punished. An important reinforcer for an athlete is the response of the crowd. The athlete expects good performance to be met with cheers and poor performance to elicit silence or boos. Indeed, this is the pattern of response when the athlete performs on the home court or in front of a friendly audience. However, the tables are turned when performing on a foreign field or in front of a hostile audience. In these cases, skillful actions bring silence or jeers while mistakes are widely cheered. The reinforcement contingencies are backward on a foreign field, and this affects the performer.

A second less obvious issue concerns the influence of familiarity. Considerable research has shown that we are comfortable with and attracted to objects and people with whom we are familiar. In one study, subjects were shown a number of photographs of others (Zajonc, 1968). Later, subjects were asked how much they liked the people in the pictures. Even though they had never met any of the people depicted, subjects were more attracted to the people they had seen most often. On the other side of the coin, events, activities, and objects that are unfamiliar to us often grab our attention. Therefore, it can be very distracting for a person to perform on unfamiliar territory because he or she is distracted by the unfamiliar surroundings.

However, before adopting the home-court advantage as a rule of thumb, consider more recent findings suggesting that there is a slight tendency for home teams to lose decisive championship games (Baumeister & Steinhilber, 1984). According to these investigators, there is a great deal of pressure on people to perform well in front of the home audience. When we add the pressure of the championship game, athletes become overly concerned with their performance. They become self-conscious and cautious and their performance suffers.

The Power of the Group

From our previous discussion, an interesting and important picture begins to emerge. On one hand, being in a group or in front of an audience can enhance the performance of even a mediocre athlete. On the other hand, the group can inhibit the performance of the most skilled player. What is the power base of the group? How can it have such wide-ranging effects? If we look carefully at the questions, we find a number of answers.

Focus of Attention

Think for a moment how you learn a new skill such as dancing. At first, you are painfully aware of each move you make. You may even look at your feet as you stumble across the dance floor. But as you progress, your attention becomes less focused on yourself, and you begin to pay attention to the music and the moves of your partner. When Ali discussed his boxing career, he described a similar pattern. Early in his learning he focused on each move he made; he paid attention to where his feet and hands were. However, as he developed these skills, he became more concerned with the results of his action and the responses of his opponent. Indeed, this may be the natural flow of events in learning and performance. But now let's add an audience to this process. To see the effect, consider the last time you stood up in front of a classroom filled with people. Even if you knew what you wanted to say and had rehearsed it in your mind, you may have felt as if your mouth were filled with cotton. Your attention began to shift to yourself: was your hair combed, did your voice sound forceful, was your zipper closed?

As we move through the day, we perform many, if not most, of our actions in a mindless fashion (Langer, 1989). We give little thought to what we are doing and how we are doing it. But this pattern becomes interrupted when we are in front of an audience. When other people focus on us, we focus our own attention on ourselves—we show objective self-awareness (Wicklund & Frey, 1980). When we "look" at ourselves, we begin to consider each behavior and compare it to a standard of what we want to do or think we should be doing. All of this may detract from our ability to carry through with our performance and/or it interrupts our ability to learn new skills. Hence, one of the influences of the group comes from the fact that it can redirect our focus of attention.

All is not lost, however. Research has shown that we can escape the negative effects of objective self-awareness if we expect to do well or are performing well-learned activities in front of the group (Greenberg & Mushman, 1981). We can also reduce the interference of self-awareness by training and by understanding the potential effects of the audience.

Concern With Evaluation

Groups not only affect the direction of our attention, but they also influence the concerns we have. When we behave in isolation from others, our major concern is the outcome of our actions. Did we achieve the desired outcome? Are we performing the way we want? But when we add the group ingredient, we add a new concern to the recipe. How are others perceiving us? Are we making a good impression on them? Will they perceive us as "showing off" or as clumsy? We develop a sense of evaluation apprehension (Worchel, Cooper, & Goethals, 1991), and consequently, we adjust our performance to meet the expectations of others.

In some cases, this apprehension may spur us to perform better. But in other cases, it may cause us to lower our performance. In an early study, Roethlisberger and Dickson (1939) examined the work output at the Western Electric Company in Hawthorne, Illinois. They found that the group developed a norm of how much each worker should produce. A worker who produced too little slowed the group down. And a worker who produced too much made the other members look bad. Over time, each worker adjusted his or her performance level to conform to the group expectations. In this way, the workers gained the approval and acceptance of the other group members.

Further research has found that the greatest evaluation apprehension occurs with new group members (Moreland & Levine, 1988) and in groups that have recently formed (Worchel, Coutant-Sassic, & Grossman, 1991). Thus, groups influence our behaviors because we want to make a good impression on others and meet their expectations.

Research has found that evaluation apprehension is very high when a new or unskilled employee is evaluated by an experienced performer.

Social Identity

Although this discussion may strike you as very sensible, let's take a step back and ask a few more basic questions. Why do we care about making a good impression on others and gaining their favor? If we fail to meet the expectations of others, will there really be any negative consequences for us? In Ali's case, why did he care how other Americans felt about his stand on the Vietnam War as long as he was able to continue boxing and earning large sums of money?

In order to answer these questions, let's begin by asking you to describe who you are. You may begin by giving your name, where you live, and some details about your physical

Men and Women in Groups

We often characterize humans as social animals, and recently there has been increasing interest in comparing the behavior of men and women in social settings. Old stereotypes portrayed women as addicted to and controlled by their social setting. Women, supposedly, were driven by the desire to join groups, and once members of the group, they easily conformed to the norms of the group. Men, on the other hand, were shown as striving for independence, often comfortable with isolation. When placed in a group, men worked to become leaders, while women were most comfortable playing the role of supportive group members. The implication of this view was that groups might bring out the best performance in men but would cause women to moderate their efforts.

As with many stereotypes, this one, too, has been shown to be inaccurate. However, the research on gender differences in social settings has uncovered some interesting differences. Overall, men belong to more groups than women, but women spend more time in their groups (Booth, 1972). Groups of women tend to be more unified and cohesive than groups of men (Winstead, 1986).

Looking more directly at performance, men tend to be more task-oriented in groups than women (Wood, 1987). Men desire to "get the job done." They focus on maximizing payoffs and on having themselves and their group perform to the highest potential. If our only concern is individual performance, the literature suggests that the group setting may enhance the performance of men.

Women in groups act somewhat differently. They, too, are concerned about performance, but they tend to be more concerned with having the group function smoothly (Wood, 1987). Women are less likely than men to take advantage of an opponent's weakness to en-

characteristics. However, you will soon find yourself giving information about the groups (family, school, social organizations, athletic team, country, state, etc.) to which you belong. This indicates that we derive a significant degree of self-identity from those groups (Tajfel & Turner, 1986). We know ourselves and others know us by the groups that we associate with. And all of us want to hold positive impressions of ourselves.

This seemingly simple situation gives rise to some far-reaching behaviors. First, we try very hard to join the most attractive groups possible. Being in an attractive group raises our self-image. Second, we attempt to do everything possible to help our own group, especially when there are competing groups. In an interesting study, Tajfel (1970) randomly divided students into two groups. He then gave each student the opportunity to divide money

hance their own performance (Forsyth, 1990). When taking the role of leader, women are more likely to adopt a democratic style, while men are more directive (Hollander, 1985). The results suggest that women may place their personal performance in a secondary position to the performance of their team.

There has been considerable discussion of gender differences as they relate to conformity. There is a slight tendency for women to conform more than men, but this difference disappears and even reverses when the task is one in which females excel (Sistrunk & McDavid, 1971). In order to explain these and other gender differences, many investigators look to early childhood training. Boys are encouraged to be independent and emphasis is put on their individual achievement. They learn very quickly that society expects them to excel, and many of their childhood games stress individual achievement (Eccles, 1991). Young girls often are given a different lesson. They are taught the importance of cooperation and schooled to consider the feelings of others. Their motor skills often develop earlier than those of boys, but they are pushed to use their talents in creative or cooperative ways, not in competition with others. They learn that society does not expect them to excel in tasks involving motor skill. In fact, those who do excel are often referred to as "tomboys."

But times are changing, and with them, childrearing practices. There is now more similarity in the ways girls and boys are reared. There is increasing acceptance, and indeed encouragement, for girls to excel in a variety of areas, including athletics. Not only do girls engage in sports that were once the sole domain of boys, but they often do so on teams that include both genders. These changes are part of an attempt to eliminate any differences in the impact of social settings on the performance of males and females.

between the two groups. One option for division gave both groups a high sum of money. The second option resulted in the individual's group getting less money, but the outgroup would be even more impoverished; the difference in the sums received by each group was greater than with the first option. Subjects chose the option that resulted in the greatest *difference* between the groups rather than the one that advantaged their group most. Subjects wanted their group to look better relative to the outgroup, even though on an absolute scale their own group received less.

A third effect of this desire to enhance our own group is the tendency to perceive our own group and its products as better than those of the outgroup. A number of investigators have found that subjects rate the performance of their own group as better than that of the outgroup when there are no clear objectives by which to judge outcome (Worchel, Lind, & Kaufman, 1975; Hinkle & Schopler, 1986). In an interesting study, Hastorf and Cantril (1954) questioned students after they witnessed a particularly brutal football game between Dartmouth and Princeton: there were numerous penalties, fights, and "dirty" tricks. Even though all students saw the same game, the Dartmouth students saw the Princeton players as violent and instigating the dirty play. However, the Princeton students saw the opposite situation; they viewed the Dartmouth players as committing significantly more infractions than the Princeton players.

Because our identity is on the line, we do everything possible to make our group appear better in comparison with other groups. But will we alter our own performance to please our group? The research on conformity suggests that we definitely will. Asch (1951) asked subjects to determine which of three comparison lines was the same length as a given standard line. As can be seen in Figure 12.2, the correct answer was very easy to find. Subjects announced their decisions in small groups, but unknown to the subjects, everyone in the group except for one naive subject was working for the experimenter. These confederates were instructed to give incorrect answers on a number of the trials. The unwary subject, who was seated second from last in the group, gave incorrect answers on nearly 35 percent of the trials. Other research showed that the more difficult the task, the more often subjects conformed (gave the incorrect answer suggested by the confederates) and conformity increased as subjects' status in the group was lower (Asch, 1952; Stang, 1972).

Thus we do alter our performance to be in line with the group to which we belong. And this conformity often protects us from being rejected by the group. Numerous studies have found that groups exclude members who deviate from the group standards (Schachter, 1951; Willis, 1972). This rejection may come in the form of not talking to the deviate or it may include forcing the member out of the group.

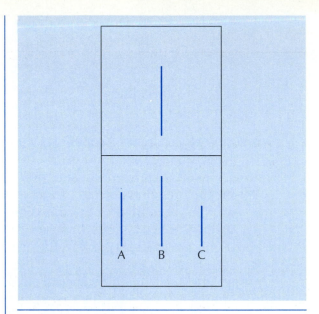

Figure 12.2 *Example of a pair of cards used in the Asch (1951) experiment to study conformity. The task is to identify which lines are the same length. Would you give the wrong answer just because others in your group gave a wrong answer?*

The point to remember here is that the group has power to influence our performance because we gain self and social identity from the groups to which we belong. We want to belong to the best groups possible to enhance our self-image, and we will go to great lengths to be accepted by "good" groups and improve the image of our groups. If we do not conform to the group's standards, we run the risk of being excluded from the group.

The groups to which we belong give us a social identity and help shape our self-image. We are motivated to join groups that will enhance our image.

FINAL COMMENT

Our social environment exercises a great deal of influence over our learning and performance. This influence involves the most basic activities as well as more complex activities. The presence of others may increase our physiological arousal, thereby influencing learning and performance. We often look to others to give us feedback about how well we are performing. And social comparison involves judging our performance by comparing it with the performance of others. We tend to compare ourselves to others who have similar abilities, although we may choose others who are not quite as skilled as we are to yield a positive comparison.

Other people influence the goals we set for our learning and performance. When we discuss these goals in groups, they often become more extreme than those we would set if making the decision alone. According to social learning theory, much of our learning results from imitating models. We can learn a wide range of behaviors through imitation. While imitation influences learning, the opportunity to gain rewards affects our performance.

The presence of others may facilitate or inhibit learning and performance. Research suggests that the presence of an audience retards our learning of new activities and our performing of complex actions. However, the audience facilitates performance of simple and well-learned behaviors. This pattern of effects may be due to the fact that others increase our arousal level, distract us from concentrating on our behavior, or increase our concern with being evaluated. Our performance level in groups is often lower than when alone. This results from the difficulty of coordinating efforts in a group. We often loaf or lower our effort in groups because we feel our personal level of output cannot be identified, we feel that the group can succeed without our input, or we feel others are reducing their efforts.

There is a tendency to perform better on familiar territory (the home-court advantage) except perhaps in critical championship games. There are many possible reasons for this effect. One is that a hostile audience reinforces our bad performance and rejects our positive performance. A second reason is that we are more comfortable with and less distracted by familiar surroundings and situations.

The group has a variety of influences on our activities. The presence of others may cause us to become objectively self-aware and focus our attention on ourselves, rather than on the outcome of our actions. We become increasingly concerned with being evaluated when performing in front of others. And groups form an important part of our identity. As a result we attempt to join the most attractive groups possible and to enhance the image of the groups to which we belong. We often adjust our behavior to conform to group standards. If we do not conform, we run the risk of being rejected from the group.

KEY TERMS

social influence	goal setting	coaction	sucker effect
arousal	level of aspiration	social facilitation	free rider effect
competition	group polarization	social inhibition	home-court
social comparison	social learning theory	social loafing	advantage

13

Theory into Practice

Paradigms: OUTSMARTING THE FUTURE

Understanding the Problem or Question

Appropriate Application of Principles

Motor Learning Checklist

Is Theory Necessary?
- *Theory: The Positive Viewpoint*
- *Theory: The Negative Viewpoint*

Basic Research and Theory into Practice
- *The Proposed Research and Communication Model*
- *Research Classifications*
- *Communication*
- *Contextual Interference Example*
- *General Concerns*

HIGHLIGHT: Chaos in the Brickyard
FINAL COMMENT
KEY TERMS

Paradigms: OUTSMARTING THE FUTURE

Joel Arthur Baker is a futurist who has a rather interesting philosophy that he uses to help corporations anticipate changes in their marketplace and develop new ideas so that they can stay current in a rapidly changing world. His lectures have helped corporations all over the world become more innovative, competitive, and successful.

What does this have to do with motor learning? One of the basic premises he uses is the paradigm. **Paradigm** is defined in Webster's New Collegiate Dictionary as "an example or pattern, especially an outstandingly clear or typical example or archetype." The philosopher Thomas Kuhn (1970) simplified this definition to a set of rules and regulations that (1) set boundaries and (2) provide rules for success within those boundaries.

Paradigms are not as abstract as they might sound; actually they are found everywhere. A parent's way of folding clothes, the coach's approach to sliding into home plate, Apple's method for learning MacIntosh—all of these are paradigms. A paradigm can be very helpful when you are learning something new, but it can be a detriment as well. Often people think that because there is an established paradigm, nothing else will work. Following are a few outstanding examples of paradigms that Mr. Baker uses in his presentations.

In sixteenth-century Italy, as in the rest of the world, people presumed that the earth was the center of the universe. Galileo, an astronomer, studied the heavens extensively with a newly perfected telescope and discovered that the earth revolved around the sun and that the sun was actually the center of our universe. When he presented this astounding discovery to his intellectual peers and the city leaders, they were so shocked that they threatened him with torture if he did not retract his abominable statement.

In 1938, a man named Chester Carlson presented a new idea to several photographic research corporations. His combination of metal plates, powdered ink, and a light bulb seemed ludicrous to them all, but Chester had faith in his new invention and gained a patent, even though no one was interested in it. Today this invention, an electrostatic copier, is con-

What do you see first—a vase or two faces? This "reversible" picture reminds us that the way we look at the world determines the way we perceive it.

- To develop a checklist of motor learning and control concepts that should be considered in designing practice sessions.

- To appreciate the positive and negative viewpoints related to the development of motor learning and control theory.

- To understand the potential breakdown in and possible solution to translating laboratory research into practice.

sidered by many to be the most popular invention in history. Copy machines are now a multibillion dollar business that saves countless working hours for almost every company.

For over a hundred years Switzerland had produced 65 percent of the entire world market share of watches and was renown as the home of the world's finest clockworks. In 1968, however, a group of Swiss researchers invented a new concept. Their quartz movement watch was totally electronic, battery powered, and much more reliable than the original spring and bearing watch. Enthusiastically they approached one Swiss watch manufacturer after another, only to be turned down by them all. Later that year two small electronics companies, one Japanese (Seiko) and one American (Texas Instruments), bought the Swiss researchers' idea. One decade later, the Swiss produced only 10 percent of the world market share of watches and over 90 percent of the employees in this trade had been laid off.

The sixteenth-century Italians, the photographic researchers of the 1930s, and the Swiss watch manufacturers of the 1960s all had one thing in common—the fear of new ideas, the fear of going beyond an existing paradigm. Established patterns can be very comfortable and easy to continue, but they can also cause people to be unreceptive to concepts that may be more effective. This is where paradigms can work to your detriment or benefit. None of us would choose to be

blind to good ideas, but we are, just the same.

Here is another, typically Texan example provided by my secretary, Leann Willoughby. In 1985, Classic Rope Manufacturing Company, a small factory owned by my secretary's family, began producing team roping lariats in a small town in Texas. Until then, this highly specialized field had been controlled by two well-established companies that had made the same limited line of good quality lariat ropes for many years. The manager and several employees of Classic Rope had worked for one of these firms for a combined 30 years and were well informed of both the strengths and weaknesses of their competitor's production lines. They started their basic line, but at the same time set out to make some modest modifications.

One of the main areas these craftsmen felt could be improved was the type of twine used in the formation of the rope. After six months of experimentation, however, Classic Rope was no closer to finding an improved product. They had tried every twine that had ever been used in team ropes, but they just had not come up with the "right feel." One of the main twine suppliers who knew the rope makers had been ordering a wide array of nylon, rayon, and Dacron twines enclosed a sample of a blue polyester twine that had been overstocked. When the cowboys unpacked the twine, they got a good laugh. No roper would be caught dead with a blue rope!

A good practical joke was all they thought

this blue twine was bound to be good for, so before they sent it back, a few "funny" ropes were made. Strangely, after they were blended and heat-treated, the ropes were not blue at all. The final product was a beautiful pale green, the color of new money. And after they experienced how well this new rope worked, they did not mind the color at all.

This "moneymaker," as it was dubbed, has since set a new precedent in the sport of team roping. For four consecutive years, it has been used at the national finals by champions who have set new arena records each year. The 1990 national champion also set a new world record by earning more money in less time than anyone else in history. Classic Rope has been two months or more behind on its production since 1986 (despite the fact that it has enlarged its production facilities and staff three times) and is by far the leader in team rope manufacturing worldwide.

Had Classic Rope not taken a chance, gone to the fringe of their paradigm, and followed a frivolous though creative urge, the sport of team roping might not have reached the heights it has today. And that company that started out as a little rope shop in the country might still be just that.

■ ■ ■

The previous chapters of this book have attempted to describe the basic principles of motor learning and control. Almost without exception these principles have been derived from experimental research. Any serious student of motor skills must ask himself or herself questions about the applicability of the information derived from laboratory tasks to everyday performances and to the processes of teaching and coaching in particular. Knowledge of the principles would be a futile academic exercise if students did not successfully utilize the information to change their own performance or that of their trainees, students, or athletes. Two factors are required for you to apply the knowledge you have learned. The first relates to understanding the problem you are dealing with and the second concerns the appropriate application of the principles. This along with some insight and creativity will go a long way toward allowing you to utilize the information that you have learned.

In order to illustrate some of the problems that may inhibit your attempts to apply your motor learning and control principles, let's begin with a few light-hearted examples.

Understanding the Problem or Question

Try to solve the three riddles below. (Answers are given at the end of this section.)

1. A farmer has 17 cows. All but nine break through a hole in the fence and wander away. How many cows are left?

2. A plane carrying 34 passengers crashes on the U.S.–Canadian border. Should the survivors be buried on the U.S. or Canadian side of the border?

3. An elderly surgeon and son were involved in a head-on crash. The surgeon died and the son was in critical condition. The boy was taken to the hospital and prepared for emergency surgery. The attending surgeon, after looking at the boy, exclaimed, "I cannot operate on him—he is my son." How could this be?

Always be sure you understand the problem or question that requires a solution. A careful analysis may be required before an appropriate solution can be found. For example, a little league batter who is consistently missing the ball may require some remedial attention. But first it is important to know *why* he or she is missing the ball. Several factors may be responsible. The problem may arise from a perceptual or motor difficulty or simply from a bat that is too heavy or a need for eyeglasses.

Make it a rule to understand the question before offering a solution. Just like a physician, we must be careful not to misdiagnose the problem or we may prescribe the wrong medicine.

Answers to the Riddles: (1) 9 cows. (2) Neither: you wouldn't bury survivors. (3) The attending surgeon was the boy's mother.

Appropriate Application of Principles

In 1942, Luchins formulated a series of problems in which subjects were given three water jars of different sizes. The subjects were to use the jars to measure an exact amount of water. Table 13.1 shows the size of the jars provided for each problem.

For example, in Problem 1 the capacities of jars A, B, and C are 21, 127, and 3 ounces, respectively, and the required amount is 100 ounces. How could you use the jars to measure exactly 100 ounces? The solution is to fill Jar B to capacity then use Jar B to fill Jar A once and Jar C twice. You then are left with exactly 100 ounces in Jar B.

What have you noticed about the problems? All the problems except number 8 can be solved by the same method: required amount = Jar B – Jar A – 2 × Jar C. Even though Problem 8 appears similar to the others, it cannot be solved by this method. Problem 8 requires a different and easier solution: required amount = Jar A – Jar C. This solution

may be difficult to "see" because we tend to rely on techniques that worked in the past. In fact, someone presented with only Problem 8 would probably find the solution more quickly than someone who had been exposed to Problems 1 to 7.

Which of these containers holds more? The child may find it hard to decide because these containers are very different in appearance. By actual measurement, however, both containers hold the same amount. Looks can be deceiving.

TABLE 13.1   **The Water Jars Problems**

Problem Number	Capacity (Ounces)			Required Amount
	Jar A	Jar B	Jar C	
1.	21	127	3	100
2.	14	163	25	99
3.	18	43	10	5
4.	9	42	6	21
5.	20	59	4	31
6.	23	49	3	20
7.	15	39	3	18
8.	28	76	3	25

Don't you wonder how many teachers and coaches are applying a solution that has worked in the past to a new problem that it does not fit? The solution to many difficult problems has appeared obvious only after the solution was known.

Motor Learning Checklist

The following is a checklist of questions to consider when planning activities to enhance the learning of motor skills. After planning a practice or activity session, it is a good idea to review the checklist to make sure you have considered the important concepts related to motor learning and control.

This ten-item checklist gives you examples of important considerations in planning teaching and coaching sessions. It is suggested that you add to or subtract from this list in order to compile one that is appropriate for the skill(s) you are teaching or coaching.

1. Are the performers appropriately aroused and motivated? What can be done to selectively change arousal and increase motivation?

2. Have I considered the factors that facilitate short- and long-term memory? What can I do to make sure the important points are remembered?

3. Have the stimuli that are important to attend to been identified?

4. Are stimulus response compatibilities clearly established and planned for?

5. What techniques can be used to increase uncertainty for the opponents and decrease uncertainty for us?

6. Does the task involve closed or open loop movements? Do speed accuracy principles affect the skill? What can be done to increase accuracy without sacrificing speed?

7. Have specific goals been established so that performance can be evaluated? What form and schedule of KR and KP will be used?

8. Are the practice sessions designed to enhance acquisition, retention, or transfer performance?

9. Have practice composition and schedule been considered in planning the teaching/practice session?

10. How do I know if my techniques are the most productive? Has research been conducted that would help me?

It is hoped that each time you read the checklist, each item will prompt you to remember the principles that have been discussed in this text. You may also find it helpful to add or delete items as you use the list.

Is Theory Necessary?

Throughout this book you have been exposed to one theory after another: closed-loop theory, schema theory, impulse variability theory—and so on. In fact the current trend in motor behavior research appears to be to value theory development and theoretical research more highly than applied research. However, there are two sides to this story.

Theory: The Positive Viewpoint

Theories are hypothetical statements of explanations for behavior under a specific set of circumstances (see Chapter 1). A theory, therefore, spells out in precise and potentially testable terms the current thinking of the scientist. A theory puts the scientist's understanding of the phenomenon on stage to be viewed by the scientific community. This community is not a passive audience but a critical and astute one. The scientific community is trained to critically evaluate theory and devise experiments to test the critical features of the theory. A theory remains intact only as long as experiments do not show assumptions and predictions to be wrong. Many tests that confirm the assumptions or predictions of a theory do not prove a theory correct, but a single demonstration of disproof causes the theory to become suspect.

In a paper on strong inference that appeared in *Science* in 1964, John Platt argued that rapid advances in science come not by the process of confirmation but by its opposite. Platt suggests that crucial experiments pit one hypothesis or theory against other hypotheses or theories. The result is that the experiment has the potential to exclude one or more of the alternatives. Platt states that all scientists should ask the following question of their theories and experiments as well as those of their fellow scientists: "what experiment could disprove your hypothesis?"; or, on hearing a scientific experiment described, "what hypothesis does your experiment disprove?" (p. 146). Platt was trying to make the point that many experiments are not very productive. Only those experiments that truly test our understanding (theories) result in substantial scientific progress.

Theory: The Negative Viewpoint

Since theories are stated precisely and logically, they can appear very convincing even when they are not correct. The scientist, in devising the theory, takes great care to present the evidence that has prompted him or her to propose the theory. It may be easy to interpret that evidence as supporting the theory. Why not? The evidence was presented for just that purpose. The important question is whether your knowledge of the theory and evidence that has been presented in its support will cloud your ability to see alternatives.

Remember the paradigm problems presented at the beginning of the chapter? Exposure to one way of thinking may cause other ideas or data to be essentially "invisible" to you. Greenwald, Pratkanis, Leippe, and Baumgardner (1986) present a number of examples in experimental psychology of what they call confirmation bias. **Confirmation bias** is the tendency for judgments based on new ideas to be overly consistent with preliminary hypotheses. This is in strict opposition to the "familiar stereotype of the scientist as an impartial observer whose hypotheses stand or fall according to the blind justice of objective data." Greenwald et al. (1986) state:

> Perhaps the most generally admired research strategy in any scientific discipline is that of testing theories. However, this admirable strategy is easily misused to produce nearly useless research conclusions. To appreciate this consider the enterprise of testing theory. . . .
>
> The theory-testing approach runs smoothly enough when theoretically predicted results are obtained. However, when predictions are not confirmed, the researcher faces a predicament that is called the disconfirmation dilemma. The dilemma is resolved by the researcher choosing between proceeding (a) as if the theory being tested is incorrect . . . or (b) as if the theory is still likely to be correct. (p. 219)

In either case, the researcher is in a difficult position: continue to support the theory with contradictory data or discount the data and try again until the data support the theory. In the former case, the researcher is left with data without an explanation.

Basic Research and Theory into Practice

The general aim of this section is to describe a research and communication model that may better promote and more efficiently accomplish the translation of basic/theoretical motor learning research into the physical education classrooms and onto athletic fields. This thesis is based on three assumptions. The first is that a critical gap currently exists between motor learning and control principles derived from basic/theoretical research and the practice of teaching and coaching motor skills. The second assumption is that recent basic research on learning issues has resulted in a number of principles that have been sufficiently developed to warrant their consideration for implementation into applied settings. Finally, it is assumed that university faculty involved with training and supervising student teachers and school system supervisors maintain a direct link with teachers and coaches in the field and are (or should be) involved in what we will define as operations research.

Figure 13.1 is an attempt to summarize our conception of the current state of research and communication relative to motor learning research and the teaching of motor skills. This topic has been reviewed by Christina (1988) and discussed by a number of experts in a 1990 issue of *Quest* (Hoffman, 1990a, 1990b; Locke, 1990; Magill, 1990; Zelaznik, 1990). Note that lines of communication (feedforward and feedback) currently exist between basic and applied researchers on one side and pedagogy (operations) researchers and teachers/coaches on the other.

The Proposed Research and Communication Model

The research and communication model to be proposed simply links the two existing lines of communication (Figure 13.2). These lines of communication must lead to and from the applied and operations researchers to be effective.

In the following discussion, basic, applied, and operations research are operationally defined within the framework of motor learning, and formal lines of communication between research levels are proposed. In addition, ex-

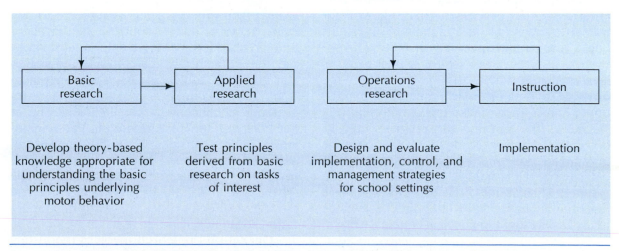

Figure 13.1 *Current state of research communication between motor learning and instruction in school and sport settings.*

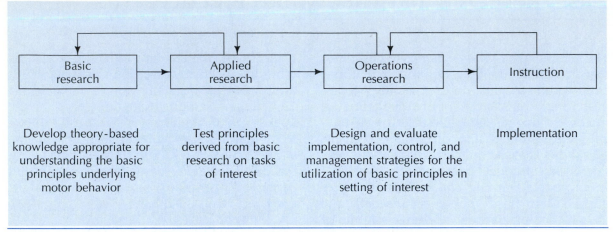

Basic research	Applied research	Operations research	Instruction

Develop theory-based knowledge appropriate for understanding the basic principles underlying motor behavior | Test principles derived from basic research on tasks of interest | Design and evaluate implementation, control, and management strategies for the utilization of basic principles in setting of interest | Implementation

Figure 13.2 *Proposed model of research communication that links basic research with instruction. Note that it is equally important to have communication move from basic research to instruction as from instruction to basic research.*

amples of basic and applied research pertaining to the principle of contextual interference are presented. Finally, we discuss our concerns about the implementation of the proposed model.

Research Classifications

Basic research in motor learning and control is concerned with the development of hypotheses, principles, laws, and theories pertaining to the processes that account for human movement and behavior. Typically, basic research is involved in testing hypotheses in laboratory settings using tasks specifically designed to involve/isolate the process(es) and/or environmental demand(s) under study. These tasks tend to be relatively *simple* so that learning can progress quickly, *novel* so the influence of past experiences is minimized, and *artificial* so that the process or environmental condition of interest can be isolated. Thus, many of the tasks used in basic research appear to have little direct relevance to the tasks taught in physical education classrooms and on athletic playing fields. In addition, the laboratory environment in which the tasks are observed during an experiment tend

to be quite different from the typical teaching or coaching environment.

Applied research is typically defined as research aimed at testing potential solutions (hypotheses) to problems that present themselves in real-world settings. Applied research should also be concerned with determining via controlled experiments the potential applications of findings derived from basic research. The tasks utilized are typically real-world tasks and the testing occurs in real-world environments. This research may, however, require some control, modification, and/or restriction of the task(s) and environment(s) found in typical physical education classrooms or athletic fields. These modifications may occur because the applied researcher is concerned that the results he or she achieves can be attributed to the manipulation under consideration. The applied researcher is concerned with whether or not the principle derived from basic research is valid for the task and in the environment of interest but is not directly concerned with implementation strategies.

Operations research involves the testing of the impact, control, and management strategies required to optimize the implemen-

Physical education teachers and coaches must work with operations researchers to determine whether instructional methods found to be productive under controlled conditions can be effectively implemented on the playing field.

tation of instructional techniques into real-world settings. Modifications to real-world tasks and environments occur only to the extent that is required for implementation and is feasible given real-world constraints. This represents the final stage of testing prior to implementation. At this level, principles discovered in the laboratory and confirmed in applied experiments may still be found impractical or too costly for implementation into the curriculum. Many techniques tested in basic and applied experiments could be beneficial to instruction but simply require expensive equipment, specialized space, too much time, or private instruction.

Communication

Basic Researcher to Applied Researcher. It is important that the basic and applied researchers communicate directly. The basic researcher must carefully distill and communicate stable findings into principles, laws, and theories. The applied researcher must determine via experiment the extent to which these findings can be applied to nonlaboratory tasks and environments. Consistent results that indicate that the application of the principles derived in the laboratory does not result in the predicted outcomes must be communicated back to the basic researcher. This may indicate boundary conditions for the principle that were not considered in the laboratory setting but represent important mediating factors. This information may be important to the basic researcher because it may lead to important experiments that may better delineate the principle under consideration.

Applied Researcher to Operational Researcher to Practitioner. When the applied researcher finds that the results from laboratory experiments are reproducible with real-world tasks and conditions, the results should be directly communicated to operational researchers. It is the operations researcher's responsibility to test the various strategies of implementing and integrating the instructional concept into the classroom or onto the playing field. If the concept can be effectively translated into instruction, it is the mission of the operations researcher to communicate these strategies to the practitioners. If not feasible, the applied research should be informed so that the applicability of the principle can be reevaluated. The practitioner, in turn, must provide feedback to the operations researcher regarding the success or failure of the implementation strategy.

It is our position that lines of communication that skip a level of research may not be as effective as the lines of communication outlined. Large volumes of basic research are collected each year. Only a small percentage of this research subsequently develops to a point that would warrant examination at the applied level. In addition, it would be inefficient for the operations researcher to evaluate implementation strategies for a principle that had not been subjected to scrutiny at the applied level. Likewise teachers and coaches could waste a great deal of time attempting to evaluate the efficacy of principles established in basic and applied research settings. Thus, the proposed model serves to systematically "cull" the number of notions derived from basic research that are prematurely translated into practice and, thus, the number of unnecessary intrusions into instruction. At the same time, researchers at all levels are provided feedback relevant to their level of study.

It is important for the operational researcher to communicate new teaching methods or strategies directly to the instructor in the field. The instructor in turn must play a part in the evaluation process.

Contextual Interference Example

An example of basic and applied research based on the phenomenon of contextual interference is provided (see Chapter 11 for further discussion). It is important to note that this phenomenon has been, and continues to be, researched at the basic and applied levels. However, contextual interference principles have not been effectively translated to instructional settings because the operational research link has failed to establish effective strategies for implementation or to communicate these strategies to teachers and coaches in the field. This is not as prevalent in industrial, agricultural, and military domains or even other areas of education in which instructional strategies consider the contextual interference phenomenon (see Melton, 1984).

Basic Research: Contextual Interference. John Shea and Robyn Morgan conducted a basic research experiment on contextual interference in 1979 (see Chapter 11). This experiment was to be the impetus for much future basic research aimed at further understanding the processes that contribute to the effect and many applied studies aimed at determining the extent to which the effect impacts applied tasks in natural environments.

The research design required subjects to learn three related motor skills under blocked (low contextual interference) or random (high contextual interference) conditions. Under blocked conditions, subjects completed all trials on one task before the next task was introduced. Subjects under random conditions were given acquisition trials on the three tasks in a random order. The task was a barrier knockdown task and required subjects to release a start button, grasp a tennis ball, then knock down three of the six barriers in an order prescribed on one of three diagrams suspended on the apparatus. A light serving as the start signal also indicated which diagram to use for that trial.

The results indicated that acquisition was poorer under high (random) than low (blocked) contextual interference conditions. However, retention was greater following acquisition under high contextual interference conditions.

This effect has been replicated many times over the years under a variety of conditions with relatively stable results. The basic researchers continue to study this phenomenon in an attempt to better understand the underlying processes that contribute to the contextual interference effect.

The basic principle derived from this research states that the retention of a series of related tasks is facilitated by random rather than blocked practice schedules.

Applied Research: Contextual Interference. In 1986 Sinah Goode and Richard Magill conducted an applied experiment based on the results of basic research on contextual interference. Subjects learned three badminton serves in either a blocked or random practice schedule. The subjects practiced the serves three days a week for three weeks. The results replicated the basic research findings. Subjects practicing under blocked conditions performed better during acquisition but subjects who had practiced under random conditions performed significantly better on tests of retention and transfer.

It is important to note that these researchers did not attempt to determine the feasibility of implementing contextual interference notions into the curriculum but rather attempted to determine the efficacy of the contextual interference principle for the learning of badminton skills. An extraordinary amount of time and energy in the badminton class was devoted to the serve. Operations research could be directed to determining the most efficient method of implementing this principle into large classes with limited time and equipment.

General Concerns

We wish to express three major concerns with the proposed model specifically and the

Chaos in the Brickyard

The following story by Bernard K. Forscher, Mayo Clinic, Rochester, Minnesota, provides a tongue-in-cheek epilogue for this chapter.

Once upon a time, the human race engaged in an activity called scientific research, and the performers of this activity were known as scientists. In reality, these scientists were builders who constructed edifices, called explanations or laws, by assembling bricks called facts. When the bricks were sound and were assembled properly, the edifice was useful and durable and brought pleasure, and sometimes reward, to the builder. But if the bricks were faulty or if they were assembled badly, the edifice would crumble, endangering the lives of innocent users of the edifice as well as the builder who sometimes was destroyed by the collapse. Because the quality of the bricks was so important to the success of the edifice, and because bricks were so scarce in those days, the builders made their own bricks. The making of bricks was a difficult and expensive undertaking and the wise builder avoided waste by making only bricks of the shape and size necessary for the enterprise at hand. The builder was guided in this manufacture by a blueprint, called a theory or hypothesis.

It came to pass that builders realized that they were sorely hampered in their efforts by delays in obtaining bricks. Thus there arose a new skilled trade known as brickmaking. These brickmakers were called junior scientists to give the artisan proper pride in his work. This new arrangement was very efficient and the construction of edifices proceeded with great vigor. Sometimes brickmakers became inspired and progressed to the status of builders. In spite of the separation of duties, bricks still were made with care and usually were produced only on order. Now and then an enterprising brickmaker was able to foresee a demand and would prepare a stock of bricks ahead of time, but in general, brickmaking was done on a custom basis because it still was a difficult and expensive process.

It came to pass that a misunderstanding spread among the brickmakers (there are some who say that this misunderstanding developed as a result of careless training of a new generation of

process of translating theory into practice in general.

1. Will the communication of the "why a method is effective" be lost as operations researchers determine "how a method can be implemented"? In any multilevel communication model, great care must be taken so that information is not distorted or lost in the

brickmakers). The brickmakers became obsessed with the making of bricks. When reminded that the ultimate goal was edifices, not bricks, they replied that if enough bricks were available, the builders would be able to select what was necessary and still continue to construct edifices. The flaws in this argument were not readily apparent, and so, with the help of the citizens who were waiting to use the edifices yet to be built, amazing things happened. The expense of brickmaking became a minor factor because large sums of money were made available, the time and effort involved in brickmaking was reduced by ingenious automatic machinery, and the ranks of brickmakers swelled with augmented training programs and intensive recruitment. It even was suggested that the production of a suitable number of bricks was equivalent to building an edifice and, therefore, should entitle the industrious brickmaker to assume the title of builder and with the title, the authority.

And so it happened that the land became flooded with bricks. It became necessary to organize more and more storage places, called journals, and more and more elaborate systems of bookkeeping to record the inventory. In all of this the brickmakers retained their pride and skill and the bricks were of the very best quality. But production was ahead of demand and bricks no longer were made to order. The size and shape was now dictated by changing trends in fashion. In order to compete successfully with other brickmakers, production emphasized those types of brick that were easy to make and only rarely did an adventuresome brickmaker attempt a difficult or unusual design. The influence of tradition in production methods and in types of product became a dominating factor.

Unfortunately, the builders were almost destroyed. It became difficult to find the proper bricks for a task because one had to hunt among so many. It became difficult to complete a useful edifice because as soon as the foundations were discernible they were buried under an avalanche of random bricks. And saddest of all, sometimes no effort was made even to maintain the distinction between a pile of bricks and a true edifice.

translation from level to level. A great tragedy would exist if teachers were taught how to teach a technique derived from basic research but did not understand the principle upon which the technique was founded. It is our opinion that the current communication system has failed in this regard. A significant number of current teaching and coaching practices have their roots in basic research. It is our opinion, however, that a relatively large percentage of the practitioners who utilize these techniques do not understand how or why they are effective.

2. Who will fill the role of applied researcher? The concern of basic researchers is not with specific applications, although we hope they are concerned that the principles they discover can be utilized in many application domains (educational, athletic, industrial, military, etc.). It should be noted that the basic research of Shea and Morgan (1979) has led to applied studies not only in physical education and athletics but also in training protocols for flight training, mathematics facts, typing skills, and mail sorting. Figure 13.3 attempts to illustrate that basic research can lead to applications in many domains. Because basic research may be utilized across application domains, it may be inefficient for the basic researcher to become too occupied with specific applications.

Then who will fill the role of applied researcher? It is our feeling that this role is best filled by applied research specialists. Some of these individuals will come from the ranks of the basic researchers and others may come from the pedagogy ranks. This role must be considered an integral part of the overall research model for universities and may become the primary research role of a portion of the universities and colleges that do not define their roles in terms of basic research.

3. Who will fill the role of operations researcher? The person who fills this role in educational settings must have research training and be in a position to access the work of the

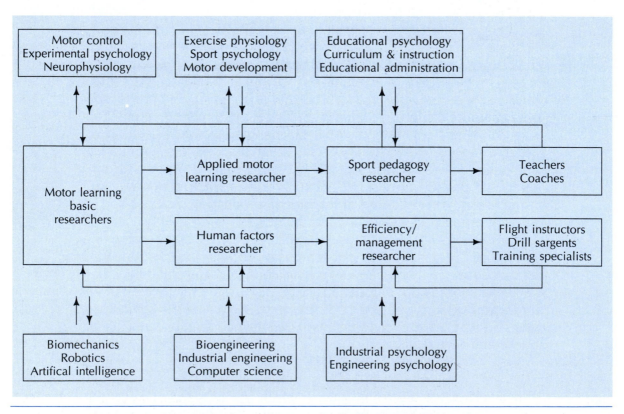

Figure 13.3 *Basic research may have application in a number of performance domains. Note also that areas of research may draw on basic research from more than one area.*

applied researchers and practitioners while at the same time having special insight into the application(s) of interest. The likely candidates are the university faculty who fill positions related to supervising student teachers. These faculty are in the business of teaching teachers how to teach! It is hoped that these researchers are concerned not only with the management of the classroom but also with the learning of the students as well.

FINAL COMMENT

It is increasingly obvious that even subtle changes in the way skills are taught have the potential to substantially impact performance and learning. Intuition and practical experiences are important to the discovery of new methods and the evaluations of those methods, but carefully conducted research is the real key. We must be careful not to close our minds to new ideas and at the same time be careful not to accept ideas just because they fit into our way of thinking.

It is also vitally important that principles established in the laboratory are subjected to evaluation in real-world settings. A communication model is presented with the goal of facilitating this process. Remember, the field of motor learning and control is changing rapidly. New ideas are being tested daily in laboratories and field settings around the world. Stay in contact with research; it has the potential to serve you well.

KEY TERMS

paradigm
confirmation bias

basic research
applied research

operations research

Appendix A

Measuring Motor Behavior

Various methods and instrumentation can be used in the measurement of motor behavior. An athlete uses his or her senses, a coach may utilize video or high-speed film, and a researcher may require electrodes and amplifiers to observe different characteristics of the same performance. The athlete may be concerned with the end result or error, the coach concentrates on the movement pattern or kinematics, and the researcher is interested in the pattern and quality of the muscular activity as indicated by electromyographic measures. In the field of motor learning and control, as in any scientific area, the questions that are asked determine the type of measurements that are taken, which in turn determines the instruments (if any) that are required.

Types of Motor Behavior Measurement

In presenting the measurements available to athletes, coaches, and researchers, we use the following classifications: physiological correlates, reaction and movement times, electromyograms, response errors, and kinematic measurements (Figure A.1). The measurements are reported in this order because they describe movement characteristics that develop at different times during the progress of the movement.

Physiological Correlates of Movement

The human body responds in many ways to physiological and cognitive demands. A student called upon to come to the front of the class to demonstrate a skill may experience a number of physiological changes. Even while approaching the front of the class, the student may experience an increase in epinephrine production (blood analysis), changes in heart rate and rhythm (electrocardiogram), an increase in metabolism (oxygen analysis), alterations in skin temperature as blood is shunted to other areas of the body (thermography), an increase in sweating that results in an increased ability of the skin to conduct electrical signals (galvanic skin response [GSR]) and perhaps even a dilation of the pupils of the eye (pupilometry). These measures are termed **physiological correlates** because they are not thought to play a direct role in the learning and control of learning of the movement. In many cases, physiological correlates are measurements of the body's attempt to prepare for

294

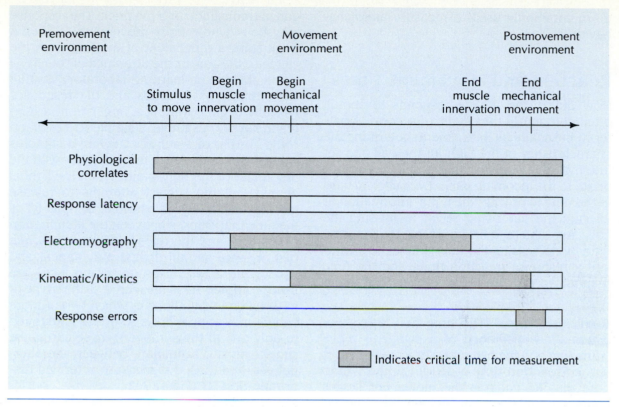

Figure A.1 *Time frame in which various measurements play an important role.*

an upcoming demand or compensate for a change in environment or work load.

The technology to monitor these physiological correlates has been available for many years. However, modern technology has made possible the sensing of many of the brain's responses to the same demands. At present many of these newer techniques are not available to teachers, coaches, or even researchers unless a medical condition requires their use in a hospital under a physician's supervision. However, the possibility of "seeing" a live, functioning brain in action is most alluring to researchers in motor learning and control.

Electroencephalography. The first available method of monitoring a working brain involved recording and amplification of the very small electrical potentials of the brain cells. The record is called an **electroencephalo-**

gram or **EEG** (see Chapter 2, Highlight). By using high-speed computers to sense and record brain-wave patterns, evoked potentials and EEG topography can be recorded. An **evoked potential** is the brain-wave pattern that appears in response to a specific stimulus such as a command to move, the starter's gun, or a pin prick. **EEG tomography** is a pictorial representation of the frequencies characteristics of the brain-wave activity across the entire brain. These methods provide recordings that look much like the CAT, PET, and MRI images that were discussed in Chapter 2.

We can better appreciate the capabilities of these new techniques having studied the biological basis for movement (Chapter 2). But it is clear that motor learning and control research could benefit from these technologies. In the next sections, beginning with reaction and movement times, we discuss techniques more commonly used to measure motor behavior.

Reaction and Movement Times

How quickly an athlete responds to stimuli often determines the degree of success. A batter in baseball has little time to determine the characteristics of the flight of the ball and set into motion a response that is uniquely appropriate to the incoming pitch. Even slight delays in the time to process the initial information or execute the bat swing result in missing the ball. An athlete quickly learns to conserve time by decreasing the time it takes to formulate a response (reaction time) and the time required to execute the response (movement time).

Reaction Time. The time that lapses between the appearance of a signal to move (stimulus) and the beginning of a movement is termed **reaction time** or **RT**. It is important to note that RT ends as the movement begins and therefore does not include the time required to move. The stimuli may be a starter's gun, a traffic light, or a pin prick. The response may be a whole body movement such as a track start, a movement of the foot from the clutch to the gas, or the utterance of "ouch!"

In the motor learning laboratory, stimuli are often lights or tones and the responses typically begin by lifting a finger from a telegraph key. For example, a simple RT condition could consist of a subject viewing a stimulus light while depressing a telegraph key with the first finger of the right hand. When the light is illuminated, the subject attempts to release the key as quickly as possible. **Simple RT** is the time that elapses between the illumination of the light and the release of the key. When two or more stimuli (lights) may appear and two or more responses (telegraph keys) are used, **complex RT** is measured. A third type of RT is taken in situations in which two or more stimuli may appear but a response is required to only one of the stimuli. In these cases, the subject must discriminate between the alternatives, and thus, this measure is termed **discrimination RT** (Figure A.2).

As you have seen in a number of chapters in this book, RT can provide a useful measure

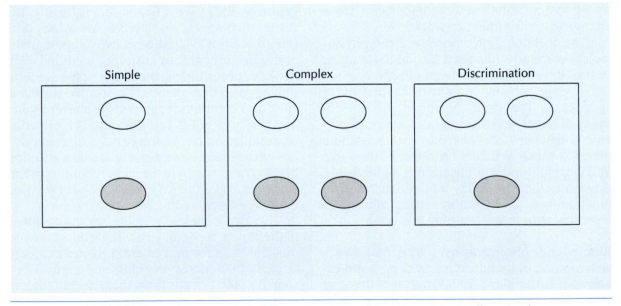

Figure A.2 Examples of stimuli (top) and response (bottom) setups to collect simple (left), complex (middle), and discrimination (right) reaction time.

of the time required to process information. Changing the type of stimuli (visual to auditory) or the complexity of the stimuli, increasing the number of alternatives to choose from (Hick, 1952), or even varying the complexity of the response to be made (Henry & Rogers, 1960) will influence RT in predictable ways.

In special cases, scientists may attempt to partition the reaction time interval into segments that represent specific categories of processing. This product is called **fractionated RT**. This method requires the measurement of evoked potentials and electromyograms (to be discussed later) to mark the onset of processing of the stimulus in the brain and the arrival of nerve impulses at the membrane of the muscle.

Movement Time.　The interval of time from the beginning to the end of the movement is **movement time** or **MT.** The sum of RT and MT is termed **response time.** It is important to note that movement time is measured solely on the basis of physical movement. That is, the motor units that produce movement may be activated a fraction of a second before the

movement begins and for some movements may cease firing well before the MT period ends (Figure A.3). The method used to detect the activity of the motor units is discussed next.

Electromyography

As a nerve impulse reaches the muscle membrane, a change in membrane potential takes place. The change in membrane potentials can be sensed by electrodes placed on the surface of the skin or by fine wire electrodes inserted by a needle into the muscle. When the signal is amplified many, many times and recorded, the product is an **electromyogram** or **EMG**. The signal that is recorded represents the sum of the motor unit activity detected by the electrodes. The EMG can be utilized in its raw form or can be transformed.

The EMG signal can be rectified and integrated or the frequency characteristics of the signal can be determined. The EMG signal is **rectified** (full-wave rectification) by calculating the absolute value of wave of electrical activity. **Integration**, a very common technique,

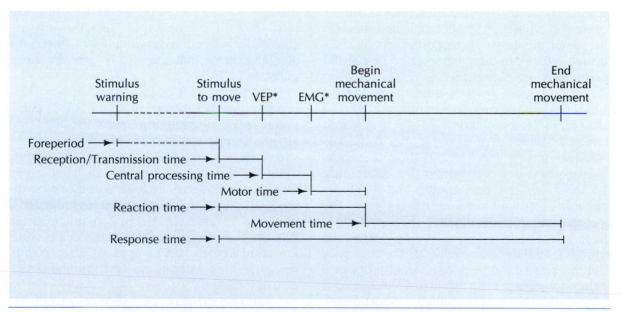

Figure A.3　*Events in a typical reaction time trial required to fractionate reaction time.*
VEP = visual evoked potential; EMG = electromyographic activity.

is accomplished by summing the rectified signal for short periods of time (e.g., 1 second). In voluntary, isometric contractions and constant velocity movements, the integrated EMG signal increases in proportion (linearly related) to the force that is being produced (Bigland & Lippold, 1954).

In recent years, a great deal of attention has been directed to the application of a mathematical technique called the fast Fourier transformation to a raw EMG signal. The **fast Fourier transformation** or **FFT** sums the frequencies contained in the signal. Remember, the EMG is the sum of the motor unit activity detected by electrodes. With surface electrodes, the number of motor units sampled may be quite large. The FFT technique is particularly interesting because different types of muscle fibers respond at different frequencies. Thus, the FFT may be used to estimate the contribution of various types of muscle fibers to the force being produced.

Response Errors

Every athlete, no matter what his or her skill level, is concerned with evaluating performance. By far the most common form of performance evaluation is accomplished through the determination of response errors. Although errors can often be detected before the movement is completed (see Closed-loop Control, Chapter 7), it is more common for these determinations to be made after the movement is terminated and the end result can be observed. For example, if a subject is asked to draw a line 6 inches long, the error, if any, can be determined by measuring the length of the line drawn. The algebraic (signed) difference between the length of the line and the goal of 6 inches is termed **algebraic error**. For a single attempt, algebraic error adequately indicates both the accuracy and the bias of the response. An attempt of 5 inches (algebraic error of –1 inch) indicates a 1-inch error (accuracy) that is too short (bias). However, when a series of attempts or trials are scored, no one algebraic error score accu-

rately summarizes the performance. Therefore, algebraic error is used to calculate a number of other error measures necessary to characterize the general performance.

A one-dimensional error refers to performance evaluation in terms of only one factor such as length, force, speed, and so on. Two-dimensional errors consider two related performance factors such as force and time. For example, two-dimensional errors are appropriate when a weight lifter attempts to apply a specific force at a specific time or an archer attempts to determine the horizontal and vertical position of an arrow relative to the bull's-eye.

One-Dimensional Errors. When performance is evaluated on only one dimension, such as force, time, or distance, algebraic errors taken over a series of trials can be used to calculate a number of measures that summarize the series of trials. For example, the student given 10 attempts at producing 5 (arbitrary) units of force against a load cell actually exerts too little or too much force on 9 trials, only "hitting" the target on one trial. In Figure A.4, algebraic errors range from –2 to +3. But the question remains: How accurate and how consistent was the performance? Was there a tendency to exert too much force? too little force? The following discussion briefly considers measures based on algebraic error that attempt to answer these questions.

Constant error or **CE** is the average error produced on a series of attempts. CE is computed as the average or mean of the algebraic errors. Note that algebraic errors with opposite signs (–3 and +3) cancel each other out. Thus, CE does not indicate accuracy but rather indicates a tendency or bias in responding. In the example, CE equals 1 unit. This indicates a tendency to produce 1 unit too much force. The absolute value of CE is termed **absolute constant error** or **ACE**. Thus, ACE represents response bias without concern for the direction of the bias.

Variable error or **VE** indicates the consistency of algebraic error on a series of attempts. VE is computed as the standard

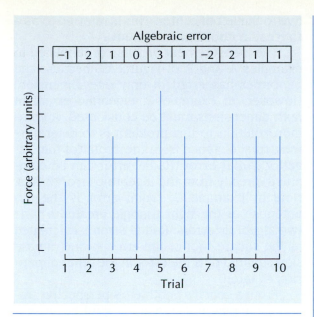

Algebraic error

| −1 | 2 | 1 | 0 | 3 | 1 | −2 | 2 | 1 | 1 |

Force (arbitrary units)

1 2 3 4 5 6 7 8 9 10
Trial

Figure A.4 *Sample performance on a force production task. The horizontal line represents the target and the vertical lines represent ten attempts to "hit" the target.*

deviation of the algebraic errors. The sample data yield a VE of 0.8 units. The section on descriptive statistics (Appendix B) discusses the computation and interpretation of standard deviations. The smaller the VE, the more consistent are the algebraic errors; the higher the value, the less consistent are the algebraic errors.

Absolute error or **AE** is a measure of accuracy that is sensitive to changes in bias (CE) and variability (VE) of the algebraic errors, but it is not calculated directly from CE and VE. AE is computed as the average or mean of the absolute value of the algebraic errors. A −1 and +1 algebraic error are both treated as 1 unit error. In the example, AE equals 1.5 units.

Total error or **E** is also a measure of accuracy and can be determined directly from CE and VE. E is computed as the square root of $CE^2 + VE^2$. As such it considers movement bias and variability equally in estimating error. The sample data yield an E of 1.2 units.

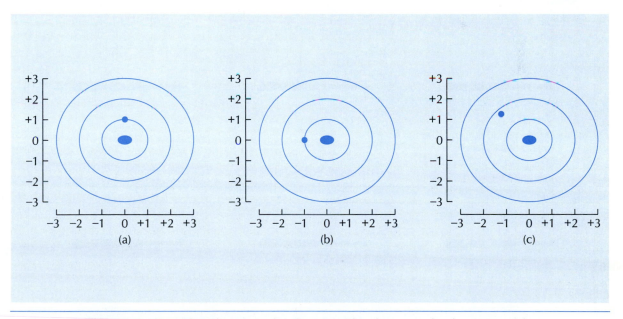

Figure A.5 *Examples of errors in dart throwing. The object is to hit the center of the target.*

Two-Dimensional Errors. Very often performance cannot be judged against a single standard. Consider the measurement problems inherent in the following three examples. In each case, the algebraic errors determined in two dimensions must be considered in order to characterize the performance. However, each example is considered separately because of the unique features that must be considered in measurement.

First, consider the measurement problems facing an archer, dart thrower, or sharpshooter (Figure A.5). Algebraic error must be determined in two dimensions. To accomplish this, the target is scaled such that the center point is considered zero in both the horizontal and vertical dimensions. In the vertical dimension a positive sign is assigned to increments above center and a negative sign to those below. Likewise, horizontal deviations are scored positive to the right of center and nega-

tive to the left of center. This is referred to as a **Cartesian coordinate system**.

The measurement problem is simplified in examples A and B of Figure A.5 because the performer has erred in only one dimension. However, in example C, algebraic errors in both dimensions must be considered. A common solution to this problem is to determine the actual distance from the center of the target or **radial error**. Radial error can be computed directly from the algebraic error scores. Note in Example C, radial error is the hypotenuse of the right triangle created by the two algebraic errors. Radial error is calculated as the square root of the error in one dimension squared plus the error in the other dimension squared.

From a coach's or athlete's perspective, radial error may not be very helpful because it may not provide the information necessary to correct the errors on subsequent attempts.

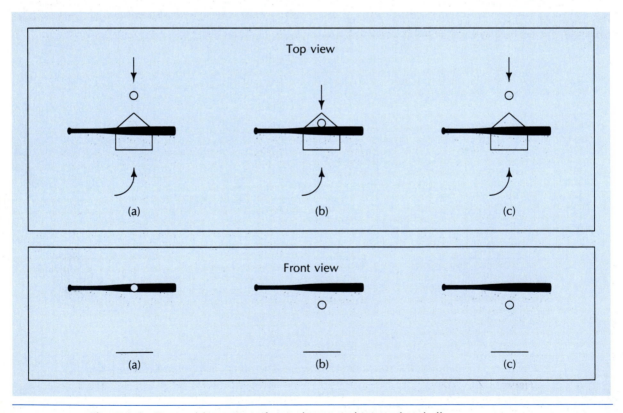

Figure A.6 *Top and front view of typical errors in hitting a baseball.*

That is, correction for wind (horizontal adjustment) and elevation (vertical adjustment) require two separate algebraic errors. A detailed discussion of the performer's use of error information is given in Chapter 10.

Second, consider measurement conditions in which errors are produced in two dimensions that are not on the same scale (e.g., time and distance). A batter must swing the bat so that it is in a position to strike the ball at the correct time. Similarly, a tennis player, a handball player, or even a receiver in football must perform a movement that must be correct in terms of both position and time. The athlete must have his bat, racket, or hand moving through a contact point at the same time that the ball arrives. Likewise, the receiver in football must adjust his stride not only to arrive at the same place as the ball but also to time the arrival coincident with the arrival of the ball.

Figure A.6 illustrates errors in batting. A timing error occurs when the bat moves through the "contact point" either before or after the arrival of the ball. Example A depicts a positive timing error because the bat arrives before the ball. Another type of error is depicted in Example B. The path of the bat swing is on a plane above (positive error) that of the ball. Note that in Examples A and B the error was in only one dimension while in Example C errors arise in both. Example C depicts a positive timing error and the path of the bat is on a plane above the ball. When errors are produced in each of two dimensions and the dimensions are not on the same scale (metric), it is not appropriate to combine the errors via radial error.

Last, consider the special two-dimensional measurement problems involved in determining tracking errors. An elementary student is asked to trace a line or letter. Whenever performance must follow a specific path or must be continuously compared to some standard, a sequential set of algebraic errors can be determined. In Figure A.7, a subject has attempted to trace the letter "V." The standard (dotted line) and actual performance (solid line) are displayed. Example A shows a hypo-

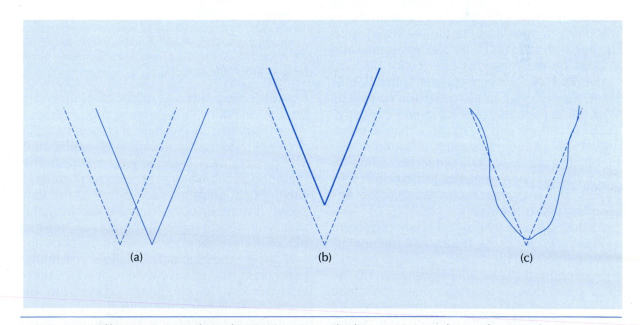

(a)   (b)   (c)

Figure A.7 *Hypothetical attempts to trace the letter "V." Example A indicates only horizontal errors, example B only vertical errors, while example C results in two-dimensional errors. The solid line is the response and the dotted line is the standard. The area between these two lines is the root mean square error.*

thetical example in which errors occur only in the horizontal dimension and Example B illustrates only vertical errors. However, in Example C, errors are made in both the horizontal and vertical dimensions. In Example C the determination of error requires measurement of the area between the lines or **root mean square error** or **RMS**. Root mean square error is used in many tracking tasks to describe performance accuracy.

Much debate has surfaced in the motor learning and control literature about the interpretation and independence of the error scores. This debate has led researchers to consider very carefully the error score(s) most appropriate for their specific conditions. Readers interested in more information concerning these issues and others related to the use and analysis of errors might consult the following: Schutz and Roy (1973), Henry (1974, 1975), Newell (1976), Schutz (1977), and Safrit, Spray, and Diewert (1980).

Kinematic Measurements

On many occasions the questions asked by the athlete, coach, or researcher center not on whether the athlete made the basket, cleared the bar, or hit the ball. The concern represents a focus on the movement itself, not the outcome. Was the movement correct, fluent, efficient? Was enough or too much force applied? Was the application of force timed correctly? These questions and many more require information about the movement of the limb segments through space and the forces acting on them. This section attempts to describe techniques and instrumentation used in the answer to these questions.

Kinematics refers to the study of motion without regard for the forces and masses involved. This is why a series of "stick figures" representing the changing positions of the body and limbs is an appropriate kinematic representation. Differences in limb length and movement are important to this type of analysis, but differences in limb circumference or mass are not. In Figure A.8 the positions of critical locations on the shoulder/arm and

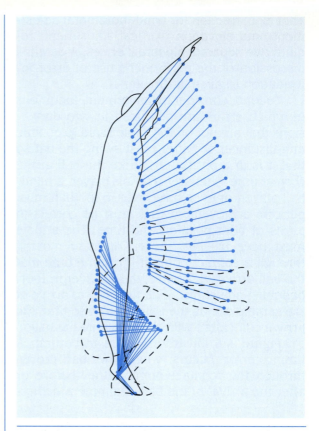

Figure A.8 *Example display of a person jumping from a squatting position. Position from various landmarks are plotted as a function of time. These positions are the basis for kinematic analysis.*

hip/leg were plotted at intervals of time during the execution of a jumping motion from a squat position. In the past this was typically accomplished by analyzing high-speed film. The process was extremely time-consuming, requiring a technician to record the position of each critical point on each frame of the film. Today, a number of instruments are available that will locate special marks or sensors placed at the critical locations on the body and will display the kinematic analysis in a matter of seconds. The relative ease with which these analyses can be conducted along with the need to ask important practical and theoretical questions concerning the kinematic qualities of movement seem to account for the increasing utilization of these techniques. Only in the last 10 years has widespread use of kinematics been seen outside the fields of biomechanics and physics.

Determining the position of the limb segments in space is, typically, only the first step in the kinematic analysis. By plotting the position of a point across time, a **displacement curve** is constructed. This is used to determine the rate of change in location across time or **velocity**. In turn, the rate of change in velocity across time is referred to as **acceleration**.

An example of kinematic data from a 17-centimeter arm movement is given in Figure A.9. The position of the subject's elbow was fixed so that a single point on the wrist accurately reflected the movement of the arm. The subject was attempting to move as quickly as possible to a target 17 centimeters from the start position. The displacement recording (top) indicates that the subject began to move at approximately 0.8 seconds into the recording. Approximately 125 milliseconds into the movement, the largest amplitude was recorded (20 centimeters), after which the subject made a small correction back to the target. The velocity recording (middle) indicates that the subject increased the velocity of the movement for the first 80 milliseconds, achieving a maximum velocity (Vm) of approximately 2.5 meters/second. The negative (below the line) velocity indicates the velocity of the movement from 20 centimeters back to 17 centimeters (target). The acceleration recording (bottom) indicates that the greatest acceleration (Am) occurred very early in the move-

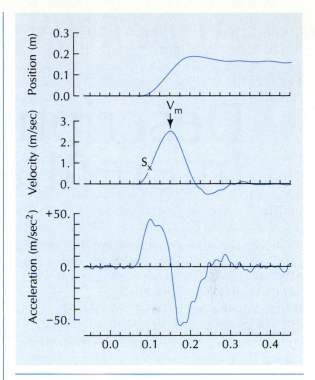

Figure A.9 *Example of position, velocity, and acceleration traces for a rapid arm movement.*

ment and the point of greatest deceleration occurred as the subject reached the 20-centimeter mark. Note that at the point of greatest velocity (Vm), there was no acceleration. The subject was in transition from acceleration to deceleration. The simultaneous recording of displacement, velocity, and acceleration permits a reasonably clear description of the movement dynamics.

KEY TERMS

physiological
  correlates
electroencephalogram
  (EEG)
evoked potential
EEG tomography
reaction time (RT)
simple RT
complex RT

discrimination RT
fractionated RT
movement time (MT)
response time
electromyogram
  (EMG)
rectified
integration

fast Fourier
  transformation
  (FFT)
algebraic error
constant error (CE)
variable error (VE)
absolute error (AE)
total error (E)

Cartesian coordinate
  system
root mean square
  error (RMS)
kinematics
displacement curve
velocity
acceleration

Appendix B

Descriptive and Inferential Statistics

Raw data can appear overwhelming. Even the simplest of experiments results in a great deal of data. The scientist uses various tools to organize and summarize the data, graphically displaying the information to best illustrate the results and then determining if relationships, trends, and/or differences exist in the data.

In this appendix, we discuss the dreaded word *statistics*. Scientists view statistics as a friendly tool—one of many they have available to help them understand and make decisions about data. It is not possible in this text, however, to dedicate much attention to statistics. Therefore, we only introduce from a conceptual standpoint the general classes of statistics that are necessary to understand the analysis experiments presented in the text. Computational techniques to calculate the statistics discussed in this section are beyond our scope.

Descriptive Statistics

Many techniques are available to help reduce large amounts of data into understandable terms. The purpose of **descriptive statistics** is to organize and summarize raw data in order to communicate the important features more effectively. The first step is to organize the data. Suppose we have the scores from a test on memory administered to three groups of 60 students each. The scores are organized from lowest to highest in a **frequency distribution**. The number of students receiving the lowest score (55) is entered first, then the number of students with the next lowest score (60), and so on. Figure B.1 presents a bar graph or histogram of hypothetical distributions for the three groups. This kind of display, for most people, is easier to understand than the raw numerical data. It is readily apparent from the histogram that the three groups did not perform equally well on the test. Group C seemed to perform best, Group B performed worst, and the scores for Group A were in between the other two groups.

Something else is apparent about the distributions. Only the scores for Group A appear to be **symmetrical**, that is, if cut in half, the two sides are identical. The other distributions are **skewed**. Group B is positively skewed because the scores "trail off" toward the high end and Group C is negatively skewed because the scores trail off at the low end.

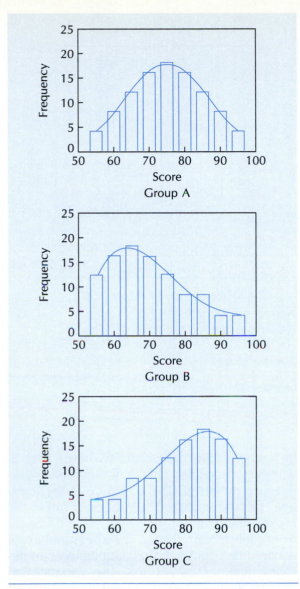

Figure B.1 *Examples of bar graphs or histograms for three groups. The data from Group A results in a symmetrical distribution while Group B results in a positively skewed distribution and Group C a negatively skewed distribution.*

	Group A	Group B	Group C
Mean	75	70	80
Median	75	65	85
Mode	75	65	85

Figure B.2 *Mean, median, and mode for data displayed in Figure B.1.*

the average, middle, or "typical" score of the distribution. There are three measures of central tendency: mean, median, and mode.

The **mean** is the arithmetic average and is obtained by adding up all the scores in the distribution and dividing that sum by the total number of scores. The **median** is the exact middle of the distribution. Half the scores fall on one side and half on the other. The **mode** is the most frequently occurring score.

These measures are provided in Figure B.2 for the three groups depicted in Figure B.1. Note that the three measures are identical for Group A. This is always the case for symmetrical distributions. However, when the distributions are skewed, the mean and the median shift apart. The mean is by far the most often used measure of central tendency; but when the distribution is skewed, the median may be the preferred measure. The mode is a crude measure of central tendency that is not often used to describe a distribution of scores or in statistical analysis. Note in Figure B.2 that the medians and modes within each group are identical. This is not always the case for skewed distributions.

Central Tendency

The histogram is useful in depicting the general characteristics of distributions, but often it is important to determine one measure that best describes the distribution. **Central tendency** refers to measures that characterize

Variability

Measures of central tendency do not always tell us all we need to know about the distribution. It is also important to determine the extent to which the scores are spread out or

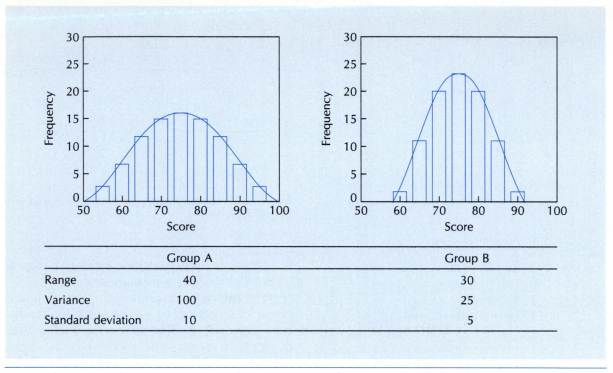

	Group A	Group B
Range	40	30
Variance	100	25
Standard deviation	10	5

Figure B.3 *Example of two symmetrical distributions with the same measures of central tendency but different measures of variability.*

variable. **Variability** refers to the dispersion or scatter of the scores. Distributions with low variability have scores that are tightly clustered, while high variability indicates a large spread among scores. Figure B.3 illustrates two distributions with the same mean, median, and mode, but they are quite different in terms of variability. Measures of variability include range, variance, and standard deviation. These measures are provided for the two groups in Figure B.3. Note that the range, variance, and standard deviation are larger for the distribution (Group A) that is more spread out or variable.

The **range** is calculated by subtracting the lowest from the highest score. With only two scores considered in the calculation, it is easy to see that the range is a crude measure of variability and that it can be greatly influenced

by a single score. The other two measures of variability consider all the scores and therefore are preferred. The **variance** is the average of the squared deviations from the mean—the sum of the squared differences from the mean divided by the number of squared deviations. If that sounds too complicated, just remember that the variance increases as the scores become more variable and decreases as the scores become less variable. The problem with using the variance is that in the calculation it is necessary to square all the deviations from the mean. Thus, the variance is not in the same unit of measurement as the raw scores. To solve this problem we turn to another and often most preferred measure of variability. The **standard deviation** is the square root of the variance. Therefore, the standard deviation is expressed in the same unit of measurement as the raw scores. As we see in the next section, the standard deviation for many distributions can provide us with more than just information about variability.

The Normal Curve

For many variables, the distribution of scores has a number of characteristics that are similar to a hypothetical distribution described by the mathematician Quetelet. This distribution, termed a **normal distribution**, is symmetrical (the left half is a mirror image of the right half) so that the mean, median, and mode are identical and the scores cluster about the mean in a very special way. A normal distribution is illustrated in Figure B.4. There are an infinite number of normal distributions, but, by definition, all have the same bell shape. This indicates that the approximate number of scores

falling under the various divisions of the normal distribution are known. For example, approximately 34.13 percent of the scores fall between the mean and 1 standard deviation above the mean. Because the distribution is symmetrical, 68.26 percent of the scores fall between ±1 standard deviation. Similarly, approximately 95 percent fall between ±2 standard deviations and approximately 99 percent between ±3 standard deviation units.

Suppose that the scores on a memory test were distributed normally with a mean of 60 and a standard deviation of 10. How could you interpret a score of 90? This would mean the score was 3 standard deviations above the mean, and you would expect 99 percent of the scores in the population to fall below the score of 90. This kind of information is quite useful. In the next section, we see that this information is useful in determining whether or not one set of scores is statistically different from another set of scores.

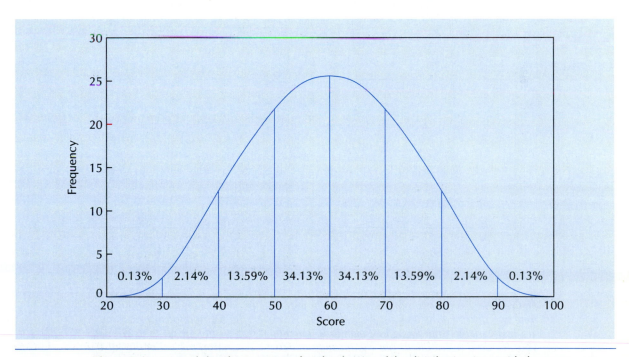

Figure B.4 *Normal distribution. Note that the density of the distribution is provided.*

Inferential Statistics

It is, in most cases, impossible to test all the subjects in a population, and yet the researcher is often interested in generalizing to the entire population. For example, the researcher uses the sample mean and standard deviation as estimates of the population mean and standard deviation. Because the descriptive statistics are only estimates of the population values, it is sometimes difficult to determine if the two means are the same or different. **Inferential statistics** are a set of procedures that can be used to make statistical judgments about population characteristics based on the characteristics of the sample. Many techniques are available, but we only briefly review two general classes of inferential statistics. The first is used to test for differences in population means and the second is used to determine if relationships exist between variables in the population.

T-Tests and Analysis of Variance

When the means for two populations are not equal, it is easy to judge that they are different. But using the sample mean as the basis for your judgment about the population mean is somewhat more difficult. Since the sample mean may not be exactly the population mean, two sample means can be different but still come from the same population. How different must two means be before we have confidence that they come from different populations? That is the pertinent question. Note the distributions illustrated in Figure B.5. In Figure B.5A the means are 20 points apart and in Figure B.5B the means are 30 points apart. Is it possible that the difference in the means for Figure B.5A is simply due to the sample

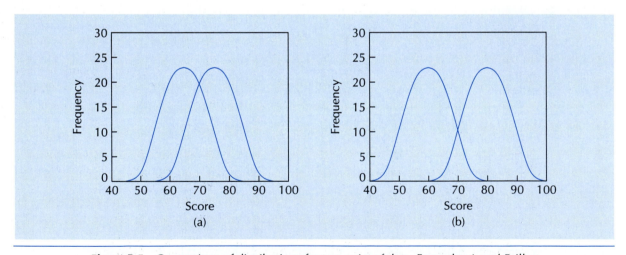

Figure B.5 *Comparison of distributions for two pairs of data. Examples A and B illustrate two distributions that are 15 units apart. However, the distributions in Example A are less variable than those in Example B. Inferential statistics are tools that will help you decide if distributions are significantly different based upon the variability of the distributions.*

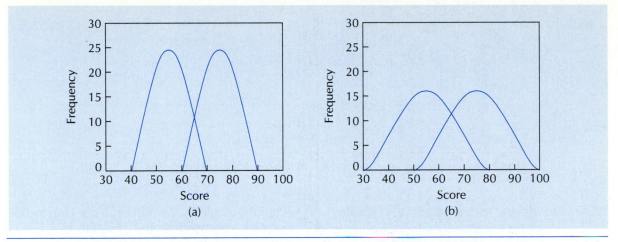

Figure B.6 *Comparison of distributions for two pairs of data. In both pairs the distribution on the left has a mean of 55 and the distribution on the right a mean of 75. Notice, however, that the distributions in Example B overlap more than the distributions in Example A.*

that we selected? How about the difference in Figure B.5B? The farther apart the means, and the less variable the scores, the more confident we become that the difference is real and not due to chance.

A procedure called a **t-test** is used to determine if two means are significantly different from each other, and a set of procedures termed **analysis of variance** can be used to test for difference in two or more means. Both procedures consider not only how far apart the means are but how variable the scores are about the mean. Consider the distribution illustrated in Figure B.6. Both the t-test and analysis of variance procedures would determine that the means in Figure B.5B are significantly different but that there is not enough evidence to conclude that the means in Figure B.5A are significantly different. Note that in both cases the means are 15 points apart but in Figure B.5A, the distributions are more variable. Relatively speaking, increases in variability decrease our confidence. That is, the differences in the means must be larger to be

judged significantly different when the variability of the distributions is greater.

Correlation and Regression

In many experiments, the researcher attempts to determine if a relationship exists between two or more variables. A **correlation** is a statistical technique that quantifies the extent to which two variables are interrelated. Variables are said to be correlated when they vary together such that a change in one variable is paralleled by a uniform, predictable change in the other. The **correlation coefficient** can range from +1 meaning that as one variable increases, the other increases in a predictable, uniform way, to 0 where the change in one variable does not indicate any predictable change in the other, to –1 meaning that the increase in one variable indicates a predictable, uniform decrease in the other variable. Figure B.7 illustrates five hypothetical relationships between two variables. Note that as the corre-

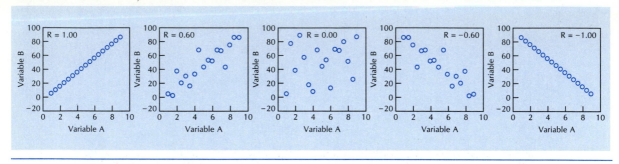

Figure B.7 *Five scatter plots illustrating correlations ranging from +1 (left) to –1 (right).*

lation increases, either positively or negatively, the points more closely approximate a straight line. When the correlation is +1 or –1, the points actually do form a straight line.

Regression is a set of statistical procedures that use, in a mathematical sense, the correlation between two or more variables to construct an equation that best summarizes the relationship(s). In many cases the relationship is linear or in a straight line, but this is not always the case. Figure B.8 illustrates the correlation between two variables. Note the line

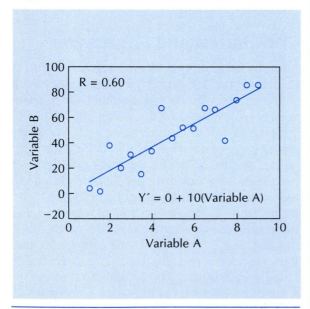

Figure B.8 *Scatter plot with regression line. Y' represents the predicted value of variable B for any value of variable A that is put into the regression equation.*

superimposed on the figure. This **regression line** best summarizes the correlation. That is, this line is placed in a position that minimizes the distances between the actual points and the corresponding points on the regression line. In fact, the sum of the distance deviations above the regression line is equal to the sum of the deviations below the regression line. This procedure assures us that no other straight line "fits" the data better.

Under special circumstances, the regression procedure can be used to predict the scores of an individual from the same population who has been tested on only one of the variables. Remember, the correlation and regression procedures use the sample data to estimate the relationship in the population. Therefore, the regression equation shown in Figure B.8 can be used to predict the performance of other members of the same population. If we select a new individual from the same population and measure performance on Variable A but not on Variable B, the regression equation can be used to predict or estimate performance on Variable B. How much confidence do we have in the predicted value? Our confidence depends on how strong the relationship is between the two variables. If the relationship or correlation is very high, we have more confidence than if the correlation is low. Still, our prediction is just that—a prediction. If the correlation is high, we would expect on the average that our prediction would be accurate.

KEY TERMS

descriptive statistics
frequency
  distribution
symmetrical
skewed
central tendency

mean
median
mode
variability
range
variance

standard deviation
normal distribution
inferential statistics
t-test
analysis of variance
correlation

correlation
  coefficient
regression
regression line

Glossary

ability. A capability or aptitude for a particular class of motor tasks.

absolute constant error (ACE). The absolute value of constant error. A measure of the magnitude of response bias.

absolute error (AE). The average error without regard for the direction of the error. A measure of response accuracy.

absolute frequency of KR. The actual number of trials for which knowledge of results (KR) is provided without consideration for the total number of trials.

absolute threshold. The least amount of stimulus energy that can be detected. Below the threshold the stimulus is not detected and above the threshold the stimulus is detected.

acceleration. The rate of change in velocity with respect to time.

acquisition. Practice experiences provided to a learner that are designed to enhance latter retention or transfer performance.

action plan. The detailed, step by step sequence of events that make up a planned movement.

active movement. Movement produced as a result of internal planning and execution processes (see passive movement for alternative).

additive effect. Occurs when an effect of an independent variable is the same regardless of whether the variable is acting alone or in combination with other variables.

afferent. Sensory neurons that carry signals to the brain or spinal cord.

after-contraction phenomenon. An increase in the amount of force produced or change in limb position as a result of a previous contraction.

agonist. Muscle that causes a joint to move in a specified direction.

algebraic error. The signed error score for a single trial.

alpha-gamma coactivation. The simultaneous setting of the intrafusal and extrafusal muscle fibers that contributes to the stretch reflex. This reflex responds very rapidly (30-40 milliseconds) to unexpected changes in muscle length.

alpha motor neuron. A neuron whose axon innervates skeletal muscle (extrafusal fiber).

ambient vision. a) is served by the entire retina, b) determines where something is, and c) is not badly degraded by low illumination.

amnesia. Partial forgetting of past events.

amplitude. The distance between the top and bottom of a sound wave; amplitude increases as sounds get louder.

analysis of variance (ANOVA). A tool used to detect if there is a difference between two or more groups. An inferential statistic with which decisions about population means are based on sample means and variability.

antagonist. A muscle that opposes the action of the agonist.

anticipation. Ability of a performer to coordinate or in some way synchronize their motor response with an external event.

antrograde amnesia. Difficulty in remembering events that happened after an injury.

applied research. Research aimed at testing potential solutions (hypotheses) to problems that present themselves in real world settings. Applied research should also be concerned with determining via controlled experiment the potential application of findings derived from basic research.

arousal. State of alertness or activation.

associative stage. An intermediate stage of learning that is concerned with performing and refining the skill. The important stimuli have been identified and their meaning is known. Conscious decisions about what to do become more automatic translations. Now the performer concentrates more on the task and response execution.

attention. The direction of mental energy or the allocation of resources to important stimuli and ignoring irrelevant ones; the process by which we notice important, meaningful, or relevant information and ignore unimportant stimuli.

autonomic nervous system. Regulates glands and organs. Divided into sympathetic and para-sympathetic divisions. Consists of nerves that stimulate and inhibit body parts to regulate functions such as heart rate, blood vessel dilation, sweating, digestion, and gland secretions, which are usually involuntary.

autonomous stage. The final stage of learning during which the information processing load appears to be reduced. The performer seems less rushed and better able to attend to other stimuli not directly related to the actual performance of the task.

axon. Long fiber that carries neural impulses away from the cell body of the neuron to the terminal branches to be passed on to other neurons. A single extension that carries neural impulses away from a cell body to thousands of other neurons.

backward masking. The ability of a stimulus to "wipe out" or mask the sensory memory of a preceding stimulus. This second stimulus, the mask, is presented within 1 or 2 seconds after the first stimulus is terminated. Presentation of a mask is an excellent way for an experimenter to control the processing time available for a stimulus.

bandwidth of KR. Involves setting some criterion range of errors within which knowledge of results is not provided and outside of which knowledge of results is provided.

bar graph. A graph in which proportional lengths of parallel bars represent the differences between sets of data.

basal ganglia. Four masses of gray matter in the brain that control background muscle tone and large, general muscle movements, part of the motor system.

basic research. Research that is concerned with the development of hypotheses, principles, laws, and theories pertaining to the processes that account for the phenomenon under study.

behaviorism. Approach to psychology based on the premise that human behavior can be described by focusing only on the observable stimulus and response.

bit. The amount of information obtained by learning which one of two equally likely alternatives is present.

Broca's aphasia. Results from damage to Broca's area of the left anterior lobe of the cortex. Characterized by speech that is slow, labored, and slightly distorted.

capacity interference. Interference arising from tasks vying for limited attentional resources.

central intermittency. Hypothesis that humans process information in discrete bursts rather than continuously.

central nervous system (CNS). Nerve tissue in the brain and spinal cord.

central pattern generators. Spinal mechanisms that control oscillatory behavior such as that involved in walking.

central processes. Information processing activities that occur in the central nervous system such as those involved in sensation/perception, response selection, and response execution.

central tendency. A single measure that represents a group of scores. Also see *mean*, *median*, and *mode*.

cerebral cortex (cerebrum). Two wrinkled hemispheres that are part of the forebrain; governs our most advanced human capabilities, including abstract reasoning and speech. Accounts for about 80% of the brain's weight.

choice reaction time. Reaction time when more than one response may be required to more than one associated stimulus.

chunking. Process of grouping elements such as letters or words into units (or chunks) that function as a whole. Chunks can be digits, letters, syllables, words, sentences, or the movement equivalents.

classical conditioning. The process whereby an originally neutral stimulus comes to elicit a response. It takes place when the neutral stimulus is repeated paired with a stimulus that elicits the response without conditioning.

closed environment. A relatively stable environment in which conditions do not change from moment to moment. An example is bowling.

closed-loop control. Control based on the comparison of feedback with a movement goal. Response produced feedback "loops" back into the information processing channel. The entire movement is not planned in advance but information processing activities are utilized to continually guide the movement to conclusion.

closed-loop theory: Adams 1971. A theory of motor learning which proposes that a memory and perceptual trace are developed as a function of practice with KR.

coaction. The presence of others independently but concurrently doing the same or similar activity. May contribute to motivation and/or arousal.

cognitive stage. The initial stage of learning when a learner is first introduced to the motor task. The learner must determine the objective of the skill as well as the relational and environmental cues that control and regulate the task to be learned.

competition. Interpersonal conflict involving an incompatibility of goals. Can result in increased motivation.

confirmation bias. The tendency for judgments based on new ideas to be overly consistent with preliminary hypotheses. This is in strict opposition to the "familiar stereotype of the scientist as an impartial observer whose hypotheses stand or fall according to the blind justice of objective data." (Greenwald et al.)

conformity. Occurs when a person changes his or her behavior or attitudes as a result of real or imagined group pressures despite personal feelings to the contrary.

constant error (CE). A measure of response bias calculated as the average score. With this measure, plus and minus errors cancel each other out.

context dependent behavior. Behavior that is more easily elicited in the environment in which it was learned.

contextual interference. The degree of functional interference found in a practice session when several tasks must be learned and are practiced together. Blocked conditions are thought to promote low contextual interference and random schedules high contextual interference.

continuous movements. Movements with no distinct beginning or ending.

control group. The subjects in an experiment who are treated exactly the same as the experimental group except that the control group is not exposed to critical levels of the independent variable and thus serves as the basis for comparison.

coordinating definition. A definition that organizes isolated observation and associated hypotheses into a coherent statement.

coordination loss. Reduced group productivity due to the group's inability to combine and use the individual member's contributions.

coordinative structure. A functional coordination of muscle groups such that they behave as a unit.

corpus callosum. Large cable of nerve fibers that connects the two cerebral hemispheres.

correlation. A method of summarizing the relationship between two variables.

correlation coefficient. The calculated value of a correlation. Value ranges from −1 to +1.

crossed-extensor reflex. A reflex whereby the extensors of one limb are activated when the flexors of the contralateral limb are activated. This reflex is thought to greatly reduce the number of central commands required in such actions as walking.

cross talk. The variety of neural communications that take place in the spinal cord and brain. Occurs at almost all levels of information transmission and processing. Simple reflexes are based on the concept of cross talk.

cutaneous senses. The senses of the skin, which include temperature, pain, and pressure sensations.

cycle. The distance between wave crests in a sound wave. Also called *wavelength*.

d' (d prime). In signal detection theory, a measure of sensory sensitivity.

decision. The process of actively choosing one response or action from among a group of viable alternatives.

deduction. The process of reasoning from a general principle or theory to an unknown, from general to specific, or from postulate to testable hypothesis.

dendrites. Short neural fibers extending out from the body of a neuron that receive impulses from other neurons and carry them to the cell body.

dependent variable. The variable that is measured in an experiment. The change in the dependent variable is assumed to be a result of the manipulation of the independent variable.

descriptive statistics. Tools for summarizing data taken from a group of objects, people, or events.

dichotic listening. An experimental procedure used to study selective attention in which earphones play separate messages in each ear. Subjects are told to ignore one message and shadow the other, which means to repeat each word immediately after hearing it.

difference threshold. The smallest difference in intensity that can be detected between two stimuli.

discrete movements. Movements with a distinct beginning and a distinct ending.

discrimination reaction time. Reaction time when more than one stimulus may be presented but a single response is made only to one associated stimulus.

displacement. The change in position over a given time period.

displacement curve. A plot of the position of a point across time.

distributed practice. Ratios of rest intervals to practice intervals of greater than one. That is, more time is devoted to the rest interval than to actual practice.

ecological validity. The degree to which the conditions of the experiment are representative of conditions encountered in real, everyday, and culturally significant situations.

EEG tomography. A pictoral representation of the frequency of brain wave activity.

effective target width (W_e). A measure that represents the spread of the movement endpoints in the direction of the movement about the target position.

effector anticipation. Ability to determine how long one's own movements or movement components will take to initiate and execute.

efferent. Motor neurons that carry signals from the brain or spinal cord.

elaboration perspective. Notion that simultaneous presence of multiple items in working memory offers the opportunity for cognitive processing that results in more robust memory for the tasks. Elaborative processing includes determining the similarities and differences between tasks being learned.

electroencephalogram (ECG). A recording of the electric potentials of brain cells.

electromyography (EMG). A recording of the voltage changes that are associated with the propagation of muscle action potentials.

empirical. Hypotheses based on observation and/or literature rather than theory.

encoding. The process of selecting and representing information in a specific form (verbally, visually, proprioceptively) in memory.

episodic memory. A person's memories about events, including the time and place they occurred.

event uncertainty. Increases as the number of equally likely alternatives is increased.

evoked potential. A pattern of brain waves in response to a specific stimulus.

experiment. An investigation in which a researcher manipulates one variable (independent) while measuring its effect on some other variable (dependent). Experiments provide evidence on which a hypothesis is either rejected or held tenable.

experimental group. The subjects in an experiment who are exposed to the critical level of the independent variable.

external validity. The extent to which the results of the experiment are generalizable.

exteroception. The perception of the environment via exteroceptors.

exteroceptors. Sensory receptors that receive stimuli which provide a description of the environment such as vision, audition (hearing), taste, and smell.

extrafusal fibers. Skeletal muscle fibers.

extrinsic feedback. External (exteroceptive) information received during and/or after the response from the environment or some additional source.

fading schedule of KR. A schedule that provides KR more frequently early in practice and then gradually reduces the number of trials for which KR is presented later in practice.

false alarm. In signal detection theory; responding that a stimulus is present when it is not.

fast Fourier transformation (FFT). A method of processing an EMG signal to determine the frequencies in the waveform.

feedback. Sensory information carried to the brain. See *afferent*.

feedforward. A process of sending information ahead of a movement so that the sensory information arising from the movement can be interpreted correctly.

final common pathway. The notion that neural commands from the brain, sensory receptors, and reflexes converge at the spinal level to produce commands to the muscles.

Fitts' law. Mathematical relationship between movement time and the index of difficulty. As the index of difficulty increases, movement time increases.

flashbulb memory. Vivid memory of unexpected and emotionally important events.

focal vision. Vision that 1) is limited to central vision, 2) has the function of determining what something is, and 3) is badly degraded by low illumination.

forgetting. An inability to remember or retrieve information from memory.

fractionated reaction time. Reaction time that is partitioned into its component parts.

free association test. Procedure in which a person looks at, or listens to, a target word and then reports other words that come to mind.

free recall test. A procedure requiring people to recall a list of words in any order they choose.

free rider effect. Explanation for social loafing that people may reduce their efforts when they observe that their contributions to the group are dispensable and that the group will succeed without them.

frequency. The number of wave crests that occur in a second; measured in cycles per second.

frequency distribution. A method of organizing scores from lowest to highest in which the number of occurrences of each score is noted.

functionalism. An approach to psychology that emphasizes the function of thought; has led to important applications in education and educational psychology.

gamma motor neuron. A neuron whose axon innervates the muscle spindle (intrafusal fiber).

generalizable motor program. A motor program that can be executed in a variety of ways depending on the parameters specified. See *schema theory*.

goal setting. A motivational technique in which performers set desired performance standards.

Golgi tendon organs (GTO). Stretch receptors located in the muscle-tendon junction that provide information about tension.

group polarization (effect). Groups tend to polarize people and move them to believe more strongly in the position they first held.

guidance hypothesis. The notion that KR can serve as a movement prescription that leads the performer to the goal. Subjects may become reliant on the guidance properties of KR to the exclusion of additional processing that may be important to learning.

Hertz (Hz). Cycles per second of a sound wave.

Hick's law (Hick-Hymen law). Defines a linear relationship between reaction time and the $\log_2$ of the number of response alternatives.

hierarchical control. A model of movement control that proposes that some higher level in the system is responsible for monitoring feedback and making adjustments while lower levels are responsible for carrying out those decisions.

hippocampus. A brain structure thought to play a critical role in short-term memory.

histogram. A graphic representation of a frequency distribution consisting of vertical rectangles whose widths correspond to a range of frequencies and whose heights correspond to the number of frequencies.

hit. In signal detection theory; responding that a stimulus is present when it is.

home court advantage. A psychological edge to playing in familiar surroundings.

hypothesis. A tentative prediction of behavior under a specific set of conditions.

imitation. Acquisition of knowledge and behavior by watching other people act and then doing the same thing.

impulse variability theory. Proposes that the variability in the muscular impulse leads to movement variability and errors.

independent variable. The variable that is manipulated in an experiment.

index of difficulty (ID). An expression of the complexity of a movement based on the amplitude of that movement and the size of the target that must be contacted. It is specified as $\log_2(2A/W)$, where A is the amplitude of the movement and W is the target width. The index of difficulty can be used to describe an individual's movement time with the following equation: $MT = a + b[\log_2(2A/W)]$. The constant "a" is termed the intercept and represents movement time when the index of difficulty is zero.

induction. Logical reasoning from isolated facts to a more general description.

inferential statistics. Tools used to test hypotheses. Utilizes samples to infer to a population.

information. Feedback that serves to reduce uncertainty.

information processing. Active cognitive operations occurring in the central nervous system. These processes result in commands transmitted to the musculature that are tailored to the specific environmental demands and the intentions of the performer.

initial conditions. In schema theory, proposed to be a description of the task requirements and environment prior to a response.

integration. A method of processing an EMG signal by summing the rectified signal over short periods of time.

interactive effect. Occurs when an effect of an Independent variable is influenced by other variables.

interference theory. An explanation offered for forgetting that proposes that prior and/or new information competes with or causes the loss or inaccessibility of information.

internal validity. The degree to which the manipulation of an independent variable in an experiment truly accounts for the changes observed by the experimenter. Internal validity increases as the experiment provides a more convincing demonstration that the observed change was a result of the experimental manipulation.

interneurons. Neurons that originate and terminate in the brain or spinal cord.

interresponse interval. The interval between responses.

intertask processing. Processing that focuses on the similarities and differences between multiple tasks.

intrafusal fibers. Small muscle fibers located at the ends of the muscle spindle that change the length of the spindle.

intratask processing. Processing that focuses on the uniqueness of a single task.

intrinsic feedback. Internal (proprioceptive) feedback normally received during and after the execution of a task.

invariant features. Characteristics that define the generalizable characteristics of the motor program. Schmidt proposes that the order of the elements, the relative timing, and the relative force are the invariant features of a generalizable motor program.

just-noticeable difference. Smallest difference in intensity between two stimuli that can be reliably detected.

KR. See *knowledge of results*.

KR delay interval. The interval of time that elapses between the completion of the response and the presentation of KR.

kinematic. A description of motion with respect to position, velocity, and acceleration without regard to mass.

kinetics. A description of motion with respect to the forces applied.

knowledge of performance (KP). Information received about the actual performance and execution of the movement (i.e., was the movement performed correctly or the way it was intended to be performed?). Often KP is presented in relation to a standard of correctness.

knowledge of results (KR). Information received concerning the extent to which a response accomplished the intended movement goal. In many textbooks KR is defined to include only augmented, verbal or verbalizable information relative to the attainment of the goal.

known probabilities. Knowledge of the probabilities with which specific alternatives occur; results in reduced average reaction time. See *Hick's law*.

KP. See knowledge of performance.

law. A statement describing a sequence of events in nature or human activities that has been observed to occur with unvarying uniformity under the same conditions.

Law of Effect. A proposal by Thorndike which states that organisms tend to repeat responses that produce a desired outcome.

learning. A relatively permanent change in capacity for behavior.

learning variable. A variable that affects learning.

levels of aspiration. See *goal setting*.

levels of processing theory. A memory perspective offered by Craik and Lockhart (1972). This perspective suggests that recall is improved by processing information to a deeper level. Processing depth is a function of elaborative processing and meaningfulness.

long-term memory. A memory system that stores information for long periods of time (perhaps permanently).

maladaptive short-term corrections. Refers to inappropriate corrections in movement production that are undertaken as a result of knowledge of results.

massed practice. Ratios of rest intervals to practice intervals of one or less. If practice intervals, perhaps practice trials, are packed together such that the time between practice is no longer than the time involved in actual practice, the session is said to be massed.

mass-spring hypothesis. A proposed mode of control based on the selection of an equilibrium point between the agonist and antagonist muscles.

mean. A measure of central tendency that is the average of the scores.

median. A measure of central tendency that is the middle score.

membrane potential. A tension that exists in a neuron between the cell's inside and outside environments. Also called *polarization*.

memory. The system and processes that enable us to retain information over time.

memory span. The number of items that we can be exposed to one time and then recall in sequence with no mistakes: 7 ± 2 items or chunks.

memory trace. A modest motor program proposed (Adams, 1971) to be responsible for initiating movement in the correct direction.

mental practice. Practice involving processes associated with rehearsing the performance of a skill in the absence of any overt physical practice.

metathetic. Sensory systems that do not follow Weber's law are said to follow a qualitative or metathetic continuum. Changes in stimuli for these senses are characterized by different receptors responding.

method of adjustment. A psychophysical method in which the subject adjusts the intensity of a stimulus until it is just barely perceived or until it is perceived to be equal to a standard stimulus.

method of constant stimuli. A psychophysical method in which the stimulus intensity is presented in random order. The subject is to respond whether the stimulus is or is not present or whether it matches or does not match a standard stimulus.

method of limits. A psychophysical method in which the intensity of a stimulus is adjusted up or down by the experimenter until it is perceived or until it is perceived to be equal to a standard stimulus.

miss. In signal detection theory; not responding that a stimulus is present when it is.

mode. A measure of central tendency that is the most frequently occurring score.

model. A mathematical or schematic representation of a process or theory.

modeling. A teaching technique in which a demonstration is used. The observers attempt to model their performance after the demonstrator.

motor control. An area of study concerned with understanding the execution of motor processes and the variables that mediate their execution.

motor learning. An area of study focusing on understanding the way in which the processes that subserve movement are developed and the factors which facilitate or inhibit the relatively permanent changes in the capacity for motor skills.

motor neuron. A neuron that innervates muscle fibers.

motor neuron pools. Group of motor neurons in the gray matter of the spinal cord that serves a related set of muscles.

motor program. A prestructured set of motor commands capable of carrying out a movement.

motor unit. A motor neuron and the muscle fibers it innervates.

movement time (MT). The interval from the initiation of a response to the termination of that response.

multiple memory theory. Theory that states there are three types of memory: sensory, short-term, and long-term.

muscle spindle. A sensory receptor arranged in-parallel with skeletal muscle fibers that monitors changes in muscle length.

neurons. Cells in the nervous system that receive and send impulses. The brain contains 100 to 200 billion neurons, and each one connects with many others.

noise. A psychological concept; in signal detection theory noise is defined as spontaneous, random sensory signals.

normal distribution. Distribution of scores in which the mean, median, and mode are the same and ± 1 standard deviation includes approximately 68% of the scores, ± 2 standard deviations includes approximately 95% of the scores, and ± 3 standard deviations includes approximately 99% of the scores.

observational learning. Learning a skill by observing others as they engage in the skill.

open environments. Environments that are continually changing. Responses cannot be planned long in advance because the conditions are subject to rapid change.

open-loop control. Motor program control. The feedback loop is left "open" during the execution of the movement, thus, all information processing must be completed before the movement is begun.

operant conditioning. A type of learning that occurs when desired responses are rewarded or reinforced and undesired responses are ignored or punished.

operations research. Research that is concerned with the testing of the impact, control, and management strategies required to optimize the implementation of instructional techniques into real world settings.

paradigm. An example or pattern for an experiment.

parallel-distributed processing. Information processing that is flexible in the order in which information is processed. The order depends on task demands, context, and past experiences.

parallel processing. Information processing in which two or more processes occur at the same time.

parallel search. A simultaneous search of all items in a memory set.

parameter. A value provided by the recall schema and applied to the generalizable motor program that defines the limits of the movement. See schema theory.

parameterize. The process of scaling the invariant features of a generalized motor program.

parasympathetic division. A part of the autonomic nervous system that controls relaxation responses. Stimulates and inhibits in a way that generally balances the pattern of the sympathetic division.

part/whole practice. A practice method in which segments of a task are practiced independently prior to their practice together.

passive movements. Movements that are produced by external forces acting on the body parts.

perception. Sensations that are given meaning. The processes involving memory by which sensations can be organized, classified, and interpreted.

perceptual anticipation. Ability to predict the occurrence of an external event that cannot be directly tracked but occurs with some degree of regularity or under a specific set of conditions.

perceptual trace. A reference of correctness proposed by Adams (1971) to represent the feedback qualities of a correct motor response.

perceptual uncertainty. Increase in response selection options as a set of stimuli or events become less easily discriminated from each other.

performance variable. A variable that affects performance.

peripheral processes. Processes that involve the activation of sensory receptors and muscles as well as the transmission to (afferent) and from (efferent) the central nervous system.

peripheral nervous system. All nerve tissue that is not in the brain and spinal cord.

physiological correlates. Physiological responses that accompany psychological events.

pitch. Difference between the low and high notes. Changes in pitch correspond to changes in frequency.

population. A subject population is comprised of all persons who meet a particular set of conditions (male, female, right-handed, blue-eyed, college student, etc.).

post KR delay interval. The interval of time that elapses between the presentation of KR and the beginning of the next response.

postulates. Theoretical assumptions or principles. Experiments that test the validity of postulates are termed *theoretical experiments*.

practice composition. Manipulations that vary the number of tasks or task variations intermingled in a practice session. Manipulations may also vary the manner in which a task is practiced: physical, mental, observational, or simulated practice.

practice distribution. Manipulations to the practice/rest intervals.

practice scheduling. Manipulations that cause a change in the conditions under which or in the context within which a specific task is executed. Manipulating the order in which tasks are learned and manipulating practice/rest intervals are examples of practice scheduling.

precision of KR. The level of accuracy with which KR is presented. For example, a timing error may be presented in seconds, tenths of a second, hundredths of a second, etc.

precue. Advance information that reduces uncertainty by reducing the number of alternatives that must be considered.

primacy effect. The tendency for the first few items in a series to be remembered better than those in the middle.

proactive inhibition. Interference of previous learning with memory for new learning.

proprioception. The perception of body part position and status via proprioceptors.

proprioceptors. Sensory receptors that receive stimuli that provide information about the current state of the body; such as the muscle spindles, Golgi tendon organs, joint receptors, as well as various pressure and temperature receptors.

prothetic. Sensory systems to which Weber's law applies are said to follow a quantitative or prothetic continuum. Increases in stimulus intensity for these senses are characterized by an increase in the number of sensory receptors that respond.

psychological refractory period. The delay in response to the second of two stimuli spaced very closely in time.

psychophysical functions. The relationship between physical energies and psychological experiences over a wide range of physical magnitudes.

psychophysics. The study of relationships between physical energies (e.g., light from a star) and psychological experiences (e.g., seeing the star).

qualitative KR. Takes two forms, depending on the task requirements; it can inform subjects that their performance is correct/incorrect or it can provide information that the subject's performance was too fast/slow, hard/soft, long/short, etc.

quantitative KR. KR which is not only indicates the direction of an error but also the magnitude of that error in some units. Quantitative KR can be presented with varying precision.

radial error. A two-dimensional error that indicates the distance from the target.

randomization. Procedure used in an experiment whereby subjects are randomly assigned to either the control or the experimental group(s). It ensures that each person has an equal chance of being assigned to each group, thus making it highly probable that subject differences will be equally distributed between groups.

range. The spread of a group of scores. Calculated by subtracting the lowest from the highest score.

rate coding. A method of controlling force by varying the frequency with which motor units are activated.

reaction time (RT). The interval from the presentation of a stimulus to the initiation of a response.

recall schema. Proposed in Schmidt's (1975) schema theory to be responsible for organizing the specific motor programs capable of initiating and controlling movements. A relationship between the sensory consequences, the initial conditions, and the outcomes that serves as the basis for selecting the parameters of the generalizable motor program. See *schema theory*.

recall test. Measures a person's ability to reproduce material. Teachers use this method with essay exams or fill-in-the-blank questions.

recency effect. The tendency for the last few items in a series to be remembered better than those in the middle.

receptor anticipation. Ability to predict the arrival of an external event when some aspect of the event can be tracked in some manner.

reciprocal inhibition. A genetically defined reflex that tends to inhibit the flexors of a joint when the extensors are activated.

recoding. The process of changing a memory representation from one form to another.

recognition processes. The cognitive operations that involve the matching of information stored in memory to sensory information. Typically information from the environment (short term sensory store) is compared with previously stored information (long term memory) in short term memory. This causes information in sensory memory to be transferred into short-term memory.

recognition schema. Proposed in Schmidt's (1975) schema theory to be responsible for evaluating the movement outcome and updating the recall schema if errors are determined.

The relationship between the sensory conse-quences, the initial conditions, and the outcomes of past movements. See *schema theory*.

recognition test. Measures a person's ability to pick the correct answer when several answers are given. Teachers use this method with multiple-choice questions.

reconstruction hypothesis. Suggests that conditions that prompt subjects to more fully process their response on each trial rather than repeat a response just executed will benefit retention. This perspective views forgetting and subsequent reconstruction as beneficial to learning.

recruitment. A method of controlling force by varying the number of motor units that are activated.

rectified. A method of processing an EMG signal by calculating its absolute value.

reflexes. Responses to stimuli that do not require information to be processed in the brain. Reflexes occur virtually automatically at the spinal level—for example, the patellar tendon reflex.

regression. Method of quantifying the relationship between two variables. An inferential statistic based on correlation.

regression line. A line resulting from a regression analysis which best reflects the actual scores.

rehearsal. Process of repeating information either physically or mentally in order to retain it in short-term memory (maintenance rehearsal) or transfer it to long-term memory.

reinforcement. An event that increases the probability of the occurrence of a response. Positive reinforcements arise from pleasant events and negative reinforcement emanates from avoidance of unpleasant events.

relative frequency of KR. Refers to the percentage of total trials for which KR is provided.

response execution. A stage of information processing that involves the formulation of the specific motor commands responsible for movement control.

response outcome. Information pertaining to the end result of a movement.

response selection. A stage in information processing in which current information and past experiences are processed to formulate a course of action or inaction.

response specifications. The requirement that results in a generalizable motor program producing a unique response.

response time. A combination of reaction time and movement time. The interval from the presentation of a stimulus to the termination of a movement.

retention. Delayed practice experiences (test or game) on a task that was experienced during acquisition, even if the conditions under which the performance is measured are altered from those of acquisition.

reticular activating system (RAS). Activates all regions of the brain for incoming sensory impulses. Plays an important part in alertness and selective attention. It performs these functions by connecting the reticular formation with other parts of the midbrain, hindbrain, and forebrain.

retrieval. The process of accessing information from long-term memory.

retrieval cues. Aids to retrieval that are often encoded with the information to be remembered; an example would be category names.

retroactive inhibition. Interference of new learning with memory for previous learning.

retrograde amnesia. Partial loss of memory for events that occurred before an injury.

reverse fading of KR. A schedule of KR that provides fewer KR trials early in practice and increases the number of KR trials as acquisition progresses.

root mean square error. The area between a desired path and an actual path.

sample. A subset of a *population*. Experimenters use a sample that is representative of the population since it is rarely feasible to test an entire population.

savings test. Measurement of a person's ability to take advantage of what was learned previously in order to relearn the same or similar material faster.

schema. An abstract representation, or rule based on experience. See *schema theory*.

schema theory: Schmidt, 1975. An open-loop theory of motor learning and control that is based on the concept of a schema and generalizable motor program. The theory proposes that a recall schema controls movement and a recognition schema evaluates the movement's success and updates the recall schema.

selective attention. The process of directing or allocating attention to specific stimuli.

semantic memory. A person's general background memory about words, symbols, concepts, and rules.

sensation. Sensory transmissions from the periphery impacting the central nervous system.

sensation-perception. A stage in information processing in which neural transmission from tens of thousands of sensory receptors are sensed and then interpreted with the help of memory.

sensorimotor coordination. The dual ability to guide motor actions by means of sensory information and to take into account motor actions when interpreting sensory information that is changed by those actions.

sensory consequences. The information from the sensory systems transmitted during the execution of a response.

sensory memory. A temporary memory store that holds sensations briefly so that they can be identified; lasts from 1 to 2 seconds. Thought to have a relatively large capacity.

sequential dependencies. Knowledge of the sequence with which alternatives occur; results in reduced average reaction time.

serial position effect. The tendency for the first (primacy effect) and the last (recency effect) items in a series to be remembered better than those in the middle.

serial processing. Processing that occurs in a specified order. One happens first, another second, another third, and so on until the processing is accomplished.

serial search. A type of one-item-at-a-time search of a memory set.

short-term memory. A memory store that holds information that has been transferred out of sensory memory or retrieved from long-term memory; lasts about 30 seconds unless information is repeated or rehearsed. Thought to have a capacity of 7 ± 2 items.

signal detection method. A psychophysical method based on the assumption that absolute thresholds are not absolute. The theory attempts to explain people's perceptual judgments by analyzing their sensitivity to sensory stimuli.

simple reaction time. Reaction time when a single known response is required to a single stimulus.

single channel hypothesis. The notion that the system can process only a single set of information at any given time.

size principle. A theory of how the recruitment of motor units depends on the size of the motor neurons. The smallest motor neurons are recruited first and the largest last.

skewed. A distribution of scores in which the *mean* and the *median* are not the same, thus the distribution is not symmetrical.

skill. Movement competency developed as a function of practice and experience.

social comparison. Using social reality to evaluate oneself—comparing oneself against the beliefs, attitudes, and behaviors of other people.

social facilitation. Performance enhancement that occurs because the presence of others tends to arouse individuals; this arousal creates an additional pool of energy that aids the performance of well-learned behaviors.

social inhibition. Situation in which the presence of an audience or co-actors hinders an individual's performance.

social loafing. Situation where the motivation to work has decreased because people are in groups in which their individual performance cannot be observed.

social learning theory. Learning by imitation.

specificity hypothesis. A proposal that motor skills are specific and only superficially resemble other similar motor skills. This implies that changing the motor task only slightly produces a new motor task for which a new motor program must be developed.

speed accuracy paradox. The finding that timing accuracy increases and movement accuracy decreases as the velocity of the stimulus to be timed increases.

speed accuracy trade-off. The fact that performers must trade-off speed in order to increase accuracy or trade-off accuracy to increase speed.

spinal cord. A cable of long nerve fibers running from the brainstem down through the backbone to the lower back, through which ascending nerves carry sensory information up to the brain and descending nerves carry commands down from the brain to the muscles.

standard deviation. A measure of the variability of a group of scores expressed in the same units of measurement as the original scores. Calculated as the square root of the variance.

stimulus-response compatibility. The degree of learned or natural correspondence between a signal or stimuli and its correct response.

structural interference. Interference arising from the simultaneous execution of motor responses that utilize the same input or output mechanisms.

sucker effect. Explanation for social loafing that argues that people will reduce their effort if they think other group members are not putting in maximum effort.

summary KR. A format for presenting knowledge of results in which a predetermined number of trials is completed before knowledge of results is presented for that set.

Suzuki method. A method for teaching the violin in which the teacher attempts to develop in the students a memory for the music before the actual practice begins.

symmetrical distribution. A distribution in which the measures of central tendency are the same, not skewed.

sympathetic division. Part of the autonomic nervous system. Favors physical activities in its pattern of stimulation and inhibition. It activates the heart and lungs, for example, because they are needed for physical activities.

synapse. A junction between two neurons. When an action potential travels to the end of an axon, it reaches a synapse. Movement of a neural impulse across this junction is called *synaptic transmission*.

synergy. The combined or cooperative action of muscle groups arising from the way muscles are organized across joints and/or resulting from spinal level reflexes.

t-test. A tool used to detect if there is a difference between a mean and a population value or between two means. An inferential statistic.

temporal uncertainty. Increased as the predictability of the time at which some critical event will occur decreases.

theoretical. Derived from theory. Theoretical implies deductive reasoning.

theory. Explanation about why behavior occurs; theories generate hypotheses that can be tested experimentally. The term *theory* implies that there is considerable evidence in support of the explanation.

timing. Generally taken to involve the timekeeping responsible for the duration of internal events such as the timing of an agonist burst or the internal timing of responses as a whole.

tonic neck reflex. A reflex apparent in infants that causes the arms and legs to alternately flex and extend as a result of turning the infant's head.

tonic neck response. Residual effects of the tonic neck reflex that influence spinal level excitability and muscle tonus as a function of head position.

total error (E). A measure of response accuracy that considers both response bias (CE) and response variability (VE).

trace decay theory. The theory that memory fades in time if its strength is not maintained through use.

transfer. The effect of practice experiences on a variation of the task or on another task that was not practiced during acquisition.

transfer appropriate processing. The notion that the processing engaged in during acquisition should be as similar as possible to that required during retention or transfer testing.

transfer paradigm. Two-phase paradigm. In the acquisition phase the independent variable of interest is manipulated. That is, different groups receive different treatments. After the acquisition phase is completed, the retention or transfer phase is conducted. Prior to this phase, a period of time is allowed to elapse so that any temporary effects of the acquisition conditions (fatigue, frustration, etc.) will dissipate

translation. A selection of a response alternative given a specific stimulus condition based on a stimulus-response association developed over practice.

uncertainty. Unknowns that require information to resolve.

variable error (VE). A measure of variability of errors calculated as the standard deviation of the raw error scores.

variability. The dispersion or scatter of the scores. Variance and standard deviation are common measures of variability.

variability of practice hypothesis. A proposal that variable but related practice experiences enhance the memory states responsible for motor control. This hypothesis was derived from schema theory.

variance. A measure of variability that is calculated as the average of the squared deviations from the mean.

variant features. The selection, scaling or parameterizing of the invariant features of a generalizable motor program. Schmidt proposes that the specific muscles to be used must be selected as well as the actual timing and actual force of the movement.

velocity. The rate of change in position with respect to time.

wavelength. The distance between wave crests in a sound wave. Also called *cycle*.

Weber's Law. A just-noticeable difference (jnd) for a given stimulus intensity is proportional to the original stimulus intensity. The law is often expressed as an equation, $\mathbf{jnd/I = K}$, in which *jnd* is the least amount of change in stimulus intensity required to reliably detect a difference, I is the original intensity, and K is a constant.

Wernicke's aphasia. Impairment resulting from an injury to the Wernicke's area of the cortex. Characterized by speech that includes wrong words and nonsense words, and shifting from topic to topic.

working memory. Short-term memory. The items held in this memory store are available for processing and accessible to consciousness.

References

Chapter 1

Adams, J. A. (1987). Historical review and appraisal of research on the learning, retention, and transfer of human motor skills. *Psychological Bulletin*, *101*, 41–74.

Donders, F. C. (1969). On the speed of mental processes. *Acta Psychologica*, *30*, 412–431.

Fitts, P. M. (1954). The information capacity of the human motor system in controlling the amplitude of movement. *Journal of Experimental Psychology*, *47*, 381–391.

Neisser, U. (1967). *Cognitive psychology*. New York: Appleton-Century-Crofts.

Pew, R. W. (1974). Levels of analysis in motor control. *Brain Research*, *71*, 393–400.

Platt, J. R. (1964). Strong inference. *Science*, *146*, 347–353.

Polya, G. (1954). *Mathematics and plausible reasoning*. Princeton, NJ: Princeton University Press.

Salmoni, A. W., Schmidt, R. A., & Walter, C. B. (1984). Knowledge of results and motor learning: A review and critical appraisal. *Psychological Bulletin*, *95*, 355–386.

Sternberg, S. (1969). The discovery of processing stages: Extensions of Donder's method. *Acta Psychologica*, *30*, 276–315.

Chapter 2

Backlund, E. D., Granberg, P. O., Hamberger, B., Sedvau, G., Seiger, A., & Olson, L. (1985). Transplantation of adrenal medullary tissue to striatum in Parkinsonism. In A. Bjorklund & U. Stemevi (Eds.), *Neural grafting in the mammalian CNS* (pp. 551–556). Amsterdam: Elsevier.

Besson, J., & Chaouch, A. (1987). Peripheral and spinal mechanisms of nociception. *Physiological Reviews*, *11*, 67–186.

Brown, J. E., & Frank, J. S. (1987). Influence of event anticipation on postural actions accompanying voluntary movement. *Experimental Brain Research*, *67*, 645–650.

Chugani, H. T., & Phelps, M. E. (1986). Maturation changes in cerebral function in infants determined by IGD position emission tomography. *Science*, *231*, 840–843.

Colt, E. W., Wardlaw, S. L., & Frantz, A. G. (1981). The effect of running on plasma beta-endorphin. *Life Sciences*, *28*, 1637–1640.

Deckel, A. W., Moran, T. H., Coyle, J. T., Sanberg, P. R., & Robinson, R. G. (1986). Anatomical predictors of behavioral recovery following fetal striatal transplants. *Brain Research*, *365*, 249–258.

Gash, D. M., Collier, T. J., & Sladek, J. R., Jr. (1985). Neural transplantation: A review of recent developments and potential applications to the aged brain. *Neurobiology of Aging*, *6*, 131–150.

Hoyenga, K. B., & Hoyenga, K. T. (1988). *Psychobiology: The neuron and behavior*. Pacific Grove, CA: Brooks/Cole.

Kalat J. W. (1988). *Biological psychology* (3rd ed.). Belmont, CA: Wadsworth.

Kolb, B., & Whishaw, I. Q. (1990). *Fundamentals of human neuropsychology* (3rd ed.). New York: W. H. Freeman.

Koslowski, M. R., & Marshall, J. F. (1981). Plasticity of neostriatal metabolic activity and behavioral recovery from vibrostriatal injury. *Experimental Neurology*, *74*, 318–321.

Marshall, J. F. (1985). Neural plasticity and recovery of function after brain injury. *International Review of Neurobiology*, *26*, 201–247.

Martini, F. (1989). *Fundamentals of anatomy and physiology*. Englewood Cliffs, NJ: Prentice Hall.

Melzack, R., & Wall, P. D. (1965). Pain mechanisms: A new theory. *Science*, *150*, 971–979.

Merzenich, M. M., Nelson, R. J., Stryker, M. P., Cynader, M. S., Schoppman, A., & Zook, J. M. (1984). Somatosensory cortical map changes following digit amputation in adult monkeys. *Journal of Comparative Neurology*, *224*, 591–605.

Olsen, Y. D., Bruhn, P., & Oberg, R. G. E. (1986). Cortical hyperprofusion as a possible cause of subcortical aphasia. *Brain*, *109*, 393–410.

Penfield, W., & Rasmussen, T. (1950). *The cerebral cortex of man: A clinical study of localization of function*. New York: Macmillan.

Sabel, B. A., Slavin, M. D., & Stein, D. G. (1984). GM1 ganglioside treatment facilitates behavioral recovery from bilateral brain damage. *Science*, *225*, 340–342.

Scherer, S. S. (1986). Reinnervation of the extraocular muscles in goldfish is nonselective. *Journal of Neuroscience*, *6*, 764–773.

Schwab, M. E., & Thoenen, H. (1985). Dissociated neurons regenerate into sciatic but not optic nerve explants in culture irrespective of neurotrophic factors. *Journal of Neuroscience*, 5, 2415–2423.

Shyne-Athwal, S., Riccio, R. V., Chakraborty, G., & In-goflia, N. A. (1986). Protein modification by amino acid addition is increased in crushed sciatic but not optic nerves. *Science, 231*, 603–605.

Sperry, R. (1970). Perception in the absence of neocortical commissures. In *Perception and its disorders* (Res. Publ. A.R.N.M.D., Vol. 48). New York: The Association for Research in Nervous and Mental Disease.

Wallin, B. G., & Fagius, J. (1986). The sympathetic nervous system in man: Aspects derived from microelectrode recordings. *Trends in Neurosciences, 9*, 63–66.

Zigmond, M. J., & Stricker, E. M. (1973). Recovery of feeding and drinking by rats after intraventricular 6-hydroxydopamine or lateral hypothalmic lesions. *Science, 182*, 717–719.

Chapter 3

Adams, J. A. (1967). *Human memory*. New York: McGraw-Hill.

Alkon, D. L. (1983). Learning in a marine snail. *Scientific American, 249*, 70–84.

Allard, F., Graham, S., & Paarsalu, M. E. (1980). Perception in sport: Basketball. *Journal of Sport Psychology, 2*, 22–33.

Atkison, R. C., & Schiffrin, R. M. (1971). The control of short-term memory. *Scientific American, 224*, 82–90.

Atkison, R. C., & Schiffrin, R. M. (1977). Human memory: A proposed system and its control processes. In G. H. Bower (Ed.), *Human memory: Basic processes* (pp. 7–113). New York: Academic Press.

Baddeley, A. D. (1981). The concept of working memory: A view of its current state and probable future development. *Cognition, 10*, 17–23.

Baddeley, A. D., & Hitch, G. (1974). Working memory. In G. H. Bower (Ed.), *The psychology of learning and motivation: Advances in research and theory* (Vol. 8, pp. 47–89). New York: Academic Press.

Barbizet, J. (1970). *Human memory and its pathology*. San Francisco: Freeman.

Bohannon, J. N., III. (1988). Flashbulb memories for the space shuttle disaster: A tale of two theories. *Cognition, 29*, 179–196.

Bower, G. H., Clark, M., Winzenz, D., & Lesgold, A. (1969). Hierarchical retrieval schemes in recall of categorized word lists. *Journal of Verbal Learning and Verbal Behavior, 8*, 323–343.

Brown, R., & Kulik, J. (1977). Flashbulb memories. *Cognition, 5*, 73–99.

Brown, R. W., & McNeill, D. (1966). The "tip-of-the-tongue" phenomenon. *Journal of Verbal Learning and Verbal Behavior, 5*, 325–337.

Chase, W. G., & Simon, H. (1973). Perception in chess. *Cognitive Psychology, 4*, 55–81.

Collins, A. M., & Quillian, M. R. (1969). Retrieval time from semantic memory. *Journal of Verbal Learning and Verbal Behavior, 8*, 240–247.

Conrad, R. (1964). Acoustic confusions in immediate memory. *British Journal of Psychology, 55*, 75–84.

Cooper, W. E. (1983). Introduction. In W. E. Cooper (Ed.), *Cognitive aspects of skilled typewriting* (pp. 1–38). New York: Springer-Verlag.

Craik, F. I. M. (1970). The fate of primary memory items in free recall. *Journal of Verbal Learning and Verbal Behavior, 9*, 143–148.

Craik, F. I. M., & Lockhart, R. S. (1972). Levels of processing: A framework for memory research. *Journal of Verbal Learning and Verbal Behavior, 11*, 671–684.

Deese, J. (1965). *The structure of associations in language and thought*. Baltimore: Johns Hopkins University Press.

Egan, D. E. & Schwartz, B. J. (1979). Chunking in recall of symbolic drawings. *Memory & Cognition, 7*, 149–158.

Engen, T. (1980, May). Why the aroma lingers on. *Psychology Today*, p. 138.

Fendrick, P. (1937). Hierarchical skills in typewriting. *Journal of Educational Psychology, 28*, 609–620.

Gold, P. E., & McGaugh, J. L. (1975). A single-trace, two-process view of memory storage processes. In P. Deutsch & J. A. Deutsch (Eds.), *Short-term memory*. New York: Academic Press.

Gold, P. E., & McGaugh, J. L. (1977). Hormones and memory. In L. H. Miller, C. A. Sandman, & A. J. Kastin (Eds.), *Neuropeptide influences on the brain and behavior*. New York: Raven.

Greenough, W. T. (1984). Structural correlates of information storage in the mammalian brain: A review and hypothesis. *Trends in Neurosciences, 7*, 229–233.

Hoyenga, K. B., & Hoyenga, K. T. (1988). *Psychobiology: The neuron and behavior*. Pacific Grove, CA: Brooks/Cole.

Johnson, P. (1982). The functional equivalence of imagery and movement. *Human Experimental Psychology, 34A*, 349–385.

Keele, S. W., & Ells, J. G. (1972). Memory characteristics of kinesthetic information. *Journal of Motor Behavior, 4*, 127–134.

Kosslyn, S. M., Ball, T. M., & Reiser, B. J. (1978). Visual images preserve spatial information: Evidence from studies of image scanning. *Journal of Experimental Psychology: Human Perception and Performance, 4*, 47–60.

Laabs, G. J. (1973). Retention characteristics of different reproduction cues in short-term memory. *Journal of Experimental Psychology, 100*, 168–177.

Leavitt, J. L., Lee, T. D., & Romanow, S. K. E. (1980). Proactive interference and movement attribute change in motor short-term memory. In C. H. Nadeau, W. R. Halliwell, K. M. Newell, & G. C. Roberts (Eds.), *Psychology of motor behavior and sport—1979* (pp. 585–593). Champaign, IL: Human Kinetics Publishers.

Lee, T. D., & Hirota, T. T. (1980). Encoding specificity principle in motor short-term memory for movement extent. *Journal of Motor Behavior, 12*, 63–67.

Loftus, E. F. (1975). Leading questions and the eyewitness. *Cognitive Psychology, 1*, 560–572.

Loftus, E. F. (1981). *Eyewitness testimony*. Cambridge, MA: Harvard University Press.

Lucariello, G., Toole, T., & Cauraugh, J. (1983). Searching short-term memory for linear positioning movements. *Perceptual and Motor Skills, 57*, 276–274.

Magill, R. A., & Dowell, M. N. (1977). Serial position effects in motor short-term memory. *Journal of Motor Behavior, 9*, 113–118.

Magill, R. A., & Lee T. D. (1987). Verbal label effects on

response accuracy and organization for learning limb positioning movements. *Journal of Human Movement Studies, 13,* 285–308.

Massaro, D. W. (1970). Perceptual auditory images. *Journal of Experimental Psychology, 85,* 411–417.

McCloskey, M., Wible, C. G., & Cohen, N. J. (1988). Is there a special flashbulb-memory mechanism? *Journal of Experimental Psychology: General, 117,* 171–181.

Miller, G. A. (1956). The magical number seven plus or minus two: Some limits on our capacity for processing information. *Psychological Review, 62,* 81–97.

Milner, B. (1970). Memory and the medial temporal regions of the brain. In K. H. Pribram & D. E. Broadbent (Eds.), *Intergroup behavior.* Chicago: University of Chicago Press.

Moray, N. (1959). Attention in dichotic listening. Affective cues and the influence of instructions. *Quarterly Journal of Experimental Psychology, 11,* 56–60.

Neisser, U. (1982). *Memory observed.* San Francisco: Freeman.

Neisser, U. (1986). Remembering Pearl Harbor: Reply to Thompson and Cowan. *Cognition, 23,* 285–286.

Olds, J. (1973). Brain mechanisms of reinforcement learning. In L. D. E. Berlyne & K. B. Madsen (Eds.), *Pleasure, reward, preference: Their nature, determinants, and role in behavior* (pp. 35–63). New York: Academic Press.

Peterson, L. R., & Peterson, M. J. (1959). Short-term retention of individual items. *Journal of Experimental Psychology, 58,* 193–198.

Rasmussen, J., & Rouse, W. B. (Eds.). (1981). *Human detection and diagnosis of system failures.* New York: Plenum Press.

Reeve, T. G., & Proctor, R. W. (1983). An empirical note on the role of verbal labels on motor short-term memory. *Journal of Motor Behavior, 15,* 386–393.

Sachs, J. S. S. (1967). Recognition memory for syntactic and semantic aspects of connected discourse. *Perception and Psychophysics, 2,* 437–442.

Schachter, D. L. (1983). Amnesia observed: Remembering and forgetting in a natural environment. *Journal of Abnormal Psychology, 92,* 236–242.

Schmidt, R. A. (1975). A schema theory of discrete motor skill learning. *Psychological Review, 82,* 225–260.

Schneider, W. (1985). Training high performance skills: Fallacies and guidelines. *Human Factors, 27,* 285–300.

Shaffer, L. H. (1975). Multiple attention in continuous verbal tasks. In P. M. A. Rabbitt & S. Dornic (Eds.), *Attention and performance* (pp. 157–167). London: Academic Press.

Shea, J. B. (1977). Effects of labeling on motor short-term memory. *Journal of Experimental Psychology: Human Learning and Memory, 3,* 92–99.

Singer, R. N. (1984). The learning of athletic skills. *International Journal of Sports Psychology, 15,* 271–282.

Smyth, M. M. (1984). Memory for movements. In M. M. Smyth & A. M. Wing (Eds.), *The psychology of human movement* (pp. 83–117). London: Academic Press.

Smyth, M. M., & Pendleton, L. R. (1989). Working memory for movements. *Quarterly Journal of Experimental Psychology, 41D,* 235–250.

Sperling, G. (1960). The information available in brief visual presentations. *Psychological Monographs, 74* (11, Whole No. 498).

Stelmach, G. E., & Kelso, J. A. S. (1975). Memory trace strength and response biasing in short-term motor memory. *Memory and Cognition, 3,* 58–62.

Sternberg, S. (1966). High-speed scanning in human memory. *Science, 153,* 652–654.

Thompson, C. P., & Cowan, T. (1986). Flashbulb memories: A nicer recollection of a Neisser recollection. *Cognition, 22,* 199–200.

Toole, T., & Lucariello, G. (1984). Attention requirements for recall and recognition. *Perceptual and Motor Skills, 58,* 939–944.

Treisman, A. M. (1960). Contextual cues in selective listening. *Quarterly Journal of Experimental Psychology, 12,* 242–248.

Tulving, E. (1972). Episodic and semantic memory. In E. Tulving & W. Donaldson (Eds.), *Organization of memory.* New York: Academic Press.

Tulving, E., & Pearlstone, Z. (1966). Availability versus accessibility of information in memory for words. *Journal of Verbal Learning and Verbal Behavior, 5,* 381–391.

Wickens, D. D. (1970). Encoding categories of words: An empirical approach to meaning. *Psychological Review, 77,* 1–15.

Wilberg, R. B., & Salmela, J. (1973). Information load and response consistency in sequential short-term motor memory. *Perceptual and Motor Skills, 37,* 23–29.

Zola-Morgan, S., Squire, L. R., & Amarai, D. G. (1986). Human amnesia and the medial temporal region: Enduring memory impairment following a bilateral lesion limited to field CA1 of the hippocampus. *Journal of Neuroscience, 6,* 2950–2967.

Chapter 4

Bjork, R. A., & Richardson-Klavehn, A. (1989). On the puzzling relationship between environmental context and human memory. In Chizuko Izawa (Ed.), *Current issues in cognitive processes.* Hillsdale NJ: Erlbaum.

Donders, F. C. (1969). On the speed of mental proceses. 1868–1869. *Attention and Performance II: Acta Psychologica, 30,* 412–431.

Fitts, P. M. (1964). Perceptual-motor skill learning. In W. Melton (Ed.), *Categories of human learning.* New York: Academic Press.

Gentile, A. M., Higgins, J. R., Miller, E. A., & Rosen, B. M. (1975). The structure of motor tasks. *Mouvement, 7,* 11–28.

Henry, F. M., & Rogers, D. E. (1960). Increased response latency for complicated movements and a "memory drum" theory of neuromotor reaction. *Research Quarterly, 31,* 448–458.

Leonard, J. A. (1959). Tactual choice reactions: I. *Quarterly Journal of Experimental Psychology, 6,* 76–83.

Neisser, U. (1976). *Cognition and reality.* San Francisco: W. H. Freeman.

Marteniuk, R. G. (1976). *Information processing in motor skills.* New York: Holt, Rinehart and Winston.

Poulton, E. C. (1957). On prediction of skilled movement. *Psychological Bulletin, 54,* 467–478.

Pribram, K. H. (1988). *Holonomic brain theory: Cooperativity and reciprocity in processing the configural and cognitive aspects of perception.* Hillsdale NJ: Erlbaum.

Sanders, A. F. (1980). Stage analysis of reaction processes. In G. E. Stelmach & J. Requin (Eds.), *Tutorials in motor behavior* (pp. 331–354). Amsterdam: North-Holland.

Smith, S. M. (1988). Environmental context-dependent memory. In G. M. Davies and D. M. Thompson (Eds.), *Memory in context: Context in memory* (pp. 13–34). New York: Wiley.

Sternberg, S. (1969). The discovery of processing stages: Extensions of Donder's method. In W. G. Koster (Ed.), *Attention and performance II* (pp. 276–315). Amsterdam: North-Holland.

Welford, A. T. (1968). *Fundamentals of skill.* London: Methuen.

Woodworth, R. S., & Schlossberg, H. (1965). *Experimental psychology.* New York: Holt, Rinehart and Winston.

Wright, D. L., & Shea, C. H. (1991). Contextual dependencies in motor skills. *Memory & Cognition, 19,* 361–370.

Chapter 5

Bach-Y-Rita, P. (1982). Sensory substitution in rehabilitation. In L. Illis, M. Sedgewick, & H. Glanville (Eds.), *Rehabilitation of the neurological patient* (pp. 361–383). Oxford: Blackwell Press.

Bach-Y-Rita, P., & Hughes, B. (1985). Tactile vision substitution: Some instrumentation and perceptual considerations. In D. Warren & E. Strelow (Eds.), *Electronic spatial sensing for the blind: Contributions from perception, rehabilitation, and computer vision.* The Hague: Martinus Nijhoff.

Bliss, J. A. (1971). A reading machine with tactile display. In T. D. Sterling, E. A. Bering, S. V. Pollack & H. G. Vaughan (Eds.), *Visual Prosthesis.* New York: Academic Press.

Bruner, J. S., & Koslowski, B. (1972). Visually preadapted constituents of manipulatory action. *Perception, 1,* 1–122.

Castillo, M., & Butterworth, G. (1981). Neonatal localization of a sound in visual space. *Perception, 10,* 331–338.

Craske, B., Crawshaw, M., & Heron, P. (1975). Disturbance of the oculomotor system due to lateral fixation. *Quarterly Journal of Experimental Psychology, 27,* 459–465.

Ebenholtz, S. M. (1976). Additivity of aftereffects of maintained head and eye rotations: An alternative to recalibration. *Perception & Psychophysics, 19,* 113–116.

Ebenholtz, S. M. (1981). Hysteresis effects in the vergence control system: Perceptual implications. In D. F. Fisher, R. A. Monty, & J. W. Senders (Eds.), *Eye movements: Cognition and visual perception* (pp. 83–94). Hillsdale, NJ: Erlbaum.

Foulke, E., & Berla E. P. (1978). Visual impairment and the development of perceptual ability. In R. D. Walk & H. L. Pick, Jr. (Eds.), *Perception and experience* (pp. 213–240). New York: Plenum Press.

Gibson, J. J. (1966). *The senses considered as a perceptual system.* New York: Houghton Mifflin.

Gordon-Salant, S. (1986). Effects of aging on response criteria in speech-recognition tasks. *Journal of Speech and Hearing Research, 29,* 155–162.

Green, D. M., & Swets, J. A. (1966). *Signal detection theory and psychophysics.* New York: Wiley.

Henry, F. M., & Rogers, D. E. (1960). Increased response latency for complicated movements and a "memory drum" theory of neuromotor reaction. *Research Quarterly, 31,* 448–458.

Lee, D. N., & Reddish, P. E. (1981). Plummeting gannets: A paradigm of ecological optics. *Nature, 293,* 293–294.

Leibowitz, H. W., Shiina, K., & Hennessy, R. T. (1972). Oculomotor adjustments and size constancy. *Perception & Psychophysics, 12,* 497–500.

Leonard, J. A. (1959). Tactual choice reactions: I. *Quarterly Journal of Experimental Psychology, 11,* 76–83.

Levy, J. (1973). Autokinesis direction before and after eye turn. *Perception & Psychophysics, 13,* 337–343.

Lipscomb, D. M. (1974). *Noise: The unwanted sounds.* Chicago: Nelson-Hall.

Mowat, F. (1963). *Never cry wolf.* Boston: Little, Brown.

National Research Council. (1986). *Electronic travel aids: New directions for research.* Washington, DC: National Academy Press.

Owens, D. A. (1985). Paper presented at the Zentrum für interdisziplinäre Forschung, Universität Bielefeld, West Germany.

Paap, K. R., & Ebenholtz, S. M. (1976). Perceptual consequences of potentiation in the extraocular muscles: An alternative explanation for adaptation to wedge prisms. *Journal of Experimental Psychology: Human Perception and Performance, 2,* 457–468.

Park. J. N. (1969). Displacement of apparent straight ahead as an aftereffect of deviation of the eyes from normal position. *Perceptual and Motor Skills, 28,* 591–597.

Regan, D. (1986). Visual processing of four kinds of relative motion. *Vision Research, 26,* 127–145.

Rock, I. (1975). *An introduction to perception.* New York: Macmillan.

Schneider, G. E. (1969). Two visual systems. *Science, 163,* 895–902.

Shebilske, W. L. (1977). Visuomotor coordination in visual direction and position constancies. In W. Epstein (Ed.), *Stability and constancy in visual perception: Mechanisms and processes.* New York: Wiley.

Shebilske, W. L. (1984b). Context effects and efferent factors in perception and cognition. In W. Prinz & A. F. Sanders (Eds.), *Cognition and motor processes.* New York: Springer-Verlag.

Shebilske, W. L. (1986). Baseball batters support an ecological efference mediation theory of natural event perception. In D. G. Bouwhuis, B. Bridgeman, D. A. Owens, W. L. Shebilske, & P. Wolff (Eds.), *Sensorimotor interactions in space perception. Acta Psychologica,* Special Volume 63, 117–131.

Shebilske, W. L. (1987). An ecological efference mediation theory of natural event perception. In H. Heuer & A. F. Sanders (Eds.), *Perspectives on perception and action* (pp. 195–213). Hillsdale, NJ: Erlbaum.

Shebilske, W. L., Karmiohl, C. M., & Proffitt, D. R. (1983). Induced esophoric shifts in eye convergence and illusory distance in reduced and structured viewing conditions. *Journal of Experimental Psychology: Human Perception and Performance, 9*, 270–277.

Stevens, S. S., & Galanter, E. H. (1957). Ratio scales and category scales for a dozen perceptual continua. *Journal of Experimental Psychology, 54*, 377–411.

Swets, J. A. (1964). *Signal detection and recognition by human observers*. New York: Wiley.

Trevarthen, C. B. (1968). Two mechanisms of vision in primates. *Psychologische Forschung, 31*, 299–337.

Turvey, M., & Carello, C. (1986). The ecological approach to perceiving-acting: A pictorial essay. *Acta Psychologica, 63*, 133–156.

Wagner, H. (1982). Flowfield variables trigger landing in flies. *Nature, 297*, 147–148.

Wetzel, M. C., & Stuart, D. G. (1976). Ensemble characteristics of cat locomotion and its neural control. *Progress in Neurobiology, 7*, 1–98.

Woodworth, R. S., & Schlossberg, H. (1954). *Experimental psychology* (2nd ed.). New York: Holt, Rinehart & Winston.

Chapter 6

Craik, K. W. J. (1947). Theory of the human operator in control systems. I: The operator as an engineering system. *British Journal of Psychology, 38*, 56–61.

Creamer, L. R. (1963). Event uncertainty, psychological refractory period, and human data processing. *Journal of Experimental Psychology, 66*, 187–194.

Drazin, P. H. (1961). Effects of foreperiod, foreperiod variability, and probability of stimulus occurrence on simple reaction time. *Journal of Experimental Psychology, 62*, 43–45.

Eithorn, A., & Lawrence, C. (1955). Central inhibition: Some refractory observations. *Quarterly Journal of Experimental Psychology, 7*, 116–127.

Fitts, P. M., & Posner, M. I. (1967). *Human performance*. Belmont, CA: Brooks/Cole.

Greenwald, A. G. (1970). Sensory feedback mechanisms in performance control: With special reference to the ideo-motor mechanism. *Psychological Review, 77*, 73–79.

Haier, R. J., Siegal, B. V., MacLachlan, A., Soderling, E., Lottenberg, S., & Buchsbaum, M. S. (1992). Regional glucose metabolic changes after learning a complex visuospatial/motor task: A positron emission tomographic study. *Brain Research, 570*, 134–143.

Hick, W. E. (1952). On the rate of gain of information. *Quarterly Journal of Experimental Psychology, 84*, 11–26.

Hymen, R. (1953). Stimulus information as a determiner of reaction time. *Journal of Experimental Psychology, 45*, 188–196.

Karlin, L., & Kestenbaum, R. (1968). Effects of number of alternatives on the psychological refractory period. *Quarterly Journal of Experimental Psychology, 20*, 167–178.

Klemmer, E. T. (1956). Time uncertainty in simple reaction time. *Journal of Experimental Psychology, 51*, 179–184.

Klemmer, E. T. (1957). Simple reaction time as a function of time uncertainty. *Journal of Experimental Psychology, 54*, 195–200.

Loveless, N. E. (1963). Direction of motion stereotypes: A review. *Ergonomics, 5*, 357–383.

Miller, J. (1982). Discrete versus continuous stage models of human information processing: In search of partial output. *Journal of Experimental Psychology: Human Perception and Performance, 8*, 273–296.

Mowbry, G. H., & Rhoades, M. V. (1959). On the reduction of choice reaction times with practice. *Quarterly Journal of Experimental Psychology, 11*, 193–202.

Mowrer, O. H. (1940). Preparatory set (expectancy): Some methods of measurement. *Psychological Monographs, 52* (233).

Quesada, D. C., & Schmidt, R. A. (1970). A test of Adams-Creamer decay hypothesis for the timing of motor responses. *Journal of Motor Behavior, 2*, 273–283.

Payne, J. W. (1976). Task complexity and contingent processing in decision making: An information search and protocol analysis. *Organizational Behavior and Human Performance, 16*, 366–387.

Reeve, T. G., & Proctor, R. W. (1984). On the advance preparation of discrete finger responses. *Journal of Experimental Psychology: Human Perception and Performance, 10*, 541–553.

Reeve, T. G., & Proctor, R. W. (1985). Nonmotoric translation processes in the preparation of discrete finger responses: A rebuttal of Miller's (1985) analysis. *Journal of Experimental Psychology: Human Perception and Performance, 11*, 234–241.

Reynolds, D. (1966). Time and event uncertainty in unisensory reaction time. *Journal of Experimental Psychology, 71*, 286–293.

Rosenbaum, D. A. (1980). Human movement initiation: Specification of arm, direction, and extent. *Journal of Experimental Psychology: General, 109*, 444–474.

Telford, C. W. (1931). The refractory phase of voluntary and associative responses. *Journal of Experimental Psychology, 14*, 1–36.

Tversky, A. (1977). Features of similarity. *Psychological Review, 84*, 327–352.

Vickers, D. (1970). Evidence for an accumulator model of psychophysical discrimination. *Ergonomics, 13*, 37–58.

Wickens, C. D. (1984). *Engineering psychology and human performance*. Columbus, OH: Charles E. Merrill.

Woodworth, R. S. (1938). *Experimental Psychology*. New York: Holt, Rinehart and Winston.

Chapter 7

Adams, J. A. (1971). A closed-loop theory of motor learning. *Journal of Motor Behavior, 3*, 111–150.

Adams, J. A. (1976). Issues for a closed-loop theory of motor learning. In G. E. Stelmach (Ed.), *Motor control: Issues and trends* (pp. 87–107). New York: Academic Press.

Bernstein, N. (1967). *The coordination and regulation of movements*. Oxford: Pergamon Press. (Original work published 1940.)

Bizzi, E., & Mussa-Ivaldi, F. A. (1989). Geometrical and mechanical issues in movement planning and control. In M. I. Posner (Ed.), *Foundations of cognitive science* (pp. 769–792). Cambridge, MA: MIT Press.

Byers, R. K. (1938). Tonic neck reflexes in children, considered from a prognostic standpoint. *American Journal of Disabled Children, 55*, 696.

Carlton, L. G. (1981). Processing visual feedback information for movement control. *Journal of Experimental Psychology: Human Perception and Performance*, 7, 1019–1030.

Chernikoff, R., & Taylor, F. V. (1952). Reaction time to kinesthetic stimulation resulting from sudden arm displacement. *Journal of Experimental Psychology*, 43, 1–8.

Dahlback, L. O., Edstedt, J., & Stalberg, E. (1970). Ischemic effect on impulse transmission to muscle fibers in man. *Electroencephalography and Clinical Neurophysiology*, 29, 579–591.

Easton, T. A. (1972). On the normal use of reflexes. *American Scientist*, 60, 591–599.

Easton, T. A. (1978). Coordinative structures—The basis for a motor program. In D. M. Landers & R. W. Cristina (Eds.), *Psychology of motor behavior and sport* (pp. 63–81). Champaign, IL: Human Kinetics.

Fukuda, T. (1961). Studies on human dynamic postures from the viewpoint of postural reflexes. *Acta Oto-Laryngologica*, 161, 1–52.

Gesell, A. (1952). *Infant development: The embryology of early human behavior*. New York: Harper & Row.

Hellebrandt, F. A., Houtz, S. J., Partridge, M. J., & Walters, C. E. (1956). Tonic reflexes in exercises of stress in man. *American Journal of Physical Medicine*, 35, 144–159.

Henry, F. M., & Rogers, D. E. (1960). Increased response latency for complicated movements and a "memory drum" theory of neuromotor reaction. *Research Quarterly*, 31, 448–458.

Hutton, R. S., Enoka, R. M., & Suzuki, S. (1984). Activation history and constant errors in human force production. *Brain Research*, 307, 344–346.

James, W. (1890). *The principles of psychology* (vol. 1). New York: Holt, Rinehart and Winston.

Keele, S. W. (1968). Movement control in skilled performance. *Psychological Bulletin*, 70, 387–403.

Keele, S. W., & Posner, M. I. (1968a). Processing of feedback in rapid movements. *Journal of Experimental Psychology*, 77, 353–363.

Keele, S. W., & Posner, M. I. (1968b). Processing of visual feedback in rapid movements. *Journal of Experimental Psychology*, 77, 155–158.

Kelso, J. A. S., Putnam, C. A., & Goodman, D. (1983). On the space-time structure of human interlimb coordination. *Quarterly Journal of Experimental Psychology*, 35A, 347–375.

Kelso, J. A. S., Southard, D. L., & Goodman, D. (1979). On the nature of human interlimb coordination. *Science*, 203, 1029–1031.

Klapp, S. T. (1980). The memory drum theory after twenty years: Comments on Henry's note. *Journal of Motor Behavior*, 12, 169–171.

Kohl, R. M., & Shea, C. H. (1992). Pew (1966) revisited: Acquisition of hierarchical control as a function of observational practice. *Journal of Motor Behavior*, 24, 32–48.

Kohnstamm, O. (1915). Demonstration einer katatonieartigen Erscheinung beim Gesunder [Demonstration of a catatonic-like phenomenon in normal subjects]. *Neurologisches Centralblatt*, 34, 290–291.

Konzem, Y. M. (1987). *Extended practice and patterns of bimanual interference*. Unpublished doctoral dissertation, University of Southern California.

Kugler, P. N., Kelso, J. A. S., & Turvey, M. T. (1982). On coordination and control in naturally developing systems. In J. A. S. Kelso & J. E. Clark (Eds.), *The development of movement control and coordination* (pp. 5–78). New York: Wiley.

Lashley, K. S. (1917). The accuracy of movement in the absence of excitation from the moving organ. *American Journal of Physiology*, 43, 169–194.

Laszlo, J. I. (1967). Training of fast tapping with reduction of kinaesthetic, tactile, visual, and auditory sensations. *Quarterly Journal of Experimental Psychology*, 19, 344–349.

Laszlo, J. I., & Bairstow, P. J. (1971). The compression block technique: A note on procedure. *Journal of Motor Behavior*, 3, 313–317.

MacNeilage, P. F., & MacNeilage, L. A. (1973). Central processes controlling speech production during sleep and waking. In F. J. McGuigan & R. A. Schoonover (Eds.), *The psychophysiology of thinking: Studies of covert processes* (pp. 417–448). New York: Academic Press.

Magnus, R., & de Kliejn, A. (1912). The adherence of the tonus of muscles to the extremities with head position. *Pluegers Archives of Physiology*, 145, 455–458.

Marsden, C. D., Rothwell, J. C., & Dell, B. L. (1984). Long-latency automatic responses to muscle stretch in man: Origin and function. In J. E. Desmdt (Ed.), *Advances in Neurology*, 39, 509–539.

Martiniuk, R. G. (1976). *Information processing in motor skills*. New York: Holt, Rinehart and Winston.

McMahon, T. A. (1984). *Muscles, reflexes, and locomotion*. Princeton, NJ: Princeton University Press.

Merton, P. A. (1972). How we control the contraction of our muscles. *Scientific American*, 226, 30–37.

Nottebohm, F. (1970). The ontogeny of bird song. *Science*, 167, 950–956.

Pew, R. W. (1966). Acquisition of hierarchical control over the temporal organization of a skill. *Journal of Experimental Psychology*, 71, 764–771.

Posner, M. I., & Keele, S. W. (1969). Attentional demands of movement. *Proceedings of the 16th Congress of Applied Psychology*. Amsterdam: Swets and Zeitlinger.

Raibert, M. H., & Sutherland, I. E. (1983). Machines that walk. *Scientific American*, 248, 44–53.

Ralston, H. J., Inman, V. T., Strait, L. A., & Shaffrath, M. D. (1947). Mechanics of human isolated voluntary muscle. *American Journal of Physiology*, 151, 612–620.

Rosenbaum, D. A. (1990). *Human motor control*. New York: Academic Press.

Salmon, A. (1916). On an interesting phenomenon of automaticity observed after muscular effort in healthy subjects. *Revue Neurologique*, 29, 27–34.

Schmidt, R. A. (1975). A schema theory of discrete motor skill learning. *Psychological Review*, 82, 225–260.

Schmidt, R. A. (1976). Control processes in motor skills. *Exercise and Sport Sciences Reviews*, 4, 229–261.

Shea, C. H., Guadagnoli, M. A., & Dean, M. (1990). Response biases: Tonic neck response and after contraction phenomenon. Paper presented at the North American Society for the Psychology of Sport and Physical Activity.

Shea, C. H., Shebilske, W. L., Kohl, R. M., & Guadagnoli, M. A. (1991). After-contraction phenomenon: Influences on performance and learning. *Journal of Motor Behavior, 23,* 51–62.

Shik, M. L., Orlovskii, G. N., & Severin, F. V. (1968). Locomotion of the mesencephalic cat elicited by stimulation of the pyramids. *Biofizika, 13,* 143–152.

Slater-Hammel, A. T. (1960). Reliability, accuracy, and refractoriness of a transit reaction. *Research Quarterly, 31,* 217–228.

Smith, J. L. (1978). Sensorimotor integrations during motor programming. In G. E. Stelmach (Ed.), *Information processing in motor control and learning* (pp. 95–115). New York: Academic Press.

Stein, R. B. (1982). What muscle variable(s) does the nervous system control in limb movements? *The Behavioral and Brain Sciences, 5,* 535–577.

Taub, E., & Berman, A. J. (1968). Movement and learning in the absence of sensory feedback. In S. J. Freeman (Ed.), *The neuropsychology of spatially oriented behavior* (pp. 173–192). Homewood, IL: Dorsey.

Thelen, M. J., Kelso, J. A. S., & Fogel, A. (1987). Self-organizing systems and infant motor development. *Developmental Review, 7,* 39–65.

Tuller, B., Turvey, M. T., & Fitch, H. (1982). The Bernstein perspective: II. The concept of muscle linkages or coordinative structures. In J. A. S. Kelso (Ed.), *Human motor behavior: An introduction* (pp. 253–270). Hillsdale, NJ: Erlbaum.

Turvey, M. T. (1977). Preliminaries to a theory of action with reference to vision. In R. Shaw & J. Bransford (Eds.), *Perceiving, acting, and knowing* (pp. 211–266). Hillsdale, NJ: Erlbaum.

Weeks, D. L., & Shea, C. H. (1984). Assimilation effects in coincident timing responses. *Research Quarterly for Exercise and Sport, 55,* 89–92.

Wilson, D. M. (1961). The central nervous control of flight in locusts. *Journal of Experimental Biology, 38,* 471–490.

Winter, D. A. (1990). *Biomechanics and motor control of human movement.* New York: Wiley.

Zelaznik, H. N., Hawkins, B., & Kisselburgh, L. (1983). Rapid visual feedback processing in single-aiming movements. *Journal of Motor Behavior, 17,* 217–236.

Chapter 8

Adams, J. A. (1971). A closed-loop theory of motor learning. *Journal of Motor Behavior, 3,* 111–150.

Adams, J. A. (1976). Issues for a closed-loop theory of motor learning. In G. E. Stelmach (Ed.), *Motor control: Issues and trends* (pp. 87–107). New York: Academic Press.

Bernstein, N. (1967). *The co-ordination and regulation of movements.* Oxford: Pergamon Press.

Chizeck, H. J. (1985). Helping paraplegics walk: Looking beyond the media blitz. *Technology Review, 88,* 55–59.

Easton, T. A. (1972). On the normal use of reflexes. *American Scientist, 60,* 591–599.

Feldman, A. G. (1966a). Functional tuning of the nervous system with control of movement or maintenance of a steady posture: II. Controllable parameters of the muscles. *Biophysics, 11,* 565–578.

Feldman, A. G. (1966b). Functional tuning of the nervous system with control of movement or maintenance of a steady posture: III. Mechanographic analysis of the execution by man of the simplest motor tasks. *Biophysics, 11,* 667–675.

Feldman, A. G. (1986). Once more on the equilibrium point hypothesis (model) for motor control. *Journal of Motor Behavior, 18,* 17–54.

Hollerbach, J. M. (1978). A study of human motor control through analysis and synthesis of handwriting. Unpublished doctoral dissertation, Massachusetts Institute of Technology, Cambridge.

Keele, S. W. (1986). Motor control. In K. R. Boff, L. Kaufman, & J. P. Thomas (Eds.), *Handbook of perception and human performance* (pp. 30.1–30.60). New York: Wiley.

Kelso, J. A. S., Putnam, C. A., & Goodman, D. (1983). On the space-time structure of human interlimb coordination. *Quarterly Journal of Experimental Psychology, 35A,* 347–375.

Kelso, J. A. S., Southard, D. L., & Goodman, D. (1979). On the nature of human interlimb coordination. *Science, 203,* 1029–1031.

Konzem, Y. M. (1987). *Extended practice and patterns of bimanual interference.* Unpublished doctoral dissertation, University of Southern California.

Kugler, P. N., Kelso, J. A. S., & Turvey, M. T. (1982). On coordination and control in naturally developing systems. In J. A. S. Kelso & J. E. Clark (Eds.), *The development of movement control and coordination* (pp. 5–78). New York: Wiley.

Mays, L. E., & Sparks, D. L. (1980). Saccades are spatially, not retinocentrically coded. *Science, 208,* 1163–1165.

Merton, P. A. (1972). How we control the contraction of our muscles. *Scientific American, 226,* 30–37.

Nickerson, R. S., Kalikow, D. N., & Stevens, K. N. (1976). Computer-aided speech training for the deaf. *Journal of Speech and Hearing Disorders, 41,* 120–132.

Polit, A., & Bizzi, E. (1978). Processes controlling arm movements in monkeys. *Science, 201,* 1235–1237.

Polit, A., & Bizzi, E. (1979). Characteristics of motor programs underlying arm movements in monkeys. *Journal of Neurophysiology, 42,* 183–194.

Rack, P. M. H., & Westbury, D. R. (1969). The effects of length and stimulus rate on tension in the isometric cat soleus muscle. *Journal of Physiology, 204,* 443–460.

Raibert, M. H. (1977). *Motor control and learning by the state-space model* (Tech. Rep. No. AI-TR-439). Cambridge: Massachusetts Institute of Technology, Artificial Intelligence Laboratory.

Rosen, M. J. (1985). The Nan Davis story: A trail of false hopes. *Technology Review, 88,* 60–61.

Rosenbaum, D. A. (1990). *Human motor control.* New York: Academic Press.

Schmidt, R. A. (1975). A schema theory of discrete motor skill learning. *Psychological Review, 82,* 225–260.

Schmidt, R. A. (1980). Past and future issues in motor programming. *Research Quarterly for Exercise and Sport, 51,* 122–140.

Schmidt, R. A. (1985). The search for invariances in skilled movement behavior. *Research Quarterly for Exercise and Sport*, 56, 188–200.

Schmidt, R. A., & McGown, C. M. (1980). Terminal accuracy of unexpectedly loaded rapid movements: Evidence for mass-spring mechanism in programming. *Journal of Motor Behavior*, 12, 149–161.

Shea, C. H., Krampitz, J. B., Tolson, H., Ashby, A. A., Howard, R. M., & Husak, W. S. (1981). Stimulus velocity, duration, and uncertainty as determiners of response structure and timing accuracy. *Research Quarterly for Exercise and Sport*, 52 (1), 86–99.

Chapter 9

Card, S. K., English, W. K., & Burr, B. (1978). Evaluation of mouse, rate controlled isometric joystick, step keys, and text keys for text selection on a CRT. *Ergonomics*, 21, 601–613.

Crossman, E. R. F. W., & Goodeve, P. J. (1983). Feedback control of hand movements and Fitts' Law. *Quarterly Journal of Experimental Psychology*, 35A, 251–278. (Original work published 1963.)

Fitts, P. M. (1954). The information capacity of the human motor system in controlling the amplitude of movement. *Journal of Experimental Psychology*, 47, 381–391.

Fitts, P. M., & Peterson, J. R. (1964). Information capacity of discrete motor responses. *Journal of Experimental Psychology*, 67, 103–112.

Hubbard, A. W., & Seng, C. N. (1954). Visual movements of batters. *Research Quarterly*, 25, 42–57.

Jagacinski, R. J., Repperger, D. W., Moran, M. S., Ward, S. L., & Glass, B. (1980). Fitts' Law and the microstructure of rapid discrete movements. *Journal of Experimental Psychology: Human Perception and Performance*, 6, 309–320.

Keele, S. W. (1986). Motor control. In K. R. Boff, L. Kaufman, & J. P. Thomas (Eds.). *Handbook of perception and human performance* (pp. 30.1–30.60) New York: John Wiley.

Kerr, B. A., & Langolf, G. D. (1977). Speed of aiming movements. *Quarterly Journal of Experimental Psychology*, 29, 475–481.

Kerr, R. (1973). Movement time in an underwater environment. *Journal of Motor Behavior*, 5, 175–178.

Langolf, G. D., Chaffin, D. B., & Foulke, J. A. (1976). An investigation of Fitts' law using a wide range of movement amplitudes. *Journal of Motor Behavior*, 8, 113–128.

McGovern, D. E. (1974). *Factors affecting control allocation for augmented remote manipulation*. Unpublished Doctoral Dissertation, Stanford University.

Meyer, D. E., Smith, J. E. K., & Wright, C. E. (1982). Models for speed and accuracy of aimed movements. *Psychological Review*, 89, 449–482.

Newell, K. M. (1980). The speed-accuracy paradox in movement control: Error of time and space. In G. E. Stelmach (Ed.), *Tutorials in motor behavior* (pp. 501–510). Amsterdam: North Holland.

Newell, K. M., Carlton, L. G., Carlton, M. J., & Halbert, J. A. (1980). Velocity as a factor in movement timing accuracy. *Journal of Motor Behavior*, 12, 47–56.

Newell, K. M., Hoshizaki, L. E. F., Carlton, M. J., & Hal-

bert, J. A. (1979). Movement time and velocity as determiners of movement timing accuracy. *Journal of Motor Behavior*, 11, 49–58.

Poulton, E. C. (1957). On prediction in skilled movements. *Psychological Bulletin*, 54, 467–478.

Schmidt, R. A. (1975). A schema theory of discrete motor skill learning. *Psychological Review*, 82, 225–260.

Schmidt, R. A., Zelaznik, H. N., & Frank, J. S. (1978). Sources of inaccuracy in rapid movement. In G. E. Stelmach (Ed.), *Information processing in motor learning and control* (pp. 183–203). New York: Academic Press.

Schmidt, R. A., Zelaznik, H. N., Hawkins, B., Frank, J. S., & Quinn, J. T. (1979). Motor-output variability: A theory for the accuracy of rapid motor acts. *Psychological Review*, 86, 415–451.

Shea, C. H., Krampitz, J. B., Tolson, H., Ashby, A. A., Howard, R. M., & Husak, W. S. (1981). Stimulus velocity, duration, and uncertainty as determiners of response structure and timing accuracy. *Research Quarterly for Exercise and Sport*, 52, 86–99.

Sherwood, D. E., & Schmidt, R. A. (1980). The relationship between force and force variability in minimal and near-maximal static and dynamic contractions. *Journal of Motor Behavior*, 12, 75–89.

Woodworth, R. S. (1899). The accuracy of voluntary movement. *Psychological Review*, 3 (Suppl. 2.).

Wrisberg, C. A., Hardy, C. J., & Beitel, P. A. (1982). Stimulus velocity and movement distance as determiners of movement velocity and coincident timing accuracy. *Human Factors*, 24, 599–608.

Chapter 10

Adams, J. A. (1971). A closed-loop theory of motor learning. *Journal of Motor Behavior*, 3, 111–150.

Adams, J. A. (1978). Theoretical issues for knowledge of results. In G. E. Stelmach (Ed.), *Information processing in motor control and learning* (pp. 229–240). New York: Academic Press.

Adams, J. A. (1987). Historical review and appraisal of research on the learning, retention, and transfer of human motor skills. *Psychological Bulletin*, 101, 41–74.

Annett, J. (1959). Learning a pressure under conditions of immediate and delayed knowledge of results. *Quarterly Journal of Experimental Psychology*, 11, 3–15.

Benedetti, C., & McCullagh, P. (1987). Post-knowledge of results delay: Effect of interpolated activity on learning and performance. *Research Quarterly for Exercise and Sport*, 58, 375–381.

Bennett, D. M., & Simmons, R. W. (1984). Effect of precision of knowledge of results on acquisition and retention of a simple motor skill. *Perceptual and Motor Skills*, 58, 785–786.

Bilodeau, I. M. (1956). Accuracy of a simple positioning response with variation in the number of trials by which KR is delayed. *American Journal of Psychology*, 69, 434–437.

Bilodeau, I. M. (1966). Information feedback. In E. A. Bilodeau (Ed.), *The acquisition of skill* (pp. 255–296). New York: Academic Press.

Bilodeau, I. M. (1969). Information feedback. In E. A.

Bilodeau (Ed.), *Principles of skill acquisition*, (pp. 255–296). New York: Academic Press.

Bilodeau, E. A., & Bilodeau, I. M. (1958). Variable frequency knowledge of results and the learning of a simple skill. *Journal of Experimental Psychology, 55*, 379–383.

Bilodeau, E. A., Bilodeau, I. M., & Schumsky, D. A. (1959). Some effects of introducing and withdrawing knowledge of results early and late in practice. *Journal of Experimental Psychology, 58*, 142–144.

Blick, K. A., & Bilodeau, E. A. (1963). Interpolated activity and the learning of a simple skill. *Journal of Experimental Psychology, 65*, 515–519.

Dees, V., & Grindley, G. C. (1951). The effect of knowledge of results on learning and performance: IV. The direction of errors in very simple skills. *Quarterly Journal of Experimental Psychology, 3*, 36–42.

Gable, C., Shea, C. H., & Wright, D. L. (1991). Summary knowledge of results. *Research Quarterly for Exercise and Sport, 62*(3), 285–292.

Hamilton, E. L. (1929). The effect of delayed incentives on the hunger drive of the white rat. *Genetic Psychology Monographs, 5*, 131–207.

Ho, L., & Shea, J. B. (1978). Effects of relative frequency of knowledge of results on retention of a motor skill. *Perceptual and Motor Skills, 46*, 859–866.

Johnson, R. W., Wicks, G. C., & Ben-Sira, D. (1981). *Practice in the absence of knowledge of results: Acquisition and transfer.* Unpublished manuscript, University of Minnesota.

Lavery, J. J. (1962). Retention of simple motor skills as a function of type of knowledge of results. *Canadian Journal of Psychology, 16*, 300–311.

Lavery, J. J. (1964). The effect of one-trial delay in knowledge of results. *American Journal of Psychology, 77*, 437–443.

Lavery, J. J., & Suddon, F. H. (1962). Retention of simple motor skills as a function of the number of trials by which KR is delayed. *Perceptual and Motor Skills, 15*, 231–237.

Lee, T. D., & Carnahan, H. (1990). When to provide knowledge of results during motor learning: Scheduling effects. *Human Performance, 3*(2), 87–105.

Lee, T. D., & Carnahan, H. (1990). Bandwidth knowledge of results and motor learning: More than just a relative frequency effect. *Quarterly Journal of Experimental Psychology, 42*, 777–789.

Lee, T. D., & Magill, R. A. (1983). Activity during the post-KR interval: Effects on performance or learning. *Research Quarterly for Exercise and Sport, 54*, 340–345.

Lindahl, L. G. (1945). Movement analysis as an industrial training method. *Journal of Applied Psychology, 29*, 420–436.

Lorge, I., & Thorndike, E. L. (1935). The influence of delay in the after-effect of a connection. *Journal of Experimental Psychology, 56*, 186–194.

Magill, R. A. (1973). The post-KR interval: Time and activity effects and the relationship to motor short-term memory theory. *Journal of Motor Behavior, 5*, 49–56.

Magill, R. A. (1977). The processing of knowledge of results for a serial motor task. *Journal of Motor Behavior, 9*, 113–119.

Magill, R. A., & Wood, C. A. (1986). Knowledge of results precision as a learning variable in motor skill acquisition. *Research Quarterly for Exercise and Sport, 57*, 170–173.

Magill, R. A. (1988). Activity during the post-knowledge of results interval can benefit motor skill learning. In O. G. Meijer & K. Roth (Eds.), *Complex motor behavior: The 'motor action' controversy* (pp. 231–246). Amsterdam: Elsevier.

Marteniuk, R. G. (1986). Information processes in movement learning: Capacity and structural interference. *Journal of Motor Behavior, 5*, 249–259.

McGuigan, F. J. (1959a). Delay of knowledge of results: A problem in design. *Psychological Reports, 5*, 241–243.

McGuigan, F. J. (1959b). The effect of precision, delay, and scheduling of knowledge of results. *Journal of Experimental Psychology, 58*, 79–80.

McGuigan, F. J., Crockett, F., & Bolton, C. (1960). The effect of knowledge of results before and after a response. *Journal of General Psychology, 63*, 51–55.

Miller, R. B. (1953). *Handbook on Training and Training Equipment Design* (pp. 53–136). U.S.A.F., Wright Air Development Center Technical Report. Dayton, OH: USAF.

Newell, K. M. (1974). Knowledge of results and motor learning. *Journal of Motor Behavior, 6*, 235–244.

Newell, K. M. (1977). Knowledge of results and motor learning. *Exercise and Sport Science Reviews, 4*, 195–228.

Newell, K. M., & Carlton, M. E. (1987). Augmented information and the acquisition of isometric tasks. *Journal of Motor Behavior, 19*, 4–12.

Newell, K. M., Quinn, J. T., Jr., Sparrow, W. A., & Walter, C. B. (1983). Kinematic information feedback for learning a rapid arm movement. *Human Movement Science, 2*, 255–269.

Nicholson, D. E., & Schmidt, R. A. (1990). *Scheduling information feedback: Gradually increasing the frequency of knowledge of results across practice degrades skill learning.* Paper presented at the annual meeting of the North American Society for the Psychology of Sport and Physical Activity. Houston, TX.

Reeve, T. G., Dornier, L. A., & Weeks, D. J. (1990). Precision of knowledge of results: Consideration of the accuracy requirements imposed by the task. *Research Quarterly for Exercise and Sport, 61*, 284–290.

Roberts, W. H. (1930). The effect of delayed feeding on white rats in a problem cage. *Journal of Genetic Psychology, 37*, 35–38.

Rogers, C. A. (1974). Feedback precision and post feedback interval duration. *Journal of Experimental Psychology, 102*, 604–608.

Salmoni, A. W., Schmidt, R. A., & Walter, C. B. (1984). Knowledge of results and motor learning: A review and critical reappraisal. *Psychological Bulletin, 95*(3), 355–386.

Schmidt, R. A. (1975). A schema theory of discrete motor skill learning. *Psychological Review, 82*, 225–260.

Schmidt, R. A., Lange, C., & Young, D. E. (1990). Optimizing summary knowledge of results for skill learning. *Human Movement Science, 9*, 325–348.

Schmidt, R. A., Young, D. E., Swinnen, S., & Shapiro, D. C. (1989). Summary knowledge of results for skill acquisition: Support for the guidance hypothesis. *Journal of Experimental Psychology: Learning, Memory, and Cognition, 15*(2), 352–359.

Shea, J. B., & Upton, G. (1976). The effects of skill acquisition of an interpolated motor short-term memory task during the KR-delay interval. *Journal of Motor Behavior, 8,* 277–281.

Sherwood, D. E. (1988). Effect of bandwidth knowledge of results on movement consistency. *Perceptual and Motor Skills, 66,* 535–542.

Smoll, F. L. (1972). Effects of precision of information feedback upon acquisition of a motor skill. *Research Quarterly, 43,* 489–493.

Swinnen, S. P., Schmidt, R. A., Nicholson, D. E., & Shapiro, D. C. (1990). Information feedback for skill acquisition: Instantaneous knowledge of results degrades learning. *Journal of Experimental Psychology: Learning, Memory, and Cognition, 16,* 706–716.

Thorndike, E. L. (1927). The law of effect. *American Journal of Psychology, 39,* 212–222.

Trowbridge, M. H., & Cason, H. (1932). An experimental study of Thorndike's theory of learning. *Journal of General Psychology, 7,* 245–258.

Winstein, C. J., & Schmidt, R. A. (1990). Reduced frequency of knowledge of results enhances motor skill learning. *Journal of Experimental Psychology: Learning, Memory, and Cognition, 16,* 677–691.

Chapter 11

Adams, J. A. (1971). A closed-loop theory of motor learning. *Journal of Motor Behavior, 3,* 111–150.

Adams, J. A. (1976). Issues for closed-loop theory of motor learning. In G. E. Stelmach (Ed.), *Motor control: Issues and trends* (pp. 87–107). New York: Academic Press.

Adams, J. A. (1986). Use of the model's knowledge of results to increase the observer's performance. *Journal of Human Movement Studies, 12,* 89–92.

Adams, J. A. (1987). Historical review and appraisal of research on the learning, retention, and transfer of human motor skills. *Psychological Bulletin, 101,* 41–74.

Adams, J. A., & Reynolds, B. (1954). Effect of shift in distribution of practice conditions following interpolated rest. *Journal of Experimental Psychology, 47,* 32–36.

Bachman, J. C. (1961). Specificity vs. generality in learning and performing two large muscle tasks. *Research Quarterly, 37,* 176–186.

Baddeley, A. D., & Longman, D. J. A. (1978). The influence of length and frequency of training session on the rate of learning to type. *Ergonomics, 21,* 627–635.

Bandura, A. (1969). *Principles of Behaviour Modification.* New York: Holt, Rinehart and Winston.

Bandura, A. (1977). Self-efficacy: Toward a unifying theory of behavioral change. *Psychological Review, 84,* 191–215.

Barnett, M. L., Ross, D., Schmidt, R. A., & Todd, B. (1973). Motor skill learning and the specificity of training principle. *Research Quarterly, 44,* 440–447.

Battig, W. F. (1979). The flexibility of human memory. In L. S. Cermak & F. I. M. Craik (Eds.), *Levels of processing in human memory* (pp. 23–44). Hillsdale, NJ: Erlbaum.

Bourne, L. E., & Archer, E. J. (1956). Time continuously on target as a function of distribution of practice. *Journal of Experimental Psychology, 51,* 25–32.

Briggs, G. E., & Waters, L. K. (1958). Training and transfer as a function of component interaction. *Journal of Experimental Psychology, 56,* 492–500.

Carroll, W. R., & Bandura, A. (1982). The role of visual monitoring in observational learning of action patterns: Making the unobservable observable. *Journal of Motor Behavior, 14,* 153–167.

Carroll, W. R., & Bandura, A. (1985). Role of timing of visual monitoring and motor rehearsal in observational learning of action patterns. *Journal of Motor Behavior, 17,* 269–281.

Carroll, W. R., & Bandura, A. (1987). Translating cognition into action: The role of visual guidance in observational learning. *Journal of Motor Behavior, 19,* 385–398.

Carson, A. V. (1969). Performance and learning in a discrete motor task under massed vs. distributed practice. *Research Quarterly, 40,* 481–489.

Carson, L. M., & Wiegand, R. L. (1979). Motor schema formation and retention in young children: A test of Schmidt's schema theory. *Journal of Motor Behavior, 11,* 247–251.

Catalano, J. F., & Kleiner, B. M. (1984). Distance transfer and practice variability. *Perceptual and Motor Skills, 58,* 851–856.

Chamberlin, C. J., & Lee, T. D. (1992). Arranging practice conditions and designing instruction. In R. N. Singer, M. Murphey, & L. K. Tennant (Eds.), *Handbook on research in sport psychology.* New York: Macmillan.

Corbin, C. (1972). Mental practice. In W. P. Morgan (Ed.), *Ergogenic aids and muscular performance* (pp. 93–118). New York: Academic Press.

Cuddy, L. J., & Jacoby, L. L. (1982). When forgetting helps memory; An analysis of repetition effects. *Journal of Verbal Learning and Verbal Behavior, 21,* 451–467.

DelRey, P., Wughalter, E. H., & Whitehurst, M. (1982). The effects of contextual interference on females with varied experience in open sports skills. *Research Quarterly for Exercise and Sport, 53,* 108–115.

Denny, M. R., Frisbey, N., & Weaver, J., Jr. (1955). Rotary pursuit performance under alternative conditions of distributed and massed practice. *Journal of Experimental Psychology, 49,* 48–54.

Ebbinghaus, H. (1964). *Memory: A contribution to experimental psychology.* New York: Dover. (Original work published 1885.)

Feltz, D., & Landers, D. M. (1983). The effects of mental practice on motor skill learning and performance: A meta-analysis. *Journal of Sports Psychology, 5,* 25–57.

Fitts, P. M. (1964). Perceptual-motor skills learning. In A. W. Melton (Ed.), *Categories of learning.* New York: Academic Press.

Fitts, P. M., & Posner, M. I. (1967). *Human performance.* Belmont, CA: Brooks/Cole.

Frederiksen, J. R., & White, B. Y. (1989). An approach to

training based on principled task decomposition. *Acta Psychologica, 71*, 89–146.

Gerson, R. F., & Thomas, J. R. (1977). Schema theory and practice variability within a neo-Piagetian framework. *Journal of Motor Behavior, 9*, 127–134.

Glenberg, A. M. (1977). Influences of retrieval processes on the spacing effect in free recall. *Journal of Experimental Psychology: Human Learning and Memory, 3*, 282–294.

Glenberg, A. M., & Smith, S. M. (1981). Spacing repetitions and solving problems are not the same. *Journal of Verbal Learning and Verbal Behavior, 20*, 110–119.

Goode, S. L., & Magill, R. A. (1986). The contextual interference effect in learning three badminton serves. *Research Quarterly for Exercise and Sport, 57*, 308–314.

Henry, F. M. (1960). Increased response latency for complicated movements and a "memory-drum" theory of neuromotor reaction. *Research Quarterly, 31*, 448–458.

Hull, C. L. (1943). *Principles of behavior*. New York: Appleton-Century-Crofts.

Kohl, R. M., Ellis, S. D., & Roenker, D. L. (1992). Alternating actual and imagery practice: Preliminary theoretical consideration. *Research Quarterly for Exercise and Sport, 63*, 162–170.

Kohl, R. M., & Roenker, D. L. (1989). Behavioral evidence for shared mechanisms between actual and imaged motor responses. *Journal of Human Movement Science, 17*, 173–186.

Kohl, R. M., & Roenker, D. L. (1990). Bilateral transfer as a function of mental imagery. *Journal of Motor Behavior, 12*, 197–206.

Kohl, R. M., & Shea, C. H. (1992). Pew (1966) revised: Acquisition of hierarchical control as a function of observational practice. *Journal of Motor Behavior, 24*, 32–48.

Lee, T. D., & Genovese, E. D. (1988). Distribution of practice in motor skill acquisition: Learning and performance effects reconsidered. *Research Quarterly for Exercise and Sport, 59*, 277–287.

Lee, T. D., & Genovese, E. D. (1989). Distribution of practice in motor skill acquisition: Different effects for discrete and continuous tasks. *Research Quarterly for Exercise and Sport, 60*, 59–65.

Lee, T. D., & Magill, R. A. (1983). The locus of the contextual interference in motor-skill acquisition. *Journal of Experimental Psychology: Learning, Memory, and Cognition, 9*, 730–746.

Lee, T. D., & Magill, R. A. (1985). Can forgetting facilitate skill acquisition? In D. Goodman, R. B. Wilberg, & I. M. Franks (Eds.), *Differing perspectives in motor learning, memory, and control* (pp. 3–22). Amsterdam: North-Holland.

MacKay, D. M. (1987). The problem of rehearsal and mental practice. *Journal of Motor Behavior, 13*, 274–285.

Magill, R. A., & Hall, E. (1990). A review of the contextual interference effect in motor skill acquisition. *Human Movement Science, 9*, 241–289.

Mané, A. M., Adams, J. A., & Donchin, E. (1989). Adaptive and part-whole training in the acquisition of a complex perceptual-motor skill. *Acta Psychologica, 71*, 179–196.

Mané, A. M., & Donchin, E. (1989). The space fortress game. *Acta Psychologica, 71*, 17–22.

Martens, R., Burwitz, L., & Zuckerman, J. (1976). Modeling effects on motor performance. *Research Quarterly, 47*, 277–291.

McCracken, H. D., & Stelmach, G. E. (1977). A test of the schema theory of discrete motor learning. *Journal of Motor Behavior, 9*, 193–201.

McCullagh, P. (1987). Model similarity effects on motor performance. *Journal of Sport Psychology, 9*, 249–260.

McCullagh, P., Weiss, M. R., & Ross, D. (1989). Modeling considerations in motor skill acquisition and performance: An integrated approach. In K. B. Pandolf (Ed.), *Exercise and sport sciences reviews* (pp. 475–513). Baltimore: Williams & Wilkins.

Moxley, S. E. (1979). Schema: The variability of practice hypothesis. *Journal of Motor Behavior, 11*, 65–70.

Naylor, J., & Briggs, G. (1963). Effects of task complexity and task organization on the relative efficiency of part and whole training methods. *Journal of Experimental Psychology, 65*, 217–244.

Newell, K. M., Carlton, M. J., Fisher, A. T., & Rutter, B. G. (1989). Whole-part training strategies for learning the response dynamics of microprocessor driven simulators. *Acta Psychologica, 71*, 197–210.

Newell, K. M., Morris, L. R., & Scully, D. M. (1985). Augmented information and the acquisition of skill in physical activity. In R. L. Terjung (Ed.), *Exercise and sport science reviews* (pp. 235–261). New York: Macmillan.

Newell, K. M., & Shapiro, D. C. (1976). Variability of practice and transfer of training: Some evidence toward a schema view of motor learning. *Journal of Motor Behavior, 8*, 233–243.

Peterson, L. R., Wampler, R., Kirkpatrick, M., & Saltzman, D. (1963). Effect of spacing presentations on retention of a paired associate over short intervals. *Journal of Experimental Psychology, 66*, 206–209.

Richardson, A. (1976a). Mental practice: A review and discussion. Part I. *Research Quarterly, 38*, 95–107.

Richardson, A. (1976b). Mental practice: A review and discussion. Part II. *Research Quarterly, 38*, 263–273.

Roland, P. E., Larsen, B., Lassen, N. A., & Skinhoj, E. (1980). Supplementary motor area and other cortical areas in organization of voluntary movements in man. *Journal of Neurophysiology, 43*, 118–136.

Salmoni, A. W., Schmidt, R. A., & Walter, C. B. (1984). Knowledge of results and motor learning: A review and critical reappraisal. *Psychological Bulletin, 95*, 355–386.

Schmidt, R. A. (1975). A schema theory of discrete motor skill learning. *Psychological Review, 82*, 225–260.

Schmidt, R. A. (1976). The schema theory as a solution to some persistent problems in motor learning theory. In G. E. Stelmach (Ed.), *Motor control: Issues and trends* (pp. 41–65). New York: Academic Press.

Scully, D. M., & Newell, K. M. (1985). Observational learning and the acquisition of motor skills: Toward a visual perception perspective. *Journal of Human Movement Studies, 11*, 169–186.

Shea, C. H., & Kohl, R. M., (1990). Specificity and variability of practice. *Research Quarterly for Exercise and Sport, 61*, 169–177.

Shea, C. H., & Kohl, R. M. (1991). Composition of practice: Influence on the retention of motor skills. *Research Quarterly for Exercise and Sport*, 62(2), 187–195.

Shea, C. H., Kohl, R. M., & Indermill, C. (1990). Contextual interference: Contributions of practice. *Acta Psychologica*, 73, 145–157.

Shea, C. H., Shebilske, W. L., Kohl, R. M., & Guadagnoli, M. A. (1991). After-contraction phenomenon: Influences on performance and learning. *Journal of Motor Behavior*, 23(1), 51–62.

Shea, J. B., & Morgan, R. L. (1979). Contextual interference effects on the acquisition, retention, and transfer of a motor skill. *Journal of Experimental Psychology: Human Learning and Memory*, 5, 179–187.

Shea, J. B., & Wright, D. L. (1991). When forgetting benefits motor retention. *Research Quarterly for Exercise and Sport*, 62, 293–301.

Shea, J. B., & Zimny, S. T. (1983). Context effects in memory and learning movement information. In R. A. Magill (Ed.), *Memory and control of action* (pp. 345–366). New York: Elsevier.

Shea, J. B., & Zimny, S. T. (1985). Representational structure and strategic processes for movement production. In D. Goodman, R. B. Wilberg, & I. M. Franks (Eds.), *Differing perspectives in motor learning, memory, and control* (pp. 55–87). Amsterdam: North-Holland.

Shebilske, W. L., Regain, H. W., Arthur, W. Jr., & Jordan, J. A. (1992). A dyadic protocol for training complex skills. *Human Factors*, 34, 369–374.

Singer, R. N. (1966). Transfer effects and ultimate success in archery due to degree of difficulty of the initial learning. *Research Quarterly*, 37, 532–539.

Stelmach, G. E. (1969). Efficiency of motor learning as a function of inter-trial rest. *Research Quarterly*, 40, 198–202.

Thorndike, E. L., & Woodworth, R. S. (1901a). The influence of improvement in one mental function upon the efficiency of other functions (I). Functions involving attention, observation and discrimination. *Psychological Review*, 8, 247–267.

Thorndike, E. L., & Woodworth, R. S. (1901b). The influence of improvement in one mental function upon the efficiency of other functions (II). The estimation of magnitudes. *Psychological Review*, 8, 384–395.

Thorndike, E. L., & Woodworth, R. S. (1901c). The influence of improvement in one mental function upon the efficiency of other functions (III). Functions involving attention, observation and discrimination. *Psychological Review*, 8, 553–564.

Turnbull, S. D., & Dickerson, J. (1986). Maximizing variability of practice: A test of schema theory and contextual interference theory. *Journal of Human Movement Studies*, 12, 201–213.

Whiting, H. T. A., Bijlard, M. J., & den Brinker, B. P. I. M. (1987). The effect of the availability of a dynamic model on the acquisition of a complex action. *Quarterly Journal of Experimental Psychology*, 39A, 43–59.

Wiesendanger, M. (1987). Initiation of voluntary movements and the supplementary motor area. In H. Heuer & C. Fromm (Eds.), *Generation and modulation of action patterns* (pp. 3–13). Berlin: Springer-Verlag.

Wightman, D. C., & Lintern, G. (1985). Part-task training for tracking and manual control. *Human Factors*, 27, 267–283.

Wood, C. A., & Ging, C. A. (1991). The role of interference and task similarity on the acquisition, retention, and transfer of simple motor skills. *Research Quarterly for Exercise and Sport*, 62(1), 27–31.

Wrisberg, C. A., & Ragsdale, M. R. (1979). Further tests of Schmidt's schema theory: Development of a schema rule for a coincident timing task. *Journal of Motor Behavior*, 11, 159–166.

Young, D. R., & Bellezza, F. S. (1982). Encoding variability, memory organization, and the repetition effects. *Journal of Experimental Psychology: Learning, Memory, and Cognition*, 8, 545–559.

Chapter 12

Allport, F. H. (1924). *Social psychology*. Cambridge, MA: Riverside Press.

Ammons, R. B. (1956). Effects of knowledge of performance: A survey and tentative theoretical formulation. *Journal of General Psychology*, 54, 279–299.

Asch, S. (1951). Effects of group pressure upon the modification and distortion of judgment. In H. Guetzkow (Ed.), *Groups, leadership, and men*. Pittsburgh: Carnegie Press.

Bandura, A. (1965). Influences of models reinforcement contingencies on the acquisition of initiative responses. *Journal of Personality and Social Psychology*, 1, 589–593.

Bandura, A. (1973). *Aggression: A social learning analysis*. New York: Holt, Rinehart and Winston.

Bandura, A., Ross, D., & Ross, S. A. (1961). Transmission of aggression through imitation of aggressive models. *Journal of Abnormal and Social Psychology*, 63, 575–582.

Bandura, A., Ross, D., & Ross, S. A. (1963). Imitation of film-mediated aggressive models. *Journal of Abnormal and Social Psychology*, 66, 3–11.

Bandura, A., & Walters, R. H. (1963). *Social learning and personality development*. New York: Holt, Rinehart and Winston.

Bandura, A., & Wood, R. (1989). Effect of perceived controllability and performance standards on self-regulation of complex decision making. *Journal of Personal and Social Psychology*, 56, 805–814.

Baumeister, R. F., & Steinhilber, A. (1984). Paradoxical effects of supportive audiences on performance under pressure: The home field disadvantages in sports championships. *Journal of Personality and Social Psychology*, 47, 85–93.

Booth, A. (1972). Sex and social participation. *American Sociological Review*, 37, 183–193.

Burnstein, E. (1982). Persuasion as argument processing. In M. Brandstatter, J. M. Davis, & G. Stocker-Kreichgauer (Eds.), *Group decision processes*. London: Academic Press.

Chen, S. C. (1937). Social modification of the activity of ants in nest-building. *Physiological Zoology*, 10, 420–436.

Eccles, J. (1991). Gender role socialization. In R. M.

Baron & W. G. Graziano (Eds.), *Social psychology.* New York: Holt, Rinehart and Winston.

Festinger, L. (1954). A theory of social comparison processes. *Human Relations, 7,* 117–140.

Forsyth, D. (1990). *An introduction to group dynamics* (2nd ed.). Pacific Grove, CA: Brooks/Cole.

Glass, D. C., & Singer, J. E. (1972). *Urban stress.* New York: Academic Press.

Goethals, G. R., & Darley, J. M. (1987). Social comparison theory: Self-evaluation and group life. In B. Mullen & G. R. Goethals (Eds.), *Theories of group behavior.* New York: Springer-Verlag.

Greenberg, J., & Mushman, C. (1981). Avoiding and seeking self-focused attention. *Journal of Research in Personality, 15,* 191–200.

Guerin, B., & Innes, J. (1982). Social facilitation and social monitoring; A new look at Zajonc's mere presence hypothesis. *British Journal of Social Psychology, 21,* 7–18.

Hastorf, A. H., & Cantril, H. (1954). They saw a game. *Journal of Abnormal and Social Psychology, 49,* 129–134.

Hinkle, S., & Schopler, J. (1986). Bias in the evaluation of ingroup and outgroup performance. In S. Worchel & W. Austin (Eds.), *Psychology of intergroup relations.* Chicago: Nelson-Hall.

Holding, D. H. (1965). *Principles of training.* Oxford, England: Pergamon Press.

Hollander, E. P. (1985). Leadership and power. In G. Lindzey & E. Aronson (Eds.), *Handbook of social psychology* (3rd ed., Vol. 2). New York: Random House.

Kerr, N. L. (1983). Motivation loss in small groups: A social dilemma analysis. *Journal of Personality and Social Psychology, 45,* 819–828.

Kerr, N. L., & Brunn, S. E. (1983). Dispensability of member effort and group motivation loss: Free rider effect. *Journal of Personality and Social Psychology, 44,* 78–94.

Knox, R. E., & Safford, R. K. (1976). Group caution at the racetrack. *Journal of Experimental Social Psychology, 12,* 317–324.

Langer, E. J. (1989). Minding matters: The consequences of mindlessness-mindfulness. In L. Berkowitz (Ed.), *Advances in experimental social psychology* (Vol. 22, pp. 137–173). New York: Academic Press.

Latané, B. (1981). The psychology of social impact. *American Psychologist, 36,* 343–356.

Lazarus, R. S. (1982). Thoughts on the relations between emotions and cognition. *American Psychologist, 37,* 1019–1024.

Locke, E. A., & Bryan, J. F. (1966). Cognitive aspects of psychomotor performance: The effects of performance goals on level of performance. *Journal of Applied Psychology, 50,* 286–291.

Moreland, R. L., & Levine, J. M. (1988). Group dynamics over time: Development and socialization in small groups. In J. E. McGrath (Ed.), *The social psychology of time* (pp. 151–181). Newbury Park, CA: Sage.

Meyers, D. G. (1982). Polarizing effects of social interaction. In H. Brandstatter, J. H. Davis, & G. Stocker-Kreichgauer (Eds.), *Group decision processes.* London: Academic Press.

Pessin, J., & Husband, R. (1933). Effects of social stimu-lation on human maze learning. *Journal of Abnormal and Social Psychology, 28,* 148–154.

Ringelmann, M. (1913). Recherches sur les moteurs animes: Travail de l'homme. *Annales de l'Institut National Agronomique, 2nd series, 12,* 1–40.

Roethlisberger, F., & Dickson, W. (1939). *Management and the worker.* Cambridge, MA: Harvard University Press.

Sanders, G. S. (1981). Driven by distraction: An integrative review of social facilitation theory and research. *Journal of Experimental Social Psychology, 17,* 227–251.

Schachter, S. (1951). Deviation, rejection, and communication. *Journal of Abnormal and Social Psychology, 46,* 190–207.

Schachter, S., & Singer, J. (1962). Cognitive, social and physiological determinants of emotional state. *Psychological Review, 69,* 379–399.

Sistrunk, F., & McDavid, J. W. (1971). Sex variable in conforming behavior. *Journal of Personality and Social Psychology, 17,* 200–207.

Smoll, F. L. (1972). Effects of precision of information feedback upon acquisition of a motor skill. *Research Quarterly, 43,* 489–493.

Stang, D. J. (1972). Conformity, ability, and self-esteem. *Representative Research in Social Psychology, 3,* 97–103.

Steiner, I. D. (1972). *Group process and productivity.* New York: Academic Press.

Stoner, J. (1961). *A comparison of individual and group decisions, including risk.* Unpublished master's thesis. MIT, School of Industrial Management.

Tajfel, H. (1970). Experiments in intergroup discrimination. *Scientific American, 22, 3,* 96–102.

Tajfel, H., & Turner, J. C. (1986). The social identity theory of intergroup behavior. In S. Worchel & W. G. Austin (Eds.), *The psychology of intergroup relations.* Chicago: Nelson-Hall.

Tesser, A. (1985). Some effects of self-evolution maintenance cognition and action. In R. M. Sorrentino & E. T. Higgins (Eds.), *The handbook of motivation and cognition: Foundations of social behavior.* New York: Guilford Press.

Travis, L. E. (1925). The effect of a small audience upon eye-hand coordination. *Journal of Abnormal and Social Psychology, 20,* 142–146.

Triplett, N. (1897). The dynamogenic factors in pacemaking and competition. *American Journal of Psychology, 9,* 507–533.

Turner, C. W., & Berkowitz, L. (1972). Identification with film aggressor (covert role taking) and reactions to film violence. *Journal of Personality and Social Psychology, 21,* 256–264.

Wallach, M., Kogan, N., & Bem, D. (1962). Group influence on individual risk taking. *Journal of Abnormal and Social Psychology, 65,* 75–86.

Whyte, W., Jr. (1956). *The organization man.* New York: Simon & Schuster.

Wicklund, R. A., & Frey, D. (1980). Self-awareness theory: When the self makes a difference. In D. M. Wegner & R. R. Vallacher (Eds.), *The self in social psychology* (pp. 31–54). New York: Oxford University Press.

Wilke, H., & van Knippenberg, A. (1988). Group performance. In M. Hewstone, W. Stroebe, J. Codol, & G. Stephenson (Eds.), *Introduction to social psychology*. Oxford, England: Basil Blackwell.

Willis, R. H. (1972). Diamond model of social response. In W. S. Sahakian (Ed.), *Social psychology: Experimentation theory and research*. Scranton, PA: International Textbook.

Winstead, B. (1986). Sex differences in same sex friendships. In V. J. Derlega & B. Winstead (Eds.), *Friendship and social interaction*. New York: Springer-Verlag.

Wood, W. (1987). Meta-analytic review of sex differences in group performance. *Psychological Bulletin*, *102*, 53–71.

Worchel, S., Cooper, J., & Goethals, G. (1991). *Understanding social psychology* (5th ed.). Monterey, CA: Brooks/Cole.

Worchel, S., Coutant-Sassic, D., & Grossman, M. (1991). A model of group development and independence. In S. Worchel, W. Wood, & J. Simpson (Eds.), *Group process and productivity*. Newbury Park, CA: Sage.

Worchel, S., Hart, D., & Buttemeyer, J. (1989). *Is social loafing a group phenomenon?* Paper presented at the Southwestern Psychological Association Meeting, Houston, TX.

Worchel, S., Lind, E., & Kaufman, K. (1975). Evaluations of group products as a function of expectations of group longevity, outcome of competition, and publicity of evaluations. *Journal of Personality and Social Psychology*, *31*, 1089–1097.

Worchel, S., & Sigall, H. (1976). There is no place like home, unless . . . *The ACC Basketball Handbook*. Charlotte, NC: VMI Publications.

Zajonc, R. B. (1965). Social facilitation. *Science*, *149*, 269–274.

Zajonc, R. B. (1968). Attitudinal effects of mere exposure. *Journal of Personality and Social Psychology*, *9*, Monograph Suppl. no. 2, pt. 2.

Zajonc, R. B. (1972). *Animal social behavior*. Morristown, NJ: General Learning Press.

Chapter 13

Christina, R. W. (1989). What happened to applied research in motor learning? In J. S. Skinner, C. B. Corbin, D. M. Landers, P. E. Martin, & C. L. Wells (Eds.), *Future directions in exercise and sports science research* (pp. 411–422). Champaign, IL: Human Kinetics.

Goode, S., & Magill, R. A. (1986). The contextual interference effects in learning of three badminton serves. *Research Quarterly for Exercise and Sport*, *57*, 308–314.

Greenwald, A. G., Pratkanis, A. R., Leippe, M. R., & Baumgardner, M. H. (1986). Under what conditions does theory obstruct research progress? *Psychological Review*, *93*, 216–229.

Hoffman, S. J. (1990a). Relevance, application, and the development of an unlikely theory. *Quest*, *42*, 143–160.

Hoffman, S. J. (1990b). Author reply. *Quest*, *42*, 202–205.

Kuhn, T. (1970). *The structure of scientific revolutions*. Chicago: U of Chicago P.

Locke, L. F. (1990). Why motor learning is ignored: A case of ducks, naughty theories, and unrequited love. *Quest*, *42*, 134–142.

Luchins, A. S. (1942). Mechanization in problem solving. *Psychological Monographs*, *54*, No. 248.

Magill, R. A. (1990). Motor learning is meaningful for physical educators. *Quest*, *42*, 126–133.

Platt, J. R. (1964). Strong inference. *Science*, *146*, 347–353.

Shea, J. B., & Morgan, R. L. (1979). Contextual interference effects on the acquisition, retention, and transfer of a motor skill. *Journal of Experimental Psychology: Human Learning and Memory*, *5*, 179–187.

Zelaznik, H. N. (1990). Commentary. *Quest*, *42*, 193–196.

Appendix A

Bigland, B. & Lippold, O. C. J. (1954). The relation between force, velocity, and integrated electrical activity in human muscles. *Journal of Physiology (London)*, *123*, 214–224.

Henry, F. M. (1974). Variable and constant performance errors within a group of individuals. *Journal of Motor Behavior*, *6*, 149–154.

Henry, F. M. (1975). Absolute error versus "E" in target accuracy. *Journal of Motor Behavior*, *7*, 227–228.

Henry, F. M., & Rogers, D. E. (1960). Increased response latency for complicated movements and a "memory drum" theory of neuromotor reaction. *Research Quarterly*, *31*, 448–458.

Hick, W. E. (1952). On the rate of gain of information. *Quarterly Journal of Experimental Psychology*, *4*, 11–26.

Newell, K. M. (1976). Knowledge of results and motor learning. In J. Keogh & R. S. Hutton (Eds.), *Exercise and Sport Sciences Reviews* (Vol. 4, pp. 196–228). Santa Barbara, CA: Journal Publishing Affiliates.

Safrit, M. S., Spray, A. J., & Diewart, G. (1980). Methodological issues in short-term motor memory research. *Journal of Motor Behavior*, *12*, 13–28.

Schutz, R. W. (1977). Absolute, constant, and variable error: Problems and solutions. In D. Mood (Ed.), *Proceedings of the Colorado Measurement Symposium* (pp. 82–100). Boulder, CO: University of Colorado.

Schutz, R. W. & Roy, E. A. (1973). Absolute error: The devil in disguise. *Journal of Motor Behavior*, *5*, 141–153.

Photo Credits

Page 3: Photofest. 6: Topham/The Image Works. 7 (left): Christopher S. Johnson/Stock, Boston; (right): Archives of the History of American Psychology, University of Akron. 8 (left): Courtesy Richard A. Schmidt; (right): UPI/Bettmann Newsphotos. 9: Courtesy Richard A. Schmidt. 23: UPI/Bettmann Newsphotos. 28: The Bettmann Archive. 29: P. Davidson/The Image Works. 31: Science Source/Photo Researchers. 32: Dr. Monty Buchsbaum. 33: Jennifer Bishop/Stock, Boston. 34: Hank Morgan/Photo Researchers. 35: Courtesy General Electric. 36: Greenlar/The Image Works. 45: Mark Antman/The Image Works. 51: NASA. 53: Day Williams/Photo Researchers. 59: Barbara Alper/Stock, Boston. 62: David Carmack/Stock, Boston. 65: J. Y. Rabeuf/The Image Works. 73: © Spencer Grant/Monkmeyer Press. 77: Michael Ochs Archives. 83: Leonel Delevingne/Stock, Boston. 90: Rhoda Sidney/Stock, Boston. 93: Dan Burns/Monkmeyer Press. 97: Eric Neurath/Stock, Boston. 103: Reuters/Bettmann. 109: Nurion Industries. 116: Bob Kalman/The Image Works. 122: K. Preuss/The Image Works. 125: Photofest. 128: Frank Siteman/Monkmeyer Press. 131: Bob Daemmrich/Stock, Boston. 132: Spencer Grant/Photo Researchers. 147: UPI/Bettmann Newsphotos. 165: Florida Department of Commerce. 167: Wright State University. 169: Mimi Forsyth/Monkmeyer Press. 171: Lynn R. Johnson/Stock, Boston. 177: Reuters/Bettmann. 183: UPI/Bettmann Newsphotos. 184: Rhoda Sidney. 190: Spencer Grant/Stock, Boston. 202: Tim Davis/Photo Researchers. 205: NASA. 206: Lance Pavalas/Texas A&M University. 210: Griffin/The Image Works. 227: AP/Wide World. 288: Photofest. 238: Gale Zucker/Stock, Boston. 241: Texas A&M. 247: Laimute Druskis. 254: Kenneth Murray/Photo Researchers. 261: UPI/Bettmann Newsphotos. 268: Lew Merrim/Monkmeyer Press. 269: Larry Kolvoord/The Image Works. 271: Mike Mazzaschi/Stock, Boston. 273: Laima Druskis. 276: Spencer Grant/Monkmeyer Press. 282: Mimi Forsyth/Monkmeyer Press. 287: Mimi Forsyth/Monkmeyer Press. 288: Rhoda Sidney.

Figure Credits

We thank the authors and publishers for permission to use the materials indicated from the following works.

Figure 2.5 From *Neuromechanical Basis of Kinesiology* (p. 156) by R. M. Enoka, 1988, Champaign, IL: Human Kinetics. Copyright 1988 by Roger M. Enoka. Reprinted by permission.

Figures 2.15 and 2.17 From *Fundamentals of Human Neuropsychology* by Bryan Kolb and Ian Q. Whishaw, third edition. Copyright © 1980, 1985 and 1990 by W. H. Freeman and Company. Reprinted by permission.

Figure 2.18 Worchel, S. & Shebilske, W. *Psychology: Principles and Applications*, 3rd ed., p. 58. Copyright © 1989 Prentice Hall.

Figure 3.4 Adapted from Peterson, J. A. & Peterson, M. J. (1959). Short-term retention of individual items. *Journal of Experimental Psychology, 58*, 193–198. In the public domain.

Figure 3.5 Worchel, S. & Shebilske, W. *Psychology: Principles and Applications*, 3rd ed., p. 231. Copyright © 1989 Prentice Hall.

Figure 3.6 Adapted from Kosslyn, S. M., Ball, T. M., & Reiser, B. J. (1978). Visual images preserve metric spatial information. *Journal of Experimental Psychology: Human Perception and Performance, 4*, 47–60. Copyright 1978 by the American Psychological Association.

Figure 3.7 Collins, A. M., & Quillian, M. R. (1969). Retrieval time from semantic memory. *Journal of Verbal Learning and Verbal Behavior*, 8, 240–247.

Figure 3.8 Adapted from Sternberg, S. (1966). High-speed scanning in human memory. *Science, 153* (5 August 1966), 652–654. Copyright 1966 by the American Association for the Advancement of Science.

Figure 3.9 Magill, R. A., & Dowell, M. N. (1977). Serial position effects in motor short-term memory. *Journal of Motor Behavior, 9*, p. 113. Copyright 1977 by Heldref Publications.*

Figure 5.7 Adapted from Turvey, M., & Carello, C. (1986). The ecological approach to perceiving-acting. *Acta Psychologica, 63*, 133–156.

Figures 5.8 and 5.9 Adapted from Worchel, S., & Shebilske, W. (1989). *Psychology: Principles and Applications*, 3rd ed., p. 99. Copyright © 1989 Prentice Hall.

Figure 5.12 Dallenbach, K. M. (1927). The temperature spots and end-organs. *American Journal of Psychology, 39*, p. 418. Copyright 1927 University of Illinois Press.

Figures 5.13 and 5.14 Weinstein, S. (1968). Intensive and extensive aspects of tactile sensitivity as a function of body part, sex, and laterality. In D. R. Kenshalo (Ed.), *The Skin as Senses*, pp. 201, 202, 204. Courtesy of Charles C Thomas, Publisher.

Figure 6.3 Hyman, R. (1953). Stimulus information as a determinant of reaction time. *Journal of Experimental Psychology, 45*, 188–196. In the public domain.

Figure 6.4 Klemmer, E. T. (1956). Time uncertainty in simple reaction time. *Journal of Experimental Psychology, 51*, 179–184. In the public domain.

Figure 6.5 Mowrer, O. H. (1940). Preparatory set (expectancy): Some methods of measurement. *Psychological Monographs, 5*(233), p. 12.

Figure 6.6 Drazin, D. H. (1961). Effects of foreperiod variability and probability of stimulus occurrence on simple reaction time. *Journal of Experimental Psychology, 62*, 43–45. In the public domain.

Figure 6.10 Miller, J. (1982). Discrete versus continuous stage models of human information processing. *Journal of Experimental Psychology: Human Perception and Performance, 8*, 273–296. Copyright 1982 by the American Psychological Association.

Figure 6.16 Fitts, P. M., & Posner, M. I. (1967). *Human Performance*. Copyright © 1967 Brooks/Cole.

Figure 6.18 Adapted from Karlin, L., & Kestenbaum, R. (1968). Effects of number of alternatives on the psychological refractory period. *Quarterly Journal of Experimental Psychology, 20*, 167–178.

Figure 7.2 Posner, M. I., & Keele, S. W. (1969). In Swets & Zeitlinger (Eds.), *Proceedings of the 16th Congress of Applied Psychology*, Amsterdam.

Figure 7.3 Data from Henry, F. M., & Rogers, D. E. (1960). Increased response latency for complicated movements and a "memory drum" theory of neuromotor reaction. *Research Quarterly*, 31, 448–458.

Figure 7.4 Slater-Hammel, A. T. (1960). Reliability, accuracy and refractoriness of a transit reaction. *Research Quarterly*, 31, p. 226. Copyright 1960 by the American Alliance for Health, Physical Education, Recreation, and Dance.

Figure 7.5 Pew, R. W. (1966). Acquisition of hierarchical control over the temporal organization of a skill. *Journal of Experimental Psychology*, 71, 764–771. Copyright 1966 by the American Psychological Association.

Figure 7.6 Winter, D. A. (1990). *Biomechanics and Motor Control of Human Movement.* Copyright © 1990 by John Wiley & Sons, Inc. Reprinted by permission of John Wiley & Sons, Inc.

Figures 7.7 and 7.8 Ralston, H. J., Inman, V. T., Strait, L. A., & Shaffrath, M. D. (1947). Mechanics of human isolated voluntary muscle. *American Journal of Physiology*, 151, 612–620. Copyright © 1947 American Physiological Society. Used by permission.

Figure 7.9 Rosenbaum, D. A. (1989). On the selection of physical actions. *Five College Cognitive Science Paper*, No. 89–4.

Figure 7.10 Shik, M. L., Severin, F. V., & Orlovskii, G. N. (1966). Control of walking and running by means of electrical stimulation of the mid-brain. *Biophysics*, 11, p. 757. Copyright 1966. Reprinted with permission from Pergamon Press Ltd., Headington Hill Hall, Oxford OX3 OBW, UK.

Figure 7.11 Shea, C. H., Shebilske, W. L., Kohl, R. M., & Guadagnoli, M. A. (1991). After-contraction phenomenon. *Journal of Motor Behavior*, 23(1), 51–62. Copyright 1991 by Heldref Publications.*

Figure 7.12 Hellebrandt, F. A., Houtz, S. J., Partridge, M. J., & Walter, C. E. (1956). Tonic neck reflexes in exercises of stress in man. *American Journal of Physical Medicine*, 35, 144–159. © by Williams & Wilkins, 1956.

Figures 8.1 and 8.2 Schmidt, R. A. (1975). A schema theory of discrete motor skill learning. *Psychological Review*, 82, 225–260. Copyright 1975 by the American Psychological Association.

Figure 8.4 Raibert, M. H. (1977). *Motor Control and Learning by the State-Space Model.* Technical report, Artificial Intelligence Laboratory, MIT (AI-TR-439), p. 50.

Figure 8.5 Shea, C. H., Krampitz, J. B., Tolson, H., Ashby, A. A., Howard, R. M., & Husak, W. S. (1981). Stimulus velocity, duration and uncertainty as determiners of response structure and timing accuracy. *Research Quarterly for Exercise and Sport*, 52(1), 86–99. Copyright 1981 by the AAHPRD.

Figure 8.6 Hollerbach, J. M. (1978). A study of human motor control through analysis and synthesis of handwriting. Doctoral dissertation, MIT, p. 53.

Figure 8.7 Rosenbaum, D. A. (1991). *Human Motor Control*, p. 215. Copyright © 1991 by Academic Press.

Figure 8.8 From *Motor Control and Learning* (p. 170) by R. A. Schmidt, 1988, Champaign, IL: Human Kinetics. Copyright 1988 by Richard A. Schmidt. Reprinted by permission.

Figure 8.9 Adapted from Kelso, J. A. S., Southard, D. L., & Goodman, D. (1979). On the nature of interlimb coordination. *Science*, 203 (March 9, 1979), 1029–1031. Copyright 1979 by the American Association for the Advancement of Science.

Figure 8.10 Kelso, J. A. S., Putnam, C. A., & Goodman, D. (1983). On the space-time structure of human interlimb coordination. *Quarterly Journal of Experimental Psychology*, 35A, 347–375.

Figures 8A and 8B Nickerson, R. S., Kalikow, D. N., & Stevens, K. N. (1976). Computer-aided speech training for the deaf. *Journal of Speech and Hearing Disorders*, 41, 120–132. Copyright 1976 American Speech-Language-Hearing Association. Reprinted by permission.

Figure 9.2 Fitts, P. M. (1964). Perceptual-motor skills learning. In A. W. Melton (Ed.). *Categories of Human Learning*, p. 258. Copyright 1964 by Academic Press.

Figure 9.6 Langolf, G. D., Chaffin, D. B., & Foulke, J. A. (1976). An investigation of Fitts' law using a wide range of movement amplitudes. *Journal of Motor Behavior*, 8, 113–128. Copyright 1976 by Heldref Publications.*

Figures 9.8 and 9.9 Schmidt, R. A., Zelaznik, H. N., Hawkins, B., Frank, J. S., & Quinn, J. T. (1979). Motor-output variability. *Psychological Review*, 86, p. 427. Copyright 1979 by the American Psychological Association.

Figure 9.10 Schmidt, R. A., Zelaznik, H. N., & Frank, J. S. (1978). In G. E. Stelmach (Ed.), *Information Processing in Motor Control and Learning*, p. 196. Copyright 1978 by Academic Press.

Figure 9.11 Sherwood, D. E., & Schmidt, R. A. (1980). The relationship between force and force variability in minimal and near-maximal static and dynamic contractions. *Journal of Motor Behavior*, 12, 75–89. Copyright 1980 by Heldref Publications.*

Figures 9.12, 9.13, and 9.14 Shea, C. H., Krampitz, J. B., Tolson, H., Ashby, A. A., Howard, R. M., & Husak, W. S. (1981). Stimulus velocity, duration and uncertainty as determiners of response structure and timing accuracy. *Research Quarterly for Exercise and Sport*, 52(1), 86–99. Copyright 1981 by the AAHPRD.

Figure 9.15 Newell, K. M. (1980). The speed-accuracy paradox in movement control. In G. E. Stelmach (Ed.). *Tutorials in Motor Behavior*, p. 505. Amsterdam: North Holland.

Figure 10.1 Bilodeau, E. A., Bilodeau, I. M., & Schumsky, D. A. (1959). Some effects of introducing and withdrawing knowledge of results early and late in practice. *Journal of Experimental Psychology*, 58, 142–144. In the public domain.

Figure 10.2 Bilodeau, E. A., & Bilodeau, I. M. (1958). Variable frequency knowledge of results and the learning of a simple skill. *Journal of Experimental Psychology*, 55, 379–383. In the public domain.

Figures 10.3, 10.4, and 10.5 Winstein, C. J., & Schmidt, R. A. (1990). Reduced frequency of knowledge of results enhances motor skill learning. *Journal of Experimental Psychology*: *Learning, Memory, and Cognition,*16, 677–691. Copyright 1990 by the American Psychological Association.

Figure 10.6 Lee, T. D., & Carnahan, H. (1990). Bandwidth knowledge of results and motor learning. *Quarterly Journal of Experimental Psychology*, 42, 777–789.

Figure 10.8 Shea, J. B., & Upton, G. (1976). The effects on skill acquisition of an interpolated motor short-term memory task during the KR-delay interval. *Journal of Motor Behavior*, 8, 277–281. Copyright 1976 by Heldref Publications.*

Figure 10.9 Lee, T. D., & Magill, R. A. (1983). Activity during the post-KR interval. *Research Quarterly for Exercise and Sport*, 54, 340–345. Copyright 1983 by the AAHPRD.

Figure 10.10 Lavery, J. J. (1962). Retention of simple motor skills as a function of type of KR. *Canadian Journal of Psychology, 16*, 300–311. Copyright 1962 Canadian Psychological Association.

Figure 10.11A Schmidt, R. A., Young, D. E., Swinnen, S. & Shapiro, D. C. (1989). Summary knowledge of results for skill acquisition. *Journal of Experimental Psychology: Learning, Memory, and Cognition, 15*(2) 352–359. Copyright 1989 by the American Psychological Association.

Figure 10.11B Schmidt, R. A., Lange, C., & Young, D. E. (1990). Optimizing summary knowledge of results for skill learning. *Human Movement Science, 9*, 325–348. Copyright 1990 Elsevier Science Publishers.

Figure 10.12 Smoll, F. L. (1972). Effects of precision of information feedback upon acquisition of a motor skill. *Research Quarterly for Exercise and Sport, 43*, 489–493. Copyright 1972 by the AAHPRD.

Figure 10.13 Reeve, T. G., Dornier, L. A., & Weeks, D. J. (1990). Precision of knowledge of results: Consideration of the accuracy requirements imposed by the task. *Research Quarterly for Exercise and Sport, 61*, 284–290. Copyright 1990 by the AAHPRD.

Figure 10.14 Lindahl, L. G. (1945). Movement analysis as an industrial training method. *Journal of Applied Psychology, 29*, 420–436. In the public domain.

Figure 10.15 Newell, K. M., Quinn, J. T. Jr., Sparrow, W. A. & Walter, C. B. (1983). Kinematic information feedback for learning a rapid arm movement. *Human Movement Science, 2*, 255–269. Copyright 1983 Elsevier Science Publishers.

Figure 10.16 Newell, K. M., & Carlton, M. E. (1987). Augmented information and the acquisition of isometric tasks. *Journal of Motor Behavior, 19*, 4–12. Copyright 1987 by Heldref Publications.*

Figure 11.2 Stelmach, G. E. (1969). Efficiency of motor learning as a function of inter-trial rest. *Research Quarterly for Exercise and Sport, 40*, 198–202. Copyright 1969 by the AAHPRD.

Figure 11.3B Baddeley, A. D., & Longman, D. J. A. (1978). The influence of length and frequency of training session on the rate of learning to type. *Ergonomics, 21*, 627–635.

Figures 11.4 and 11.5 Shea, J. B. & Morgan, R. M. (1979). Contextual interference effects on the acquisition, retention, and transfer of a motor skill. *Journal of Experimental Psychology: Human Learning and Memory, 5*, 179–187. Copyright 1979 by the American Psychological Association.

Figure 11.6 Lee, T. D., & Magill, R. A. (1983b). The locus of contextual interference in motor skill acquisition. *Journal of Experimental Psychology: Learning, Memory, and Cognition, 9*, 730–746. Copyright 1983 by the American Psychological Association.

Figures 11.7 and 11.8 Shea, C. H., Kohl, R. M., & Indermill, C. (1990). Contextual interference: Contributions of practice. *Acta Psychologica, 73*(2), 145–157.

Figure 11.9 Shea, C. H. Shebilske, W. L., Kohl, R. M., & Guadagnoli, M. A. (1991). After-contraction phenomenon: Influence on performance and learning. *Journal of Motor Behavior, 23*(1), 51–62. Copyright 1991 by Heldref Publications.*

Figure 11.10 McCracken, H. D., & Stelmach, G. E. (1977). A test of the schema theory of discrete motor learning. *Journal of Motor Behavior, 9*, 193–201. Copyright 1977 by Heldref Publications.*

Figures 11.11, 11.12, and 11.13 Shea, C. H., & Kohl, R. M. (1990). Specificity and variability of practice. *Research Quarterly for Exercise and Sport, 61*(2), 169–177. Copyright 1990 by the AAHPRD.

Figure 11.14 Data from Shea, C. H., & Kohl, R. M. (1991). Composition of practice: Influence on the retention of motor skills. *Research Quarterly for Exercise and Sport, 62*(2) 187–195.

Figure 11.15 Data from Shea, C. H., & Kohl, R. M. (1991). Lag and spacing effect in motor skills. *Journal of Human Movement Studies, 31*, 41–51.

Figure 11.17 Data from Kohl, R. M., & Roeneker, D. L. (1980). Bilateral transfer as a function of mental imagery. *Journal of Motor Behavior, 12*, 197–206.

Figure 11.18 Kohl, R. M., & Shea, C. H. (1992). Pew (1966) revised: Acquisition of hierarchical control as a function of observational practice. *Journal of Motor Behavior, 24*, 32–48. Copyright 1992 by Heldref Publications.*

Figure 12.1 Locke, E. A., & Bryan, J. F. (1966). Cognitive aspects of psychomotor performance. *Journal of Applied Psychology, 50*, 286–291. Copyright 1966 by the American Psychological Association.

*Figures from articles in the *Journal of Motor Behavior* published by Heldref Publications are reprinted with permission of the Helen Dwight Reid Educational Foundation, 1319 Eighteenth St., N.W., Washington, D.C. 20036-1802.

Author Index

Adams, J. A., 19, 52, 143, 149, 150, 168, 169, 170, 209, 211, 214, 236, 237, 245, 246, 247, 253, 254, 257
Alkon, D. L., 71
Allard, F., 63
Allport, F. H., 269
Amarai, D. G., 71
Ammons, R. B., 264
Annett, J., 221
Archer, E. J., 236
Arthur, W., Jr., 254
Ashby, A. A., 174, 197, 198
Atkinson, R. C., 54, 55

Bachman, J. C., 247
Bach-Y-Rita, P., 119
Backlund, E. D., 47
Baddeley, A. D., 56, 238, 239
Bairstow, P. J., 151
Ball, T. M., 60
Bandura, A., 257, 264, 267, 268
Barbizet, J., 72
Barnett, M. L., 246
Battig, W. F., 240
Baumeister, R. F., 272
Baumgardner, M. H., 284
Beitel, P. A., 197
Bell, A. G., 112
Bellezza, F. S., 250
Bem, D., 266, 267
Benedetti, C., 220
Bennett, D. M., 212
Ben-Sira, D., 214
Berger, H., 32
Berkowitz, L., 267
Berla, E. P., 119
Berman, A. J., 152
Bernstein, N., 6, 156, 161, 177
Besson, J., 27
Bigland, B., 298
Bijlard, M. J., 258
Bilodeau, E. A., 212, 218
Bilodeau, I. M., 212, 218, 220, 223

Bizzi, E., 159, 175, 176
Bjork, R. A., 94
Bliss, J. A., 119
Bohannon, J. N., III, 73
Booth, A., 274
Bourne, L. E., 236
Bower, G. H., 64
Braille, L., 118-19
Briggs, G. E., 254
Brown, J. E., 36
Brown, R. W., 67, 72
Bruhn, P., 46
Bruner, J. S., 107
Brunn, S. E., 270
Bryan, J. R., 265
Buchsbaum, M. S., 135
Burnstein, E., 266
Burr, B., 191
Burwitz, L., 258
Buttemeyer, J., 271
Butterworth, G., 114
Byers, R. K., 164

Card, S. K., 191
Carello, C., 108
Carlton, L. G., 152, 153, 196, 199
Carlton, M. E., 229
Carlton, M. J., 196, 199, 254
Carnahan, H., 217
Carroll, W. R., 257
Carson, A. V., 236
Carson, L. M., 247
Cason, H., 212
Castillo, M., 114
Catalano, J. F., 248
Cauraugh, J., 66, 67
Chaffin, D. B., 188
Chakraborty, G., 47
Chamberlin, C. J., 252, 254
Chaouch, A., 27
Chase, W. G., 62, 63
Chen, S. C., 269
Chernikoff, R., 153
Chizeck, H. J., 168

Christina, R. W., 285
Chugani, H. T., 34
Clark, M., 64
Cohen, N. J., 72
Collier, T. J., 47
Collins, A. M., 64
Colt, E. W., 27
Conrad, R., 59, 60
Cooper, J., 273
Cooper, W. E., 58
Corbin, C., 257
Coutant-Sassic, D., 273
Cowan, T., 72
Coyle, J. T., 47
Craik, F. I. M., 57, 67
Craik, K. W. J., 144
Craske, B., 108
Crawshaw, M., 108
Creamer, L. R., 144
Crossman, E. R. F. W., 189
Cuddy, L. J., 250
Cynader, M. S., 46

Dahlback, L. O., 151
Darley, J. M., 265
de Kliejn, A., 164
Dean, M., 165
Deckel, W. W., 47
Dees, V., 219
Deese, J., 63, 64
Dell, B. L., 152-53
DelRey, P., 245
den Brinker, B. P. I. M., 258
Denny, M. R., 236
Dewey, J., 8, 9
Dickerson, J., 243
Dickson, W., 273
Diewart, G., 302
Donchin, E., 253, 254
Donders, F. C., 14, 88
Dornier, L. A., 223
Dowell, M. N., 67
Drazin, P. H., 133

Easton, T. A., 160, 177
Ebbinghaus, H., 52, 79, 236
Ebenholtz, S. M., 108, 111
Eccles, J., 275
Edstedt, J., 151
Egan, 63
Eithorn, A., 144
Ells, J. G., 57
Engen, T., 57
English, W. K., 191
Enoka, R. M., 162, 164

Fagius, J., 48
Feldman, A. G., 175
Feltz, D., 257
Fendrick, P., 58
Festinger, L., 264
Fisher, A. T., 254
Fitch, H., 161, 162
Fitts, P. M., 8, 90, 140, 185, 186, 187, 188, 203, 245
Fogel, A., 159
Forsyth, D., 264, 275
Foulke, E., 119
Foulke, J. A., 188
Frank, J. S., 36, 189, 192, 193, 194, 203
Frantz, A. G., 27
Fredricksen, J. R., 254
Frey, D., 273
Frisbey, N., 236
Fukuda, T., 164, 165

Gable, C., 223
Galanter, E. H., 103, 104
Gash, D. M., 47
Genovese, E. D., 236, 237
Gentile, A. M., 93, 94
Gerson, R. F., 247
Gesell, A., 164
Gibson, J. J., 107, 122
Ging, C. A., 243
Glass, B., 189
Glass, D. C., 264
Glenberg, A. M., 250
Goethals, G. R., 265, 273
Gold, P. E., 74
Goode, S., 289
Goodeve, P. J., 189
Goodman, D., 177
Gordon-Salant, S., 102, 103
Graham, S., 63
Granberg, P. O., 47
Green, D. M., 102
Greenberg, J., 273
Greenough, W. T., 70, 71
Greenwald, A. G., 127, 284
Grindley, G. C., 219
Grossman, M., 273

Guadagnoli, M. A., 162, 163, 165, 245
Guerin, B., 269

Haier, R. J., 135
Halbert, J. A., 196, 199
Hall, 242, 243, 244
Hamberger, B., 47
Hamilton, E. L., 218
Hardy, C. J., 197
Hart, D., 271
Hawkins, B., 150, 152, 189, 192, 193, 194, 203
Hellebrandt, F. A., 164, 165
Hennessy, R. T., 108
Henry, F. M., 9, 89, 153, 246, 247, 297, 302
Heron, P., 108
Hick, W. E., 129, 138, 297
Higgins, J. R., 93, 94
Hirota, T. T., 61
Hitch, G., 56
Ho, L., 214
Hoffman, S. J., 285
Holding, D. H., 264
Hollander, E. P., 275
Hollerbach, J. M., 174
Hoshizaki, L. E. F., 199
Houtz, S. J., 164, 165
Howard, R. M., 174, 197, 198
Hoyenga, K. B., 24, 71
Hoyenga, K. T., 24, 71
Hubbard, A. W., 201
Hughes, B., 119
Hull, C. L., 237
Husak, W. S., 174, 197, 198
Husband, R., 269
Hutton, R. S., 162, 164
Hymen, R., 129, 130, 137

Indermill, C., 243, 245
Ingoflia, N. A., 47
Inman, V. T., 158
Innes, J., 269

Jacoby, L. L., 250
Jagacinski, R. J., 189
James, W., 152
Johnson, P., 57
Johnson, R. W., 214
Jordan, J. A., 254

Kalat, J. W., 47
Kalikow, D. N., 178, 179
Karlin, L., 142
Karmiohl, C. M., 111
Keele, S. W., 57, 150, 151, 152, 162, 178, 190

Kelso, J. A. S., 70, 159, 177
Kerr, B. A., 188, 189
Kerr, N. L., 270
Kestenbaum, R., 142
Kirkpatrick, M., 250
Kisselburgh, L., 150, 152
Klapp, S. T., 153
Kleiner, B. M., 248
Klemmer, E. T., 131
Knox, R. E., 266
Kogan, N., 266, 267
Kohl, R. M., 156, 162, 163, 165, 228, 245, 248, 250, 251, 252, 257, 258
Kohnstamm, O., 162
Konzem, Y. M., 180
Koslowski, B., 107
Koslowski, M. R., 47
Kosslyn, S. M., 60
Krampitz, J. B., 174, 197, 198
Kugler, P. N., 177
Kuhn, T., 279
Kulik, J., 72

Laabs, G. J., 61
Landers, D. M., 257
Lange, C., 221, 223, 225
Langer, E. J., 272
Langolf, G. D., 188, 189
Larsen, B., 257
Lashley, K. S., 152
Lassen, N. A., 257
Laszlo, J. I., 151
Latané, B., 270
Lavery, J. J., 221, 223
Lawrence, C., 144
Lazarus, R. S., 264
Leavitt, J. L., 69
Lee, D. N., 107
Lee, T. D., 60, 61, 68, 69, 217, 220, 236, 237, 240, 242, 243, 250, 251, 252, 254
Leibowitz, H. W., 108
Leippe, M. R., 284
Leonard, J. A., 89
Lesgold, A., 64
Levine, J. M., 273
Levy, J., 108
Lindahl, L. G., 228
Lintern, G., 252
Lippold, O. C. J., 298
Lipscomb, D. M., 113
Locke, E. A., 265
Locke, L. P., 285
Lockhart, R. S., 57
Loftus, E. F., 64
Longman, D. J. A., 238, 239
Lorge, I., 218
Lottenberg, S., 135
Loveless, N. E., 140

Lucariello, G., 57, 66, 67
Luchins, A. S., 282

McCloskey, M., 72
McCracken, H. D., 247
McCullagh, P., 220, 257, 258
McDavid, J. W., 275
McGaugh, J. L., 74
McGovern, D. E., 191
McGown, C. M., 176
McGuigan, F. J., 219
MacKay, D. M., 257
MacLachlan, A., 135
McMahon, T. A., 156, 157
MacNeilage, L. A., 155
MacNeilage, P. F., 155
McNeill, D., 67
Magill, R. A., 60, 67, 68, 219, 220,
    223, 240, 242, 243, 244, 250,
    251, 285, 289
Magnus, R., 164
Mané, A. M., 253, 254
Marsden, C. D., 152-153
Marshall, J. R., 46, 47
Marteniuk, R. G., 81, 156, 219
Martens, R., 258
Massaro, D. W., 55
Mays, L. E., 176
Mazziotta, 34
Melzack, R., 42, 43
Merton, P. A., 172
Merzenich, M. M., 46
Meyer, D. E., 189
Meyers, D. G., 266
Miller, E. A., 93, 94
Miller, J., 136
Miller, R. B., 221
Miller, T. A., 63
Milner, B., 71
Moran, M. S., 189
Moran, T. H., 47
Moray, N., 58
Moreland, R. L., 273
Morgan, R. L., 239, 240, 242-43,
    289, 292
Morris, L. R., 258
Mowat, F., 97, 98
Mowbry, G. H., 142
Mowrer, O. H., 132
Moxley, S. E., 247
Mushman, C., 273
Mussa-Ivaldi, F. A., 159

National Research Council, 119
Naylor, J., 254
Neisser, U., 18, 72, 73, 79
Nelson, R. J., 46
Newell, K. M., 196, 199, 200, 203,

211, 212, 228, 229, 247, 254,
    257, 258, 302
Nicholson, D. E., 215
Nickerson, R. S., 178, 179
Nottebohm, F., 152

Oberg, R. G. E., 46
Olds, J., 71
Olsen, Y. D., 46
Orlovskii, G. N., 160
Owens, D. A., 105

Paap, K. R., 108
Paarsalu, M. E., 63
Park, J. N., 108
Partridge, M. J., 164, 165
Payne, J. W., 127
Pearlstone, Z., 67, 69
Pendleton, L. R., 61
Pessin, J., 269
Peterson, J. R., 188
Peterson, L. R., 56, 57, 68, 250
Peterson, M. J., 56, 57, 68
Pew, R. W., 19, 20, 151, 156
Phelps, M. E., 34
Platt, J. R., 12, 284
Polit, A., 175, 176
Polya, G., 11
Posner, M. I., 140, 150, 151, 152,
    162, 245
Poulton, E. C., 92, 196
Pratkanis, A. R., 284
Pribram, K. H., 84
Proctor, R. W., 60, 136
Proffitt, D. R., 111
Putnam, C. A., 177

Quesada, D. C., 134
Quillian, M. R., 64
Quinn, J. T., 189, 192, 193, 194,
    203, 228

Rack, P. M. H., 175
Ragsdale, M. R., 247, 248
Raibert, M. H., 157, 173
Ralston, H. J., 158
Rasmussen, J., 74
Reddish, P. E., 107
Reeve, T. G., 60, 136, 223
Regain, H. W., 254
Regan, D., 107
Reiser, B. J., 60
Repperger, D. W., 189
Reynolds, D., 144
Rhoades, M. V., 142
Riccio, R. V., 47
Richardson, A., 257

Richardson-Klavehn, A., 94
Ringelmann, M., 270
Roberts, W. H., 218
Robinson, R. G., 47
Rock, I., 107
Roenker, D. L., 257
Roethlisberger, F., 273
Rogers, C. A., 223
Rogers, D. E., 89, 153, 297
Roland, P. E., 257
Romanow, S. K. E., 69
Rosen, B. M., 93, 94
Rosen, M. J., 168
Rosenbaum, D. A., 136, 159, 175
Ross, D., 246, 257, 267
Ross, S. A., 267
Rothwell, J. C., 152-53
Rouse, W. B., 74
Roy, E. A., 302
Rutter, B. G., 254

Sabel, B. A., 46, 47
Sachs, J. S. S., 61
Safford, R. K., 266
Safrit, M. S., 302
Salmela, J., 63
Salmoni, A. W., 15, 16, 162, 208,
    211, 212, 219, 235
Saltzman, D., 250
Sanberg, P. R., 47
Sanders, A. F., 84
Sanders, G. S., 269
Schachter, D. L., 73
Schachter, S., 264
Scherer, S. S., 47
Schiffrin, R. M., 54, 55
Schlossberg, H., 89
Schmidt, R. A., 15, 16, 65, 69, 91,
    133, 134, 149, 152, 154, 162,
    170, 172, 176, 180, 189, 192,
    193, 194, 203, 208, 209, 211,
    212, 214, 215, 216, 219, 221,
    223, 225, 228, 235, 246, 247,
    250, 251
Schneider, G. E., 107
Schoppman, A., 46
Schultz, R. W., 302
Schumsky, D. A., 212
Schwab, M. E., 47
Schwartz, B. J., 63
Scully, D. M., 257, 258
Seng, C. N., 201
Severin, F. V., 160
Shaffer, L. H., 58
Shaffrath, M. D., 158
Shapiro, D. C., 221, 223, 225, 247
Shea, C. H., 94, 156, 162, 163, 165,
    174, 197, 198, 223, 228, 239,
    240, 242-43, 243, 245, 248,
    250, 251, 252, 258

Shea, J. B., 60, 61, 214, 219, 289, 292
Shebilske, W. L., 108, 110, 111, 162, 163, 165, 245, 254
Sherrington, C., 6
Sherwood, D. E., 194, 216
Shiina, K., 108
Shik, M. L., 160
Shyne-Athwal, S., 47
Siegal, B. V., 135
Sigall, H., 271
Simmons, R. W., 212
Simon, H., 62, 63
Singer, J. E., 264
Singer, R. N., 58, 247
Sistrunk, F., 275
Skinhoj, E., 257
Skinner, B. F., 7, 79
Sladek, J. R., Jr., 47
Slater-Hammel, A. T., 153, 154
Slavin, M. D., 46, 47
Smith, J. E. K., 189
Smith, J. L., 151
Smith, S. M., 94, 250
Smoll, F. L., 223, 264
Smyth, M. M., 61
Soderling, E., 135
Southard, D. L., 177
Sparks, D. L., 176
Sparrow, W. A., 228
Sperling, G., 55, 56
Sperry, R., 38
Spray, A. J., 302
Squire, L. R., 71
Stalberg, E., 151
Stein, D. G., 46, 47
Stein, R. B., 160
Steiner, I. D., 270
Steinhilber, A., 272
Stelmach, G. E., 70, 236, 247
Sternberg, S., 14, 66, 84
Stevens, K. N., 178, 179
Stevens, S. S., 103, 104
Stoner, J., 265
Strait, L. A., 158
Stricker, E. M., 47
Stryker, M. P., 46
Stuart, D. B., 122
Suddon, F. H., 223
Sutherland, I. E., 157
Suzuki, S., 162, 164

Swets, J. A., 102
Swinnen, S., 221, 223, 225

Tajfel, H., 274
Taub, E., 152
Taylor, F. V., 153
Telford, C. W., 142, 143
Tesser, A., 265
Thelen, M. J., 159
Thoenen, H., 47
Thomas, J. R., 247
Thompson, C. P., 72
Thorndike, E. L., 209, 218, 247
Todd, B., 246
Tolson, H., 197, 198
Toole, T., 57, 66, 67
Travis, L. E., 269
Treisman, A. M., 59
Trevarthen, C. B., 107
Triplett, N., 268, 269
Trowbridge, M. H., 212
Tuller, B., 161, 162
Tulving, E., 63, 67, 69
Turnbull, S. D., 243
Turner, C. W., 267
Turner, J. C., 274
Turvey, M. T., 108, 161, 162, 177
Tversky, A., 134

Upton, G., 219

van Knippenberg, A., 269
Vickers, D., 133

Wagner, H., 108
Wall, P. D., 42, 43
Wallach, M., 266, 267
Wallin, B. G., 48
Walter, C. B., 15, 16, 208, 211, 212, 219, 228, 235
Walters, C. E., 164, 165
Walters, R. H., 267
Wampler, R., 250
Ward, S. L., 189
Wardlaw, S., 27
Waters, L. K., 254
Weaver, J., Jr., 236

Weber, E. H., 104
Weeks, D. L., 162, 223
Weigand, R. L., 247
Weiss, M. R., 257
Welford, A. T., 8, 81
Westbury, D. R., 175
Wetzel, M. C., 122
White, B. Y., 254
Whitehurst, M., 245
Whiting, H. T. A., 258
Whyte, W., Jr., 266
Wible, C. G., 72
Wickens, C. D., 144
Wickens, D. D., 69
Wicklund, R. A., 273
Wicks, G. C., 214
Wiesendanger, M., 257
Wightman, D. C., 252
Wilberg, R. B., 63
Wilke, H., 269
Wilson, D. M., 152
Winstead, B., 274
Winstein, C. J., 214, 215, 216, 228
Winter, D. A., 158
Winzenz, D., 64
Wood, C. A., 223, 243
Wood, R., 264
Wood, W., 274
Woodworth, R. S., 89, 128, 129, 185, 189, 203
Worchel, S., 271, 273
Wright, C. E., 189
Wright, D. L., 94, 223, 251
Wrisberg, C. A., 197, 247, 248
Wughalter, E. H., 245
Wundt, W., 7

Young, D. E., 221, 223, 225
Young, D. R., 250

Zajonc, R. B., 269, 272
Zelaznik, H. N., 150, 152, 189, 192, 193, 194, 203, 285
Zigmond, M. J., 47
Zimny, S. T., 240, 251
Zola-Morgan, S., 71
Zook, J. M., 46
Zuckerman, J., 258

Subject Index

Absolute constant error, 298
Absolute error, 299
Absolute frequency, of knowledge of results, 211-12
Absolute threshold, meaning of, 99
Accommodation, visual, 105
Acetylcholine, actions of, 27
Acquisition, meaning of, 235
Action plan
    definition of, 127
    in information processing approach, 84
Action potential
    meaning of, 25
    and synaptic transmission, 25-26
Active interlocked modeling, 254
Active movements, 61
Afferent neurons, function of, 27
After-contraction effect, 162-64
Aging effect, temporal uncertainty, 133
Algebraic error, 298
Alpha-gamma coactivation, 160
Alzheimer's disease, and amnesia, 73-74
Ambient vision, 106
Amnesia
    antrograde amnesia, 71, 72
    retrograde amnesia, 71
Analysis of variance, 309
Anticipation
    effector anticipation, 196
    influencing factors, 196-97
    perceptual anticipation, 196
    receptor anticipation, 196
    and speed-accuracy tradeoff, 196-97
Aphasia, 78
Applied research, nature of, 286
Arousal
    and competition, 264
    physiological aspects, 264
    social component of, 264
Associative stage, of learning, 91
Attention

dichotic listening experiment, 58-59
    meaning of, 58
Audience effects, on performance, 272-73
Autonomic nervous system, 45, 48-49
    parasympathetic division, 48-49
    sympathetic division, 45-48
Autonomous stage, of learning, 91
Axons, 24

Backward chaining, 254
Backward masking, 55
Bandwith of KR (knowledge of results) procedure, 216-20
    KR delay interval, 218-20
    and relative frequency, 217
    and response stability, 217
Basic research, nature of, 286
Behavioral approach, 18-20
    nature of, 20
Behaviorism
    basic premise in, 7, 79
    conditioning in, 79
Blind, reading methods for, 119
Braille alphabet, 119, 120
Brain, 31, 36-38
    basal ganglia 36, 43, 45
    cerebellum, 31
    cerebral cortex, 31, 36-38, 45
    corpus callosum, 36, 38
    hypothalamus, 31
    left and right hemisphere functions, 36, 38
    medulla, 31
    midbrain, 31
    motor cortex, 37, 45
    occipital lobe, 37
    parietal lobe, 37
    pons, 31
    somatosensory cortex, 37, 38
    thalamus, 31

Brain damage, recovery from, 46-47
Brainstem, functions of, 45
Broca's aphasia, 38

Canadian Society for Psychomotor Learning and Sport Psychology, 9
Catch trials, 133
Catecholamines, actions of, 27
Central intermittency, meaning of, 8
Central nervous system, 31, 36-43
    brain, 31, 36-38
    spinal cord, 39-43
Central pattern generator, function of, 159-60
Central processes, information processing approach, 81, 82-84
Central tendency measures, 305
    mean, 305
    median, 305
    mode, 305
Chunking, memory, 62-63
Classical conditioning, 79
Closed environment, 92-93
Closed-loop control, 91, 149-52
    Adam's closed-loop theory, 168-70
    advantages/disadvantages of, 151
    evidence for, 150-51
Closed-loop theory, (Adam's 1971) 168-70, 209
    criticisms of, 169-70
    memory trace in, 169
    perceptual trace in, 169
Coaction, 269
Cognitive stage, of learning, 90-91, 245
Competition
    and arousal, 264
    and performance, 269

Confirmation bias, meaning of, 284
Conformity, and groups, 276
Constant error, 298
Constructive theories, of sensorimotor coordination, 107, 108
Context dependent behavior, 94
Contextual interference, 239-45
  applied research of, 289
  basic research of, 289
  extended practice, 243-45
  internal context manipulation, 245
  meaning of, 240
  reconstructive hypothesis, 240-42
  same versus different motor program, 242-43
Continuous movements, nature of, 95
Control group, 14-16
  function of, 14
Coordinating definitions, 11
Coordination loss, and social loafing, 270
Coordinative structures, movement production, 177
Crossed-extensor reflex, 159
Cross-talk, meaning of, 87
Cutaneous senses, 115-19
  distribution of sensitivity, 115-17
  and sensorimotor control, 118-19
  sensory receptors, 118

Deaf
  boilermaker's deafness, 113
  teaching speech to, 178-79
Debriefing, and experimental subject, 17
Deception, and experimental subject, 17
Decisions, as response selection, 83, 127
Deduction, reasoning, 12
Delay interval, knowledge of results, 218-20
Dendrites, 24
Descriptive statistics, 12, 304-7
  central tendency, 305
  frequency distribution, 304
  normal distribution, 307
  purpose of, 304
  variability, 305-6
Dichotic listening, attention experiment, 58-59
Difference threshold, meaning of, 99
Discrete movements, nature of, 95

Distributed practice, 236

Ear
  deafness, 113
  parts of, 113
Ecological validity, meaning of, 18
Effective target width (W_e),192-94
Effector anticipation, 196
Efferent neurons, function of, 27
Electroencephalography (EEG), 32-33, 295
Electromyography
  fast Fourier transformation, 298
  integration, 297-98
  rectified signal, 297
Empirical experiments, 11
Encoding, 58-61
  in long-term memory, 61
  movement codes, 60-61
  in short-term memory, 58-61
  verbal codes, 59-60
  visual codes, 60
Endorphins, actions of, 27
Environment
  closed environment, 92-93
  environmental context dependent memory, 94
  open environment, 93-94
Episodic memory, 63, 65
Ethics and experimentation, 16-17
  deception and debriefing, 17
  informed consent, 16-17
  privacy, 17
Event uncertainty, 128-31
  Hick-Hymen law, 129
  and number of alternatives, 129
  and reaction time, 129
  shell game, 129-30
Evoked potential, 295
Expectancy theory, nature of, 143
Experimental group, 14-16
  function of, 14
Experiments, 11, 12-18
  control group and experimental group in, 14-16
  critical experiments, 12
  empirical experiments, 11
  ethical issues, 16-17
  experimental paradigms, 13-16
  process in, 12-13
  sampling, 13
  statistics used in, 12-13
  validity, 17-18
  variables in, 14
Extensors, 39
External validity, meaning of, 18
Exteroception, meaning of, 98, 104
Exteroceptors, 82
Extrinsic feedback, 208

Eye
  light receptors, 105
  parts of, 104-5

Fading schedule, KR, 215
Fast Fourier transformation, 298
Feedback
  extrinsic feedback, 208
  importance of, 207
  intrinsic feedback, 208
  in motor control, 149-55
  spinal cord, 42
  See also Information feedback
Feedforward, spinal cord, 42
Final common pathway, meaning of, 6
Fitts' law, 8
  accounts for, 189
  application to control of machines, 190-91
  index of difficulty in, 187, 188-89
  speed-accuracy tradeoff, 185-86, 189
Flashbulb memories, 72
Flexors, 39
Focal vision, 105-6, 107
Force-force variability relationship
  accounts for, 194
  speed-accuracy tradeoff, 194-95
Forgetting, 68-70
  definition of, 68
  interference theory, 68, 69-70
  trace decay theory, 68-69
Fractionation, part-whole practice, 252-53
Free association test, memory test, 63-64
Free recall test, memory test, 64
Free rider effect, and social loafing, 270
Frontal lobe, functions of, 36-37
Functionalism, basic premise in, 8-9
Functional neuromuscular stimulation, 167-68

Gating, spinal cord, 42
Generalizable motor program, 170
Goal setting, 265-66
  and learning and performance, 265-66
  meaning of, 265
Golgi tendon organs, 122-23
Groups
  and conformity, 276
  effects on self-awareness, 272-73
  effects on self-evaluation, 273
  gender differences and group behavior, 274

group polarization, explanations for, 266
and social identity, 273-76
See also Social influences
Guidance hypothesis, processing of feedback, 211

Hearing, 109, 112-15
ear, parts of, 113
loss, and loud sounds, 112
and sensorimotor coordination, 113-15
sound, characteristics of, 109, 112
Hemispheres of brain
and corpus callosum, 36, 38
left and right functions, 38
Hick-Hymen law, 129
Hierarchical control, motor control, 155-56
Hippocampus, and memory loss, 71
Home-court advantage, 271-72
explanations for, 271-72
Hook's law, 175
Huntington's disease, 45
Hypothesis
and experimentation, 11-12
meaning of, 11

Ideomotor theory, 127
Imaging methods
computerized axial tomography (CAT) scan, 32, 33
magnetic resonance imaging (MRI), 35
positron emission tomography (PET) scan, 34
Impulse variability theory
effective target width measure, 192-94
speed-accuracy tradeoff, 192-94
Independent variables, 14
Index of difficulty, and speed-accuracy tradeoff, 186-87, 188-89
Individual differences
aspects of, 19
and theory formation, 19
Induction, reasoning, 11
Inferential statistics, 12-13, 308-10
analysis of variance, 309
correlation, 309
correlation coefficient, 309-10
purpose of, 308
regression, 310
t-test, 309
Information feedback
feedback sources, 207-8

guidance hypothesis, processing of feedback, 211
knowledge of performance, 208, 228-30
knowledge of results, 207-8, 211-25
and motivation, 209-10
and reward, 209-10
Information processing approach, 20
action plan in, 84
anticipation, effects of, 92
basic premise in, 79
central processes, 81, 82-84
environmental effects, 92-95
learning effects in, 90-91
model for, 80-81, 85
movement time, effects of, 91
parallel-distributed processing, 85, 87
parallel processing, 85
perception in, 82-83
peripheral processes, 81, 82
reaction time, 87-90
response execution, 83-84
response selection in, 83
sensation in, 82
serial processing, 84-85
task effects in, 95
Informed consent, and experimental subject, 16-17
Initial conditions, nature of, 170
Interference theory
forgetting, 68, 69-70
proactive and retroactive inhibition in, 69-70
Internal validity, meaning of, 17-18
Interneurons, 39
function of, 27
Interresponse interval, 218
Intrinsic feedback, 208
Invariant features, motor program, 171-72

Journal of Motor Behavior, 9
Just-noticeable difference, 104

Kinematic KR (knowledge of results), 228
Kinematics, 302-3
nature of, 302
use of data in, 303
Kinesthesia
meaning of, 120
See also Proprioception
Knowledge of performance, 208, 228-30
compared to knowledge of results, 228
types of, 228

Knowledge of results, (KR), 207-8
absolute and relative frequency of, 211-12
bandwidth of KR, 216-20
error measure used, effects of, 225
fading schedule, 215
information KR, 228
kinematic KR, 228
precision of KR, 223-25
qualitative KR, 223
quantitative KR, 223
relative frequency, 212, 214
reverse fading, 215
summary KR, 220-23
Known probabilities, 137-38
definition of, 137
and reaction time, 138
Korsakoff's syndrome, and amnesia, 72-73

Language disorders
aphasia, 78
Broca's aphasia, 38
Wernicke's aphasia, 38
Lateral geniculate nucleus, 107
Law, scientific, formation of, 12
Law of Effect, 209
Learning
associative stage, 91
autonomous stage of, 91
cognitive stage of, 90-91, 245
learning variables, 208
meaning of, 208
compared to performance, 208
performance effects, 269-70
Levels of processing theory, of memory, 57-58, 63
Limbs, multilimb control in movement, 177, 180
Locomotion, processes involved in, 156
Long-term memory, 57
encoding in, 61
and neurons, 70-71
organization of, 63-65
and rehearsal, 57
retrieval from, 67-68
types of, 63
types of information of, 57

Maladaptive short-term corrections, 216
Massed practice, 236, 237-38
Mass-spring hypothesis, of movement production, 175-76
Membrane potential, meaning of, 25

Memory
    chunking, 62-63
    definition of, 52
    electrical and chemical regulation of, 74
    encoding, 58-61
    environmental context dependent memory, 94
    episodic memory, 63, 65
    flashbulb memories, 72
    levels of processing theory, 57-58, 63
    long-term memory, 57
    for movement, 60-61, 65, 67, 68
    multiple memory theory, 54, 61
    and neurons, 70-71
    recoding, 62
    recognition processes, 55
    retrieval, 66-68
    semantic memory, 63-65
    sensory memory, 54-55
    short-term memory, 55-57
    tests for study of, 52-54
Memory loss
    amnesia, types of, 71
    disease caused amnesia, 72-74
    forgetting, 68-70
    and hippocampus damage, 71
Memory span, 63
Memory trace, 169
Mental practice, 255, 257
Methathetic continuum, 104
Minor motor anomalies, sensorimotor coordination, 108-9
Motivation
    and information feedback, 209-10
    loss from social loafing, 270
Motor behavior measurement
    electroencephalography (EEG), 295
    electromyography, 297-98
    kinematics, 302-3
    movement time, 297
    physiological correlates, 294-95
    reaction time, 296-97
    response errors, 298-302
Motor control, 149-62
    closed-loop control, 149-52
    closed-loop theory, 168-70
    closed/open loop continuum, 154-55
    hierarchical control, 155-56
    meaning of, 5
    mechanical factors in, 156, 158-59
    neurological-reflexive factors in, 159-60
    open-loop control, 152-54
    schema theory, 170-74
    synergies in, 160-62

Motor control system, 43, 45
Motorneuronal pool, 28
Motor neurons, 27, 27-28
Motor program
    definition of, 152
    research related to, 152-53
Motor units, 28
    motor-unit recruitment, process of, 28-29
    muscle fibers of, 28
    rate coding, 29
    tonic and phasic units, 29
Movement production, 162-65
    after-contraction effect, 162-64
    coordinative structures, 177
    mass-spring hypothesis, 175-76
    multilimb control, 177, 180
    response outcome, 171
    sensory consequences of, 171
    temporal and spatial aspects, 174
    tonic neck response, 164-65
Movement time, 297
    effects on information processing, 91
    meaning of, 88, 91, 297
Multiple memory theory, 54, 61
Muscle force
    neural control of, 27-29
        motor neurons, 27-28
        motor-unit recruitment, 28-29
    rate coding, 29
    and spinal reflex, 39-43
Muscles
    receptors of, 120-21
    serial elastic components of, 158
Muscle spindles, 120, 122
Myelin sheath, 24-25

Negative transfer, 253
Nervous system
    autonomic nervous system, 45, 48-49
    central nervous system, 31, 36-43
    motor control system, 43, 45
    overview of, 30
    peripheral nervous sysem, 31
    reticular activating system, 43
Neurons, 24-27
    function of, 24
    and memory, 70-71
    muscle force, control of, 27-29
    neural impulses, 25
    parts of, 24-25
    recovery from brain damage, 46-47
    synapse, 25-26
Neurotransmitters, 26-27

acetylcholine, 27
catecholamines, 27
endorphins, 27
norepinephrine, 27
Noise (signal detection)
    meaning of, 100
    noise distribution, 100-102
Norepinephrine, 27
North American Society for the Psychology of Sport and Physical Activity, 9

Observational practice, 257-59
Open environment, 93-94
Open-loop control, 152-54
    advantages/disadvantages of, 153-54
    evidence for, 152-53
Operant conditioning, 79
    goal of, 7
Operations research, nature of, 286-87
Opticon, 119
Order of elements, 172

Paradigm, definition of, 279
Paradoxical cold, 116
Parallel-distributed processing, nature of, 85, 87
Parallel processing, nature of, 85
Parallel search, of short-term memory, 66-67
Parameterized motor program, 172, 173
Parasympathetic division, autonomic nervous system, 48-49
Parkinson's disease, 45
Part-whole practice, 252-54
    active interlocked modeling, 254
    effectiveness of, 254
    fractionation, 252-53
    segmentation, 253-54
    simplification, 253
Passive movements, 61
Patellar tendon reflex, 40, 41, 87
Perception
    cutaneous senses, 115-19
    hearing, 109, 112-15
    meaning of, 82-83, 98
    proprioception, 120-23
    vision, 104-9
Perceptual anticipation, 196
Perceptual trace, 169
Perceptual uncertainty, 133-34
    experiments in, 133-34
Performance
    effects of learning on, 269-70
    and goal setting, 265-66

compared to learning, 208
  performance variable, 208
Peripheral nervous system, 31
Peripheral processes, information
  processing approach, 81, 82
Pew task, 155, 156
Phasic motor units, 29
Physiological correlates, motor behavior measures, 294-95
Postulates, nature of, 12
Practice
  contextual interference, 239-45
  of continuous tasks, 236
  of discrete tasks, 236
  distributed practice, 236
  elaborative perspective, 240
  information processing activities
    after, 135
  interaction of task and practice
    distribution, 237-38
  massed practice, 236, 237-38
  mental practice, 255, 257
  observational practice, 257-59
  part-whole practice, 252-54
  practice composition, 234
  practice distribution, 236-39
  practice scheduling, 234
  purpose of, 234
  and retention, 235, 248-50
  specificity hypothesis, 246-47
  and transfer, 235, 247-48
  variability of practice hypothesis,
    247
Precision of KR (knowledge of results), 223-25
Precuing, 134, 136-37
  definition of, 134, 136
  experiments in, 136
  and reaction time, 136-37
Primacy effects, recall of memory,
  67
Privacy, and experimental subject,
  17
Proactive inhibition, in forgetting,
  69
Probe trials, 110
Problems, application of principles
  to, 282
Professional organizations, related
  to motor learning and control, 9
Progressive part practice, 253-54
Proprioception, 120-23
  meaning of, 6, 98, 120
  receptors in, 120-22
  and sensorimotor control, 122-23
Proprioceptors, 82
Prothetic continuum, 104
Psychological refractory period,
  142-43
  definition of, 142

and reaction time, 142-43
Psychology, concept of motor control in, 7
Psychophysics
  nature of, 99
  psychophysical functions, mea-
    surement of, 103
  psychophysical questions, types
    of, 99
  Weber's Law, 104
Pure part practice, 253

Qualitative KR (knowledge of results), 223
Quantitative KR (knowledge of results), 223

Radial error, 300
Randomization, in sampling, 13
Rate coding, and muscle force, 29
Reaction time, 87-90, 296-97
  complex reaction time, 297
  discrimination reaction time,
    297
  and event uncertainty, 129
  fractionated reaction time, 297
  and known probabilities, 138
  meaning of, 88, 297
  and precuing, 136-37
  and psychological refractory pe-
    riod, 142-43
  and sequential dependencies,
    138-39
  simple reaction time, 297
  and stimulus-response compati-
    bility, 140, 142
  and temporal uncertainty,
    131-32
Reactive inhibition, 237
Reasoning
  deduction, 12
  induction, 11
Recall, levels of, 67
Recall schema, 170, 172
Recall tests, memory test, 52
Recency effects, recall of memory,
  67
Receptor anticipation, 196
Reciprocal inhibition, definition of,
  159
Reciprocal innervation, meaning
  of, 6
Recoding, memory, 62
Recognition processes, memory,
  55
Recognition schema, 170
Recognition tests, memory test,
  52-53
Reconstructive hypothesis, 240-42

Rectified signal, electromyography,
  297
Reflexes
  crossed-extensor reflex, 159
  definition of, 87
  and motor control, 159-60
  spinal, 39-43
  stretch reflex, 160
  tonic neck reflex, 164
Refractory period, 143
Refractory theory, nature of, 143
Regression, 310
Regression line, 310
Rehearsal
  and long-term memory, 57
  and short-term memory, 56
Reinforcement, effects of, 267-68
Relative frequency
  and bandwith of KR (knowledge
    of results) procedure, 217
  of knowledge of results, 211-12
  knowledge of results, 212, 214
Research and communication
  model, 285-93
  communication of researchers
    in, 287-89
  contextual interference example,
    289
  translation of theory into prac-
    tice, 290-93
Research
  applied research, 286
  basic research, 286
  operations research, 286-87
Response errors, 298-302
  absolute constant error, 298
  absolute error, 299
  algebraic error, 298
  constant error, 298
  one-dimensional errors, 298-99
  radial error, 300
  root mean square error, 302
  total error, 299
  two-dimensional errors, 300-302
  variable error, 298-99
Response execution
  experiment, reaction time, 89-90
  in information processing ap-
    proach, 83-84
  meaning of, 149
  motor control, 149-62
  movement production, 162-65
Response outcome
  of movement, 170
  movement production, 171
Response selection
  decisions in, 83, 127
  definition of, 127
  expectancy theory, 143
  experiment, reaction time, 88-89
  in information processing, 83

known probabilities, 137-38
precuing, 134, 136-37
psychological refractory period, 142-43
refractory theory, 143
sequential dependencies, 138-39
single channel theory, 143
stimulus-response compatibility, 139-42
translation in, 83, 127
and uncertainty, 127-34
Response specifications, nature of, 170
Response stability, and bandwith of KR (knowledge of results) procedure, 217
Response time, 297
Restless-leg syndrome, 31
Retention
meaning of, 235
and practice, 248-50
and variability of practice, 248-50
Reticular activating system, 43
Retrieval, 66-68
from long-term memory, 67-68
retrieval cues, 67-68
from short-term memory, 66-67
Retroactive inhibition, in forgetting, 69-70
Reverse fading, knowledge of results, 215
Reward, and information feedback, 209-10
Risky-shift dilemmas, 267
Root mean square error, 302

Sampling
population in, 13
process of, 13
randomization process, 13
Savings tests, memory test, 53
Schema, 65
information abstracted in, 170-71
meaning of, 170
recall schema, 170
recognition schema, 170
Schema theory, 170-74, 192, 209
generalizable motor program in, 170
invariant features, 171-72
parameterizing, 172, 173
sources of schema information, 170-71
spatial and temporal movement demands in, 174
variant features, 172
Scientific approach, 10-18
bottom-up process, 10, 12

experiments, 11, 12-18
hypothesis formation, 11-12
law, formation of, 12
postulates in, 12
reasoning processes in, 11, 12
theory in, 12
top-down process, 11, 12
Segmentation
part-whole practice, 253-54
progressive part practice, 253-54
pure part practice, 253
Semantic memory, 63-65
Sensation
meaning of, 82, 98
measurement of, 99-104
Sensation-perception experiment, reaction time, 88
Sensorimotor control, and cutaneous senses, 118-19
Sensorimotor coordination
constructive theories of, 107, 108
and hearing, 113-15
minor motor anomalies, 108-9
nature of, 98-99
stimulus theories of, 107
and vision, 107-9
Sensory consequences
of movement, 170
movement production, 171
Sensory memory, 54-55
backward masking in, 55
recognition processes in, 55
Sensory neurons, 39
Sensory receptors, types of, 82
Sequential dependencies, 138-39
definition of, 138
and reaction time, 138-39
Serial position effects, recall of memory, 67
Serial processing, nature of, 84-85
Serial search, of short-term memory, 66
Short-term memory, 55-57
encoding, 58-61
memory span, 63
and neurons, 70-71
and rehearsal, 56
retrieval from, 66-67
searches of, 66-67
testing of, 56-57
working memory, 56
Signal detection method, sensation measure, 100-102
Simplification, part-whole practice, 253
Single channel theory
nature of, 143
single channel hypothesis, meaning of, 8
Size principle, of motor-unit

recruitment, 28-29
Social comparison, 264-65
process of, 265
Social facilitation effect, on performance, 269, 270
Social identity, 273-76
and groups, 274-76
Social influences
audience effects, 272-73
group polarization, 266
home-court advantage, 271-72
on arousal, 264
on goal setting, 265-66
reason for study of, 263
social comparison, 264-65
social facilitation effect, 269, 270
social inhibition effect, 269, 270
social loafing, 270-71
Social inhibition effect, on performance, 269, 270
Social learning theory, 267-68
basis of, 267
reinforcement in, 267-68
Social loafing, 270-71
and coordination loss, 270
and feelings about group, 270-71
and free rider effect, 270
and motivation loss, 270
sucker effect, 270
Sound, 109, 112
Specificity hypothesis, practice, 246-47
Speed-accuracy tradeoff
anticipation in, 196-97
batting example, 200-202
Fitts' law, 185-86, 189
force-force variability relationship, 194-95
impulse variability theory, 192-94
and index of difficulty, 186-87, 188-89
meaning of, 185
speed-accuracy paradox, 196
and stimulus velocity, 197-99
and timing, 199-200
timing in, 196
Spinal cord, 39-43
feedback, 42
feedforward, 42
gating, 42
injuries, and functional neuromuscular stimulation, 167-68
spinal reflexes, 39-40
Statistics
descriptive statistics, 12, 304-7
inferential statistics, 12-13, 308-10
Stimulus-response compatibility, 139-42

definition of, 140
and reaction time, 140, 142
Stimulus theories, of sensorimotor
coordination, 107
Stretch reflex, 40, 41, 122-23
functions of, 160
Stroke, recovery from, case example, 23-24
Sucker effect, and social loafing,
270
Summary KR (knowledge of results), 220-23
Sympathetic division, autonomic
nervous system, 45-48
Synapse, 25-27
firing rate, 26
and neurotransmitters, 26-27
synaptic transmission, process
of, 25-26
types of, 27
Synergy
definition of, 161
in motor control, 161-62

Tactile Visual Substitution System,
119
Temporal lobe, functions of, 37
Temporal uncertainty, 131-33
aging effect, 133
experiments in, 131-33
and reaction time, 131-32
warning interval, 131
Tendons
parallel elastic components of,
158
receptors of, 120
Theory

and confirmation bias, 284
formulation of, 12
nature of, 283-84
negative view of, 284
positive view of, 283-84
Timing
influencing factors, 196-97
and speed-accuracy tradeoff,
199-200
use of term, 196
Tip-of-the-tongue phenomenon,
67
Tonic motor units, 29
Tonic neck reflex, 164
Tonic neck response, 164-65
Total error, 299
Trace decay theory, forgetting,
68-69
Transfer
meaning of, 235
negative transfer, 253
of practice, 247-48
transfer paradigm, 235
Transfer test, 219
Translation, as response selection,
83, 127

Uncertainty, 127-34
event uncertainty, 128-31
meaning of, 127
perceptual uncertainty, 133-34
temporal uncertainty, 131-33

Validity, 16-18
ecological validity, 18
external validity, 18

internal validity, 17-18
Variability measures, 305-6
range, 306
standard deviation, 306
variance, 306
Variability of practice hypothesis,
247
retention in, 248-50
transfer in, 247-48
Variable error, 298-99
Variables
dependent variables, 14
independent variables, 14
Variant features, motor program,
172
Verbal-motor stage, 245
Virtual environments, 226
Vision, 104-9
ambient vision, 106
eye, parts of, 104-5
focal vision, 105-6, 107
and sensorimotor coordination,
107-9
visual pathways, 105-7
Visual motor coordination, and
dart throwing, 110-11
Voluntary motor control system,
43, 45
organization of, 44

Walking machines, 157
W_e, See Effective target width
Weber's law, 104
application to sensations, 104
jnd (just-noticeable difference),
104
nature of, 104
Wernicke's aphasia, 38